D1156619

The Education Reform Act, 1988
Its Origins and Implications

The Education Reform Act, 1988
Its Origins and Implications

Edited by

Michael Flude and Merril Hammer

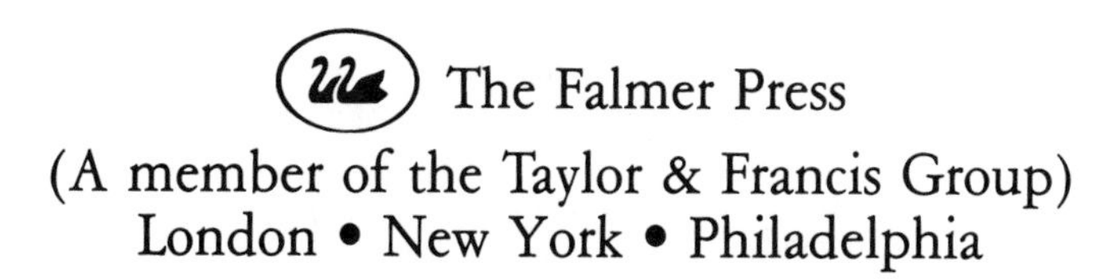

The Falmer Press
(A member of the Taylor & Francis Group)
London • New York • Philadelphia

UK The Falmer Press, Rankine Road, Basingstoke, Hants RG24 0PR

USA The Falmer Press, Taylor & Francis Inc., 1900 Frost Road, Suite 101, Bristol, PA 19007

First published 1990

British Library Cataloguing in Publication Data

The Education Reform Act, 1988: its origin and
implications
1. England. Education. Law: Education Act 1988
I. Flude, Michael II. Hammer, Merril
344.204′7

ISBN 1–85000–553–2
ISBN 1–85000–554–0 pbk

Library of Congress Cataloging-in-Publication Data

The Education Reform Act, 1988: its origins and
implications/edited by Michael Flude and Merril Hammer.
p. cm.
ISBN 1–85000–553–2. -- ISBN 1–85000–554–0 (pbk.)
1. Educational law and legislation--Great Britain.
2. Education and state--Great Britain. I. Flude, Michael.
II. Hammer, Merril.
KD3600.A75E35 1990
344.41′07--dc20 90–37681
[344.1047] CIP

Jacket design by Caroline Archer

Typeset in 10/12 Garamond by
Chapterhouse, The Cloisters, Formby L37 3PX

Printed in Great Britain by
Redwood Burn Limited, Trowbridge, Wiltshire

Contents

Introduction

Michael Flude and Merril Hammer

> Our education system has operated over the past 40 years on the basis of the framework laid down by Rab Butler's 1944 Act, which in turn built upon the Balfour Act of 1902. We need to inject a new vitality into that system. It has become producer-dominated. It has not proved sensitive to the demands for change that have become ever more urgent over the past ten years. This Bill will create a new framework, which will raise standards, extend choice and produce a better-educated Britain. (Kenneth Baker's opening speech in the Second Reading debate on the Education Reform Bill in the House of Commons, 1 December 1987, quoted in Haviland, 1988)

Acknowledged by friend and foe as a radical break with the past, the passing of the 1988 Education Reform Act heralds both a restructuring of the basic power bases of the education system and a decisive break with the political priorities that informed the drafting and passing of the 1944 Education Act and the subsequent 'partnership' that evolved between central state institutions, local authorities and teachers. Although in the early 1980s the imagery of partnership was frequently evoked by Secretaries of State, this was little more than a rhetorical device in a context where the centralization of state power was making rapid advances. With the passing of the 1988 Education Reform Act, no longer do a concern for equality of opportunity and the ideals of a fully comprehensive system of state education figure highly in national educational programmes and initiatives. Instead, the emphasis has come to be placed on parental choice and competition, the management of resources, people and institutions in an increasingly cost-conscious environment, and the extension of a new battery of central controls that establish a strong regulatory framework for state education.

In this collection of critical papers the contributors have sought to place the Act (and its various sections) within a broader socio-political and cultural context and to reflect critically on its origins and implications; on what the Act sets out to do and on its possible effects, intended or unintended. We regard the book as an early contribution to critical discussion, research and debates, within both the educational community and the wider public. Writing so soon after the Act was passed, authors have not simply had to be tentative about the outcomes of its implementation but have had to deal with a constantly changing influx of data — on National Curriculum requirements, on testing arrangements, on numbers and types of schools voting to opt out, on local management of schools regulations, on responses from teachers, parents and governors, etc.

We have attempted to give a full coverage of the major issues and dimensions of the legislation, and of the accompanying circulars that had been published at the time of writing. We are aware, however, that the coverage is not all-inclusive. In particular, we do not have a chapter addressing the abolition of the Inner London Education Authority (but see below); nor have we directly addressed the role of and the effects on the work of teachers in the implementation of the Act, although a number of contributors (particularly Whitty and Brehony) do address these issues, pointing to the immense array of new pressures and demands to be made on teachers: the implementation of a National Curriculum and assessments; the increasing competitiveness between schools with open enrolment and a grant-maintained sector; the institution of local management in schools and its possible consequences for job security. And all this at a time when teachers have lost their negotiating rights over pay and conditions of service and when schools are increasingly facing a shortage of qualified staff.

A further question not dealt with is whether the Education Reform Act can be seen as a measure which will allow for harmonization with Europe prior to the implementation of a unified market in 1992. As McLean's (1988) analysis shows, certain of the proposed changes closely mirror European practice, in particular the National Curriculum which 'presages, if not a common content of school education throughout the European Community, then at least a clearly identified set of equivalences' (ibid.) and, with the new central government powers to determine the curriculum, makes European-wide curriculum adjustment possible through concerted action by the governments of member states. Further, if the Education Reform Act is viewed as a stage in the destruction of Local Education Authorities, then the concomitant strengthening of both national and school level authority might also be seen as a move in a European direction. Other aspects of the Act cannot, however, be interpreted so clearly in terms of harmonization. Whatever the possibilities for harmonization within the Act, McLean clearly views the ideological underpinning as radically different:

> But the political philosophy underpinning the Act — a new version of the nineteenth century 'social contract' — diverges sharply from the 'corporatism' which continues to underlie educational policy in most other European countries. How can administrative marriage with Europe co-exist with philosophical divorce? (ibid.)

The contributors to this volume are not wholly negative about the Act nor about the possibilities for the future. Nor are they always in agreement with each other. Thus there is found support, in principle at least, for *a* National Curriculum and for greater accountability of schools to the local community. But one unifying feature of all contributions is their opposition to the ideologies of the New Right, whose influence on the Act is traced. In our overview below, we have not followed the organizing principles of the book: discussion of the provisions of the Act as they relate to schools; issues of concern for schools; Local Education Authorities; and the post-school sectors. The issues raised are not as discrete as this organization might suggest, so we have attempted to draw together some of the common themes in what follows.

Overview

In the opening chapter, Stewart Ranson considers the historical context and significance of the Education Reform Act and analyzes how it introduces a radical recasting of the powers and responsibilities of parties to the government of education: central and local government institutions, governors and parents. He argues that the distinctiveness of these changes can only be grasped as part of a broader reconstituting of the social and political order, the organizing principles of which celebrate the values of individual rights and choice. Ranson traces the growing influence of the New Right on educational and social policy in the 1980s and the way in which its vision of individual rights in a consumer democracy has sought to displace the post-war tradition of social justice and opportunity within a social democratic state. Whilst the greater emphasis placed on public involvement and accountability is welcomed, Ranson questions the appropriateness of consumerism in education. He concludes by proposing alternative conditions for realizing an active citizenship within the government of education.

Various chapters point to the ways in which changes in the ideological context of schooling have exerted a major influence in restructuring educational priorities. Some signs of this restructuring can be found in the Black Papers of the 1960s and 1970s, Callaghan's Ruskin College speech of 1976 and the so-called Great Debate of the mid-1970s. Shifts in the political agenda for state schooling intensified with the return of a Conservative government in 1979, although educational reform did not figure highly in the government's order of priorities until the mid-1980s. The advance of New Right ideologies, reflected in the growing influence of groups such as the Centre for Policy Studies and the Education Unit of the Institute of Economic Affairs, importantly created the space for the advocacy of new policies that not so many years earlier would have been discussed as eccentric and impractical. The 'successes' and 'popularity' of the government's privatization policies in industry and the sale of council houses also contributed to creating a socio-political context in which it was possible to extend these principles to other public sector services (Flude and Hammer, 1989).

There is by no means a clear and homogenous ideology that unifies the New Right. At least two major strands may be identified: the neo-liberal advocacy of the 'free market mechanism in economic and social policy on the one hand, and the proponents of social order, authority and traditional values on the other' (Salter and Tapper, 1985). Some commentators have seen these different tendencies within the New Right as giving rise to contradictions between the consumerist and centralizing provisions of the Education Reform Act. Geoff

Whitty's chapter takes as its starting point the apparent tension between the imposition of a National Curriculum and the stress on parental choice and market forces in determining the shape of the new curriculum. Differences within the New Right over the issue of the school curriculum are explored and Whitty points to ways in which neo-liberal and neo-conservative positions may ultimately be reconciled. Findings from a recent research project on the Assisted Places Scheme are drawn on by Whitty to consider some possible consequences of allowing market forces to determine the nature of the school curriculum. Finally, following his analysis of the 'atomization of decision-making' that marks government policy on open enrolment, local management of schools and grant-maintained schools, Whitty sees the National Curriculum as the 'one remaining symbol of a common education system'. This, he suggests, offers a potential site for collective struggles to tackle the injustices faced by groups and individuals whose aspirations and interests have been marginalized in recent years. Yet, as Hartnett and Naish (forthcoming) point out, it is more accurately described as a 'statutory' rather than a 'national' curriculum since it 'applies only to a part of the UK and then only to state-funded schools'.

In his chapter Whitty suggests that neither the neo-liberal nor the neo-conservative positions of the New Right may prove attractive to the government's industrial sponsors who wish the curriculum to be more responsive to the needs of industry. These conflicts within Conservatism between what Jones (1989) calls the 'traditional and modernizing tendencies' are further explored in the chapter by Hickox and Moore. The process of 'vocationalization' of education, as expressed particularly in the Technical and Vocational Education Initiative (TVEI) is discussed by the authors by reference to the 'crisis in liberal education'. This is seen to result from various trends associated with the expansion of education in the post-war period. It is argued that this expansion undermined liberal education in two ways. First, the effect of credit inflation in the labour market 'imposed increasing requirements for credentials without bringing individuals any net gain' in terms of improved employment or mobility. Second, the need to accommodate increasing numbers of young people in extended educational careers led to a diversification of courses and teaching styles which weakened traditional definitions of what counted as education. These two factors are seen to have created conflicts with, on the one hand, the predominantly instrumental interest which most people have in education (an interest in direct contrast to the liberal view of education as *intrinsically worthwhile*) and, on the other, with the traditional, grammar school model of 'excellence'. For Hickox and Moore these conflicts are currently reflected in the contradictory demands that education becomes either more vocational or more traditional. These demands are related to conflicts within the New Right between neo-conservative and neo-liberal traditionalists and the technicist manpower planners of the Training Agency (previously the Manpower Services Commission [MSC]). These groups are seen by Hickox and Moore as having in common only a shared desire to constrain the professional autonomy of teachers which is expressed in the way in which the Education Reform Act is reconstructing the system of control over education.

The major importance of the introduction of a National Curriculum is reflected elsewhere in the collection. Kevin Brehony's chapter looks at the National Curriculum in terms of its likely implications for primary schools. Like Whitty, Brehony stresses the importance of seeing the National Curriculum within its broader structural and political context. He examines the extent to which the National Curriculum may be seen as specifically addressing the issues raised in the debates about the primary school curriculum which have taken place since the late 1970s. Using a simple model for analyzing educational policy making (comparing what it claims to do with what it can do), the National Curriculum as it applies to primary schools is assessed from the point of view of its educational rationality. By this test, Brehony finds it lacking on a number of counts. It is argued that, insofar as it has anything to do with primary schools, the problems it is supposedly a response to are mainly political in origin, having been constructed principally by the New Right. HMI are shown also to have played a role in this, but that role mainly consisted in providing evidence which could be distorted and utilized by the New Right to further its aim of privatizing the education system. Moreover, Brehony suggests, in its disregard of the question of how the National Curriculum is to be implemented, by refusing to take account of the lack of human and material resources which it requires, the government has demonstrated that the National Curriculum, as it affects primary schools, has not an educational rationale, but a political one.

In their chapter, Hardy and Vieler-Porter point to some of the major implications of the market-directed provisions of the Education Reform Act for the black community. Thus, in the present political and media climate which stresses ideals of the individual and family above community and society and which depoliticizes, individualizes and pathologizes disadvantage, it is difficult for institutions to deliver social justice or even to win the ideological ground necessary to set about doing so. They consider how the National Curriculum and regulations governing the teaching of religious education and school assemblies seek to reconstruct through education a national identity based on a narrowly defined notion of 'Englishness'. This is seen to stand in stark contrast to the political ideals and aspirations of justice and equality which underlie the anti-racist movement. Despite the tight controls imposed by the Act, Hardy and Vieler-Porter suggest that it will be possible for those committed to an anti-racist perspective to subvert imaginatively the nationalistic intentions that their analysis of the Act highlights.

Miles and Middleton's chapter evaluates the case put forward by some liberal-feminists that the National Curriculum could promote equal opportunities by giving girls access to traditionally masculinized subject areas and occupations. Some of the factors which might inhibit the implementation of equal opportunities (such as classroom processes, teacher recruitment and training, and pupil attitudes to subject content and testing) are considered, and it is argued that in some respects at least, the Act will prove deleterious in its effects. Miles and Middleton also suggest that the differing strands of conservative ideology represented in the Act may have contradictory implications for girls' education. The National Curriculum is the DES's response to employer demands for an educated workforce that would provide a wider pool of ability regardless of gender, but the preference for traditional, subject-based forms of education may in fact prove damaging both to training efficiency and equal opportunities. Furthermore, it is suggested that the conservative commitment to traditional family life, as reflected in the Act by the call for greater parental 'choice', may conflict with moves that could improve career prospects for girls. Finally, Miles and Middleton argue that the liberal-feminist conception of equal opportunities that has informed much of the discussion around the National Curriculum is limited by its failure to address class and ethnic differences between girls.

Philippa Russell describes the National Curriculum as 'the cornerstone of the 1988 Act' and argues that in certain respects the Act may reinforce the concept of entitlement and participation for all children, including those with special educational needs. However, the notion of attainment targets and programmes of study are seen to pose potentially serious threats to the flexibility introduced by the 1981 Education Act and its procedures. The 1981 Education Act made radical changes in the organization and philosophy of special education. It introduced the concept of a continuum of special educational needs, abolished categories of handicap, emphasized the importance of multi-professional assessment and gave parents new rights and responsibilities with regard to involvement in the assessment of their child's special educational needs. Most importantly, the 1981 Act gave local authorities a dynamic strategic role in orchestrating a range of multi-professional services to ensure that children's needs were met in the most appropriate way. It is suggested that, with the passing of the 1988 Act, the devolution from LEA to schools *may* encourage a grassroots service concern for meeting the needs of all children. However, valuable local authority resources and expertise, and the wider perspective on special needs, may be lost. Although the National Curriculum Council has emphasized the importance of involving all children within the new curriculum, Russell points out that it remains to be seen whether the National Curriculum is one for all children or whether the 1988 Act will have a retrogressive effect on the recent trend towards integration.

Various chapters in the collection discuss ways in which the Act increases competition and introduces the philosophy and values of a market economy into state education. An essential component of this change is the need for performance indicators to inform the activities of consumers in the market place. The system of national assessments has a vital role in this respect. Roger Murphy traces the evolving framework of national assessment, including the guidelines presented by the Secretary of State's Task Group on Assessment and Testing. He also looks at some of the tensions between the desire to make national assessments into simple performance indicators, and the fear that they could become crude and misleading measurements of the real achievements of pupils. Murphy gives particular attention to the role of teachers in the national assessments and to the wider purposes national assessments could fulfil if they are truly to reflect the achievements of all pupils in relation to the full breadth of the National Curriculum.

The 1986 Education Act, which extended the power of school governors, and the proposals for setting up city technology colleges announced in October 1986, prefigured the Education Reform Act's push to diversify the provision of schooling and subject educational institutions to a demand-led environment. In their chapter on grant-maintained schools, Flude and Hammer explore proposals to establish this new category of schools in a series of papers published by New Right groups. The support given to freeing schools from local authority control is seen as an important constituent element within an incrementalist strategy for 'liberating' consumer interests, and as a means of moving towards a system of educational vouchers. The progress of the proposal for grant-maintained schools to the statute book is traced, and subsequent circulars and financial regulations are examined and evaluated. Flude and Hammer argue that the combined effects of the inability of local authorities to plan provision, the possible financial gains for grant-maintained schools and the inherent pressures for selection in a system of different categories of schools point to the development of a hierarchy of schools. At the same time, the development of a grant-maintained sector is seen to extend further the processes of privatization in education.

That aspects of the Education Reform Act are consistent with a move towards a system of educational vouchers is taken up in other chapters. Hywel Thomas argues that it is essential to distinguish local financial management (LFM) from local management of schools (LMS) as a prerequisite for a proper understanding of the changes in the Act. LMS is described as creating a framework for a system of educational vouchers. The various elements of this voucher economy comprise financial delegation, formula funding, open enrolment, staffing delegation and performance indicators. Thomas goes on to analyze the role of markets in shaping the delivery of LMS and also reviews the place of professional commitment as an influence upon outcomes. Arising from this is a discussion of the training implications for those with responsibility for managing schools within a more competitive environment.

Similarly to Hywel Thomas, Andrew Stillman sees open enrolment and local management of schools offering a backdoor voucher system. Along with the introduction of grant-maintained schools, these initiatives are the latest developments in a series of legislative measures since 1980 that subject the education system to greater parental choice and accountability. The government's strategy of seeking improvements in education by subjecting schools to market forces is critically evaluated. Following his discussion of the parliamentary history of parental choice, Andrew Stillman draws on the findings of an NFER-sponsored research project to evaluate the implementation of the 1980 Education Act, and to question whether open enrolment and the increased variety of schools will increase parental choice.

Another ongoing strategy for increasing consumer choice has been changes in the composition and responsibilities of school and college governing bodies. These changes are examined by Rosemary Deem with respect to schools and by Lorna Unwin in the post-compulsory sector. Deem's chapter begins by tracing the history of school governing bodies since 1944, before moving on to consider the impact of the 1986 and 1988 Education Acts. The 1986 Act reshaped governing bodies, reducing LEA nominations and increasing parental and co-opted membership whilst also giving new powers and duties to governors. The 1988 Education Reform Act, especially in relation to local management of schools, open admissions, charging and the National Curriculum, has added to the heavy responsibilities the new governing bodies carry in their oversight of schools. Drawing on recent and continuing research, Deem goes on to look at who has become a governor since Autumn 1988 and whose interests are thereby represented or under-represented. Also explored are some of the assumptions underlying the reforming of the membership of governing bodies and the coping strategies being used by school governors to manage these responsibilities.

Lorna Unwin's chapter considers the impact of the 1988 Education Reform Act on further and adult education (FE/AE) in the light of other key initiatives which have served over the past decade to transform the post-compulsory sector. She argues that in contrast to its treatment of the school sector, the Act does not address the FE/AE curriculum but concentrates instead on restructuring the balance of power and control. The FE/AE curriculum, however, is already being reshaped by the National Council for Vocational Qualifications (NCVQ) and the Training Agency, a development which the Act does not seek to challenge. Although the Act does not directly offer FE/AE institutions, unlike schools, the choice of 'opting out', it stipulates the creation of new industry-dominated governing bodies who may, in the near future, be keen to seek independence from their Local Education Authorities. Unwin characterizes the Act as taking a broad brush approach to FE/AE and implies there is an acceptance that interpretation can be left to local agencies. Placed in context alongside other centrally orchestrated developments such as the switch to competence-based qualifications, Training and Enterprise Councils and the move away from state-funded public sector services, the Act is seen as completing the jigsaw of educational provision for the 1990s and beyond. Like other chapters that have pointed to the Act extending the process of privatization in state education, Unwin regards it as a significant policy mechanism enabling the government to push forward the wholesale privatization of both further and adult education, a move which has major implications for tutors, students, parents, local authorities, community groups and employers.

Whereas some commentators in this collection and elsewhere (e.g., Troyna, 1988; Walton, 1988) have pointed to the erosion of local authorities' policy-making function and responsibilities, these aspects of the Act's impact are regarded by Wallace as less significant than the strengthening of local authorities' planning functions, especially those concerning the implementation and delivery of the National Curriculum. Wallace writes from the point of view of a local authority adviser engaged in implementing the Act locally. He largely approves of the establishment of a National Curriculum, although the implementation of this is seen to be dependent on adequate resourcing. His analysis points to the restructuring of local authority powers and responsibilities: the enhancement of these with respect to the delivery of the National Curriculum; the shedding of managerial responsibility for institutional and non-educational activities; and, by implication, the marginalization of local democratic influence on the policy process and goals. In contrast to Hywel Thomas' chapter, Wallace views local management of schools as a largely peripheral matter in relation to local authorities' influence over schools.

Whatever the merits of Wallace's argument that LEAs have been given 'a much more interventionist and influential role in relation to schools and colleges' through the Education Reform Act, the history of and arguments about the Inner London Education Authority show clearly that there are strong pressures within the New Right for removing the powers of local authorities. Surviving proposals in 1979, 1981 and 1983 to abolish the Authority, ILEA became a directly-elected single-purpose authority in 1985 following abolition of the Greater London Council. Then, in 1987 in the Education Reform Bill consultation papers, with the justification that 'the new ILEA has shown little sign that it is ready to tackle the root causes of its educational and financial problems' (DES, 1987), the government proposed that individual boroughs would be able 'to apply to become LEAs for their areas. ILEA will continue to be the local education authority for the areas of those boroughs who do not choose to take advantage of this opportunity' (ibid.). Between publication of the Bill and the passing of the Act, the legislative provisions changed. Michael Heseltine and Norman Tebbit, ex-ministers in the Thatcher government, joined forces at the Committee stage in the House of Commons to move an amendment which replaced the opting-out clause with a simple proposal for immediate abolition and transfer to the boroughs. 'Faced with the prospect of defeat at the hands of their own back-benchers, ministers bowed to the inevitable and submitted their own amendments along these lines' (Maclure, 1988). Thirteen new borough-based LEAs would be established on 1 April 1990.

The arguments for the abolition of ILEA bear a close resemblance to those of the New Right for creating grant-maintained schools: 'The ILEA incurs excessive costs; it displays overall poor standards of attainment, which moreover vary enormously from school to school; it has tolerated or even encouraged a politicised curriculum and the introduction of politicised appointments and teachers' (Hillgate Group, 1987). And for the Centre for Policy Studies, the demise of the ILEA is seen as only a first step in the right direction:

> For here is an opportunity to tackle one of the most serious threats to education reform — the dominance of Local Education Authorities (LEAs) in running the school system. As long as LEAs continue to control the life of individual schools through their extensive bureaucracy and support services, the aims of reform will be frustrated. Higher standards for pupils, greater responsibility for schools and more choice for parents, will remain illusory. The root of the problem is the LEA system itself, which must not be left intact... Abolition of the ILEA provides the occasion for the necessary reduction of the powers, scope and role of the LEAs (Lawlor, 1988).

The final chapter in the collection considers the Education Reform Act alongside other radical changes occurring in British higher education in the 1980s. Gareth Williams argues that the main provisions of the Education Reform Act with respect to higher education — the removal of the polytechnics and colleges from local authority control and the establishment of the Universities Funding Council (UFC) and the Polytechnic and College Funding Council (PCFC) — were an almost inevitable result of tensions in the system since the time of Robbins and Crosland's announcement in 1965 of the binary policy. For the future, Williams argues that there is no inevitability about the UFC and PCFC coming together: indeed, he suggests it is more likely that they will grow apart with the two sectors of higher education performing different functions. It is claimed that the dominant influence on British higher education during the 1990s will be the dramatic fall in the school-leaving population following the decline in the birth rate between 1965 and the end of the 1970s. It is acknowledged that it is not easy to predict what the effects of this will be. On the one hand, there will almost certainly be fewer traditional applicants for higher education; on the other, there is likely to be a severe shortage of graduates by the mid-1990s which will raise the private rate of return to higher education very considerably. This will encourage enrolment rates to rise. Governments, it is argued, will face similar conflicts. There will be pressures to shift public expenditure towards the needs of an ageing population and, at the same time, there will be pressure to increase expenditure on higher education in order to meet the needs of a growing economy in an age of rapidly expanding technology. Williams concludes with an expression of concern about the quality of higher education and claims that mass higher education is a mirage if it simply means increased access to under-resourced and low quality universities, polytechnics and colleges.

References

DEPARTMENT OF EDUCATION AND SCIENCE (1987) *Consultation Paper: The Organisation of Education in Inner London*, London, HMSO.

FLUDE, M. and HAMMER, M. (1989) *Changing Schools, Changing Curriculum*, Units 9/10, E208 *Exploring Educational Issues*, Milton Keynes, The Open University Press.

HARTNETT, A. and NAISH, M. (forthcoming) 'The sleep of reason breeds monsters: The birth of a statutory curriculum in England and Wales', *Journal of Curriculum Studies*.

HAVILAND, J. (Ed.) (1988) *Take Care, Mr Baker!*, London, Fourth Estate.

HILLGATE GROUP (1987) *The Reform of British Education*, London, The Claridge Press.

JONES, K. (1989) *Right Turn: The Conservative Revolution in Education*, London, Hutchinson Radius.

LAWLOR, S. (1988) *Away with LEAs: ILEA Abolition as a Pilot*, London, Centre for Policy Studies.

MACLURE, S. (1988) *Education Re-Formed*, London, Hodder and Stoughton.

MCLEAN, M. (1988) 'The Conservative education policy in comparative perspective: Return to an English golden age or harbinger of international policy change', *British Journal of Educational Studies*, *XXXVI*, 3, pp. 200–17.

SALTER, B. and TAPPER, T. (1985) *Power and Policy in Education: The Case of Independent Schooling*, Lewes, Falmer Press.

TROYNA, B. (1988) 'The dawn of a new ERA? The Education Reform Act; "race" and LEAs'. Paper given at Conference, Local Authorities and Racial Equality, Policies and Practice, University of Warwick, 24–25 September.

WALTON, B. (1988) 'The impact of government's educational legislation upon local government', *Local Government Studies*, January/February.

1
From 1944 to 1988: Education, Citizenship and Democracy

Stewart Ranson

The Education Reform Act (29 July 1988) proposes the most radical redirection of the service since 1944. Yet the 1988 Act will seek to emulate as well as replace its revered predecessor. For the intention of both pieces of legislation was and is not only to recreate the form of education government but to do so as the significant part of a broader reconstituting of the social and political order. Within this Act, as elsewhere, there is the vision of a consumer democracy that is intended to replace the purported weary assumptions of the liberal democratic state which have lasted for a generation and more.

This chapter seeks to understand the Act in this historic context and to separate out what will contribute to, as against diminish, the education service. I shall argue that the principal shift in direction — towards public involvement and accountability — is to be acclaimed, although the means chosen are often to be derided.

Beginning with the terms which will shape the analysis of the chapter, I shall describe the context of the Act before discussing its historic role. The chapter critically evaluates the market philosophy which informs the Act and concludes by arguing for a different set of conditions for active citizenship within the government of education.

Understanding education and the political order

The significance of education is very deep-seated historically. Church and state have struggled to control its form and purpose. Understandably, because the process of learning can shape not only the purposes of individuals but through them beliefs about the ordering of society and polity. The shaping of individuals is at the same time the shaping of a generation. Choices about the purpose of education take on a wider significance as an expression of social and political purpose (Williams, 1965). The vehicle for the elaboration of educational aims as social purpose is found in the structuring of government which constitutes distinctive values in policies and in its supporting organizational forms. For some the government of education possesses the distinctive role in articulating and embodying the vision of society's future (Centre for Contemporary Cultural Studies 1978). The restructuring of the government of education in 1988 as much as in 1944 reveals a similar objective, though informed by opposed visions, of social as well as educational regeneration. This understanding of forms of government constituting and reconstituting a moral and political order derives from Weber (1968). A review of these analytical ideas can clarify the framework which shapes the ensuing argument.

Weber wanted to grasp the uniqueness of modern society while appreciating the similarity of social processes within different historical periods. For him all social forms exhibit a 'dominant order' of beliefs and values which legitimate the structure of power and organization. Societies reveal a distinctive pattern of power, values and organization. Power, the capacity to make people comply, is organized through appropriate forms of administration. But, typically, men and women obey not because of coercion or custom or material gain, but because the organizing and exercise of power are based upon consent and thus acquire authority. A form of rule is accepted because it is informed by a moral order which is perceived as legitimate. It is the legitimate authority of this dominant order of values and beliefs which provides an historical period with its distinctive character and uniqueness.

Weber was aware that the organizing principles of a dominant order would endure not only because they reflected shared ideal values embedded in appropriate forms, but also because the enduring structure was sustained by and grounded in a 'constellation of interests'. The ruling order results in a distribution of advantage, status and power which favours some groups in society; these groups, in turn, strive to perpetuate an order which serves their interests. The fairer the distribution the more likely the order will persist through time.

An emerging system of government, therefore, reveals a distinctive order of ruling values and interests which hold sway because men and women believe them to be legitimate. Power and organization are authorized in agreement about the form of rule (Figure 1). The elements of analysis can be set out in a simple model which describes the constituting of a social and political order[1]. The argument of the chapter is that the 1944 Education Act and the 1988 Education Act were and are about shaping educational purpose and government in order to secure the constituting of a (ruling) social and political order. The upshot of the ensuing analysis, however, will be that the shift in ruling values could be posed as a

Figure 1 A Model for Analysing the Social and Political Order

ORGANIZING PRINCIPLES	CONSTITUTIVE SYSTEM	SOCIETY
• Values • Beliefs • Ideas	The form of government organization and procedure	• Interest groups • Power

complementary development while the current debate is posed in terms of conflict and mutual rejection.

The 1944 Education Act: justice as fairness

The 1944 Education Act was aimed at radical change as Halsey, Heath and Ridge (1980) have argued. It was a great Act which formed a system of education government that has lasted for forty years. What enabled it to sustain such an achievement? Its accomplishment was, firstly, to express a sophisticated understanding of power in relation to the tasks to be undertaken and, secondly, to express values and interests which were perceived as legitimate and achieved a consensus across society which has lasted a generation.

Power and responsibilities were distributed amongst the parties to education so as to form, as Briault (1976) has called it, 'a triangle of tension, of checks and balances'. Legislators held beliefs not just about the importance of diffusing power over educational decision-making so as to prevent unwarranted concentration of control over such a vital service, but also to organize power in a way that was appropriate to the task. Thus the Education Ministers and their Department were to control and direct education, but through clarifying and promoting broad policy objectives and by securing the appropriate volume of national resources. The Local Education Authority was the 'providing' authority — building, staffing and maintaining schools, and planning a local function in relation to local needs and demands and statutory responsibilities:

> It shall be the duty of the LEA for every area, so far as their powers extend, to contribute towards the spiritual, moral, mental, and physical development of the community . . . .(Section 7, 1944 Education Act)

The development of the curriculum and appropriate teaching methods were regarded as largely the professional responsibilities of teachers in schools guided by university syllabuses. Parents had a duty to send their children to school although the LEA had a duty to make schooling responsive to parents: 'Pupils are to be educated in accordance with the wishes of their parents' (S.76). In short, Whitehall was to promote education, Town and County Hall was to plan and provide, teachers were to nurture the learning process so as to meet the needs of children and the wishes of parents. The constitutive system of the government of education formed a complex, 'polycentred'[2] division of power and responsibility appropriate to differentiated tasks. Divided power was designed to ensure partnership between necessary and equal parties to the government of education.

It became, nevertheless, a decentralized system constituted in a way which reflected dominant beliefs about the key relationship between teacher and child. Centre, locality and profession were accorded the necessary authority to support that relationship:

> The keynote of the new system will be that the child is the centre of education and that, so far as is humanly possible, all children should

> receive the type of education to which they are best adapted. (HMSO, 1943).

The system of education embodied in the 1944 Education Act was constituted to implement radical change in educational purposes and values.

Before the 1944 Education Act most young people only received an elementary schooling. The Act realized for the first time Tawney's ideal of universal free secondary education for all directed to the needs and capacities of youngsters rather than dependent upon the material well-being, status and power of their parents. The Act established the universal right to personal development through education.

If these radical ideas for the expansion of educational opportunities are to be fully understood, however, they have to be located within a broader context of social reconstruction and reform which began during the Second World War. There was a groundswell of social and political opinion that there could be no returning to the social order of the 1930s: idleness, poverty, disease, ignorance and squalor had to give way to employment, income, personal dignity, health and opportunity. The unity which had won the war would recreate a new more just, open and modern society. While Keynes offered the design for economic planning and Beveridge shaped the blueprint for universal welfare support, Butler provided the framework for educational opportunity and the possibility of social mobility that could dissolve a rigid, outmoded, class-divided society:

> The state came to be seen as something vaster and more beneficent . . . as the real guarantor of reform and reconstruction . . . .(Middlemas 1979)

The state was constituting the institutional conditions for citizenship: common membership and dignity which derives from contributing to the wealth production of community in which one lives; the universal right to health and welfare services in times of need; equality of educational opportunity to fulfil personal powers and capacities; and the right to franchise and representation within the polity. Archbishop Temple articulated the importance of the 1944 reforms to creating an educated democracy of citizens who would form the only safeguard against the memories of encroaching fascism in the 1930s:

> Until education has done far more than it has had the opportunity of doing, it cannot have society organized on the basis of justice: for this reason there will always be a strain . . . between what is due to a man in view of his humanity with all his powers and capacity and what is due to him at the moment as a member of society with all his faculties underdeveloped with many of his tastes warped and with his powers largely crushed. Are you going to treat a man as what he is or what he might be? That is the whole work of education. Give (the man) the full development of his powers and there will no longer be conflict between the claim of the man as he is and of the man as he might become. And so you can have no justice as the basis of your social life until education has done its full work . . . and you cannot have political freedom any

> more than you can have moral freedom until people's powers have developed, for the simple reason that over and over again we find that men with a cause which is just are unable to state it in a way which might enable it to prevail . . . There exists a mental form of slavery that is as real as any economic form. We are pledged to destroy it . . . If you want human liberty you must have educated people. (Archbishop Temple, 1982)

Yet the unity which framed the post-war educational and social reconstruction was a political settlement, a contract between the estates of the realm: capital, labour and the state (Middlemas, 1979). Bullock (1960) recalls the belligerence of Bevin in forging a social and political partnership for peace: 'Why should the working class lend the government money for war with no guarantee of employment or improvement after.' Kogan (1978) and Maclure (1985), as well as Middlemas (1979), have recalled the great radical move to create a social and political order that afforded justice and opportunity. As Butler described in his *The Conservatives*: 'Our contribution, flanked by the Worker's Charter, attempted to give capitalism a human look'.[3] This was the orthodoxy of the wise and the good in the immediate post-war years.

This post-war partnership, though contracted, had widespread political appeal and formed a cross-party consensus for a generation. A state, a system of rule, had been constituted which endured. Its organizing of power and task were legitimated by a moral and political order whose primary value was justice as fairness: the foundation stone of common citizenship. If the 'contract' had received a philosopher's seal it would, in retrospect, have been Rawls' (1971). If men and women were to decide the foundation charter of their society — that is, the basic institutional structure of rights and duties, of advantage and disadvantage — they would, in the 'original position' where none know their advantage or how society will turn out, choose to create a fair society. They would constitute a just structure which would provide the conditions for equal citizenship and the inviolability of each person. Individual freedom and well-being for all required agreement about the basic constitutive rules that would ensure a society based upon justice as fairness. Those contracting a foundation charter would choose a just structure in order to secure freedom. Freedom requires justice, argued Rawls.

An interlude through time

Nurturing young citizens

It was in the 1960s that the institutional conditions for equal educational opportunities really began to be developed. The invidious selective system which labelled and excluded 'failures' gave way to schools committed to a comprehensive education for all; the expansion of higher education opened up opportunities previously restricted to an elite. At the same time, primary education promoted the child-centred learning which could deliver the promise of the 1943 White Paper.

The emphasis upon the education of each individual pupil reinforced the original bias to decentralization within the system. Only the professional judgement of teachers in the classroom could identify the learning needs of each pupil and release their talents and capacities. Other partners needed to support their fragile relationship. Young citizens had to be nurtured in a caring environment by professionals dedicated to public service.

Education, like other services although more reluctantly, began to reach out to its public and consult them about proposals for comprehensive reorganization. It was often at the level of informing the public.

Structural change and surplus capacity

The liberal democratic state was shaken by a transformed context from the early 1970s. The oil crisis precipitated a recession and a 'fiscal crisis' in public expenditure as the cost of services outgrew the political will to pay for them. Contraction seemed inevitable. Yet such economic changes were overshadowed by even more significant structural changes in employment. Massey and Meegan (1982) produced a powerful account of the mechanisms of industrial intensification, rationalization and technical innovation which explain the anatomy of 1980s job losses. The revolution in the nature of work created by these new information technologies seems finally to be emerging. The shedding of surplus capacity through the restructuring of work began to raise fundamental questions about the necessity and distribution of work: was work an intrinsic part of personal identity, dignity and citizenship? These cyclical and structural changes in the economy parallel and reinforce changes in society: growing poverty as well as division between north and south fragment family patterns, often reflecting the changing relations between men and women; a multicultural society with black and ethnic minorities striving for greater equality; boredom as well as anxiety and alienation; and a more politicized world as differences about ways of resolving economic and social problems begin to sharpen.

The corporate response: rationalizing opportunities

Economic crisis created 'steering problems' for the state. To maintain control and integration the state progressively extends its boundaries of intervention. The corporate state strives to achieve national unity and order by increasingly concentrating and rationalizing its control. In education, from the mid-1970s, government challenged the dominant ethos of personal development and promoted in its place the vocational preparation of young people for their future economic roles. Education in the future must be accountable to society and economy. Given a contracting labour market it was deemed sensible to rationalize educational opportunities accordingly. Idle, educated hands. . . .Power shifted rapidly to the centre as Whitehall administrators extended their control at the expense of the local authorities and the teachers. The struggle focused upon whether the Manpower Services Commission (MSC) or the DES would prevail.

The pamphleteers of consumer rights and accountability

The transformed context had generated a review of the purposes and practices of the education service as well as the roles and relationships between the education partners. There was growing agreement about the need for change and redirection of the service. For some,[4] the upholders of comprehensive education, the emphasis was upon reforming and developing existing practice: celebrating more diverse aims of learning, broadening the curriculum, and reforming assessment. For others,[5] the New Right, the reform of education required a rejection of the whole post-war scheme of things. For them the original 'charter' was misguided. It is this second critique which has come to dominate the polity and has informed the preparations for the 1988 Education Reform Act. The analysis which underlies this critique needs to be made clear before the Act can be described and understood.

The challenge to the post-war ruling order in education, as in the polity, grew over an extended period; its views were increasingly articulated and influential. Three main overlapping phases can be analysed: the first phase (1969–77) consisted of a number of Black Papers which attacked the quality of comprehensive schooling and the need to strengthen the voice of parents in education. In the second phase (1974–84), Conservative Party education leaders developed a 'parents charter', a theory which tied educational quality to consumer accountability, and an initial phase of legislative reform — the 1980 Education Act — which presented parents with extensive information about schools, allowed them limited discretion in choosing schools, and strengthened their representation on school governing bodies. In the third period (1984–8) a revolution in parental power is conceived, culminating in Parliament in 1987–8 with the new Education Reform Act. Here I wish to draw out the common and developing thread in the argument about the need to radically expand the role of parents in the education service.

This growing critique of post-war education focuses upon purported failures of achievement, on inadequate and distorted curricula, and the root causes of the problems — said to be the stifling control of professional bureaucracies. Standards have fallen is the cry. Test scores and exam results have declined because comprehensive schools have replaced IQ selection and tripartism.[6] Child-centred learning has distracted children from the three Rs and, moreover, is to blame for the lack of discipline within schools. By the 1980s the attack of the pamphleteers had shifted to the politicization of the curriculum ('anti-racism', 'peace studies', and so on) and the emphasis on 'soft', artificial subjects (for example, life and social skills). Indeed, the whole purpose of schooling has, it is claimed, been distorted by its preoccupation with equality. Such social engineering and egalitarianism is mistaken: education is intrinsically individual and inequality of achievement inescapable.

These failures of education, it is argued, derive from professionals and (local) politicians appropriating control of the service from its proper source — the parents. The 'producers' have taken over and pursue their own purposes at the expense of the needs of the 'consumers' of the service. The Adam Smith Institute's Omega File on Education generalizes the problems facing education in common with other state monopolies as those of 'producer capture': 'whereby the service comes to be organized more to suit the needs of producers than consumers'. The professionals create a technical language which serves only to bamboozle ordinary people and they organize the system for their convenience rather than to respond to the demands of its consumers. The result is inertia and resistance to change.

The pamphleteers call for action and change: 'Nothing short of radical measures are needed to improve the state maintained system of education and to placate its growing critics, the parents, the employers and the children themselves' (Sexton, 1987). The solution lies in new values and beliefs about education and the reconstituting of the government of education to suit.

The values of the New Right pamphleteers emphasize that the education system must be built upon the principles of public choice and accountability. Individual parents have an inalienable right to choose the education which their children receive. The values articulate beliefs about educational achievement which assert that a system which is accountable and responsive to the choices of individual consumers of the service will improve in quality as a necessary consequence. As in other forms of market exchange, the products which thrive can only do so because they have the support of consumers. Those products which fail the test of the market place go out of business. The astringent experience of the market can be the test of quality in schooling as much as in the production of chocolate bars.

For consumers to fulfil their allotted role as quality controllers in the market place they require some diversity of product, information about the scope of choice and the quality of performance, as well as the opportunity to choose.

If schools were made to respond to the market 'there would be a built-in mechanism to raise standards and change forms and types of education in accordance with that market demand':

> In short, it supposes that the wisdom of parents separately and individually exercised, but taken together becoming the collective wisdom is more likely to achieve higher standards more quickly and more acceptably to the public than the collective wisdom of the present bureaucrats, no matter how well meaning those bureaucrats may be. (Sexton, 1987)

Creating this direct accountability between consumer and producer is the secret, it is argued, to renewal in education. To shift from a producer to a consumer led system will take time but placing public choice at the heart of the system will release the quality which is at present alleged to be submerged under the weight of administration.

Radical reforms are proposed for the government of education in order to reconstitute it according to these new organizing principles and values. The pamphleteers propose to dismantle the present system of education government. For some, even the DES will become 'superfluous' over a period of time as the routines of the market establish themselves. The Omega File, however, envisages a continuing and strengthened role for HM Inspectorate to ensure standards are maintained and teaching is of an acceptable quality. For the Hillgate Group, the state becomes an essential guarantor of the nation's traditional culture and values,

> safeguarding our educational tradition . . . a repository of knowledge, an inheritance that survives only if it is enshrined in durable institutions which have the means and purpose to pass it on. (The Hillgate Group, 1986)

A variety of strong, increasingly independent institutions are proposed which will provide a differentiated system of schools and colleges that will allow diversity of choice for parents. The independent sector would be reinforced, the direct grant schools recreated, 'magnet' and city technology schools established, grammar and secondary moderns restored *de facto*.

The root of the current problems, argue the pamphleteers, lies with the LEAs which should be stripped of their powers and eliminated from the system of education government. In time it is proposed that the ownership of all schools and the management of teachers should transfer to independent trusts or boards. This would create self-governing institutions under the control of parent governors and subject to consumer pressures in the market place. The survival of schools

> should depend on their ability to satisfy their customers. And their principal customers are parents, who should therefore be free to place their custom where they wish in order that educational institutions should be shaped, controlled and nourished by their demand. (The Hillgate Group, 1986)

Strengthening the rights of individual consumers is the secret to improved educational quality.

Rights and choice in a new social order

The values and reforms express a conception of good government of education but also play a key part in reconstituting a new social and political order. The organizing principles of the new order espouse the values of individual rights and choice.

'There are only individual people with their own individual lives', argues Nozick (1974). Individuals are morally self-sufficient and their dignity derives from expressing their unique individuality. What property and skills they possess they are entitled to keep and deploy as they choose. These are natural, inalienable rights, as Locke proposed. The notion of Rawls, that inherited skill forms a common asset to mankind, is unintelligible according to this perspective.

The general well-being of society is best served when individuals are allowed to pursue their self-interest. Although individuals only enter society and form associations to further their self-interest, nevertheless, the unintended consequence — guided by a hidden hand — is the general well-being of all in society. When individuals are free to compete with each other in the market place they can exchange goods and services to mutual advantage while the efficiency of this allocation secures benefit for all.

If individuals are to acquire the necessary freedom to calculate their interests then government needs to be constrained. For some (for example, Nozick) the 'minimal state' should be 'limited to the narrow function of protection against force, fraud, enforcement of contracts, and so on . . . ' (*ibid.*). Others, such as Bentham, believe that if the market place is to be protected then the state requires a few extra powers to regulate the deviations of social misfits. The surveillance of the panopticon has its place.

The legitimacy of this moral order derives from its protection of individual interests but also from enabling freedom of choice. The values encourage an active polity whose members are conceived not as passive, dependent, creatures but as agents reflecting upon and actively developing their interests. Government is made to serve and to account to the market place.

From pamphlets to legislation: the 1988 Education Act

The Education Reform Act is indeed a radical recasting of the education service constituting in its proposals many of the principles and values of the new liberalism outlined above. The Bill, which was presented to Parliament on 20 November 1987, conforms closely to a series of consultative papers published during that summer. The passing of the Act on 29 July 1988 can be seen as the culmination of a decade's campaigning to strengthen the rights of parents in the government of education. The pamphleteer's proposals had now passed through the precincts of Parliament. Introducing the legislation in Parliament, the Secretary of State said the reforms would

> galvanise parental involvement in schools. Parents will have more choice. They will have greater variety of schools to choose from. We will create new types of schools. Parents will be far better placed to know what their children are being taught and what they are learning . . . And (they) will introduce competition into the public provision of education. This competition will introduce a new dynamic into our schools system which will stimulate better standards all round.[7]

Parent power in a market place of schools that are made more accountable to their consumers will improve educational standards. Yet in the transformed system of government the Education Secretary realizes the lost powers of 'control and direction', institutions are strengthened and the LEA diminished. I shall review the Act's provisions in terms of their implications for the constituencies of education decision-making.

Parents are to be brought centre-stage in the establishing of an education market place. Parents are accorded choice, influence over governing bodies and control — if they choose — of new grant-maintained (GM) schools. 'Open' enrolment is designed to end the LEAs' capacity hitherto to place artificial limits on admission to schools. 'The government is committed to securing wider parental choice within the system of state schools'. To this end schools will be allowed to recruit up to their available capacity defined as physical capacity or 'the standard number' admitted in 1979 (when schools were largely full) or, if it is higher, the number admitted in the year before the legislation takes effect. If a governing body decides it wishes to accept a larger number of pupils it can apply to the Secretary of State. Moreover, local electors can object to the Education Secretary if they believe an LEA has set the limit too low.

Parents are to acquire a determining influence over school governing bodies. The 1986 Education (No.2) Act gave parents an equal representation with the LEA on governing bodies. Now the new Act gives governors responsibilities for school budgets, the appointment and dismissal of staff as well as the ability to overrule an LEA on redeployment of staff. The Act extends such proposals to the governing bodies of colleges. The representation of college consumers — for example, business and commerce — are increased 'to ensure that the governing body is, and is seen to be, properly independent of the maintaining LEA'.

Parents are to be granted the capacity to acquire control of schools if they choose:

> The Government is taking action to increase the autonomy of schools and their responsiveness to parental wishes....The Government considers that it should... respond to the numerous indications it has received that groups of parents want responsibility of running their schools as individual institutions. It proposes to provide an additional route to autonomy by introducing legislation... to enable governors of county and voluntary maintained schools, with the support of parents, to apply to the Secretary of State for maintenance by grant from Central Government, instead of maintenance by LEAs. The Government believes that this proposal... will add a new and powerful dimension to the ability of parents to exercise choice within the publicly provided sector of education. The greater diversity of provision which will result should enhance the prospect of improving education standards in all schools. Parents and local communities would have new opportunities to secure the development of their schools in ways appropriate to the needs of their children and in accordance with their wishes, within the legal framework of a national curriculum. (DES, 1987b)

These schools will receive grant directly from the Secretary of State and will form a new type of independent school within the maintained sector and, initially at least, they will retain their existing form (a comprehensive cannot opt out and immediately become a grammer school). Governors of the larger primary schools as well as of all county and voluntary secondary schools can apply to opt out. Circular 10/88 (DES, 1988) describes how parents, if necessary, can override the opposition of governors and pursue their own application according to the same rules. Parents will have a determining influence on the governing bodies of newly-formed GM Schools.

Other independent schools, known as city technology colleges (CTCs) will accompany GM schools in creating much greater variety of institutions for parents to choose from in the market place. As McLeod (1988) discusses, CTCs will be established by the Secretary of State who 'may enter into agreement with any person' to provide such urban schools. They will offer free education for pupils of different abilities with a broad curriculum given an emphasis on science and technology. CTCs have more discretion in relation to the national curriculum than other LEA schools although they must broadly adhere to it as a condition of receiving grant.

Schools and colleges are to be granted more autonomy so that they can become more responsive and accountable to their consumers. The Act delegates financial responsibilities to school governors:

> (i) To ensure that parents and the community know on what basis the available resources are distributed in their area and how much is spent on each school; (ii) to give the governors of all county and voluntary secondary schools and of larger primary schools freedom to take expenditure decisions which match their own priorities and the guarantee that their own school will benefit if they achieve efficiency savings. (DES, 1987a)

Circular 7/88[8] describes how LEAs will be required to submit to the Secretary of State 'schemes' which will describe how they propose to delegate financial resources to schools including the allocation formula to be used. Parents will be able to assess the efficiency of each school:

> At the end of each year the LEA would be required to publish information on actual expenditure at each school which could be compared to the original plans. This information together with that required of governors relating to the achievement of the national curriculum would provide the basis on which parents could evaluate whether best use had been made of the resources available to the governors.[9]

Colleges, also, are to be governed by equivalent formula funding arrangements and performances indicators are to be used to assess their efficiency.[10]

In the past, the allocation of resources has been a closed professional affair. Now it is likely that the criteria as well as the distribution of resources will become a subject of public debate as consumers enquire why one institution received more than another or was more efficient than another (Thomas, 1989). If consumers are to express their preferences in the market place then their choices need to be informed. Strategic direction is given to the new system through proposals for the Education Secretary to prepare a National Curriculum of core and foundation subjects that will make explicit the goals pupils are to pursue, the curriculum followed and the learning levels which have been achieved against national targets.

> Parents will be able to judge their children's progress against agreed national targets for attainment and will also be able to judge the effectiveness of their school. (DES, 1987c)

Clarity of purpose, process and achievement will make schools accountable to their consumers and as a result reinforce standards of learning and teaching. Circular 1/89 (DES, 1989) on complaints, and the draft Circular on information requirements,[11] describe the processes of responding to parents' concerns as well as keeping them informed.

The new National Curriculum has been criticized for possessing too restricted a view of core and foundation subjects (Walton, 1988; Ouseley, 1988), and for imposing a repressive regime of assessment tests at 7, 11, 14 and 16. As Murphy (1988) explains, such tests may limit the progression in learning which the National Curriculum purports to encourage.

Thus the working of the market place is not to be left entirely to the hidden hand of competitive self-interest. Rather, it is to be interpreted and guided by the 'public' hand of the Secretary of State who will be granted an extraordinary new range of regulatory powers that will more reflect Bentham's panopticon than Nozick's minimal state. The market will be monitored by ministers. Schools may be 'privatized' progressively but their reproduction of culture (the curriculum) will be nationalized (or anglicized). (The pamphlet from Hillgate clearly has been more influential than that from the Adam Smith Institute or the IEA.)

Between the emerging forces of market and hierarchy[12] it appears that the centre piece of the 1944 legislation — the Local Education Authority, and the local government of education — has been considerably reduced in status and authority. Its former powers and responsibilities are largely dissolved or redistributed. The way the education profession often liked to describe education — as a national service locally administered — was mistaken then but seems to be a reality now. The LEA may no longer be a tier of government but be limited to efficient implementation of national plans or accurate reading of market trends.

Towards education for citizenship

The Education Reform Act is a centrepiece in the constituting of a new moral and political order of individual rights and public accountability of government to consumer choice in the market place. It is a moral order of individual self-interest in a market society.

The Act encourages a number of beneficial developments: the return to a general education for all; the centre, clarifying common educational purposes, which have public agreement; and schools being granted financial discretion to meet their needs. Each of these require more elaborate discussion.

Here, however, I wish to focus on and acclaim what I take to be the major innovation of the Act: the intention to celebrate more active public choice and accountability. (Many will argue that this is the rhetoric which masks the extraordinary growth in state power accelerating for a decade but now reinforced and secured in this Act. But this statism, I argue, is that of Bentham and designed for detailed scrutiny and regulation of the market place. The statism and the market go together. What is new and requires analysis is the role of the market. What needs to be critically evaluated is the conception of public choice embodied in the legislation.)

Consumers are not citizens

The organizing principle of the new order values active public participation and choice. This strategic development is necessary and timely for our polity and will set the political agenda for the next two decades. Indeed there is, arguably, already considerable agreement across the policital spectrum that our democracy needs reinvigorating. The issue here is whether the organizing principles and constitutive systems of the Act and its underlying moral order can achieve this intended objective. If it can, the 1988 Act will indeed emulate its revered predecessor and last a generation. But I believe it cannot achieve such legitimacy because it is flawed in means and conception.

The moral and political order informing the Act proposes competitive self-interest in the market place as the best means of realizing both individual choice and quality in the provision of goods and services. Yet it needs to be examined whether the market place is an appropriate mechanism for every purpose. The assumption can exist that all goods and services are discrete products which can be purchased in the market. Yet the market can actually change certain goods. If I purchase a chocolate bar or take out an Austen novel from the library my 'purchase' has no effect on the product although pressure may be placed upon production or delivery. But my preference for a school, privately expressed, together with the unwitting choices of others, will transform the product. A small school grows in scale with inevitable consequences for learning style and administrative process. The distinctive ethos which was the reason for the choice may be altered by the choice. Some of the most important writing (Sen, 1982; Parfit, 1984; Elster, 1979, 1983) in the human sciences is preoccupied with the unintended public consequences of private decision-making — with the growing realization, especially in many public services, that self-interest can be self-defeating. It is likely in education, moreover, that choice will not only change the product but eliminate it. Choice implies surplus places, but if market forces fill some schools and close others then choice evaporates leaving only a hierarchy of esteem with little actual choice for many. But assuming that choice is a continuing reality, is education a 'product' which can be marketed?

If education is no more than acquiring a social status which schools can readily confer then it may be a discrete product which can be purchased in the market place. If education, however, is regarded more as an unfolding learning process which is adapted continuously to suit the needs of particular individuals then it is neither a product nor a process which is appropriate to the market place. The changing needs of individuals cannot be packaged and marketed nor can the institution which is a vehicle for their realization because it is changed and damaged by the market. Let the market place be supported wherever it is appropriate but its limits be understood.

Whatever the product exchanged in the market, however, it is its unique social functions which are of fundamental importance. The market is formally neutral but substantively interested. Individuals come together in competitive exchange to acquire possession of scarce goods and services. Within the market place all are free and equal, differentiated only by their capacity to calculate their self-interest. Yet, of course, the market masks its social bias. It elides, but reproduces, the inequalities which consumers bring to the market place. Under the guise of neutrality, the institution of the market actively confirms and reinforces the pre-existing social order of wealth and privilege. The market is a crude mechanism of social selection. It can provide a more effective social engineering than anything we have previously witnessed in the post-war period.

But consumerism in education is not only flawed as an instrument for achieving its purported objectives, it is misconceived in its purposes. Consumerism is not citizenship. Nor can it achieve 'public choice'. A consumer expresses self-interest registered privately and with uncertain (though often malign) public consequences. A citizen, however, has a concern for the well-being of others as well as the health of society, and both should become the subject of public debate in order to constitute a public choice.

The conditions for citizenship

The reform of education is timely, and it is fitting that it should be such a significant part of a larger re-forming of the social and political order that seeks to create a more active public accountability. The time is ripe for the establishing of a more active democracy. Yet the measures proposed cannot achieve this end. What can? What conditions are needed to develop the citizenship which the proposals strive for?

Such conditions presuppose a more complex set of organizing principles and values than those we have been presented with, because they will reflect greater understanding of the complexity of society and polity. Arguably, the whole post-war project can be conceived as developing, at each stage, some of the necessary conditions for citizenship. The challenge of reform facing our polity is to integrate and synthesize the essential contribution of each period. That is, an institutional framework committed to equal opportunities and a progressive professionalism, to support the present challenge to develop active public participation.

The institutional conditions for citizenship

This involves protection and support of the basic preconditions for personal development and citizenship: the rights and duties that define common membership, work and earned income, health and equal educational opportunities that are not dependent upon wealth, status or power. These conditions formed the post-war settlement and are as valid to-day if we still seek to constitute a fair society. They form Rawls' foundation contract, or charter, for a just society based upon the understanding that one cannot be a person nor take advantage of liberty unless there is justice. Even Dworkin (1977, 1984) who wants us to 'take rights seriously', argues for the inescapable importance of a just distribution that can enable all to contribute equally in a market society.

The enabling profession

The post-war contract for a liberal democratic society of equal opportunities for all was delegated to skilled professionals to provide for people. Services have sometimes, however, been perceived as those of the profession rather than the people. A balance needs to be restored. But denigrating professional expertise can only undermine the development of (young) citizens. A new perspective of the enabling professional offering and negotiating specialist skills can provide a necessary condition for releasing the potential of citizens.

Active citizens

The government seeks to encourage active public choice and accountability, but they are conceived as consumerism rather than citizenship. This is the next step that is required, but building upon the virtues of each of the previous stages.

The public needs to be involved in education as citizens because education is a *public as well as a private good* — a good, that is, in which we are all interested because of its pervasive, collective consequences as well as its personal significance. It is a good, therefore, which because of its public characteristics, cannot be determined by individuals acting in isolation from each other. Thus, education is a good which should be the subject of *public, collective, choice* which is *accountable* to the public as a whole (Ranson and Stewart, 1989).

This public choice will be accountable if it reflects the interests of the public as a whole, that is if it relates to the common good. Public choice which secures wide public agreement will acquire legitimate authority because it is grounded in the consent of the public.

If choice is to be public choice it requires the opportunity for citizens to express their view, for their voice to be heard, so that the inescapably diverse constituencies of education are enabled to present, discuss and negotiate their account. Public choice presupposes public participation and mutual accountability.

These organizing principles and values for an active citizenship presuppose arenas in which citizens can become involved collectively and form the partnership which is a precondition for public choice and agreement about education. The constitutive conditions for an active democracy require extensive consultation, and participation on governing bodies and in local community forums. It implies, as Sallis (1988) has argued, developing governing bodies as a forum for partnership rather than consumer power as in the Government's legislation. Community polling could be developed as a form of listening to the views of the public.

A learning democracy, therefore, is one that listens, enables expression and strives for understanding. Its conditions are a charter for justice, an enabling profession and an active citizenship involved in and shaping public choice. A learning democracy which facilitates public choice will need the institutional capacity to bring the diversity of views together in common choice in the public interest. The 'duality of publicness' — the unity as well as the variety of 'a public' — requires a strong tier of local government to enable the integration of views that can allow public choice.

In the Education Reform Act the LEA has lost direct control of its institutions. Nevertheless, it retains significant responsibilities and it can create a role of strategic influence (Stewart, 1987) in enhancing the public conditions for learning quality. Working within the national framework, the LEA's role can be to serve the schools and colleges: advising on educational leadership and progress; encouraging clear and consistent thinking; enabling policy planning in schools; helping them to set standards and disseminate good practice; managing progression between the stages of learning; making staff development suit the needs of schools and encouraging good management at institutional level. In this way the LEA can ensure the achievement of quality in the learning process.

Yet this reinforcing of learning quality will only improve public confidence if the LEA continually seeks to involve the public at every stage and become accountable to the public. The role of the LEA is to facilitate public accountability and participation by presenting information, evaluating performance, thereby enabling public discussion about achievement and educational purpose.

Out of this can return a renewed confidence in the institution of local government and democracy as the necessary condition for public choice and accountability in education. Our society and polity will have to rediscover local democracy. A system which allows only one tier of representative democracy possesses a disturbing monopoly of power that is ill-suited to its public purpose. And a system which acclaims rights as self-interest in the market against the virtues of justice is a system committed to inequality that is unlikely to acquire the consent of the public as a whole. In its misuse of public power and its implicit valuing of unfairness and inequality this Act seems unlikely to emulate its revered 1944 predecessor. Nevertheless, in its commitment to an active public, this Act properly sets the agenda for years to come.

Acknowledgement

This paper is based on an earlier version in *Local Government Studies*, Vol. 14, No. 1, January/February 1988.

Notes

1. These ideas are being elaborated in a forthcoming book.
2. A term used by David Regan.
3. Quoted in *The Times Literary Supplement*, 13 March 1987.
4. The Hargreaves Report (1984) *Improving Secondary Schools*, ILEA.
5. *The Omega File on Education* (1984) Adam Smith Institute; The Hillgate Group (1986) 'Whole schools: a radical manifesto'; Sexton, S. (1987), 'Our schools — a radical policy', Institute of Economic Affairs
6. For alternative interpretations readers should consult the research of J. Gray at Sheffield University; and A. Macpherson at the University of Edinburgh.
7. DES press release, 20 November 1987.
8. Circular 7/88, Education Reform Act 1988: Local Management of Schools, DES.
9. *Financial Delegation to Schools* (1978).
10. Drawing upon the DES — Local Authority Associations Report, Managing Colleges Efficiently, DES, 1987.
11. Draft Circular Education Reform Act 1988: Information Requirements relating to the School Curriculum and Assessment, DES, 23 September 1988.
12. Beginning since the early 1980s. See Ranson, S. Jones, S. and Walsh, K. (Eds) *Between Centre and Locality: The Politics of Public Policy*, London, Allen and Unwin, 1985.

References

BRIAULT, E. (1976) 'A distributed system of educational administration: An international viewpoint', *International Review of Education*, Vol. 22, No. 4.

BULLOCK, A. (1960) *The Life and Times of Ernest Bevin*, Vol. 2, London, Hodder and Stoughton.

CENTRE FOR CONTEMPORARY CULTURAL STUDIES (1978) *Social Democracy, Education and the Crisis*, University of Birmingham.

DEPARTMENT OF EDUCATION AND SCIENCE (DES) (1987a) *Financial Delegation to Schools*, A Consultative Paper.

DES (1987b) *Grant Maintained Schools*, A Consultative Paper.

DES (1987c) The National Curriculum 5–16, A Consultative Document.

DES (1988) Circular 10/88, Education Reform Act 1988: Grant Maintained Schools.

DES (1989) Circular 1/89, Education Reform Act: Local Arrangement for the Consideration of Complaints.

DWORKIN, R. (1977) *Taking Rights Seriously*, Duckworth.

DWORKIN, R. (1984) 'Liberalism', in Sandel, M. (Ed.) *Liberalism and its Critics*, Oxford, Blackwell.

ELSTER, J. (1979) *Ulysses and the Sirens*, Cambridge, Cambridge University Press.

ELSTER, J. (1983) *Sour Grapes*, Cambridge, Cambridge University Press.

HALSEY, A.H., HEATH, A.F. and RIDGE, J.M. (1980) *Origins and Destinations*, Oxford, Oxford University Press.

HMSO (1943) Educational Reconstruction, Cmnd 6458.
KOGAN, M. (1978) *The Politics of Educational Change,* London, Fontana.
MASSEY, D. and MEEGAN, R. (1982) *The Anatomy of Job Loss,* London, London University Press.
MACLURE, S. (1985) 'Forty years on', *British Journal of Educational Studies,* Vol. 33, No. 2.
MCLEOD, J. (1988) 'City technical colleges — a study of the character and progress of the educational reform', *Local Government Studies,* Vol. 14, No. 1.
MIDDLEMAS, K. (1979) *Politics in Industrial Society*, London, Deutsch.
MURPHY, R. (1988) 'Great Education Reform Bill proposals for testing — a critique', *Local Government Studies,* Vol. 14, No. 1.
NOZICK, R. (1974) *Anarchy, State and Utopia,* Oxford, Blackwell.
OUSELEY, H. (1988) 'Reforming Education: Equal Opportunities Lost', *Local Government Studies* Vol. 14, No. 1.
PARFIT, D. (1984) *Reasons and Persons,* Oxford, Oxford University Press.
RANSON, S. and STEWART, J. D. (1989) 'Enabling citizenship and government: the challenge for management in the public domain', *Political Studies,* Vol. 37, No. 1.
RAWLS, J. (1971) *A Theory of Justice,* Oxford, Oxford University Press.
SALLIS, J. (1988) *Schools, Parents and Governors: A New Approach to Accountability,* London, Routledge.
SEN, A. (1982) *Choice, Welfare and Measurement,* Oxford, Blackwell.
STEWART, J. D. (1987) 'The management of influence', Local Government Training Board, Luton.
ARCHBISHOP TEMPLE, in Butler, R. A. (1982) *The Art of Memory,* London, Hodder and Stoughton.
THOMAS, H. (1989) 'Local management of schools', Cosin, B., Flude, M. and Hales, M. (Eds) *School, Work and Equality,* London, Hodder and Stoughton.
WALTON, B. (1988) 'The impact of the Government's legislation upon local government', *Local Government Studies,* Vol. 14, No. 1.
WEBER, M. (1968) *Economy and Society*, edited by Roth, G. and Wittich, C., Berkeley, University of California.
WILLIAMS, R. (1965) *The Long Revolution,* Harmondsworth, Pelican.

2
The New Right and the National Curriculum: State Control or Market Forces?*

Geoff Whitty

> I sometimes think that a study of the life and teachings of Adam Smith should be compulsory in all schools. (Bob Dunn addressing the IEA in July 1988 [quoted in *Education,* 8 July 1988]).

In one of the many consultation papers isssued during the passage of the Education Reform Bill, the government asserted that it was 'taking action to increase the autonomy of schools and their responsiveness to parental wishes' (DES, 1987). The provisions in the Education Reform Act on open enrolment, financial delegation, grant-maintained (GM) schools and city technology colleges (CTCs) were all presented by the Government as consistent with this aim. They were presented as building upon the parental choice and accountability provisions of the 1980 Education Act and, more particularly, those of the 1986 Education (No.2) Act, which enhanced the powers of governors and increased the influence on governing bodies of parents and members of the local business community. The Government claimed, for example, that GM schools would 'add a new and powerful dimension to the ability of parents to exercise choice within the publicly provided sector of education' and 'parents and local communities [would] have new opportunities to secure the development of their schools in ways appropriate to the needs of their children and in accordance with their wishes. However, significantly, it added 'within the legal framework of the national curriculum' (DES, 1987).

---

*This paper was first presented at the International Sociology of Education conference at Newman College Birmingham 3–5 January 1989 and published in the *Journal of Education Policy,* Vol. 4, No. 4 (1989). Parts of the paper draw upon work carried out with Tony Edwards and John Fitz, in the context of our study of the Assisted Places Scheme (ESRC Award No. C00230036), and with Ian Menter, Nick Clough, Veronica Lee and Tony Trodd, my fellow members of the Bristol Polytechnic Education Study Group. However, none of these colleagues should be held responsible for the arguments put forward in this paper.

Then, during the passage of the Bill in the House of Commons, Norman Tebbit argued that:

> This Bill extends choice and responsibility. Some will choose badly or irresponsibly, but that cannot and must not be used as an excuse to deny choice and responsibility to the great majority. Today, only the wealthy have choice in education and that must be changed. (Norman Tebbit, quoted in *The Daily Telegraph*, 2 December 1987)

Yet the exercise of choice and responsibility was to be denied to the majority of parents in the field of the curriculum, where (given the exclusion of independent schools from the legislative imposition of a national curriculum and system of testing), only the wealthy would continue to have choice.

Tensions within the Education Reform Act

As a result of this, many commentators suggested that there was something of a paradox or contradiction within an Act which increasingly gave market forces their head within whole areas of policy which had previously been subject to detailed regulation and planning by central and local government, yet suddenly introduced prescription into the one area of education where hitherto there had been autonomy, save in the case of Religious Education which was mandatory under the 1944 Education Act. Of course, that autonomy had essentially been professional autonomy rather than the autonomy of consumer choice, but why should consumer choice replace LEA and teacher judgement in most matters, but ministerial prescription take over from it in the area of curriculum decision-making. Given the tendency of most ministerial statements on the curriculum to portray the curriculum as a commodity, which presumably could be marketed just like other goods, the paradox seemed especially puzzling.

Some critics have resolved the paradox by suggesting that the devolution proposals are themselves as much about increasing central government control, at the expense of the teaching profession and local government, as they are about increasing the power of local communities which are linked with parents in the government's rhetoric (Demaine, 1988). Indeed, with the demise of any significant LEA function in relation to GM schools, it can surely be argued that the role of the local people (except current parents) in relation to such schools is diminished rather than enhanced. Thus, the argument goes, the rhetoric of decentralization is a cover for centralization. The atomization of decision-making and the removal or marginalization of intervening arenas of political mobilization, such as LEAs and trade unions, effectively removes any chance of a collective challenge to the government, thus enhancing its ascendent position. And this is then consistent with an enhanced central government role in the curriculum. But again the question remains — if that is the aim, why not employ a consistent strategy? Either go for direct government management of the whole enterprise or let market forces decide the fate of everything including the curriculum.

Of course, while this paper is largely about the position of the New Right, it is also the case that, in government, the rhetoric of the New Right is tempered by other considerations (Demaine, 1988) — indeed other political forces have to be taken into account even by a Thatcher government and I will return to this point later. But yet another way of resolving the paradox has been to see different fractions within the so-called New Right itself as influencing different areas of policy. It has now become a commonplace to identify two main strands within New Right thinking — namely neo-liberal and neo-conservative. Thus, Andrew Gamble, amongst others, argues that what is distinctive about Thatcherism as a force within British conservatism is its capacity to link the neo-conservative emphasis on tradition, authority and national identity/security with an espousal of neo-liberal free market economics and the extension of its principles into whole new areas of social activity including the provision of welfare (Gamble, 1983b; see also Levitas, 1986). In analyzing education, Demaine's discussion of the New Right (Demaine, 1988) focuses mainly on its neo-liberal elements, while another recent paper that recognizes this distinction places most of its emphasis on neo-conservative influences (Quicke, 1988).

As New Right ideology is based on a blend of moral and economic academic and philosophical doctrines, they are sometimes complementary, but sometimes in tension, particularly in its mediated political versions (see Edwards *et al.*, 1984; Whitty and Menter, 1989). It has also been pointed out that, provided the discourse of the New Right as political rhetoric strikes a chord and can command assent, its internal inconsistencies and its eclectic philosophical roots are something of an irrelevance (Ball, forthcoming). So greater consumer power over choice and management of schools, a neo-liberal response to criticisms of LEA bureaucracies, and a national curriculum, a neo-conservative response to charges that trendy teachers are subverting traditional moral values and selling the nation short, may both resonate with popular experience and be electorally attractive even if the whole package does not add up.

However, even if all this is true, there may also be a principled sense in which the various policies are at least broadly reconcilable. Gamble has suggested that the paradox of at one and the same time building a strong state through increased expenditure on the military and the apparatuses of law and order, while at the same time using state power to roll back state intervention from whole areas of social activity, does have a degree of consistency. This is because the state needs to protect the market from vested interests and restrictive practices and prevent the conditions in which it can flourish being subverted either from without or within (Gamble, 1983a). On this basis, the government's curriculum policies may not necessarily be as much at variance with its policies on the structure of the education system as is sometimes suggested even at the level of principle. The contrast between apparent centralization in one sphere and apparent decentralization in the other may not be the paradox it at first appears. Schools which are responsive to choices made by parents in the market are believed by the

Government to be more likely than those administered by state bureaucrats to produce high levels of scholastic achievement, to the benefit of both individuals and the nation. The strength of the state therefore has to be used to remove anything that interferes with this process or with the development of an appropriate sense of self and nation on the part of citizens who will be making their choices in the market. Thus, not only does the traditional partnership with LEAs and teachers' trade unions need to be abandoned in favour of the discipline of the market, it also becomes imperative (at least in the short term) to police the curriculum to ensure that the pervasive collectivist and universalistic welfare ideology of the post-war era is restrained. In this way, support for the market, self-help, enterprise and the concept of the 'responsible' family and a common 'national identity' can be constructed. Hence, for example, whether or not Bob Dunn's intriguing suggestion that there should be compulsory teaching of free market economics was offered tongue in cheek, it may merely be an extreme example of a more general approach to the problem confronting the political project of Thatcherism within education (Hall, 1988). In other words, the overt ideology of the curriculum needs to be addressed directly before the ideology of the new structure is sufficiently developed to do its work. So, in this sense, there may actually be an ideological congruity rather than incongruity between the national curriculum proposals and other aspects of the Education Reform Act.

Neo-liberal and neo-conservative approaches to the curriculum

Although certainly in some respects rather too neat both theoretically and empirically, this reading does actually gain credence from a study of the internal debate going on between the various pressure groups associated with the New Right. The contribution of the Hillgate Group (1986, 1987), comprising Caroline Cox, Jessica Douglas-Home, John Marks, Laurie Norcross and Roger Scruton, is particularly significant here and the apparent contradictions within it more explicable than some commentators imply (Demaine, 1988; Ball, forthcoming). Rather than being the product purely of muddled thinking, these contradictions derive from an attempt to consider both short-term and long-term strategies and this is what leads to their adoption of both neo-liberal and neo-conservative policies to achieve long-term ends that will be broadly acceptable to both. Heavily influenced by neo-conservative critiques of progressivism, members of the Hillgate Group are attracted by the idea of prescription at the level of the curriculum in order to defend traditional standards and values. However, they also see parents as a potent force against progressivism and embrace — and indeed wish to extend — the government's espousal of market forces in open enrolment, opting out, and so on, as the best way of improving educational standards. But their political allies in the latter cause, including some of those closest to them, such as Keith Joseph, Stuart Sexton and Dennis O'Keefe, have argued that if market forces are to be efficacious in these other areas, why not in determining the curriculum?

O'Keefe, for example, in what he claims to be a libertarian view of government policy (O'Keefe, 1988), says that open enrolment, opting out and financial delegation are all entirely to the good and so is testing, in principle, providing it is conducted independently on behalf of the taxpayers and not controlled by the educational establishment. But a prescribed curriculum is both 'alien to the British tradition' (and hence presumably should be questioned by neo-conservatives as well as neo-liberals) and looks like being controlled via that 'network of in-house trading and special interest' which has controlled our quasi-syndicalized educational culture of recent years — and incidentally by the very same personnel who are especially culpable for pulling a fast one over the government with the GCSE. This group is usually referred to disparagingly by the New Right as the 'liberal education establishment', though they sometimes suggest that its members are 'socialist' (e.g., O'Keefe and Stoll, 1988). They fear that it could still subvert the new proposals from within and O'Keefe would presumably see the mathematics, science and English working group reports (DES, 1988a, 1988b, 1988c), as well as the reports of the Task Group on Assessment and Testing (TGAT, 1987, 1988), as vindicating this view.

Far better than anything prescribed by such groups, or even by ministers and civil servants, would be a 'free enterprise curriculum' — or that mixture of contents and styles that a 'free citizenry' plumps for. As O'Keefe puts it himself, 'if you do not like the groceries at one supermarket, try another. The system which has utterly outperformed all others in history in the production of a wide range of goods and services needs trying out in the field of education too' (O'Keefe 1988: 19). (Incidentally, I would argue that the emphasis of the neo-liberals, like some sections of the New Left, on devising new ways of arriving at a curriculum model rather than providing an alternative blueprint, is one of the reasons why, when it comes to concrete thinking about the curriculum, such as that demanded of the National Curriculum working groups, the educational establishment usually gets its way.)

Stuart Sexton, a former adviser to Keith Joseph and now Education Director of the Institute of Economic Affairs, places a particularly strong emphasis on finding an appropriate neo-liberal mechanism for determining the curriculum. Thus, he has argued a similar case to O'Keefe's against a centralized and bureaucratically set 'Nationalized Curriculum', at the same time as regarding the main elements of the National Curriculum proposals as what most reasonable parents would actually want. But he points out that 'for the independent schools . . . the "market" of parental demand dictates that they do provide such a "national curriculum" '. So if a more self-managing state sector emerges from the government's other proposals, it too will 'have to respond to parental demand to provide an acceptable curriculum' (Sexton, 1988a). This would allow for choice and diversity and local variation and remove the dangers of a Secretary of State imposing a straitjacket on enterprising schools on the say-so of the fifteen or so experts on the National Curriculum Council (Sexton, 1988b). That is why Lord Joseph moved an amendment to make the whole National Curriculum discretionary rather than mandatory, and why when that failed there were attempts by Sexton and his colleagues to persuade the government to make only the list of subjects mandatory and the programmes of study etc. discretionary. One of the arguments Joseph used in the Lords' debate against a legislated and inflexible national curriculum was that it might not meet the needs of either non-academic or gifted children (Blackburne, 1988). And Sexton has recently expressed concern that schools should remain free to teach Scottish examinations or the International Baccalaureate — or even a revived GCE O-level to able pupils if they wanted to and if boards wished to offer it — and he particularly deplores those parts of the Education Reform Act that allow the Secretary of State, or effectively the School Examinations and Assessment Council, to determine what examination courses children in maintained schools can follow. He regards it as absurd that, while independent schools may teach non-GCSE courses if they and the parents want them to, state schools could be legally debarred from doing so whatever the parents might wish (Sexton, 1988b, 1988c).

Sexton (1988c) calls for 'more intellectually rigorous examinations' and his own preference for a return to GCE O-level is also something which the Hillgate Group and its close associates desire (Hillgate Group, 1987; North, 1987). However, because they are strongly linked to neo-conservative forces at the same time as having connections with advocates of a free market, they have rather more time than Sexton or O'Keefe for the idea of government prescribing a national curriculum in some way rather than leaving it to market forces. The Hillgate Group sympathizes with the government's proposals to control the curriculum, because the eternal vigilance of parents is neither to be expected nor desired, though in the long run would prefer a proper system of examinations as a more appropriate and less contentious means of control than some of the detail of the present proposals. They firmly back the government's desire to set attainment targets, though they are less convinced about its way of developing the detailed programmes of study. But given what has happened with GCSE they are particularly supportive of the government specifying proper subjects as the basis of the curriculum and not those which are either intellectually vacuous or a cover for political indoctrination or both. One of their central concerns in this field is, at the same time as giving members of minority groups opportunities to run their own schools, to integrate them fully into the national culture and ensure a common political loyalty — in other words to provide a common framework of knowledge and values within which atomised decision-making can take place. There is therefore, for example, a need for attainment targets in history that 'ensure a solid foundation in British and European history and ... no concessions to the philosophy of the global curriculum currently advocated by the multi-culturalists' (Hillgate Group, 1987). So, although any actual programmes of study emerging from government will no doubt reflect other mediating influences, the neo-conservative strand of the New Right does clearly wish government curriculum policy to support a particular view of society and citizen. As Anne Sofer, until recently the education spokesperson of the Social and Liberal Democrats has put it, the 'draconian control' now to be exercised over the curriculum by the Secretary of State as a result of the Education Reform Act has to be seen in a context where:

> The prevailing philosophy is one that does get excited about Christianity being absolutely predominant in RE, about the need to make sure British history prevails over other sorts of history and to stamp on anything that has the label anti-racism attached to it. (quoted in *Education*, 8 July 1988)

In the light of this comment, it is interesting to note that, in launching the National Curriculum Working Group on History, Kenneth Baker stated that 'the programmes of study should have at the core the history of Britain, the record of its past and, in particular, its political, constitutional and cultural heritage' (quoted in *The Times,* 14 January 1989).

The other major concern of the Hillgate Group, and associated groups such as the Campaign for Real Education, is to rid the system of the influence of the educational establishment which, of course, has traditionally regarded the curriculum as its own territory. They therefore want advisory bodies to include several members from outside the educational establishment (which they see as including DES officials and especially HMI). While they accept O'Keefe's argument that curriculum prescription is alien to the British educational tradition, they believe that a national curriculum is necessary so that the government, on behalf of consumers, can rid us of the influence of the educational establishment 'which, prey to ideology and self-interest, is no longer in touch with the public'. It is 'time to set aside . . . the professional educators and the majority of organized teacher unions [who rather than classroom teachers] are primarily responsible for the present state of Britain's schools' (Hillgate Group, 1987). Hence their broad support for a national curriculum — though not necessarily the current working groups which apparently contain 'the student radicals of the 1960s, who have marched through to leading positions in departments of education' (CRE, 1989) — at the same time as accepting with enthusiasm, though wanting to take further, all the other elements of government policy designed to devolve power to consumers. A prescribed curriculum can be used in the short-term to re-educate consumers to use their new-found power responsibly and free them from dependency upon professional experts, while in the longer term the ideological work of exercizing their new responsibilities will ultimately produce changes in consciousness that will begin to render even the prescription of a national curriculum unnecessary.

So, particularly given that governments can change in our system, once a curriculum appropriate for maintaining a sense of self and nation fitted for a free market society has been established, and once the last vestiges of the influence of the liberal educational establishment have been removed, the Hillgate Group might well then be content to let market forces determine the curriculum in the manner suggested by Sexton and O'Keefe. And a similar view may actually be reflected in government policy, which implies that independent schools do not need a legislated national curriculum because they already respond to market forces and, in most cases, teach that curriculum. The argument that they are excluded purely because they are not in receipt of public funds is less than convincing, partly because equally stringent requirements have been imposed on certain privatised utilities, but more particularly because those independent schools in the Assisted Places Scheme are effectively in receipt of public funds (in some cases now to a considerable degree) and because of this the 1980 Education Act required them to publish examination results in the same way as maintained schools. Furthermore, city technology colleges (CTCs), which will certainly be in receipt of public funds, only need to adhere to the broad substance of the national curriculum presumably because, at least originally, they were conceived of as entirely new schools with new traditions set up in ways that would make them peculiarly responsive to market forces from their industrial sponsors as well as their parental clients. GMs, though, will have to conform to the letter of the National Curriculum, but then they will still be staffed by teachers schooled in and reflecting the traditions of the old LEA establishment and may need time to purge themselves of former working practices. But, in the longer term, they might be freed from such requirements as the market is trusted to undertake more of the task. In that situation, it could eventually be only LEA maintained schools that will have a highly prescriptive National Curriculum.

The irony is that, if it is anything like the present National Curriculum, Lord Joseph (amongst others) might well regard it as unsuitable for the particular clientele who are likely, by that stage, to be left in many LEA maintained schools (Bristol Polytechnic Education Study Group, 1989). This issue brings to light a further tension within government curriculum policy which I have discussed at greater length elsewhere (Bowe and Whitty, 1988). However, one of those other mediating influences on government education policy that I mentioned earlier is that of the industrial lobby. Although there is a lack of coherence both in the nature of such a group and what it does or does not require of the school curriculum, there is certainly an unresolved debate in and around government about the extent to which the National Curriculum is based upon an appropriate curriculum model for the late 20th century. In particular, there are those who ask whether it is an appropriate model for all pupils. Even with the amendment allowing certain pupils with special educational needs to be exempted from its provisions, there are many like Lord Joseph who doubt it.

The curriculum and the needs of industry

Furthermore, the attack by the Hillgate Group on 'relevance' in the curriculum appears to go against all the arguments of the last few years about the need for relevance to the needs of industry at all levels of the system and against the argument that the traditional curriculum was partly, or even largely, to blame for the decline of Britain's industrial spirit (Callaghan, 1976; Wiener, 1981; Barnett, 1986). There are many who fear that the National Curriculum provisions of the Education Reform Act and the Hillgate Group's attack on 'relevance' will spell the end of the positive innovations brought about by Technical and Vocational Education Initiative (TVEI), ironically an essentially corporatist policy introduced under Keith Joseph. Jamieson and Watts have argued that, in curricular terms, the traditionally oriented Hillgate Group rather that Lord Young and the advocates of the enterprise culture have been winning the battle for the high policy ground (Jamieson and Watts, 1987). Although the initial National Curriculum working group reports seemed to allay some of these fears both in content terms, but more particularly in the freedom they offered for different modes of curriculum delivery, the New Right's suspicion that they, like GCSE and TVEI, had been hi-jacked by the liberal educational establishment may perhaps be part of the explanation for Kenneth Baker's reservations about them and the amendments made to them by the National Curriculum Council and the Secretary of State (DES, 1989a, 1989b).

The continuing tensions were also evident in a recent speech by Anne Jones, director of education programmes for the Training Agency, the successor to the Manpower Services Commission/Training Commission. She emphasized that, while the National Curriculum was a set of important knowledge, the process of learning offered by TVEI was also important, so that Knowledge + Process equalled Capability. But she was apparently less than convinced by the government's own commitment to the view that TVEI remains a fruitful source of ideas about the delivery of the National Curriculum. Perhaps indicating some sympathy with others at the same conference, who suggested that what has ultimately emerged from the NCC and Kenneth Baker from the consultation exercises over the maths and science reports looks suspiciously like the same boring old school subjects, she told her audience of TVEI teachers and coordinators to 'hang on in there and see what can be done .... The dinosaur system of schools will not do any more' (quoted in *Education,* 16 December 1988). Change would come from employers, if not from the government, she asserted.

While Roger Dale (1983) has pointed out that the industrial trainers have always had an uneasy relationship with the core groups constituting Thatcherism — and many industrialists' lack of enthusiasm for CTCs perhaps supports this view (Nash and Hugill, 1988) — the New Right is clearly aware that there might be a degree of embarrassment if their views were to be wholly rejected by those who claimed to speak for the nation's wealth creators. Despite the fact that the CBI was one of the few groups to welcome the original consultation document on the National Curriculum virtually without reservation, CBI representatives have recently criticized some aspects of the implementation of the National Curriculum, particularly the Secretary of State's revisions to the curriculum working group reports (Slee, 1989). They are particularly concerned that he has given 'too much importance to narrow academic knowledge and too little to the fostering of transferable skills and learning ability' (Jackson, 1989).

However, those associated with the Hillgate Group attempt to bridge any gap between their position and that of the government's industrial supporters by suggesting that, within the school curriculum, an emphasis on practical skills and training for life has actually become a veil for the promulgation of a 'progressive egalitarian ideology', which is ultimately a threat to enterprise (North, 1987). And echoing some of the arguments, in the Black Papers before them, they argue that the National Curriculum, with its emphasis on traditional subjects, actually provides a much better grounding in the basic skills of reading, writing and comprehension which, although not taught with industrial relevance in mind, will ultimately provide industry with the properly educated recruits it currently claims to lack. Not all contributors to the Black Papers would regard a subject-based curriculum as appropriate for all pupils, though, and it is interesting in the light of our earlier discussion that Bantock, a neo-conservative in many other respects, sees differentiation between types of curricula as best arising from parental choice (Bantock, 1977).

Nevertheless, the construction of a meeting of minds between the Hillgate Group and the industrial lobby is clearly necessary if the government is to reconcile the demands of what Dale (1983) terms the industrial trainers with his old Tories, privatizers, moral entrepreneurs and populists. Indeed, any substantial failure to do so would expose one of the central assumptions in the government's approach to curriculum policy, which is that it is only professional educators in the liberal educational establishment who are out of step and that its own proposals are a distillation of what would be demanded of schools by all reasonable clients. The question of who those clients are is neatly sidestepped and the assumption made that parents and the business community have common interests (both separately and collectively) and that the combination of government prescription, parental choice and the enhanced role of parent and business governors will sort everything out.

The consequences of a market-led curriculum

This brings us to the question of what sort of curriculum a free market approach as advocated by O'Keefe and Sexton would actually produce. Would parents opt for something akin to the National Curriculum? Would it be regarded favourably by industry? And, would it be regarded favourably by the pupils, whose absence from most contemporary discussions of consumer choice (with the exception of the Hillgate Group as it happens) is interesting in itself? At the moment, we cannot answer those questions because we do not have a free-market situation in the curriculum and the government is not actually proposing one. We can only rely on data from what parents tell us they want from a school and what we know about how far that actually influences choice. A future task is to analyze the mass of data on these issues which we collected from both private and public sectors in the course of our recent research on the Assisted Places Scheme (Edwards *et al.*, 1989). Then we might have some clearer answers as to what sort of curriculum a free market might produce. In the meantime, what follows is based on a very preliminary analysis of that data to help point up some of the issues which seem to be raised by the idea of letting the market set the curriculum.

Certainly amongst the parents of pupils likely to be interested in assisted places, there was widespread demand for a traditional curriculum model. And amongst many of those parents, a suspicion of too overt a vocational or even pre-vocational orientation to education. This was certainly the view of the heads of many comprehensive schools and, of course, it would be primarily in the light of their conception of what the market wanted that schools would construct their curricula in a free market situation. We certainly came across heads who had avoided TVEI because they saw it, rightly or wrongly, as watering down the curriculum that had most appeal to parents. And schools which saw themselves as wanting to compete with independent schools for academically able pupils were very much influenced by their model and some of them admitted that this might well be to the disadvantage of other market segments that they, unlike the independent schools, were expected to serve. It does seem likely, then, that the cultural pull of the public or grammar school curriculum (or rather the public perception of that curriculum) would distort the market with consequences that would not please the advocates of 'relevance' as an organizing principle for the curriculum. (In this context, it will be interesting to see how the curricula of City Technology Colleges develop).

The head of what we have called in our study Thomas Darby High School, an inner city TVEI school with very few pupils with VRQ scores over 105 and badly affected by falling rolls, told us recently:

> What I think we have got is parents who are opting for an education system which they experienced 20 or 30 years ago. When Kenneth Baker talks about needing to recruit more people for science and technology and when we get vast amounts of money spent on records of achievement, TVEI and so on, it isn't the schools who are dragging their feet on this, it is the parent expectations that are dragging on this. I mean . . . the parents who send their children to the other schools predominantly want something that is very safe, secure, dull and predictable to make them happy — and a school (like this) that is offering them something else is seen to be experimental and threatening. (Fieldwork interview, October 1988).

On the other hand, this head felt that his own school's parents were more enthusiastic about TVEI than they were about most things, but then they were largely those inner city parents who had chosen the school because it was local rather than on any specific curricular considerations. In other words, most of those who had made positive curriculum choices had gone elsewhere.

That sort of dynamic was certainly clear in one of our three local study areas and it was present to some extent, though in a less clearcut way, in the other two. If it proved to be at all typical, then O'Keefe's free-enterprise curriculum might produce a situation in which inner city schools were the only ones experimenting in curricular terms. Now Lord Joseph would presumably argue that that was a good thing, because the market would then create a relevant curriculum for those unable to cope with the traditional academic one. On this model, schools with an unattractive curriculum for any market segment would eventually wither away. This assumes that curriculum provision is an important factor in choice of schools, whereas in fact many schools are currently chosen because they are local or because friends are going to them. This is particularly true in the case of those parents whose children attended schools like Thomas Darby and, in such cases, the discipline of the market might not have any clearly beneficial effects in curricular terms and it would certainly not necessarily limit the freedom of teachers to experiment. This may well explain the government's current rejection of a free enterprise approach to the curriculum for such schools.

Indeed, we saw earlier that, in the absence of a totally market-centred approach to curriculum policy and given the mixed mode approach currently favoured by government, it might well be that in practice, in the longer term, LEA schools like those in the inner city could actually become the only ones to have the National Curriculum imposed on them, while others arrived at it through market forces. We need then to consider how far such an imposition would be desirable. The Hillgate Group would presumably justify it on the basis that some inner city dwellers are amongst those most in need of a prescribed initiation into a common national culture and a common political loyalty, because they 'might not yet be aware of its strengths and advantages' (Hillgate Group, 1987: 4). But, whatever one thinks about that particular argument, even opponents of a National Curriculum on the left would need to think carefully about the position of kids left in under-resourced inner city schools if there was no National Curriculum. If everyone else was getting the National Curriculum through parental choice, then the arguments in terms of equity might well point in the direction of insisting that those pupils had access to it as well, rather than providing them with a separate curriculum based on 'relevance', particularly if parents had not expressed a positive preference for it — and perhaps even if they had. Otherwise, Martyn Shipman's strictures of ten years ago about trendy teachers experimenting on other people's children while exposing their own to the most traditional curriculum imaginable might well remain appropriate (Shipman, 1980). Even so, this raises a major dilemma, since treating people who are different in the same way can actually be a major source of inequality in itself, and this certainly needs to be taken very seriously when addressing the modes of delivery of any national curriculum.

The issue of what is appropriate curriculum provision in residual or 'sink' schools becomes a particularly significant one in the context of current government policies because the non-curricular elements of the Education Reform Act are eventually likely to produce an even more hierarchical and differentiated system of schooling than we have at the moment, with independent schools at the top, with CTCs and GM schools and perhaps Voluntary Aided (VA) schools below them, with county maintained schools at the bottom (Bristol Polytechnic Education Study Group, 1989). In that situation, LEA or 'Council' schools would again become the paupers of the system and the preserve of those unable or unwilling to compete in the market. As such, they might well become straightforward institutions of social control for the inner cities, though the legitimacy of the system and the notion of an open society would still be maintained by devices such as the Assisted Places Scheme, which can be seen as legitimating inequality by ostensibly offering opportunities to 'worthy' disadvantaged children to 'escape' from their backgrounds, while actually (on the evidence available so far) attracting mainly middle-class children and enhancing the market appeal of the private sector (Edwards *et al.*, 1989).

The head of another inner city school we interviewed in connection with the Assisted Places research reported that a leading member of the neo-liberal tendency of the New Right had said openly at a meeting of heads recently that any market produces casualties and that the children left in 'sink' schools in the period before they went to the wall would unfortunately be amongst them (fieldwork interview at Knotley High School, October 1988). Some people, as Norman Tebbit said in the quotation cited earlier, make 'irresponsible' choices and, in this case, children will presumably have to suffer for their parents' irresponsibility. Any suggestion that their choices might be structured by influences beyond the family, for which compensation should be made, has been largely rejected by the government because, as Kenneth Baker said in a speech at Crawley during the passage of the Education Reform Act: 'For too long we have accepted socio-economic causes for why families should not be doing certain things' (quoted in *The Financial Times*, 12 December 1987). Hence the government's guidelines for funding formulae for local management of schools place little stress on socio-economic factors of the sort that have influenced education funding formulae in many urban LEAs in the past (Bristol Polytechnic Education Study Group, 1989).

As market forces come to define all aspects of provision other than the curriculum, those in inner city schools may become increasingly disadvantaged. As a leading Conservative critic of the government's market-oriented initiatives pointed out when they were first mooted, they 'all help most those children with parents best able to play the system to escape from poor schools. They do nothing for the quality of education of [those] who remain behind' (Argyropulo, 1986). This explained his own broad support, and that of the Conservative Educational Association, for a National Curriculum to offset the worst effects of the other government policies on these schools. Yet the government's own insistence that such schools should teach the National Curriculum could also be seen as a cynical ploy to make it appear that there was a measure of equal treatment for all pupils when the structures that emanate from the other measures all conspired to deny it having any meaningful effect.

However, that does not seem a good reason for saying that it would be better to strip away the legitimating veil of the National Curriculum and let the market do its best — or worst. One of the results of market oriented social and economic policies is, as the Archbishop of Canterbury's Commission on the inner city pointed out, that a distinct group separated from the rest of society emerges (Archbishop of Canterbury's Commission, 1985). It thereby becomes further divided even from the rest of the working class and its political movements which in the past have fought, amongst other things, for a common system of education. In the current, virtually universalistic, system of state provision, it is at least possible to conceive of groups opposed to the injustices of the system combining to fight for gains that individually they could never hope to win. The atomisation of decision-making that is a feature of current government policies on open enrolment and so on threatens not only the negative conception of collectivism associated with inhuman state bureaucracies; it also constitutes an attack on the very notion that collective action is a legitimate way of struggling for social justice.

In that situation, one can argue that, however cynical its imposition might appear, we should be thankful that the National Curriculum is there as the one remaining symbol of a common education system and specifiable entitlement which people can struggle collectively to improve, rather than letting all provision emerge from the individual exercise of choice (or non-choice) in the market-place. To that extent, the influence of the neo-conservatives within the New Right may ultimately prove fortuitous. But, of course, for those who reject both the neo-liberal and the neo-conservative visions of the world, the present National Curriculum will need changing. Even then, it will not be enough to work together to develop an alternative version of the National Curriculum, and certainly not enough to substitute Keynes or Marx in Bob Dunn's statement which heads this paper. The much more daunting task will undoubtedly be to find ways of developing an alternative structure for the education system which is consistent with an alternative political project and which will command electoral consent. What does seem quite clear is that neither welfare state versions of collectivism nor the atomized market approach of Thatcherism will serve that purpose and that a National Curriculum delivered in either of those contexts will effectively be discredited however good it appears on paper. And, to that extent, it is the neo-liberals who are right to remind us of the importance of considering what are the appropriate democratic mechanisms for arriving at a National Curriculum, rather than just what we as 'experts' from the liberal educational establishment think it ought to consist of.

References

ARCHBISHOP OF CANTERBURY'S COMMISION ON URBAN PRIORITY AREAS (1985) *Faith in the City,* London, Church House Publishing.

ARGYROPULO, D. (1986) 'Inner city quality', *The Times Educational Supplement*, 1 *August.*

BALL, S. (forthcoming) *Politics and Policy-making in Education,* London, Routledge.

BANTOCK, G. (1977) 'An alternative curriculum', in Cox, C. B. and Boyson, R. (Eds) *Black Paper 1977,* London, Temple Smith, pp. 78–86.

BARNETT, C. (1986) *The Audit of War,* London, Macmillan.

BLACKBURNE, L. (1988) 'Joseph's curriculum revolt fails', *The Times Educational Supplement'*, 6 May.

BOWE, R. and WHITTY, G. (1989) 'The Re-opening of the GCSE "Settlement": Recent Developments in the Politics of School Examinations', *British Journal of Sociology of Education*, Vol. 10, No. 4.

BRISTOL POLYTECHNIC EDUCATION STUDY GROUP (1989) 'Restructuring the Education System?', in Bash, L. and Coulby, D. (Eds) *The Education Reform Act,* London, Cassell.

CALLAGHAN, J. (1976) 'Towards a national debate', *Education,* 148 (17).

CAMPAIGN FOR REAL EDUCATION (1989) 'Cause for concern?', *Newsletter,* 3 (1).

DALE, R. (1983) 'Thatcherism and Education', in Ahier, J. and Flude, M. (Eds) *Contemporary Education Policy,* London, Croom Helm, pp. 233–55.

DEMAINE, J. (1988) 'Teachers' work, curriculum and the New Right', *British Journal of Sociology of Education,* Vol. 9, No. 3, pp. 247–64.

DES (DEPARTMENT OF EDUCATION AND SCIENCE) (1987) Grant Maintained Schools: Consultation Paper, London Department of Education and Science.

DES (1988a) *Mathematics for Ages 5 to 16,* London, Department of Education and Science.

DES (1988b) *Science for Ages 5 to 16,* London, Department of Education and Science.

DES (1988c) *English for Ages 5 to 11*, London, Department of Education and Science.

DES (1989a) *Mathematics in the National Curriculum,* London, HMSO.

DES (1989b) *Science in the National Curriculum,* London, HMSO.

EDWARDS, A., FULBROOK, M. and WHITTY, G. (1984) 'The state and the independent sector: policies, ideologies and theories', in Barton, L. and Walker, S. (Eds) *Social Crisis and Educational Research,* London, Croom Helm, pp. 118–50.

EDWARDS, A., FITZ, J. and WHITTY, G. (1989) *The State and Private Education: A Study of the Assisted Places Scheme,* Lewes, Falmer Press.

GAMBLE, A. (1983a) *Education under Monetarism,* London, World University Service.

GAMBLE, A. (1983b) 'Thatcherism and Conservative politics', in Hall, S. and Jacques, M. (Eds), *The Politics of Thatcherism*, London, Lawrence and Wishart, pp. 109–31

HALL, S. (1988) *The Hard Road to Renewal: Thatcherism and the Crisis of the Left,* London, Verso.

HILLGATE GROUP (1986) *Whose Schools? A Radical Manifesto,* London, Hillgate Group.

HILLGATE GROUP (1987) *The Reform of British Education,* London, Claridge Press.

JACKSON, M. (1989) 'CBI struggles to "save" curriculum from Baker', *The Times Educational Supplement*, 24 March.

JAMIESON, I. and WATTS, T. (1987) 'Squeezing out enterprise', *The Times Educational Supplement,* 18 December.

LEVITAS, R. (Ed) (1986) *The Ideology of the New Right,* Oxford, Polity Press.

NASH, I. and HUGILL, B. (1988) 'Industrial giant spurns Baker CTC approach', *The Times Educational Supplement,* 27 May.

NORTH, J. (Ed) (1987) *The GCSE: an Examination,* London, Claridge Press.

O'KEEFE, D. (1988) 'A critical look at a national curriculum and testing: a libertarian view'. Paper presented to American Educational Research Association, New Orleans.

O'KEEFE, D. and STOLL, P. (1988) 'Postscript' to Sexton, S. (Ed) *GCSE: A Critical Analysis,* Croydon, IEA Education Unit.

QUICKE, J. (1988) 'The "New Right" and education', *British Journal of Educational Studies,* Vol. 26, No. 1, pp. 5–20.

SEXTON, S. (1988a) 'No nationalized curriculum', *The Times*, 9 May.

SEXTON, S. (1988b) 'Squeezing out choice at the grassroots', *Education,* 9 September.

SEXTON, S. (Ed) (1988c) *GCSE: a Critical Analysis,* Croydon, IEA Education Unit.

SHIPMAN, M. (1980) 'The limits of positive discrimination', in Marland, M. (Ed.) *Education for the Inner City,* London, Heinemann, pp. 69–92.

SLEE, P. (1989) 'Redundant reforms', *Education,* 13 January.

TGAT (TASK GROUP ON ASSESSMENT AND TESTING) (1987) *A Report,* London, Department of Education and Science.

TGAT (1988) *Three Supplementary Reports,* London, Department of Education and Science.

WHITTY, G. and MENTER, I. (1989) 'Lessons of Thatcherism: education policy in England and Wales, 1979–88', *Journal of Law and Society*, Vol. 16, No. 1, pp. 42–64.
WIENER, M. (1981) *English Culture and the Decline of the Industrial Spirit 1850–1980*, Cambridge, Cambridge University Press.

3
National Assessment Proposals: Analyzing the Debate

Roger Murphy

National assessments as performance indicators

The various chapters in this volume have explored different dimensions of the Education Reform Act, and have repeatedly pointed to a set of basic philosophies that lie behind it. Several authors have referred to an implied assumption that there is a crisis within the public education system, which the Act is designed to solve. This crisis, so the argument runs, needs to be confronted by major reforms — the essential aspects of the curriculum need to be defined and enforced in all schools, and the consumers (who are often thought of as being parents) need to be given greater power to make sure that their needs are being met. Greater public choice and accountability are seen as the linchpin towards raising educational standards. Increased parent power is presented as the force which will ensure that schools and teachers provide a better service. In a free-market economy parents will vote with their feet (and in some cases their cheque books). The 'producers' who do the best job of persuading the 'consumers' that they are offering them a good deal will prosper while others, who are less successful, will decline and eventually go out of business.

Stuart Ranson (in Chapter 1) has in particular developed this analysis and has indicated how consumer choice depends both on a diversity of products — the alternative of independent schools now being supplemented by city technology colleges (CTCs) and grant-maintained (GM) schools and on a system of quality control, allowing the consumers to have both the opportunity for choice and some information upon which to base their choices. Finding out about the quality of schools has always been an elusive exercise as far as many parents have been concerned (NFER, 1988). Many have been prepared to assume that the product that costs the greatest amount of money must be the best. Others have been denied that choice, by economic and social factors, and have had to be content with whatever the state education system had on offer in their locality. No-one has been really sure which schools were the most effective, although some estate agents have managed to push house prices up in certain catchment areas by claiming that they had the 'best school in the area'.

The public/private divide in education has been a dominant feature in Britain for a long time, and many analysts (such as Pring, 1987) read into the current reforms a desire to extend the ethos of 'private enterprise' into the maintained education system. Thus parents, opting to stay within the maintained system, who have always had the right to apply for places for their children in schools outside their catchment area, are to be encouraged to do so both by the principle of 'open enrolment' and by the creation of a greater variety of types of school within the maintained system. Another vital factor is the fuelling of a market forces mentality within the maintained system, by providing simple market indicators to allow the consumers to look for 'best buys' and to see 'market trends'. This is the reason why the notion of national assessments with published results for all maintained schools (but *not* independent schools) and all children at specific ages is so central to the philosophy of the Act. Market indicators are the life-blood of any market, and, whether it is the Financial Times Index for the Stock Exchange, or the average monthly sunshine and temperature figures for holiday resorts, the principles remain the same. Useful market indicators need to be precise, reliable, sensitive to change, and give the consumer a rapid insight to help guide choices within the market place. Thus a particular focus for this chapter is the role that national assessments at 7, 11, 14 and 16 will play in providing market indicators within the reformed education system. They are seen as having a key role within the overall philosophy of an Act which is aiming to raise educational standards by giving greater choice to the consumers, and encouraging them to use this by supplying them with clearer, and more regular, information about pupils' attainments.

The months that have followed the first articulations of this idea, in early 1987, in speeches by both the Prime Minister and the Secretary of State for Education and Science, have seen the unfolding of a lively debate over the nature of market indicators that could be produced. Strong support has been forthcoming from right wing quarters, such as the Hillgate Group and the Centre for Policy Studies, for the idea that simple indicators can easily be produced. Others have been more concerned about the nature of the indicators and whether output measures can be interpreted at all unless they are accompanied by input measures, for example those which could focus on the potential of pupils entering a school as well as their achievements by the time they leave (Goldstein, 1988). Others have been concerned over the impact that judging schools and pupils in relation to such restricted targets could have, and have stressed the need to make sure that any system of national assessments should reflect both something of the complexity of the nature of educational achievement, and the factors which lie behind the different patterns of achievement of individual pupils and schools around the country.

The educational progress of an individual child, and the collective achievements of all the children in an individual school or Local Education Authority can easily enough be summarized in a few words, or come to that numbers. However, like any brief account of a complex phenomenon, much important detail necessarily has to be overlooked in such an account. A recent book (Hill, 1987) written for parents in Australia to guide them in relation to the increased choice they too are being offered between different types of schools, provides a simple checklist, of fifty-seven features of any school, which would be worth thinking about in making such a choice. Not many of those fifty-seven features would be discernible from published national assessment results at 7, 11, 14 and 16, and this in itself raises a fundamental question about the extent to which national assessment results will satisfy the perceived need of parents for more information about schools.

Now it could well be that many parents would be happy to work with a shorter list than Brian Hill's 'fifty-seven varieties' of ways of judging between different schools. Indeed many would undoubtedly welcome the provision of simple information either putting the schools in their area in some kind of 'league table' or providing a Consumer Association type of list of 'star buys', 'good buys' and 'worth thinking about'. All of this comes back to the value systems individuals are happy to operate with, and basic questions about what schooling and education within a developed society are for. If schooling is largely about providing pupils with an opportunity to develop their abilities in relation to an agreed set of basic, easily defined and measured, attributes then a simple system of national testing may reveal all that needs to be known (although the evidence from other countries who have tried that approach is not encouraging in terms of either technical feasibility of the idea or the overall effects on teaching in schools). However, there is a widely-held view that education is about much more than that. Thus the provision of simple information relating to achievement in relation to a restricted set of basic skills purporting to represent a good 'market indicator' could create both confusion amongst those who attempt to use the information, and a distortion of good practice in schools in response to this new breed of market indicators.

Similar points can also be made about the relationship between models of assessment and models of pupil learning. Simple systems of reporting assessment results tend to imply that learning progresses in a simple way as well. For example progress through a set of ten levels (such as those proposed by the TGAT group) can be thought to imply that pupils' learning progresses in a straightforward linear fashion, whereas all that we know about learning is that it is much more complex than that, and involves all sorts of fits and starts, U-turns and even apparent periods of regression before further progress is made (Driver, 1983). Thus the quest for simple assessment results is fraught with difficulties all along the way. Both the nature of educational achievement, and the way in which individual children acquire their own distinctive conglomeration of achievements are complex. Those who attempt to provide a simple picture of this complex set of phenomena do so both at their own peril, and at the peril of those they seek to describe.

The international quest for simple indicators of educational performance

Despite current trends towards systems of assessment which can provide more detailed and specific information in relation to the achievements of individual pupils (Murphy and Torrance, 1988), there has been a long history of simplifying educational achievement into single grades or pass/fail examinations. Broadfoot (1984) and others have pointed to the substantial selection function that educational assessment has performed, and the preoccupation with simple assessment results at the key points where decisions have to be made about access to future educational opportunities and/or training and employment. In Britain the 11+ examination and the major school leaving public examinations have characterised this role. In some respects the system of issuing separate grades for individual GCSE and A-level subjects represents a greater level of detail than is often available in other countries where 'aggregate scores' or 'grade point averages' have reduced the overall outcomes of eleven or more years of full-time education to a single numerical score. Nevertheless the emphasis throughout the world has been on assessment results providing simple information to be used as a rough and ready guide to making selection choices. The fact that examination grades are known to have low predictive validity is generally recognised but dismissed as an argument, in a situation in which choices have to be made and there needs to be a quick and easy basis for making them.

Throughout the world the interest in educational assessment has extended beyond its role in fulfilling selection functions within different societies, to offering the possibility of monitoring and evaluating schools, school systems, and whole nation's educational programmes. Cohen (1987) has pointed critically to the large amount of resources that has been channelled into large-scale testing programmes, both within nations, through schemes such as the Australian Studies in Student Performance (ASSD), the National Assessment Educational Progress (NAEP) in the USA, and the Assessment of Performance Unit (APU) in the UK, and across nations, through schemes such as those mounted by the International Association for the Evaluation of Educational Achievement (IEA). Cohen along with many others is critical of such systems of evaluating education, pointing to the way in which such schemes have to make massive compromises in the way in which they define the educational standards that they set out to monitor. Comparative results can only be produced by ignoring regional and local differences in curriculum provision and learning experiences, and in many cases this is done by focusing solely on a few discrete parts of the curriculum experienced by the pupils included in the studies. Thus at the end of the day politicians may be satisfied by such attempts to make it look as though 'standards' are being monitored in a uniform way across whole systems, while educators have to live with the knowledge that the results reveal very little about the actual achievements of pupils within the various parts of the system. So wherever crude indices of educational achievement are produced it will always be at the expense of riding roughshod over an enforced analysis of real educational experience. Cohen summarizes his position as follows:

> The accurate and valid assessment of standards indeed represents a complex professional set of challenges. The seeming precision of published quantitative data mask the difficulties of adequately selecting or determining and representing the range of criteria which truly reflect educational standards (Cohen, 1987).

Thus the history of attempts to introduce national schemes of assessment, and the decreasing prominence of the Assessment of Performance Unit (APU) results in Britain, has paralleled a similar diminished lack of influence of national testing programmes elsewhere. Nevertheless the current plans contained within the Education Reform Act seem set to outstrip any attempts towards developing national assessments that have ever been attempted anywhere else in the world. Rarely can any country have attempted to introduce such an ambitious and comprehensive system of assessment covering such a wide range of age points and areas of the curriculum.

The evolving model for national assessments in Britain

As already mentioned in the previous section a fascination with systems of national assessment has been present in a number of countries, including USA, Australia and England and Wales since the end of the 1960s (Cohen, 1987, Gipps, 1989). In each of these countries attempts have been made to introduce large-scale monitoring of educational standards through programmes of national testing. In England and Wales the APU has, since 1975, attempted to monitor various aspects of the achievements of children at 11, 13, and 15 years of age. None of these schemes has apparently gone very far towards meeting the political desire for educational performance indicators. Technical difficulties over issues such as the comparability of different tests have made it very difficult to draw anything other than very general conclusions from the results. Furthermore the possibility of making any real attempt at answering the question of whether educational standards were rising or falling over a period of years has remained the hardest nut of all to crack.

National assessments carried out by the APU have principally focused on a set of skills within the three major survey areas of mathematics, language and science, and now assess these achievements amongst a national sample of pupils every five years. These testing activities have been substantially reoriented over the years to attempt to maximize the potential feedback to teachers in relation to specific obstacles to progress within particular areas of the curriculum. The APU has therefore become less a source of national performance indicators than was originally anticipated, and the resources are now being used to bolster curriculum-focused in-service work with teachers. Thus the emphasis has swung away from statistical comparisons of national aggregate scores towards the production of more detailed commentaries on particular features of the tests results, which could be used by teachers to inform future classroom practice.

The role of the APU has always been a confused one and it is clear that the purpose of APU activities has had to be re-thought and dramatically altered on several occasions during its existence (Gipps, 1987). At no point did it ever come close to providing a detailed national accountability-type scrutiny of the performance of individual pupils, teachers, schools and LEAs. However, the fears which were some years ago articulated in relation to what the APU might become, are now much more clearly being stated as the specific purposes of the national assessments, which are proposed in the Education Reform Act.

The key role of publically-available assessment results of pupils at several age points was clearly to be a linch-pin of the government's reform of the education system right from the first speeches that alluded to it early in 1987. Both the Prime Minister, and her Secretary of State for Education and Science, made repeated references to the introduction of a nationally prescribed curriculum accompanied by compulsory benchmark tests which would be taken by all pupils in maintained schools at certain key ages. These tests, it was claimed, would show parents and other interested parties, exactly what each pupil knew, understood and could do. This proved to be good election speech material, and a national opinion poll later in the year revealed the testing proposals as one of the most popular parts of the proposed reform. Overall, 71 per cent of parents supported such tests with only 24 per cent against (Gallup Poll, 1987).

With a good measure of public and political support behind them the proposals for introducing national assessments seemed destined to be implemented. There were however very strong reservations being expressed by educationalists, and assessment experts in particular (Hargreaves, 1987; Nuttall, 1987; Denvir, Brown and Eve, 1987; and Murphy, 1987 and 1988a), about the possible implications of such a system on both classroom practice and on the future health of the education system as a whole. Furthermore there was widespread fear amongst teachers about what they were in store for, and at an early stage in the proceedings the biggest teachers union, the National Union of Teachers (NUT), threatened to boycott the entire assessment process.

The early fears that were expressed in relation to the introduction of 'benchmark tests' alongside the new national curriculum, grew rapidly as more detail about the proposals began to unfold. The term 'benchmark test' was gradually dropped however, as a model of an assessment system linked to specific attainment targets at defined ages was developed. What appeared to be certain was that there would be a national system of assessment, combining some teacher assessment results with external test results and leading to nationally available results for all pupils at a number of fixed ages. The precise ages to be chosen was a point of some conjecture, and the original idea of 7, 9, 11, 14, and 16, was later modified to 7 (or thereabouts), 11, 14, and 16.

When the National Curriculum 5–16 consultation document (DES, 1987) was published in July 1987, the assessment proposals occupied a major part of it, and extravagant claims were made about the role assessment was going to have in the process of reforming the education system and raising educational standards. It was claimed that the system of assessment proposed was a 'proven and essential way towards raising standards of achievement' (DES 1987: 10), although no-one was very sure where the evidence existed for demonstrating the success of such a system anywhere else in the world. Another point of controversy that emerged at this stage was over the role that teachers were going to have in the assessment process. Despite earlier assurances from the Secretary of State that the assessments would all be set and marked by teachers, the consultation document stated that 'at the heart of the assessment process there will be nationally prescribed tests done by all pupils to supplement the individual teachers' assessments' (DES, 1987: 11).

Writing towards the end of 1987 I attempted to summarize six main reservations about the proposals as they were emerging at that stage:

1. The *purpose* of the tests is confused — the results are almost certain therefore to be *misused*.
2. The attainment targets will not encapsulate more than *isolated fragments* of the whole National Curriculum.
3. The tests are bound to encourage an *extremely narrow* approach to teaching and learning, even with respect to the broad aims of the National Curriculum.
4. There is little justification for prescribing attainment targets in relation to *fixed ages*. Optimum attainment levels should be recorded and rewarded regardless of the age when they are reached by individual pupils.
5. The assessment system is likely to be dominated by 'nationally prescribed tests' to the detriment of the assessments to be carried out by teachers.
6. The pressure to keep the proposed system *simple* is likely to result in the worst kind of *norm-referenced tests* which will produce results, on a three (or five) point grading scale, which will convey little or no information in relation to the attainment targets anyway. (Murphy, 1988a: 42–43).

Subsequently the Secretary of State set up a Task Group on Assessment and Testing (TGAT), who devised a model that at least made some attempt to address some of these early concerns. However all remain valid issues to focus on in the post-TGAT era, when the first attempts are made to put national assessment ideas into practice. In particular, reservations 1, 2, 3 and 5 are of paramount concern to those who are aware of the potential damage that could occur through certain types of national assessment being implemented.

The TGAT group was given little more than three months to advise Kenneth Baker 'on the overriding requirements which should govern assessment and testing in schools for children of all abilities at the key ages of around 7, 11, 14 and 16' (DES Press Release, 30 July, 1987). Their work was to complement that of the National Curriculum subject working groups, who were concentrating on the identification of specific attainment targets at each of the prescribed ages. The group clearly had a difficult task from the start and the members of it, who were selected by the Secretary of State, had to try to come up with an assessment framework which avoided some of the worst pitfalls feared by those within the education system, but which would also meet the requirements of the consultation document. That they managed to produce a report at all within the timescale was remarkable, and the fact that it was widely acclaimed by all of the main political parties and teacher unions was quite extraordinary (Murphy, 1988b).

The TGAT report (DES, 1988) was recognized as being based on sound educational principles, and went a long way to subtly change the way in which the national assessments were being conceived. Its most major contribution was in relation to the way in which the assessment results were to be conceived. Up until that time it had been assumed that each key age point would have its own grades (say A to E or 1 to 5), and there was widespread fear that pupils who got low grades at 7 years of age could be easily de-motivated by the prospect of getting the same grades again when they were 11, 14 and 16. The TGAT proposal was for a single-grading system, involving ten levels, which would span all of the age points. Thus although it would be anticipated that pupils at age 7 would be somewhere within the range from Level 1 to Level 3, they could progress higher if they were ready to, and pupils at subsequent ages would then be assessed in relation to whichever level of the scale they had then reached. This idea drew very heavily on the work of the graded assessment and testing projects (Pennycuick and Murphy, 1988) and provided a much more positive basis for recording the progress of those who were inevitably going to achieve different levels of attainment at different ages.

The other surprise that the TGAT group pulled out of their bag was the idea of Standard Assessment Tasks (SATs). These were a kind of half-way house between conventional externally devised written tests and coursework assessment undertaken by teachers. The group argued that externally-prepared paper and pencil tests would have too many limitations to adequately assess the range of attainment targets that would be developed within the National Curriculum. They therefore proposed an approach to external assessment which encompassed a wide variety of ways of delivering questions to pupils, various kinds of pupil activities, and a selection of ways in which pupils might respond to tasks.

> The art of constructing good assessment tasks is to exploit a wide range (far wider than those normally envisaged for tests) of modes of presentation, operation and response, and their numerous combinations, in order to widen the range of pupils' abilities that they reflect and so to enhance educational validity. (DES, 1988, Para. 48)

Thus the TGAT group appeared to have done a Houdini-like act of escaping from an impossible situation. They had produced a report which appeared to satisfy nearly everyone! It was however clear that all they had provided was a theoretical framework and their report certainly contained proposals for assessment practices that had never before been implemented anywhere in the world. What they did was come up with some clever compromise solutions and then pass a substantial baton to the subject working groups, and other bodies, who were to be given the task of putting the ideas into practice, within the emerging framework of individual subject attainment targets.

However within a few more weeks the TGAT group had received much more national attention than they had ever expected for their efforts. A leaked letter from the Prime Minister's Office indicated that she had been studying the TGAT proposals, which the Secretary of State had already welcomed, and felt that the report was proposing a system that was too complicated, too costly, and too far removed from the type of traditional externally-devised written tests that she was hoping for. It was clear from the letter that she wanted a much simpler system of assessment that could be implemented quickly and cheaply, and she urged the Secretary of State to think again about whether to embark along the TGAT road. This apparent rift between the Prime Minister and Kenneth Baker was the subject of considerable media attention, and was front-page news in the national newspapers for several days. It became clear that the approach that Kenneth Baker was adopting towards national assessment was a good deal 'softer' than was being advocated by more right-wing elements within the Conservative Party.

Despite this high-level attack on the TGAT recommendations, they have remained the major basis for the advice to the National Curriculum subject working parties, and more recently to the consortia who have been commissioned to start developing the Standard Assessment Tasks (SATs). The fact that £6 million was allocated to three consortium groups for the development of SATs for 7-year-olds at the end of the first key stage, in December 1988, was seen as a firm indication that the TGAT model was to be pursued.

At the time of writing the focus of much of the discussion about the national assessments is upon these SATs, which are expected to play a major part in the overall assessment process. The concept of SATs is a new one, and the consortia who have been commissioned to develop them will have a major task ahead of them in terms of producing tasks that can operate practically within schools throughout England and Wales. The SATs will need to encapsulate the important features of the main subjects within the National Curriculum and provide a fair basis for assessing the achievements of pupils regardless of gender, ethnic background and social-class factors.

The time that will be needed to develop and trial SATs means that no real details will emerge about the likely format of the national assessments for any of the key stages until 1990 at the earliest. Even then the SATs developed will only relate to the assessment of 7 and 14-year-olds in a restricted range of National Curriculum subjects. It will then be well into the mid 1990's before the full range of assessments relating to all of the four key stages and both the core and foundation subjects come into operation. Furthermore in all of the timetables that have been drawn up little allowance has been made for the possibility that problems may be encountered with the development of SATs. Presumably as it has been accepted that the SATs need to be trialled before they can be put into operation, then it follows that the trials may reveal deficiencies in the SATs that would suggest that they were unsuitable as the major basis for assessing the nation's children at the ages of 7, 11, 14 and 16. All of the available evidence that we have, from studies such as Denvir, Brown and Eve (1987), suggests that the development of acceptable SATs within the timescale laid down will be a difficult, if not impossible, challenge.

Meanwhile alongside the major development work on SATs, teachers will also be expected to start their own school-based assessment of pupils against the published attainment targets, starting from 1989. Far less attention is being paid to this part of the assessment process, and there remains a fear that the assessment operation will be seen to depend largely on SATs, and that less status will be given to the regular classroom assessments. If this turns out to be the case it will be a major departure from the implied philosophy of the TGAT report, which attempted as far as it could to integrate the National Curriculum assessment processes into everyday classroom practices, and avoid the unhealthy and artificial separation of assessment from teaching and learning.

If teachers are to be given a proper professional responsibility for assessing pupils against the attainment targets of the National Curriculum, then a considerable amount of attention needs to be given to the support they will need to develop reliable assessment, recording and reporting processes. Furthermore if the Education Reform Act is really about improving education then improved classroom assessment of pupils' progress needs to be seen as an essential component of that. The development of good quality SATs could assist that process, but cannot replace the need to build much further on the progress that has been made through GCSE coursework and the Profiling and Records of Achievement developments. These recent assessment initiatives have done much to change the face of educational assessment into something that is much more pupil-centred, organic and integrated into everyday teaching and learning (Murphy and Torrance, 1988), and national assessments could, depending on how they evolve, either harness that potential or destroy it.

Conclusions

In the preceding sections of this chapter I have argued that the package of reforms contained within the Education Reform Act assume that greater competition within the education system will improve its overall effectiveness. Readily available and simple performance indicators, in the form of national assessment results, have therefore been highlighted as a vital component in fuelling greater competition between pupils, teachers, schools and LEAs. Thus the political interest in getting simple standard assessment information into the envisaged new market place of the reformed state education system is urgent and strong. It is anticipated that the presence of readily available performance indicators will allow instant judgements to be made of the progress of individual pupils, and the respective qualities of individual teachers, schools and LEAs. Furthermore it is expected that as the consumers respond to this newly-available market information then the system as a whole will improve in response to the pressure of the consumers wanting better results and choosing to go where they think they are most likely to get them.

The entire logic of this market indicators argument rests among other things on the assumption that simple valid and reliable indicators can be produced. In this respect a historical and comparative analysis of the quest for simple performance indicators is not encouraging. The desire for a simple gauge of the effectiveness of education has been around for a long time in many countries, but where simple measures of assessment have been produced they have rarely been seen to carry with them much credibility in terms of providing a good summary of progress.

At the heart of the debate about national assessments is the conflict between those who believe that the essential aspects of achievement are by definition simple, and those who believe that both the nature of educational achievement and the context within which it needs to be interpreted are by their nature complex. It would be all too easy to administer basic tests of numeracy and literacy to 7, 11, 14 and 16-year-old pupils throughout the country. Indeed many LEAs already have extensive programmes of blanket testing of pupils in operation (Gipps *et al.* 1983). However the National Curriculum is about much more than literacy and numeracy. The working groups that have been charged with the responsibility of creating attainment targets for each of the key stages for each of the core and foundation subjects are unveiling an overall curriculum that is broad, diverse and complex. Individual children will in time progress in very different ways through the various parts of the curriculum, and their teachers will hopefully be given the chance to develop the necessary skills to assess the progress they are making, as well as diagnosing any difficulties that they are having in particular areas.

The essential requirements for a national assessment system that will support the laudable aim of encouraging every child to make as much progress as possible in relation to the entire National Curriculum are that:

1. The assessment results relate in a meaningful way to specific aspects of the National Curriculum, and are not so global as to be devoid of meaning in relation to particular attainment targets.
2. The overall assessment procedures adequately cover all of the National Curriculum subjects, and are not allowed to remain focused exclusively on core subjects alone.
3. Individual children are given a reasonable opportunity to demonstrate what they know, understand and can do. This will involve providing a variety of opportunities, for them to demonstrate evidence of their achievements, which avoid the various sources of assessment bias.
4. The involvement of pupils and teachers in the assessment process is a positive and motivating experience, which provides helpful feedback about progress at regular intervals, so that the information can be useful in planning future teaching and learning strategies.
5. The unique position of teachers in the assessment process is capitalised

upon and that moderation methods are adopted which recognise, promote, and develop the potential of teachers as the assessors of their own pupils.

6. Where summaries are provided about the achievements of individual pupils, teachers, schools or group of schools, these are provided in relation to other contextual information which allows them to be interpreted meaningfully. (Goldstein, 1988)

Only time will tell whether an improved version of national assessment will come to fruition and meet these ideals. If that is to happen then the preoccupation with getting simple results into the market place must be made to become subservient to the much more serious need of making sure that national assessments relate to the whole of the National Curriculum and not just parts of it, and that the assessment processes assist rather than damage the day-to-day classroom practices of teachers and pupils.

The current preoccupation with putting resources into developing SATs, and the concentration on developing a restricted range of attainment targets and profile components within little beyond the core subjects, are seen as an early indication that the euphoria that greeted the TGAT report may have been more of a trick than a treat (Gipps, 1988). Once the objective is met of getting simple performance indicators into existence, however tenuous their connection with the full range of attainments laid out within the National Curriculum, it may become very hard to pursue the overall plan of the national assessment system which was outlined in the TGAT report.

References

BROADFOOT, P. M. (1984) *Selection, Certification and Control*, Lewes, Falmer Press.

COHEN, D. (1987) 'Evaluating standards: is there a better way?' Mimeo, Macquarie University, Australia.

DENVIR, B. BROWN, M. and EVE, P. (1987) *Attainment Targets and Assessment in the Primary Phase: Mathematics Feasibility Study*, DES, London.

DES (Department of Education and Science) (1987) *The National Curriculum 5–16. A Consultation document*, DES, London.

DES (1988) *National Curriculum: Task Group on Assessment and Testing: A Report*, DES, London.

DRIVER, R. (1983) *The Pupil as Scientist?*, Milton Keynes, Open University Press.

GIPPS, C. (1989) 'National assessment: a comparison of English and American trends', in Broadfoot, P. Murphy, R. J. L. and Torrance, H. (forthcoming), *International Changes in Educational Assessment*, Multilingual Matters.

GIPPS, C. (1987) 'The APU: From Trojan Horse to Angel of Light?' *Curriculum*, Vol. 8, No. 1.

GIPPS, C. (1988) 'The TGAT Report: Trick or Treat', *Forum*, Vol. 31, No. 1, pp. 4–7.

GIPPS, C., STEADMAN, S., BLACKSTONE, T. and STIERER, B. (1983) *Standardized Testing in Local Education Authorities and Schools*, London, Heinemann.

GOLDSTEIN, H. (1988) 'Comparing schools', in Torrance, H. (Ed.) *National Assessment and Testing: A Research Response*, BERA occasional publication.

HARGREAVES, D. (1987) 'Getting the mixture right', *The Times Educational Supplement*, 11 September.

HILL, B. V. (1987) *Choosing the Right School*, Sydney, ATCF Books.

MURPHY, R. J. L. (1987) 'Assessing a National Curriculum', *Journal of Education Policy*, Vol. 2, No. 4, pp. 317–23.

MURPHY, R. J. L. (1988a) 'Great Education Reform Bill proposals for testing — a critique', *Local Government Studies*, Vol. 14, No. 1, pp. 39–45.

MURPHY, R. J. L. (1988b) 'TGAT a change of heart?', in Torrance, H. (Ed.) *National Assessment and Testing: A Research Response*, BERA occasional publication.

MURPHY, R. J. L. and TORRANCE, H. (1988) *The Changing Face of Educational Assessment*, Milton Keynes, Open University Press.

NFER, (1988) *Quality in Schools: A Briefing Conference*, Slough, NFER.

NUTTALL, D. L. (1987) 'Testing, Testing, Testing . . .' *Education Review*, Vol. 1, No. 2, pp. 32–5.

PENNYCUICK, D. and MURPHY, R. J. L. (1988) *The Impact of Graded Tests*, Lewes, Falmer Press.

PRING, R. (1987) 'Privatization in education', *Journal of Education Policy*, Vol. 4, No. 2, pp. 289–99.

RANSOM, S. (1989) 'From 1944 to 1988: Education, Citizenship and Democracy' (Chapter 7 in this volume).

4
Opting for an Uncertain Future: Grant-Maintained Schools

Michael Flude and Merril Hammer

Introduction

In this chapter we explore the ideological roots and justification for setting up a new category of grant-maintained (GM) schools, as well as discussing their likely impact and the wider implications for the education service as a whole. Like other developments, notably the Assisted Places Scheme and the attempts to establish a network of City Technology Colleges (CTCs), the emergence of this new category of schools will further blur the boundaries between public and private schooling and widen the scope of the process of privatization occurring within education.

Before the Education Reform Act the support on the political right for freeing schools from local authority control was part of an evolving strategy that sought to challenge the alleged 'producer domination' exercised by the educational establishment, by means of enhancing 'consumer' interests and influence. Campaigns mounted by New Right groupings, especially in the run-up to the 1987 election, had the effect of creating the ideological space for a series of interlinked legislative measures contained in the Education Reform Act that not so many years earlier would have been dismissed as eccentric and impractical. Although there are some apparently contradictory strands within a hastily assembled, complex and wide-ranging piece of legislation, the main thrust of the Act lies in the substantial changes it seeks to bring about in the culture and ethos of schooling. Not only does the Act widen the scope of the process of privatization; the combined effect of GM schools, open enrolment and local management of schools seeks to open up what is at present a predominantly publicly-funded service to the priorities and values of an enterprise culture. In this respect at least it can be argued that the possibility for schools to opt out of local authority control may in the end prove more significant than the number of schools that eventually become grant-maintained. In our discussion of the main features and implications of grant-maintained schools, we draw on the comments of Andrew Turner, Director of the Grant Maintained Schools Trust, in an interview carried out early in 1989.[1]

Origins and antecedents

The origins of the proposals to establish a new category of GM schools that were announced by the DES Consultation Paper of July 1987 are to be found in a series of earlier papers published by New Right pressure groups. Although specific and detailed proposals for the establishment of schools free from local authority control (including CTCs) emerged in the 1980s, the sustained attack on state schooling during the previous decade was organized around a number of themes that prepared the ground for the radical educational agenda of the New Right.

Some considerable continuity is evident in the attacks made on state schooling from the Black Paper movement of the 1960s and 1970s, to the later publications by the Hillgate Group and the Education Unit of the Institute of Economic Affairs. However, whereas the Black Paper polemicists operated largely on the fringes of major policy developments, various New Right groupings in the late 1970s and 1980s have exerted a major influence in shifting the 'dialogue of discourse' (Neave, 1989) and in promoting a radical restructuring of state education. The criticisms of state schooling that have prompted this restructuring have been centred around the claimed decline of educational standards, particularly following the ending of selective secondary education, and the move by primary schools towards child-centred methods (see Brehony, Chapter 7 in this volume).

Both earlier and later publications in their diagnosis of the problem of declining standards display an antipathy to central and local state control of education and various educational trends informed by egalitarian policy goals. Within the Black Paper movement support is found for the introduction of a system of educational vouchers or credits, a return to selective education and the strengthening of parental choice in education. Writing in the final Black Paper publication Stuart Sexton called for the removal of those 'political constraints and directions which seek to distort the pattern of educational supply and demand', the reinstatement of direct grant grammar schools as a means of establishing a network of academic schools throughout the country, and 'the elimination of bureaucratic direction between parents and schools that affect choice of school' (Sexton, 1977). In seeking to promote educational change via enhancing the influence of the consumer, Sexton also calls for a greater variety of schools and devolved administration from local authorities to schools. Although the proposal is not developed Sexton concludes by supporting what appears to be an embryonic version of the GM school: 'There is no reason why a maintained school should not be an independent unit just as in the private sector' (Sexton, *ibid.*).

There is evidence also that tactically New Right groups came mainly to embrace a gradualist approach to the long term aim of replacing a 'producer-led system' to a 'consumer-led system' through the introduction of a system of educational vouchers or credits. Supporting a phased introduction of such a system Sexton writes:

> Both politically and financially it would not be possible or desirable to make a *sudden change*, countrywide, to an education credits system from the current sysem of education provision and finance.

> Politically it requires the public at large to reach the logical conclusion for themselves, namely that education credits are the only sensible way to proceed . . .
>
> What the phased introduction of education credits does is first to adapt the structure and finance of education so that a full education credit scheme, by common consent logically and legitimately, springs from it. (Sexton, 1987)

A number of policy developments and proposals from the early 1980s mark the beginnings not only of moves to extend parental choice as discussed in the chapters of Ranson and Stillman, but also to diversify the range and types of schools. The 1980 (No.2) Education Act established the Assisted Places Scheme as a partial replacement for direct-grant grammar schools which had been phased out after 1976, albeit in a more restricted form than had originally been envisaged (Whitty and Menter, 1989). Providing financial support directly to parents on a means tested basis rather than to the institutions themselves, the Assisted Places Scheme increased the pool of able pupils for the private sector, as well as marginally extending parental choice of schools. As Tapper and Salter put it, 'The Assisted Places Scheme offered the [Conservative] Party the opportunity of combining the traditional support of schools committed to academic excellence with its newly found interest in parental choice. The scheme was preferable to the restoration of direct grant as few independent schools could be expected to embrace the status that had already been abolished by government fiat' (Tapper and Salter, 1986).

In the first half of the 1980s various proposals that were examined by Sir Keith Joseph and his policy advisers can also be seen as precursors of CTCs and GM schools. First, consideration was given to the funding of a small number of direct grant primary schools. This appeared to replicate for the primary sector the Prime Minister's support of direct grant funding of academically selective schools (*Guardian,* 18 November 1985). Second it was reported in 1986 (*Times,* 1 April 1986) that plans had been drawn up to establish a network of directly funded and administered Crown schools to serve primarily inner city areas. This scheme proposed transferring initially fifty or sixty comprehensive schools out of local authority control into central control, and for such schools to act as models of superior teaching and thereby stimulate higher standards in local authority schools. It appears that this proposal was being promoted within the Department of Education and Science as an alternative to the growing influence being exerted by the New Right's call for radically extending the process of privatization within state education (Pring, 1986). Third, at a time when a process of privatization by stealth was becoming marked in the state sector, with schools being increasingly forced to rely on private sources of funding, active consideration was being given to the adaptation of American magnet schools to the British context. Caroline Cox argued that such schools would:

> . . . help alleviate the all-too-familiar problems of providing secondary

> education in our inner city areas: scarce resources, especially of teachers in certain subjects, underachievement . . . and falling rolls . . . The primary objectives of magnet schools is to offer high quality education within the state system, based on voluntary choice by the student and parents with open access beyond the immediate neighbourhood catchment area. Each school strives to offer high quality education in all main subjects but each also has a distinctive curriculum based on a special theme. (Cox, 1985).

The announcement of the setting up of CTCs in 1986 marked a major development in the funding and control of schools. The proposal brought together a number of strands associated with different policy groups on the political right. It combined support for establishing a new category of schools independent of local authority control financed by private sector sponsorship and government funds, a technically oriented curriculum focused primarily on improving educational standards in inner city areas, and an admissions procedure that reintroduced selection. While it was the stated intention that City Technology Colleges would admit pupils across the full ability range, entry would nevertheless be selective insofar as account was to be taken of pupils' achievements and aptitudes and their parents' commitment to full-time education or training up the age of 18. Importantly, as McLeod (1988) has pointed out, the initiative to establish CTCs was part of an evolving strategy that advocated greater parental choice across a more diversified range of schools as a means of raising educational standards.

The development of the embryonic idea of state funded schooling free from local control can be traced through a series of New Right publications. The pamphlet *No Turning Back* published in 1985 by a group of Conservative MPs called for a radical package of educational reforms, including a scheme to allow parents and teachers to start their own schools and to receive state monies for doing so (Brown *et al,* 1985). On lines similar to magnet schools it was envisaged that these schools would offer greater specialization and would bring 'extra choices into areas which were badly served by the existing schools' (*ibid.*). The 'radical agenda' for schools outlined in *No Turning Back* was developed and extended in the group's later pamphlet *Save our Schools*. This reiterated the familiar criticisms of state schooling associated with the political right, and saw that 'the key to reform lies in the introduction of opportunities for consumer input' (Brown *et al.*, 1986). It was argued that this had to be a more thorough going change than expanding the independent sector if the quality of education was to be improved for the majority of parents. Another possible route to reform, the adoption of a voucher scheme, was rejected as being politically unrealistic.

> It alienates or deters the various interest groups involved, and does not immediately construct interest groups on the other side to outweigh them. It changes everything at once, and forces change on those who might not feel equipped to handle it. A more viable system might seek to provide opportunities for change and allow the incremental decisions

> of parents to build the new reality cumulatively, instead of overnight. (Brown *et al.*, 1986).

Three interrelated reforms were proposed as part of this incrementalist strategy for liberating consumer interests and establishing something approaching an 'internal market' within state education by simulating market conditions within a framework of a state-financed education system. It was proposed that newly constituted school governing bodies would have responsiblity for administering schools and determining policy priorities. The second proposal was that schools should be directly funded by central government (as well as drawing on private sources of finance). It was suggested that this would 'give effect to the independence of the school by changing the method of finance' (*ibid.*). Finally, open entry was sought allowing parents to send their children to any school that would accept them. Within this package of reforms financial delegation to schools was regarded as critical if schools were to operate as independent and autonomous units. Although no reference is made to the future establishment of a fully-fledged voucher system the implications of these proposals for such a scheme are clear.

Two further papers extend and refine the suggestions made in *Save our Schools*. A broad-ranging educational manifesto issued by the Hillgate Group called for the ownership of schools to be transferred to individual trusts, with schools being financed by central grants. As in the previous document open entry was advocated in order to give parents freedom of choice, as well as giving parents 'partial control over the financing of the schools their children will attend' (Hillgate Group, 1986). The manifesto presented two ways in which parents could exercise this choice. First, by giving the parents the option of a place at a direct grant school or by granting to parents a credit that could buy a place at a private school. Second, by taking steps to blur the distinction between public and private schools by subsidizing private schools on a per capita basis.

Extending the process of privatization within state schooling is also for Sexton the means of moving to the phased introduction of credit vouchers. In progressing towards an eventual free market in schooling a series of interlocked proposals are made to establish the conditions in which a scheme could operate and have wide acceptance. These include per capita educational expenditure, devolved school budgets, the phasing out of national salary scales for teachers, and steps to diversify the range of schools via the reintroduction of direct grant primary and secondary schools, the expansion of the Assisted Places Scheme and the possibility for some maintained schools to change their status. Once again the proposal to free schools from local authority control is tied into the introduction of a voucher or credit scheme:

> Most of such newly independent schools may then be expected to become part of the new direct grant system . . . and, in the longer run still, schools at which education credits may be spent. This is a way of freeing a number of maintained schools, especially in the inner cities, from current party political control. It can even be considered as a 'management buy-out' scheme. (Sexton, 1987).

Within the pamphlets and articles surveyed that have emanated from New Right groups we find a number of insistent messages. There is the claim that educational standards and the quality of education for the mass of the population will not improve until state controls, particularly those of the local state, are drawn back to a level compatible with maximizing parental choice. Following from this there is the argument that further major steps need to be taken to diversify the provision of schooling in order that parental choice and consumer accountability can determine the supply of schooling. In order to achieve this schools must be enabled to move outside local authority control and stand as relatively autonomous institutions in their own right. For Cooper, CTCs and GM schools constitute a step towards the privatization of schooling. It is claimed that these schools will have similar effects to magnet schools in the United States: 'enhanced choice for parents, greater competition, productivity, and efficiency for schools; and an improved educational service for all' (Cooper, 1987). It is quite clear that for policy groupings on the New Right a new direct grant status is supported as a means of moving towards something approaching a market economy in education. From such a neo-liberal perspective (Levitas, 1987) with its emphasis on individual choice, minimal government and the supremacy of the market in the distribution of goods and services, an additional advantage accrues to this package of radical reforms. It potentially undermines and destabilizes comprehensive systems of secondary schooling, and does so in a way which avoids those problems surrounding earlier attempts to reintroduce selective education in a number of local authorities (Hargreaves and Reynolds, 1989).

Whilst both Sexton, as Director of the Education Unit of the Institute of Economic Affairs, and the Hillgate Group put their trust in parental and employer demands and influence in raising educational standards, one important difference is apparent in the strategy they advocate. Sexton rejects the imposition by the government of a National Curriculum on local authority and grant-maintained schools. He argues that 'the most *effective* National Curriculum is that set by the market itself, that set by the *consumers* of the education service' (Sexton, 1988). On the other hand, the Hillgate Group support the introduction of a National Curriculum. Government prescription in this respect is accepted by the Hillgate Group, at least in the short term, as the means of eliminating the influence and ideology of the educational establishment. As Whitty has suggested in this volume, this 'presumably implies that they will take time to throw off their local authority origins and develop the new responsive working practices that the government would like to see develop'. In contrast to the neo-liberalist stance taken by Sexton, the policies and strategy advocated by the Hillgate group give expression to a 'neo-conservatism' in New Right thinking which prioritizes notions of 'social authoritarianism, the disciplined society, hierarchy and subordination, the nation and strong government' (Quicke, 1988). For the Hillgate Group government intervention and prescription at least in the area of the curriculum and assessment is a justifiable means for Parliament to recover 'the powers of wrongly constituted or abusive bodies' (Hillgate Group, 1987) before power is devolved back to the consumer.

Interestingly some of the themes that are found in New Right publications emerged in the recommendations made in the Second Report of the Public Schools Commission (The Dennison Report), which considered the relationship and future of direct grant grammar schools in the context of the movement to establish comprehensive secondary education (Public Schools Commission, 1970). A significant body of opinion within the Commission sought to maintain the distinct identity of such schools and their separateness from local authority schools. One of the two schemes recommended in this report proposed that direct grant grammer schools become 'full grant' schools offering a free education to all pupils, and that their current and capital expenditure be met out of central funds to be administered by a newly-constituted Schools Grant Committee. It was recommended that this body would also have the additional function of negotiating the role such schools would play in local authority schemes of comprehensive reorganization. It was the belief of those on the Commission that supported this scheme 'that there is value to the national system of education in the diversity provided by having a group of schools which combine self-government with central control of finance . . . ' (*ibid.*). In the event it was the other scheme that was adopted and direct-grant grammar schools were phased out following the Direct Grant Grammar Schools (Cessation of Grant) Regulations 1975. We find in the Report not only nearly half of the Commission supporting a scheme designed to secure a distinct status for direct grant schools, but the Report as a whole lending its weight to all schools in the maintained sector being given more freedom and responsibility.

> Within the general framework of public control, we think that the governors and the head should be left to run the school. The central and local authorities' legitimate financial concern is to ensure that the school's overall expenditure is kept within approved limits and that they get good value for the money they spend (Public Schools Commission, 1970).

From consultation to implementation

It was in the run up to the election held in June 1987 that the Government declared its commitment to a major package of changes in the education system. The intention to allow local authority schools to opt out of LEA control and to become independent charitable trusts was declared in the Conservative Party manifesto *The Next Moves Forward.* This along with other policy proposals attested to the behind-the-scenes influence of New Right policy groupings, and their skilful manipulation of the media to prepare the way for major structural changes in the delivery and control of state education. Prior to the election the dominant justification for such schools was to allow parents and schools an alternative to left-wing controlled LEAs.

In the summer of 1987 a series of consultation papers issued by the DES foreshadowed the main provisions of the Education Reform Bill published in the following November. Of all the changes that were signalled it was the proposal to establish a new category of GM schools that created greatest controversy. The proposal to establish GM schools, along with devolved school budgeting and open enrolment, reflected a new philosophy about how state schooling as a public service should operate. As Cordingley and Wilby put it, these measures 'represent a proposal for a fundamental shift in how the education service works, a shift essentially from the principles that underlay a universal, non-market service to those which underlie a selective, privatised (and hence differentiated and inequitable) market service' (Cordingley and Wilby, 1987). No longer were local authorities to have a predominant role in identifying educational needs and planning how these are to be met. John Tomlinson has drawn attention to the loss of local authorities' strategic planning function as schools become 'organised as semi-autonomous competitive units' (Tomlinson, 1988).

The DES Consultation Paper saw action to establish grant-maintained schools as adding 'a new and powerful dimension to the ability of parents to exercise choice within the publicly provided sector of education. The greater diversity of provison which will result should enhance the prospect of improving education standards in all schools' (DES, 1987b). It was claimed also that this proposal was a response to the numerous indications it had received that groups of parents wanted the responsibility for running schools as individual institutions *(ibid)*. The basis for this claim seems tenuous. In the event it was only New Right groups that welcomed the Government's proposal and then with some reservations about the composition of governing bodies of grant-maintained schools and the failure to allow existing or new independent schools to 'opt-in' and become direct grant schools (Hillgate Group, 1987; Sexton, 1988). With the exception of the Professional Association of Teachers which remained uncommitted, all of the major educational groups declared their opposition to the Government's proposals. Various national and local surveys of public opinion published between June 1987 and January 1988 revealed high levels of parental satisfaction with the standard of education provided by local state schools, and low levels of support for schools in their area to opt out of local authority control.

Grant-maintained schools and local authority planning

Under the provisions of the Education Reform Act, and as elaborated in DES Circular 10/88, the option of seeking grant-maintained status is open to all LEA secondary schools, and primary schools with more than 300 pupils. The Act gives the Secretary of State the power either to substitute a lower number or make all primary schools eligible. Circular 10/88 indicates that all future decisions about the widening of eligibility will be made 'in the light of experience of grant-maintained schools and of the progress of local management within smaller primary schools' (DES, 1988a). Schools which are not eligible to apply for grant-maintained status are special schools and schools where proposals for closure have already been agreed. Schools facing local authority closure or amalgamation plans that have not been approved are eligible to apply. The possibility that schools facing closure or change of character would consider this option was reinforced by the Secretary of State suspending decisions on reorganization proposals between the Education Reform Act gaining Royal Assent on July 29th, 1988, and the end of November 1988. This provided the opportunity for schools facing reorganization to decide whether or not to ballot parents about applying for grant-maintained status. By mid-May 1989, thirty-eight schools had balloted in favour of opting out, whereas thirteen had rejected this possibility. The prominent reasons for considering GM status amongst this first batch of schools was to escape the threat of closure or amalgamation or, in the case of the grammar schools, the effects of changes in the selection policy of local authorities and plans either in the present or future for comprehensive reorganization.

Amongst the many implications for local authorities of the establishment of a new category of GM schools is the critical problem of how they respond to the need to rationalize school provision at a time of falling secondary numbers and per capita led financing. National targets for the removal of surplus places, especially in the secondary sector, were announced by the DES in 1987:

> The removal of the 850,000-odd places between 1987–88 and 1991–92 implies a continuation of the removal of places at about the same annual aggregate rate as at present . . . In order to maintain the momentum LEAs will need to look particularly now to the rationalization of secondary provision. There are long lead-times which means that no time must be lost if the necessary reductions in capacity are to be achieved to target. Progress in the removal of surplus places by individual LEAs will continue to be monitored annually and is to be the subject of increasing attention from LEAs' external auditors (DES, 1987a).

In the short term at least the priority attached to the removal of surplus places by the DES comes into conflict with the Secretary of State's concern to promote the grant-maintained sector. It is interesting to note, given this conflict, that the government's expenditure white paper published in January 1989 announced that the earlier targets for the removal of surplus places in 1989–90 were to be revised downwards, and later targets abandoned. Nevertheless, given the continued budgetary constraints, the pressure remains on local authorities to achieve rationalization in secondary school provision, especially as over the next three years secondary numbers are expected to fall by 3.8 per cent (*Guardian,* 31 January 1989).

From its remit to review the economy, efficiency and effiectiveness with which local authorities deploy their resources, the Audit Commission's response to the consultation paper on GM schools neatly encapsulates the problem:

> The Commission has consistently taken the view that the best insurance policy against waste and inefficiency is strengthened accountability at

> local level. It has drawn attention to the failure of most local authorities properly to address the issues posed by the decline in the number of children of secondary school age. It is one of the principal obstacles in the way of the optimal utilization of resources. The commission is concerned that the proposals may slow down the process of schools rationalization rather than the reverse. There is a risk that local authorities will not propose schools for closure if they suspect that schools so scheduled will then try to opt out of local authority control . . . It would be unfortunate, to say the least, if the net effect of these proposals were to perpetuate a wasteful distribution of resources and perpetuate schools which could only provide good education, particularly within the Government's proposals for a national curriculum, at exaggerated cost. Competition can only further efficiency if schools which are demonstrably less successful in attracting pupils are closed. Unless this happens surplus capacity will simply be shuffled around (quoted in Haviland, 1988).

A similar set of concerns has also been expressed by the Association of Metropolitan Authorities both before and after the passing of the Education Reform Act. The AMA has reported the impact of the uncertainty of how many schools will seek GM status on the implementation of local authority reorganization plans (AMA, 1988). Similarly, Neil Gill, director of education for Barnet, and faced with two comprehensives that have successfully balloted for GM status, has commented: 'The more schools opt out, the more serious the problem will become. With each school that leaves the authority, unit costs rise and eventually a critical point is reached where it no longer makes financial sense to have an authority' (*Independent,* 23 February 1989). There have been many other local examples of the disruptive effects on authority planning of the possibility of one or more of its schools seeking GM status. In Dudley, for example, the authority's attempts to complete reorganization and rationalize the variety of secondary schools of different sizes and age-ranges has been disrupted as a number of schools considered the possibility of opting out (Copus, 1989). The case of Dudley illustrates that it is not only schools facing the potential loss of sixth form provision that may consider this option, but also voluntary aided schools and sixth form colleges, many of which, under nominally comprehensive systems of schooling, operate with selective entry. In such cases the primary motive for opting out appears to derive from the concern of governors and parents to preserve a school's distinctive ethos and social character that in large measure is seen as dependent on maintaining the forms of academic and social selection already in existence.

Funding arrangements and their implications

The financial basis of GM schools involves the transfer of land and property from the local authority to the school's governing body, and the direct funding of the school's running costs by the payment of a maintenance grant. Before local management schemes are implemented the maintenance grant paid to GM schools will be calculated on the basis of the historic expenditure of the LEA to the school. After financial delegation is fully implemented the maintenance grant will be set by reference to the LEA's allocation formula, which, as Hywel Thomas discusses, (Chapter 5 in this volume) will be substantially based on pupil numbers together with a notional share of the LEA's central service costs. The maintenance grants paid to schools are to be recovered from the LEA mainly by deductions from the Rate Support Grant. Within the Education Reform Act there is also provision for the Secretary of State to provide special purpose grants to schools' governing bodies 'for or in connection with educational purposes of any class or description so specified' (Education Reform Act, 1988). It is the stated intention through this provision to support specific activities in grant-maintained schools paralleling local authority run programmes financed under the Urban Programme, the Local Authority Training Grants Scheme, Education Support Grants and Section 11 of the 1966 Local Government Act (DES, 1988a). GM schools will also be able to participate in TVEI (Technical and Vocational Education Initiative), either as individual schools, or as members of consortia arrangements alongside local authority schools. Special grants will also be available during the first year of a school becoming grant-maintained to enable the restructuring of school staff in order that it will match better the school's new management structure and priorities' (DES, 1989). This has been criticized by the teacher unions on the grounds that severance payments could be made to teachers who opposed opting out (*Times Educational Supplement,* 17 March 1989). Furthermore this marks a discrepancy in the treatment of grant-maintained and local authority schools for no such grants for staff restructuring are available to the latter. The concern expressed by critics about the open-ended wording of the Act with respect to special purpose grants is not likely to be assuaged by the Draft Financial Regulations for GM schools. Although it is the stated intention that local authority and grant-maintained schools will be treated equitably, the regulations provide 'power for the Secretary of State to pay special purpose grants on a contingency basis where he considers it necessary to assist a school to meet an emergency need, resulting from circumstances beyond its control' (DES, 1989). There are similar anxieties about how the Secretary of State will consider applications for capital funding where 100 per cent grants will be available to GM schools for approved projects. The Draft Financial Regulations state that capital grants will be used to fund the grant-maintained sector at the same level on average nationally as LEA-maintained schools' (DES, 1989). This presumably means that schools that seek grant-maintained status in local authorities where capital grants are below the national average will do rather better once they have opted out of local authority control.

The increased discretionary powers of the Secretary of State exemplified in these financial arrangements are a clear example of the potential centralizing aspects of the Education Reform Act (Flude and Hammer, 1989; Hargreaves and Reynolds, 1989; Simon, 1988). A possible consequence of this, despite reassurances to the contrary, is a widening discrepancy in the treatment of grant-maintained and local authority schools by central government.

Various statements made by DES officials have suggested that there will be no financial inducements to persuade schools to opt out of local authority control. Asked whether he thought it was likely that central government might offer schools financial inducements to opt out, Andrew Turner of the Grant Maintained Schools Trust commented: 'I don't think that is at all likely. The inducement is in the opportunity to do better things with the same amount of money.' Irrespective of the possibility of financial incentives to opt out through the allocation of capital and special purpose grants, there has been considerable discussion about the possible financial benefits and costs of schools becoming grant-maintained. Dennison (1988), for example, has argued that the financing of grant-maintained schools already provides sufficient incentives for some schools to consider changing their status. Others (Houlden and Tipple, 1988) have disputed this pointing to a range of heavy administrative costs that will have to be borne by individual schools.

The linking of grant-maintained and local authority school budgets will inevitably mean that the financing of grant-maintained schools will be subject to considerable variation. In addition, year by year changes in local authority funding of schools will create an uncertain financial environment in which GM schools will operate. This may well lead to pressure for GM schools to be funded independently of local authority levels of finance. Asked to comment on this, Andrew Turner pointed to a number of virtues in the chosen method of financing GM schools:

> ... The present system keeps the DES as far as possible out of particular arguments about what should be spent in a particular area. Any national set level of funding, if it was set over the country as a whole, just wouldn't work, because of the variation of cost in different areas. If it were authority by authority, or region by region, it would be a new rate support grant. I just think it is fairly neat to use the Authority's method. It keeps ministers out of the debate.

GM schools must provide free education. However, once governing bodies are incorporated into this sector, the pressures to raise additional income — from voluntary donations from parents or the community and by entering into sponsorship deals with industrial and commercial firms — will undoubtedly increase. As John Webster, head of Skegness Grammar School, stated in February 1989 when his school was given approval for grant-maintained status: 'We now have to regard ourselves as a business' (quoted in *Guardian*, 23 February 1989). This is likely to widen even further the financial disparities between local authority maintained schools and schools that will comprise the grant-maintained sector, although we recognize that there may be similar pressures to raise income in schools operating local management schemes. GM schools will also be free to make investment decisions about income and assets that will not be available to the LEA sector. It can plausibly be suggested that schools with previous experience of operating relatively autonomously under local management schemes, or schools that have successfully drawn on privatized sources of funding, may well figure prominently among those schools favourably inclined towards GM status. It is necessary also to acknowledge the potential financial benefits that accrue to voluntary schools through the availability of 100 per cent capital grants. Voluntary-aided schools that become grant-maintained will no longer have to raise 15 per cent towards capital expenditure, while voluntary controlled schools may seek this status as a 'means of escaping threats of closure or grudging ministrations from an unsympathetic Local Authority' (National Society, 1988). In general, church authorities maintained a critical stance towards the opting out proposal in the Education Reform Bill, and following the passing of the Act they have urged individual schools to weigh up carefully the implications of becoming grant-maintained. The Church of England, for example has stated:

> Although at first sight attractive, [it] could work to the disadvantage of Church schools as a whole. Apart from the question of whether it is right or not for the Church to have certain privileges for its schools without bearing significant costs (and some people argue that 15 per cent is already too low notwithstanding the fact that the Church in the past met the original capital cost), the absence of any continuing financial input from the Church could strengthen the arm of any future government wishing to abolish Church schools. (National Society, 1988)

Change of character?

There is a second area of potential disparity between grant-maintained and LEA-maintained schools. Views from across the political spectrum point to the inherent pressures in a system of grant-maintained schools, with open enrolment, for moves towards greater selection, whether on the basis of ability or of social criteria such as ability to contribute financially to the school, motivation, social class or ethnic background (e.g. Professional Association of Teachers, Social Democratic Party, the Conservative-controlled London Borough of Barnet, Society of Education Officers, National Union of Teachers — see Haviland, 1988, Chap. 4).

Throughout the consultation period and the passage of the Bill through parliament, Baker attempted to give reassurances that 'grant-maintained schools will continue to form part of a local system serving local people. A school which becomes grant-maintained will retain its previous character' (speech to North of England Conference, reported in *Times Educational Supplement*, 8 January, 1988). But, as The Observer cynically commented on earlier reassurances, 'He is . . . anxious to point out that schools cannot change from being a comprehensive to a grammar. Well, not 'for a few years' anyway. And they can't change their intake policy. Unless, of course, he gives them permission' (*Observer*, 21 May 1987). In fact, the promises by Baker that schools would have to maintain their pre-existing character (in terms of size, selection criteria and religious basis) for at least five years was included in neither the Bill nor the Act, although they will have to follow the same procedures as LEAs (as specified in sections 12 and 13 of the 1980 Education Act) in order to change their character. It is in Circular 10/88 that qualified support for the five year period is given: 'the Secretary of State would not *normally* approve proposals for a change of character within five years of its acquiring grant-maintained status' (DES, 1988a, our emphasis).

What this will mean in the long-term is difficult to assess. In the short-term, it can already be seen as a measure that will protect existing selective provision. Of the thirty-eight schools that have balloted successfully for grant-maintained status (all in England) ten are grammar schools i.e. 26.3 per cent, whereas only 3.7 per cent of the total number of secondary and middle deemed secondary schools in England are grammar (from January 1988 figures provided by the DES).

In the longer term much will depend on the priorities of the Secretary of State and the government, the extent to which pressures from the New Right continue to find a sympathetic ear, and the effectiveness of lobbying by grant-maintained schools themselves. While Baker has asserted that the legislation is not intended to provide a back-door route to selection, he has also said 'I think there has got to be, within any education system, an element of selection' (interview with Stuart Maclure, *Times Educational Supplement*, 3 April 1987). Thatcher has consistently shown that she is anxious to reinstate selective education and 'believes opting out would open the door to this' (*The Observer,* 20 November 1987). For the New Right the present proposals must be seen as a significant step towards their preferred scenario: individual 'consumer' choice, minimal government and the supremacy of the market. Selection *per se* no longer has the priority it had in the early discourse, most notably that of the Black Paperites. The priority now is 'to encourage as many grant-maintained schools to emerge as soon as possible' (Hillgate Group, 1987) in the interests of creating a sufficiently diversified choice for 'consumers'. Nonetheless, within this scenario, it would seem necessary to create the scope for producers to tailor their 'products' to match consumer demand. The arguments of the Conservative Family Campaign exemplify this New Right scenario:

> The one major area where we would disagree with the current proposal is that the school is not going to be allowed to change its character. This seems to us an unnecessary restriction . . . a change from, for example, comprehensive to selective should be allowed and indeed could be one of the major reasons why parents would wish to see a school opt out of the LEA.

The Hillgate Group thus return us to a central issue raised at the opening of this chapter:

> All the desired objectives in the consultation paper could be achieved, and more besides, and for all parents, if the Government were to commit itself to a system of education vouchers. (in Haviland, 1988).

What pressures might come from grant-maintained schools and the Grant

Maintained Schools Trust are not clear. Given public concern shown in responses to the consultation document (e.g. Haviland, 1988) at the possibility of reintroducing selection on whatever basis, and the reassurances from the Secretary of State, it would clearly be impolitic *at present* for schools considering grant-maintained status to argue publicly for new selective admissions procedures.

Regardless of publicly expressed policy intentions, critics of the Act have expressed fears of creeping selection. The principal mechanism for retaining the character of the school lies in the admissions arrangements which 'will be independent of, but similar in nature to, the arrangements operating for local authority schools in the area' (DES, 1988a). 'Independence' and 'similarity' are, of course, difficult to determine, and the only monitoring of this lies in the approval of admissions arrangements to be given by the Secretary of State. One issue we have not seen addressed is how, or whether, these admissions arrangements will be expected to apply 'catchment area' criteria where a school is oversubscribed. The wider the catchment area, the greater the choice for the school, and 'if you can attract [the pupils] to put their names forward then you can have them', as Andrew Turner of the Grant-Maintained Schools Trust has stated.

Asked more generally about introducing 'selection by stealth', Turner acknowledged: 'Any system that is operated has those dangers, but there are considerable safeguards, and if it were to be done on any systematic or long-term basis it would be spotted.' The 'considerable safeguards' are, apparently, the approval of admissions arrangements by the Secretary of State and the ability of dissatisfied parents to appeal to what Turner calls an 'independent' appeals committee. In fact, the appeals committee is to be *'established by the governors'* and to have 'independent representation *as well as members of the governing body'* (DES, 1988a, our emphasis). The proposal for grant-maintained status from The London Oratory School (a voluntary-aided comprehensive in Inner London) provides an indication of the possible scope for selection by stealth:

> Normally the headmaster makes arrangements for all applicants to be interviewed . . . [the interview's] main function is to assess whether the aims, attitudes, values and expectations of the parents and the boy . . . are in harmony with those of the school. The places available will be offered to the most suitable candidates . . . (Proposal for the Acquisition of Grant-Maintained Status by The London Oratory School, February 1989)

And amongst the factors to be taken into account is a 'commitment by the parents and by the boy to 11–18 schooling and an undertaking to remain at the school for the sixth form' *(ibid.)*. Thus, the purposes of the interview clearly open the way for selection on motivational and social criteria (aims, attitudes, values and expectations) while the requirement that parents and pupils commit themselves to remain at school for the sixth form potentially opens the way for selection by ability. It is difficult to see how anything other than maladministration could be used to overturn a decision by the school not to admit a pupil, given these admission criteria (now accepted by the Secretary of State). The same concerns about creeping selection can be applied to permanent exclusions, where appeals committees are to be similarly constituted. The LEA, however, will continue to have the duty to educate pupils rejected by or excluded from GM schools.

Developing a grant-maintained sector

The combined effects of the inability of local authorities to plan provision, the possible financial gains for grant-maintained schools and the pressures for selection point to the development of a hierarchy of schools ranging from the fully independent and privatized sector through city technology colleges and GM schools to 'a minority sector comprising a rump of council schools . . . .a safety-net service for those who cannot survive in the market' (Cordingley and Wilby, 1987). The extent to which this happens will depend on how many schools opt out of local authority control. At this stage any analysis of the numbers and types of schools must remain tentative. All secondary schools, and primary schools with over 300 registered pupils, are entitled to apply. Yet, at the time of writing, only fifty-one schools have held ballots and of these thirteen have gone against opting out. There is one middle school catering for 9–13 year olds and one high school for 11–14 year olds. None have been primary schools.

Gay (1988) has provided an interesting analysis of the scope for primary schools to acquire grant-maintained status. Based on the DES statistical returns for January 1986, only 10.9 per cent of all primary schools will be eligible to opt out of local authority control, but these are very unevenly distributed across LEAs and the effects on the county sector are potentially greater (13.9 per cent eligible) than for the voluntary sector (5.4 per cent). Based on the assumption that for the immediate future the opting out figure remains at 300 or above for primary schools, Gay concludes that opting out will have little overall effect on the primary sector. Because of the very uneven distribution of large primary schools between LEAs it is unlikely to be an effective curb on 'the power of left wing LEAs' (Haringey, ILEA and Liverpool, for example, would be barely affected) and is likely to 'significantly affect some loyal Conservative LEAs' (*ibid.*). Impact is likely to be greater in the county than the voluntary sector and

> to have a very small effect on the Church of England's primary schools as only 4.5 per cent will be eligible to apply for grant-maintained status. This conclusion, coupled with the Anglican's slim involvement in the secondary school sector, contrasts with some of the criticism that the Church of England's opposition to the grant-maintained legislation has been launched largely out of self-interest (Gay, 1988).

Both the Government and New Right pressure groups have been keen to see the rapid development of the grant-maintained sector. For the Hillgate Group potential candidates are: successful schools threatened by closure or amalgamation; schools with threatened sixth forms; village schools; and schools 'threatened by politicisation of the curriculum, or by the imposition of lessons offensive to parents' (The Hillgate Group, 1987). Interestingly, they do not mention grammar schools facing comprehensive re-organization or changes in selection procedures, yet schools in this category together with comprehensives facing closure or amalgamation constitute the bulk of those schools voting to opt out. Of the thirty-four schools for which information was available, only eleven (32.4 per cent) gave greater independence or greater control of resources as the reasons for opting out. When we look at political control, there is little evidence that schools are opting out of 'hard left' Labour authorities. Of the thirty-eight who have voted to opt out there are only fifteen from *all* Labour authorities, with fifteen in Conservative and eight in Democrat or hung councils.

From the outset, the Government's commitment to promoting grant-maintained status has been clear. The consultation paper proposed the 'creation of an association or trust independent of the Department of Education and Science to *promote* the development of grant-maintained schools' (DES, 1987b, our emphasis), and in July 1988 the Grant-Maintained Schools Trust was launched. In September 1988 the DES circulated a glossy brochure subtitled 'How to become a grant-maintained school' (DES, 1988b) to all chairs of school-governing bodies. Despite a key amendment in the House of Lords that an absolute majority of all parents eligible to vote be obtained for a school to be considered for grant-maintained status, the Government reinstated the requirement for a simple majority of those voting providing that 50 per cent of registered parents take part. If fewer than 50 per cent vote, a second ballot is to be held but, irrespective of turnout, this ballot will be conclusive. Further, although 'interested parties will be free to make their own views known to parents and others as they think fit' (DES, 1988a) there is no mechanism for *ensuring* that this is done.

The glossy brochures from the DES and the establishment of the Grant Maintained Schools Trust are both examples of a trend towards the use of public funds by central government to promote the restructuring and privatization of public services 'in defiance of its own strictures on the use of public money' (Aitken in *Guardian,* 20 February 1989). According to Andrew Turner:

> [The Trust's] principal role is to give advice — independent advice — that is, not political particularly, although obviously, with a small p, this is a political activity for parents and everyone involved. But advice on the consequences of grant-maintained status, on how to get it, and I try to be as objective as possible. So I have a funny kind of dual role there. We are not supported by the DES at the moment, that is financially. We hope to be supported shortly as far as the non-political activities are concerned but not as far as the advice I give is concerned . . .

He explained, further, how it was financed:

> Principally — almost entirely at the moment — by about half a dozen wealthy contributors who have given us £25,000 or so each . . . Some have given through charitable trusts money which we cannot actually get

> our hands on at the moment because we're not a charity, or they have offered their money like Grand Metropolitan.

While charitable status is still being pursued (see *The Independent,* 18 February 1989; Hansard, 20 March 1989), in early February 1989 Mr Baker laid down regulations giving himself powers to award grants to the Trust. The independence of the Trust from the Conservative government is open to challenge on other counts as well: the chair, Steven Norris, is Conservative MP for Epping Forest and Andrew Turner is a Conservative councillor in Oxford and a former member of the Conservative Party research department.

However much the Thatcherite wing of the Conservative Party wants a significant and established grant-maintained sector, there are still dilemmas to be resolved by the Secretary of State in granting approval. For the Government grant-maintained schools must be seen to be successful — early failures will not encourage others to opt out.[2] At the time of writing fifteen applications for grant-maintained status have been considered by the Secretary of State. Two have been rejected. Both had their applications turned down because of doubts about viability. The concern for viability is also reflected in the decision that each school applying will be subject to a confidential HMI report.

Privatization extended?

Public rhetoric from government spokespersons has tended to avoid the term 'privatization' when referring to education, unlike statements on many other publicly provided services. When, within days of the publication of the Conservative manifesto in May 1987, Thatcher suggested that opted-out schools might become fee-paying and selective, her comments caused 'uproar' among even her own supporters and she was forced to retract her statements (*London Daily News,* 28 May 1987). Yet the processes of privatization within the education service have been in evidence for some time.

Hargreaves and Reynolds (1989) have identified two broad aspects to privatization in British education: the increasing privatization of the financial means for purchasing or gaining access to good quality education and the privatization of decision making in relation to the supply and demand of educational services with deregulation of direct state involvement in education. These are manifest in three major ways:

> . . . in development of, and support for, private provision outside the state system, in shifting of responsibility for certain kinds of provision within the state system to private sources and in reorientation of the style and pattern of state operation and provision towards market economy principles. (Hargreaves and Reynolds, 1989)

While not in themselves private schools, GM schools are clearly seen by Conservative supporters as a half-way house between the state and private sectors, as 'independent state schools' to quote Thatcher (speech to the Conservative Party Conference at Blackpool, 9 October 1987). Similarly, Andrew Turner has suggested that support for grant-maintained schools (in the form of sizable donations to the GMS Trust) has come from people 'who have gone through the state system, have done well and want good state schools to continue to be available. And . . . don't see why people in many areas should almost be forced into the private sector'.

The role of private sources of provision must almost inevitably increase more significantly within a grant-maintained sector, in both the acquisition of additional resourcing and in the purchase of services to the schools:

> Competition in the provision of education, and for that matter in the availability of educational services to schools, is a roundabout consequence of opting out. If schools can buy-in advisers from wherever they like, and can buy-in in-service training from wherever they like, it improves the quality, or is likely to improve the quality: whereas at the moment they're tied to local authority provision. (Andrew Turner)

> We [the GMS Trust] talked to the Independent Schools Joint Council and the Independent Schools Bursars Association. We have been offered, and some of our schools have been offered, help by the independent schools, for instance over in-service training. And we have been offered help over advice on where services can be obtained . . . from the ISJC. (Andrew Turner)

This blurring of the distinction between public and private is seen by Turner as beneficial not only to GM schools:

> It actually helps the independent schools to be more a part of the national education system if they are not isolated. Grant-maintained schools are likely, I think, to have links in both directions.

But it is in the area of 'market economy principles' that a grant-maintained sector most strongly reflects the growing privatization of education. Schools are to compete for the 'consumers' of education and parents are to exercise choice between producers:

> I want to see a greater variety of schools in addition to the present range of independent schools, voluntary-aided schools, special agreement schools, voluntary controlled schools and county schools. That is why two new types of school, grant-maintained schools and city technology colleges, will gradually become available to add to the present variety . . .

> With grant-maintained schools, we now seek to carry the concept of parental choice to the heart of our education system. True choice should not simply be the privilege of the rich. It should be available to all. Governors and parents should be able to run schools themselves without

> being forced to finance the enterprise from fees. Parents should not have to accept second best within a local authority monopoly of free education.
>
> If the product is not all that it should be, parents should not be put in the position of having to like it or lump it. Grant-maintained schools will be a threat to the complacent and to the second best. They will challenge all within the service to do better. (Kenneth Baker, speech to North of England Conference, reported in *Times Educational Supplement*, 8 August 1988)

A concomitant feature of this market philosophy is what Whitty and Menter have described as 'the atomization of decision-making' which

> threatens not only the negative conception of collectivism associated with inhuman state bureaucracies; it also constitutes an attack on the very notion that collective action, rather than the individual exercise of supposedly free choice in an unequal society, is a legitimate way of struggling for social justice. (Whitty and Menter, 1989)

For GM schools, decision-making will be devolved entirely to the individual headteacher and governing body (albeit within the constraints imposed by central government), severely limiting the extent to which education policy can be influenced by interest groups in the wider society. With the school as the individual employer of staff, the capacity of trade unions to organize collectively to defend employment and conditions of service will be threatened and the possibility arises that unions will not be recognized, with no-strike agreements being instituted as a condition of employment (as has been mooted for Nottingham CTC). Parents are to take individual responsibility for their child's education through choice of an appropriate school. Education is no longer a community responsibility.

> As far as the pupils are concerned, there is a very nice sort of question here: whose responsibility it is — whether it is the parents' responsibility. If the parents want to send them to a school with only 200 pupils, they are allowed to do so. It is their decision. All that is in question is whether it is right for an authority to maintain a school of that size. So I don't regard it as an educational question. That's a financial question. I don't think pupils will suffer because parents can, if they want to, take them elsewhere (Andrew Turner).

Thus, the market philosophy is linked to another major strand in current Conservative thinking — the dominance of the family.

While the education producers are to be fragmented and diversified, the market is nonetheless to operate within centrally defined controls — the national curriculum and its associated testing (with publication of results).

> All, it seems, are to have the same curriculum, in whatever type of school, though the government's cherished city technology colleges are

> to be exempt, as are (unsurprisingly) the 'independent' schools. This is a curriculum for the masses. Its purpose is control (Simon, paper presented at BERA Conference, September 1987).

Nevertheless, given the continued influence exerted by the market economy ideology, there is the future prospect of grant-maintained schools becoming more diversified and specialized institutions, of breaking away from the constraints of the national curriculum (Flude and Hammer, 1989; Whitty, Chapter 2 in this volume). As Thatcher has claimed, 'those schools are meant to be schools where children receive a different form of education' (quoted in *The Independent*, 23 May, 1987). The question remains to be answered of whether this shift in the distribution of educational power and responsibility signals a move towards the preferred scenario of the New Right, or alternatively, strengthens the bureaucratic control of the central state giving to the DES and the Secretary of State 'executive authority over a whole category of schools' (Maclure, 1988).

Notes

1. Andrew Turner, Director of the Grant Maintained Schools Trust, was interviewed by one of the authors on 12 January 1989. The quotations from Andrew Turner used in this chapter are all taken from this interview. For the full interview see M. Hammer and M. Flude 'Grant-maintained schools are nothing to do with party politics': an interview with Andrew Turner, Director of the Grant Maintained Schools Trust (*Journal of Education Policy*, Vol. 4, 1989).
2. However GM schools develop, success in the short term is likely to be judged in terms of the continuing viability of the school which will depend largely on ability to recruit pupils.

References

ASSOCIATION OF METROPOLITAN AUTHORITIES (1988) *Grant Maintained Schools, Independence or Isolation?*, London, AMA.

BROWN, M., CHOPE, C., FALLON, M., FORSYTH, M., HAMILTON, N., HOWARTH, G., JONES, R., LEIGH, E., LILLEY, P., MAUDE, F., PORTILLO, M., RUMBOLD, A. and TWINN, I. (1985) *No Turning Back*, London, Conservative Political Centre.

BROWN, M., CHOPE, C., FALLON, M., FORTH, E., FORSYTH, M., HAMILTON, N., HOWARTH, A., JONES, R., LEIGH, E., LILLEY, P., PORTILLO, M., and TWINN, I. (1986) *Save Our Schools*, London, Conservative Political Centre.

COOPER, B. S. (1987) *Magnet Schools*, Warlingham, Institute of Economic Affairs.

COPUS, M. (1989) 'Partnership wreckers', *Teacher* No. 30/16, January, p. 11.

CORDINGLEY, P. and WILBY, P. (1987) *Opting our of Mr. Baker's Proposals*, London, Education Reform Group.

COX, C. (1985) 'Many attractions of the magnet', *The Times Educational Supplement*, 15 March.

DENNISON, B. (1988) 'No need to sugar the pill', *The Times Educational Supplement*, 25 November.

DES (Department of Education and Science) (1987a) *Providing for Quality: the pattern of organization to age 19*, London, DES.

DES (1987b) *Grant Maintained Schools: Consultation Paper*, London, DES.

DES (1988a) *Education Reform Act 1988: Grant-Maintained Schools* (Circular 10/88), London, DES.

DES (1988b) *School governors: how to become a grant-maintained school,* London, DES.

DES (1989) *Consultation Paper: Grant Maintained Schools: Financial Arrangements,* London, DES.

FLUDE, M. and HAMMER, M. (1989) *Changing Schools, Changing Curriculum,* Units 9/10 from E208 *Exploring Educational Issues,* Milton Keynes, The Open University Press.

GAY, J. (1988) *Opting Out: Grant Maintained Primary Schools,* Culham College Institute Occasional Paper Number 9, Abingdon, Culham Educational Foundation.

HARGREAVES, A. and REYNOLDS, D. (1989) 'Decomprehensivization', in Reynolds, D. and Hargreaves A. (Eds) *Education Policy: Controversy and Critiques,* Lewes, Falmer Press.

HAVILAND, J. (1988) *Take Care, Mr. Baker! A selection from the advice on the Government's Education Reform Bill which the Secretary of State for Education invited but decided not to publish,* London, Fourth Estate.

HILLGATE GROUP (1986) *Whose Schools? A radical manifesto,* London, Hillgate Group.

HILLGATE GROUP (1987) *The Reform of British Education: from principles to practice,* London, Claridge Press.

HOULDEN, R. and TIPPLE, C. (1988) 'The bitter pill', *The Times Educational Supplement,* 16 December, p. 16.

LEVITAS, R. (1987) 'Ideology and the New Right', in Levitas, R. (Ed.) *The Ideology of the New Right,* Cambridge Political Press, pp. 1–24.

MACLURE, S. (1988) *Education Re-formed: a guide to the Education Reform Act 1988,* London, Hodder and Stoughton.

MCLEOD, J. (1988) 'City Technology Colleges: a study of the character and progress of educational reform', *Local Government Studies,* Vol. 31, No. 2, pp. 75–82.

NATIONAL SOCIETY (1988) *Grant-Maintained Status and the Church School,* London, The National Society (Church of England) for Promoting Religious Education.

NEAVE, G. (1989) 'Education and social policy: demise of an ethic or change of values?', *Oxford Review of Education,* Vol. 14, No. 3, pp. 273–83.

PRING, R. (1986) 'Privatization and education', in Rogers R. (Ed.) *Education and Social Class,* Lewes, Falmer Press.

PUBLIC SCHOOLS COMMISSION (1970) *Second Report, Volume 1: Report on Independent Day Schools and Direct Grant Grammer Schools,* London, HMSO.

QUICKE, J. (1988) 'The ''New Right'' and education', *British Journal of Educational Studies,* Vol. 26, No. 7, pp. 5–20.

SEXTON, S. (1977) 'Evolution by choice', in Cox C.B. and Boyson R. *Black Papers 1977,* London, Temple Smith, pp. 86–9.

SEXTON, S. (1987) *Our Schools — A Radical Policy,* Warlingham, Education Unit, Institute of Economic Affairs.

SEXTON, S. (1988) *A Guide to the Education Reform Bill,* Warlingham, Education Unit, Institute of Economic Affairs.

SIMON, B. (1988) *Bending the Rules: The Baker 'reform' of education,* London, Lawrence and Wishart.

TAPPER, T. and SALTER, B. (1986) 'The Assisted Places Scheme: a policy evaluation', *Journal of Education Policy,* Vol. 1, No. 4, pp. 315–31.

TOMLINSON, J. (1988) 'Curriculum and market: are they compatible?' in Haviland, J., *op. cit.*, pp. 9–13.

WHITTY, G. and MENTER, I. (1989) 'Lessons of Thatcherism — education policy in England and Wales 1979–88', *Journal of Law and Society,* Vol. 16, No. 7, pp. 42–64.

5
From Local Financial Management to Local Management of Schools

Hywel Thomas

Introduction

One characteristic of local financial management (LFM) schemes is at once general and misleading. This general characteristic is that LFM moves some decisions on the use of resources away from the 'centre' and closer to the school. This can be a misleading characteristic because LFM schemes are always more than a form of delegation of budgetary responsibility so that, without describing and understanding the other elements of what is always a set of changes, there is a serious risk of misunderstanding the uniqueness of individual schemes. Thus, with respect to the local management of schools (LMS) framework defined by the 1988 Education Reform Act, decentralisation in England and Wales is not fundamentally about enhancing the control of schools over the deployment of resources. If account is taken of all the elements in the LMS package — financial delegation, formula funding, open enrolment (better understood as part of the LMS package rather than an unconnected change), appointment and dismissal of staff and assessment of performance — we have a change which is about making teachers more accountable to parents and the local community; a framework which, with the probable exception of the pivotal position of the headteacher, reduces rather than enhances the powers of the professionals in the education service.

It is by focusing on the differences as much as the similarities between the Act's LMS framework and existing practice of LFM, that this chapter seeks a deeper understanding of the implications of the LMS changes and their consequences for educational provision, process and performance. This is done in the following four sections. There follows a description and discussion of the five elements of the Act's LMS framework and how they interact to bring about a change which has at least as much to do with accountability and the standards of education than value for money. This is followed by a section on the place of competition and professionalism as influences upon the quality of education and the nature of accountability. From this, the discussion moves onto a section which reviews the staff development and training implications for securing quality and accountability. The chapter ends with brief concluding section.

Local management of schools defined

LMS is best understood as creating a framework for a system of educational vouchers in our schools to be phased in from April 1990. There are *five* elements to this voucher economy.

First, *financial delegation* gives schools more day-to-day control over their budgets. This is the national extension of practice in places such as Cambridgeshire (Downes, 1988) and Solihull (Thomas, 1987) and also represents an international trend (see Caldwell and Spinks, 1988). It includes power of virement over the budget, which means that schools can move money away from its original allocation by the Local Education Authority (LEA) and commit spending to those areas which the school regards as a priority. Delegation also includes more flexibility in deciding who will be employed to do certain jobs. For example, on grounds and buildings maintenance, schools can obtain quotations for jobs and decide upon contractors. There is also more scope for choosing suppliers of educational materials and equipment. Delegation also means that it is the school which decides priorities for decorating and arranging for such work to be done at times which are convenient for the smooth running of the school.

While the framework for financial delegation is set out in the government's Circular (DES, 1988a), the degree of freedom will vary somewhat as between LEAs. It is already clear, after reading draft schemes prepared by several LEAs, that some will delegate to schools a higher proportion of the *general schools budget* than others. This arises from the flexibility, albeit limited, allowed to LEAs over those items which may either be retained centrally or delegated to schools. While a regulation limits total expenditure on these *discretionary exceptions* to 7 per cent of the general schools budget by 1993, there is no regulation which prevents an LEA reducing its centrally controlled spending below that level.

Nonetheless, even considerable delegation will not mean that the school will be completely free to make its own judgements about the commitment of resources. LEAs and schools will still be bound by national agreements on the salary and conditions of staff. Legislation on Health and Safety, on Employment Protection and so on will still apply. Expenditure on in-service training funded from Educational Support Grants (ESG) and LEA Training Grants (LEATGS) cannot be included in the delegated budget and must be managed by the LEA. The schools also remain the responsibility of the LEA and, if the delegated powers are mismanaged by a school, the LEA may revoke its authority over the budget, although this is not a power which LEAs are expected to use frequently and, in any event, governors have the right of appeal to the Secretary of State.

This delegation of financial responsibility is based on the uncertain premise that schools make better decisions than LEAs when identifying resource priorities

(Thomas, 1987). It is a change which is important and staff at all levels must be properly trained for their new responsibilities, an issue to be discussed in a later section. However, while financial delegation is an important component of the changes, preparation for it alone will not be an adequate response to the range of changes.

Linked to the Education Reform Act's version of financial delegation is *formula funding*, a new system for funding schools which will be introduced over four years from 1st April 1990. This change applies to all schools, irrespective of size and whether they are to have financial delegation. The formula is a pupil-driven system of funding schools in which a *minimum* of 75 per cent of the money allocated by formula must be tied to a pupil so that '... schools have a clear incentive to attract and retain pupils' (Circular 7/88, Para. 105). This is the basic voucher, linked to the pupil so that as pupil numbers alter so will the school's budget.

The formula which each LEA must include within its LMS scheme must have regard to certain principles. Section 36 of the Act notes that they should be

> (a)... simple, clear and predictable in their impact... (b) should be based on an assessment of schools' objective needs... [and a] (c) central determinant of those needs should be the numbers of pupils in each school, weighted for differences in age.

A fourth principle recognizes that LEAs may wish to take account of other factors, such as school size and the socioeconomic characteristics of the intake. A *maximum* of 25 per cent of the money allocated by formula can be used to meet those needs which are not tied to pupil numbers and age.

The introduction of a funding formula within an LEA, which will be expected to be explicit and public in nature, signals a major change in the practice of resourcing schools in England and Wales. Hitherto, for example, staffing levels have been determined largely by rules such as pupil–teacher ratios or curriculum staffing models (Audit Commission, 1986), so that appointment committees do not need to take account of the actual salary costs of applicants. On maintenance, an earlier Audit Commission study (1984) on non-teaching costs in secondary schools drew attention to the poor quality of information on the costs of school maintenance, in a more general critique of the work of direct labour organizations. As to energy costs, while some LEAs have energy monitoring systems and schemes which reward those schools which keep costs down, many simply pay the bills and give little attention to monitoring usage in different schools.

A characteristic of these methods of resourcing schools is that, typically, LEAs in England and Wales have not known the costs of individual schools. A study by Hough (1981) illustrated the state of general ignorance within LEAs about the costs of schools in the later 1970s, findings supported by a later study of my own in the early 1980s (Thomas, 1988). Contact with several LEAs in the early months of 1989 suggest that the situation has changed little, presenting a major problem as LEAs attempt to write a funding formula and to compare its effects with the existing costs of schools. There is little UK experience to draw upon as LEAs prepare their formulae. Even the leading exponents of financial delegation in England and Wales (Cambridgeshire and Solihull) have managed their schemes by basing resourcing largely on historical costs; only in April 1988 did Cambridgeshire introduce a formula which, in any event, only applied to secondary schools.

The Act also requires LEAs to consult with the headteachers and governing bodies of schools before deciding upon the elements of their formula, a change which may well influence spending priorities. What is being introduced, therefore, is not only a major change in the techniques and processes for formulating budgets but also in the cast of characters required to take some part in the decisions. It is a change which will reduce the discretion which education officers have often had in allocating resources to schools.

How will priorities be determined under these new procedures? Will there be more or less support for younger pupils? Will governing bodies tend to favour generous support for small schools or will they wish to concentrate support on larger schools? Will the process of consultation lead to more or less support for children from socially disadvantaged backgrounds? Answers to these questions will determine how pupils and/or schools are *weighted*, a concept which shows that apparently remote and unexciting funding formulae are not neutral in their effects. They are not intended to be neutral. The *purpose* of weighting formulae is to ensure that more resources go to those groups defined as having greater need, however need might be defined.

How LEAs resolve these issues will have a direct effect on the distribution of educational opportunities, insofar as these are linked to the distribution of educational resources. That formula funding will have an impact upon the funding of schools should not be doubted. It is an impact which will be enhanced because of the parallel changes in enrolment regulations.

Link the formula change to more *open enrolment* (better thought of as the third element of LMS and not an unconnected change) and we see emerging a voucher system which enables parents to move children to more popular schools knowing that much of the money effectively follows the child. The change on enrolment policy is at once modest and potentially significant. The Act ends the powers of LEAs and governing bodies to cite 'efficiency' arguments for imposing admissions limits below the capacity of a school. In future, most schools must admit pupils to their physical capacity. Exceptionally, selective schools and church schools can set a lower admissions limit if the children admitted as a result of setting a higher admissions figure are deemed to alter the character of the school. For example, in a period of falling rolls, maintaining the admissions number of a selective school may alter the range of pupil ability traditionally admitted to the school.

The change in admissions policies may have a big impact in those LEAs which have avoided school closures and used admission limits to distribute pupils across the system. However, what might be expected as a result of these changes is more fully discussed by Andy Stillman (Chapter 6 in this volume).

Now tie the formula and the enrolment change to the crucial fourth element of *staffing delegation*. The Act gives to boards of governors of individual schools the powers of appointment, suspension and dismissal over those teaching and non-teaching staff attached to the school and paid from the delegated school budget. These radically extend the powers and responsibility of governors in county schools, redefined as recently as the 1986 Education Act, and place major limitations on the powers of the LEA over its staff in schools; nonetheless, the LEA remains the employer.

The Act makes it clear that the decisions of governing bodies to dismiss a member of their teaching or non-teaching staff override any local 'no redundancy' agreements with teacher unions, so that the member of staff cannot simply be kept on the LEA payroll. In the event of a dismissal decision, the Circular declares that 'the LEA would then be under a duty to issue a notice of dismissal within 14 days of the date of notification of the LEA by the governing body' (DES, 1988a).

This considerable change in the employment conditions of teachers and non-teaching staff in schools will have an effect upon relationships between the several interests affected. What strategies will LEAs develop to try and *manage* their school staffs in these new circumstances? How will the relationships between headteachers and governing bodies, on the one hand, and teaching and non-teaching-staff, on the other, be affected by the change? What strategies might trade unions and professional associations devise in response to the new conditions? If those involved with LMS are to make a success of the change, these are issues which they must consider and for which they must prepare. Such preparation must also take place in the uncertain context created by proposals such as the licensed teacher and in conditions of growing concern over the availability of teachers in certain subject areas.

The staffing element of LMS emphasizes the purpose of the Act in strengthening the accountability of teachers for the service they provide. If teachers and schools are unable to maintain enrolment, their claim to employment would seem to be forfeited. The voucher economy emerges: in a funding system which will be largely pupil-driven, fewer pupils will mean less money and will require schools to dismiss teachers in post. The basis upon which parents decide whether schools are performing effectively leads on to the place of published data on school performance.

The relationship between the budget and performance on the national assessment is made clear in the consultation paper on financial delegation:

> At the end of the year the LEA would be required to publish information on actual expenditure at each school, which could be compared to the original plans. This information together with that required of governors relating to the achievement of the national curriculum would provide the basis on which parents could evaluate whether best use had been made of the resources available to the governors. (DES, 1987)

It is a statement which suggests a view of parents as 'cost-effectiveness analysts', comparing the expenditure choices of a school against its performance on the national assessment. Whether this is a wholly realistic view of many parents is, in some respects, less important than the position it adopts about the rights of parents to receive information about the effective use of resources in schools. In principle, there can surely be little argument against the rights of parents to have more information about the performance of their children and of the schools which their children attend. It is in converting principles into practice that difficulties arise.

There are certainly grounds for concern about the nature and quality of some of the information on performance about schools which may be published. The use of information from the national assessment is a case in point. While it is desirable that parents receive information on the actual performance levels of their children, as proposed in the TGAT Report (DES, 1988b), is it appropriate to use the same data as a basis for assessing the effectiveness of schools, another recommendation of the Report? It would seem more appropriate to publish data which reflects *what schools do* with children rather than data which may say much more about the *original quality* of pupils enrolling in a school; a distinction helpfully summarized by John Gray as the difference between 'progress' and 'standards' (see Plewis *et al.*, 1981).

The case for recording data which reflects the 'progress' of children, as against the 'final standards' which they obtain, can be illustrated by the figures in Table 5.1. The data is drawn from a study of the cost-effectiveness of A-level provision in

Table 5.1

Institution	Unadjusted A-level score for each institution	A-Level scores adjusted for differences in O-level and CSE records of candidates
Upton SFC	2.46	2.12
Rossthwaite SFC	1.56	2.02
Weston SFC	1.78	2.10
Acreidge HS	1.26	1.54
Beeches HS	1.80	1.72
Marshfield School	1.79	1.57
Whitefield HS	0.98	1.25
Winson Heath HS	1.52	1.72
Yule Green School	1.62	1.70
Upton CoT	1.45	1.82
Weston CoT	1.54	1.88
East March College	2.11	2.18
Grand mean	1.99	

Notes: The A-level results have been calculated by converting grades into the numbers used by higher education institutions, so that A = 5, B = 4, C = 3, D = 2, E = 1 and 'o' and 'f' = 0. The final average score is quite low because of the effect of including zero scores for all the candidates who obtained only an O-level pass or a fail grade. The highest pass rate, for example, was 84 per cent at Upton SFC.

different institutions (Thomas, 1988) and shows the effect on performance when the 'raw' results are adjusted for differences in the intake of students. For example, the first column shows Upton SFC having an average A-level grade of 2.46 (split C/D grade) per entry, a figure which is adjusted to 2.12 when account is taken of how the O-level and CSE qualifications of its students compare with those of the other schools and colleges in the study.

It is the second column of results which is a more reliable indication of how well teachers and lecturers have worked with the students. When the A-level scores are adjusted for differences in the O-level and CSE records of candidates, they provide data which can be used for comparing the *learning value-added* achieved by schools and colleges. This data can more properly be used as a basis for *institutional* comparisons and are a more convincing basis for holding teachers to account for their achievements. Thus, one feature of such data is that sharp differences in the raw scores of the three sixth form colleges are 'washed out' when the results are adjusted for intake differences. However, there remain significant differences when the effectiveness of school sixth forms are compared with the sixth-form colleges.

Examination results and the results of the National Assessment tests are only one part of the sets of data which the government expect schools and LEAs to publish. An early signal of the intentions of devising a wider range of *performance indicators* was provided by the Coopers and Lybrand Report (DES, 1988c). This included an Appendix on Performance Indicators and from it developed a pilot study where seven LEAs cooperated with the DES to test the applicability of various indicators. By March 1989 this had progressed to the stage where the DES is likely to produce a consultation paper in the late Spring/early Summer. Informal contact with some of the parties involved suggests that there is little likelihood of the DES being deflected from its desire to require schools to publish more information about themselves.

It would be surprising if it were otherwise because *performance indicators* are an essential element of the voucher system. Parents entering the education market need data on school performance if they are to make informed choices and these indicators are seen as providing the necessary information.

The unity of the LMS package is impressive, well integrated and carefully and coherently constructed. It creates a framework for more competition between schools which is designed to improve standards and the *quality* of education, and also to make the education service more *accountable*, primarily to parents-as-clients. However, the *delivery* of quality education to *all* the nation's children and effective accountability to parents of all social groups is less certain and depends, in some degree, on the preparation for local management.

Preparing for local management

At one level, LMS secures quality and accountability automatically, through the inter-action of its five elements in the education 'market-place'. On this argument, the competition to attract pupils will lead to more emphasis on standards of attainment and a general improvement in the measured outcomes of schools. Those schools which fail might be viewed as less effective and, if their teachers lose their jobs, this will be no more than they 'deserve' for failing to provide a more satifactory education.

However, the superficial elegance of this market solution to concerns about educational standards should not inhibit a proper analysis of some associated difficulties. Competition may well raise standards but in the *imperfect* education market the distribution of those improvements are likely to be uneven. What will happen to those youngsters attending failing schools whose parents do not act swiftly and effectively to move their children to better schools? How long will such a school have to decline before it is closed?

Will competition lead to the commitment of too much energy into marketing the school with the consequent diversion of resources from the curriculum? What will be the ethics of competition and what messages are we conveying to our children if they see their teachers engaged in 'advertising' which breaches codes of honesty and integrity?

Stewart Ranson (Chapter 1 in this volume) notes the differences between the nature of education for a citizen democracy and that for a consumer democracy. Those tensions are not examined further in this chapter but it is worth emphasising that LMS is the gearing in the Act for a consumer democracy and makes it more difficult to secure some of the desirable characteristics of a citizen democracy.

Identifying these issues provides legitimate reminders that most education innovations have costs as well as benefits; LMS will be no different in this respect. Securing the benefits and minimizing the costs can be assisted by effective preparation of those most involved in making the new system work. It is this which brings me to the second — and possibly more profound — level upon which the quality of education and the substance of accountability will depend. This concerns the quality of professional commitment and how it is manifested in schools and LEAs. Within schools, what are the structures and processes of management which need to be created if LMS is to improve quality and accountability? Outside schools, what is the role of the LEA within this new system? Preparing for LMS is relevant to four main areas of practice.

First, the effect of LMS on the quality of education in schools will depend upon how well the school budget is managed. Integrating the budget process with the educational needs of the schools is a precondition to the achievement of quality. The budgets of schools should be an expression of their educational priorities and not financial statements detached from educational needs.

Second, the quality of education will also depend upon the ways in which governors and head teachers manage their new responsibilities over staffing. Teaching and non-teaching staff are the key budgetary resource and the effectiveness of education depends upon how their roles are fulfilled.

Third, by creating a more competitive environment for schools, LMS will make it more difficult for schools to collaborate. Yet, innovations such as TVE

Extension, GCSE and National Assessment moderating processes require more collaboration between schools. Managing this tension so that teachers from different schools can continue to work effectively together must form an important element of a training package.

Fourth, improved accountability depends upon the availability of more information on school performance. The provision of information — and performance indicators — by and about schools will be a further new responsibility on schools. It is an area where schools will require knowledge and guidance.

If governors and head teachers are to be effective in their management of LMS, preparation in these four areas of practice may be a prerequisite. They might be achieved through an approach to training which is outlined in the following six elements, beginning with an assumption of little knowledge and building towards a more elaborate and holistic view of the locally managed school.

A training agenda for LMS

Managing the budget: getting started

Training must recognize the anxiety and uncertainty with which many heads and governors will approach their new budgetary responsibilities. It is important, therefore, for training sessions to contain some information on the more technical aspects of budget setting and monitoring. Areas to be covered could include: arriving at the total budget; the linkage of formula and pupil numbers to a cash budget; possible other sources of funds; the effect of cash limits, inflation and incidence of spending; areas of flexibility and inflexibility. However, even here, the emphasis must be on showing how the construction of budgets should reflect a school's educational priorities. Training must also consider issues of *who* is to be given *what* responsibilities for *managing* the budget and for its *administration*.

The budget and the curriculum

Effective management of school budgets as statements of educational purposes cannot be assumed. Training must make heads, governors and others aware of the relationship between the budget and a school's educational needs and priorities. It is important to avoid the budget becoming an activity which is separate from the school's main decision-making structure.

Training should provide opportunities for reviewing the relationships between the balance of the curriculum and the budget. For example, the budgetary effect of making different assumptions on teacher contact time or class sizes. It should consider the effect of different types of resource mix, such as the trade-offs between teachers and secretarial support. As experience, knowledge and confidence grow, training programmes might begin to ask more sophisticated questions on budget management. Governors, heads and others could be given opportunities for discussing options and resolving disagreements on alternatives.

Managing staff

An effective school depends upon the commitment of its staff, and training must consider the impact of LMS upon that commitment. The delegation to governing bodies of powers of appointment, suspension and dismissal profoundly alters the relationship between the head and governors on the one hand and teaching and non-teaching staff on the other. It will push the head towards becoming the 'chief executive' while s/he must still act as the 'leading professional' (Hughes, 1985) if the quality of education is to be maintained or improved.

Training must review the forms of consultation and participation of staff which are relevant under LMS, and to consider their impact upon quality and accountability. What are the implications of these changes in context for the tensions which can develop for the performance review of individuals and teams, and the development of effective teamwork? What impact will these changes have on the role of senior and middle management within schools?

For example, how might a locally managed school deal with the effects of having a weak head of department? If governors expressed concern about standards in the subject area and asked the head to begin a review of alternatives, what are the options which arise? Moreover, how does the new *competitive environment* of LMS impact upon the concerns for standards? A different problem would be a review of staffing options in a school which has suffered a decline in pupil numbers. How are these problems to be managed and who should be involved within the school, the LEA and the teacher associations?

Competition and collaboration

A greater emphasis on competition between schools is one of the means by which LMS is designed to improve quality and be more accountable to its parents. The nature and form of competition between schools might vary greatly and training should provide opportunities for governors, heads and others to consider alternative approaches to competition and the practical and ethical problems associated with them.

At a practical and self-interested level, training programmes need to raise awareness of the benefits of inter-school collaboration. This would include identifying the benefits of collaboration on activities such as GCSE moderation and TVE Extension. Relevant also might be the argument that marketing can be wasteful of resources which could be directed into the curriculum.

At a more difficult and ethical level, there is the impact of competition on the less successful schools and, most pertinently, the quality of education for children attending them. To what extent is it reasonable, or realistic, to expect the governors and head in one school to take account of the needs of youngsters in schools other than their own? The competitive environment of the 1990s will present these ethical problems to the managers of schools.

Training sessions might provide opportunities for examining approaches to marketing a school, with a review of how its work and achievements should be presented to the community. Positive and negative effects of competition could be reviewed as well as the means by which cooperation and collaboration between schools can be sustained. This module would also provide an opportunity for discussing the place of fund-raising by schools and sponsorship by the private sector, areas which might be regarded as improving a school's competitive position by strengthening its resource base. On this topic, the role of the LEA might be prominent as it seeks to manage the tensions which will arise from the pressures to compete with the need for maintaining collaboration between schools.

Managing information

One of the means by which schools will be held more accountable for their performance will be through the provision of greater information about themselves. This may be basic descriptive data, information on the local context, performance data and information on school management. It will be important to consider the purpose of the information. Some may be required nationally, others by the LEA and the school will itself have to provide information to its parents and its community.

What will be the nature of this data and to whom and how will schools report them to others? Most important may be performance indicators. What are they and what indicators might be selected by the DES and LEA? What criteria would schools select as part of a process of self-reporting?

What significance will the choice of indicators have on activities within schools? What processes will schools set up for reporting to parents and what role might an LEA play in constructing methods of reporting? How will schools and LEAs use the performance indicators to inform their management of schools? How might schools develop indicators which reflect their own views on educational priorities and how they try and communicate these to their parents.

Training in this area would be an ideal vehicle for elaborating the role of the LEA as monitor of performance and adviser to schools, drawing upon PIs about schools to inform its management of quality. Training sessions might show how PIs on a school could trigger an LEA response in terms of staff development support through use of LEA Training Grants, or the use of funds from an LEA's fund for supporting new initiatives.

Local management in action

A stage-by-stage approach to training would allow trainees to develop their thinking on LMS to the point where it is understood as a framework for a new approach to school management, where school-based managers are the pivotal actors. Integral to the process should be a review of the respective roles of these actors. For example, how can unpaid and volunteer governors make an effective contribution to the process of management without it becoming unduly burdensome on them and excessively intrusive on the executive discretion of the head and staff? A no less important issue is how a balance is to be achieved so that the enhanced powers over staffing and the budget do not, by default, go to the head and are not shared with others.

The ideal is surely the devlopment of a partnership, so that a team of governors, head teacher and others could produce and review a school development plan of which they have a sense of joint ownership. Such a plan could include projecting the school's circumstances over the coming three or five years and modelling the effects of different assumptions on circumstances and priorities. It would be a process which would show the flexibility and the constraints of budget management and how options must take account of the nature of the environment in a more open and competitive system. Identifying these areas for decision draws attention to the range of new demands which LMS places upon the leadership of schools in the 1990s, the quality of which is critical to the effects of LMS on our children's education.

Conclusion: schools at the centre

Local Management presents a major challenge to the education service. At the heart of the response will be the requirement upon head teachers to acquire new and unfamiliar skills, related to finance, staff and competition. While this is happening, there is little doubt that they will also play the crucial role in assisting most governing bodies come to terms with their new responsibilities. In addition, headteachers must provide the professional leadership necessary for the implementation of the National Curriculum and the National Assessment programmes, while simultaneously managing the introduction of schemes of teacher appraisal. It is a daunting list to which some may respond with every success. However, it is likely that others will fail to maintain the quality of education under the weight of such a range of changes, although others will be helped by the support of LEA inspectors and advisers. It may be, though, that the key to a successful response lies within the school.

The range of new skills and expectations upon schools cannot be handled effectively by the headteacher alone or, indeed, by a small team of senior teachers and enthusiastic governors. Schools must draw upon expertise from within its teaching and non-teaching staff and governing body, irrespective of the status of the personnel involved. Such an approach, with its emphasis on participation and the idea of a shared enterprise, would also help to counter the divisive effects of the delegation of staffing powers to governors, advised by headteachers. It is ironic that a package of educational change which is based upon the assumptions that professionals cannot be relied upon, and that markets style solutions can raise standards automatically, may depend upon the quality and depth of professional commitment for its success.

References

AUDIT COMMISSION, THE (1984) *Obtaining Better Value in Education: Aspects of Non-Teaching Costs in Secondary Schools,* London, HMSO.

AUDIT COMMISSION, THE (1986) *Towards Better Management of Secondary Education,* London, HMSO.

CALDWELL, B.J. and SPINKS, J.M. (1988) *The Self-Managing School,* Lewes, Falmer Press.

COOPERS & LYBRAND (1988) *Local Management of Schools,* A Report prepared by Coopers and Lybrand for the DES. London, DES.

DES (Department of Education and Science) (1987) *Financial Delegation to Schools: consultation paper,* London, DES.

DES (1988a) *Education Reform Act: Local Management of Schools.* Circular 7/88. London, DES.

DES (1988b) *National Curriculum Task Group on Assessment and Testing: A Report,* London, DES.

DES (1988c) *Local Management of Schools.* A Report to the Department of Education and Science by Coopers and Lybrand. London, DES.

DOWNES, P. (1988) *Local Financial Management,* Oxford, Blackwell.

HOUGH, J.R. (1981) *A Study of School Costs,* Windsor, NFER.

HUGHES, M. (1985) 'Leadership in Professional Staffed Organisations', in Hughes, M., Ribbins, P. and Thomas, H. (Eds) *Managing Education: The System and the Institution,* London, Cassell.

PLEWIS, I., GRAY, J., FOGLEMAN, K., MORTIMORE, P., BYFORD, D. and DISCUSSANTS (1981) *Publishing School Examination Results: A Discussion.* Bedford Way Papers No. 5. London, University of London Institute of Education.

THOMAS, H. (1987) 'Efficiency and opportunity in school finance autonomy', in Thomas, H. and Simkins, T. (Eds) *Economics and Education Management: Emerging Themes,* Lewes, The Falmer Press.

THOMAS, H. (1988) *The cost-effectiveness of A-level provision in different types of educational establishment.* Unpublished PhD. thesis, University of Birmingham.

6
Legislating for Choice

Andrew Stillman

Introduction

Education has had an enhanced political and media profile ever since 1976 when the Labour Prime Minister, James Callaghan, set off a round of soul-searching conferences with his well known Ruskin College speech. But the Labour Government was not in a powerful parliamentary position and seeking educational reform during an economic crisis proved difficult. Few educational changes came about at that time as a result of those conferences. However, in 1979 Mrs Thatcher and the Conservative Party came into office. In doing so, they took over the same perceived problems and much the same agenda for change, and ever since education has been the target of an enormous cultural and legislative onslaught. A series of Education Acts (1979, 1980, 1981, 1986 and 1988) set out to change the whole fabric of the system. The main thrusts of this legislation operate in seven major areas:

- The various relationships between parents, schools, LEAs and central government;
- The role, constitution and membership of schools' governing bodies;
- The nature and frequency of the mandatory information for parents, the press and other interested parties;
- The entire system of LEAs' and schools' financial management, ie, Local Management of Schools (LMS) and Competitive Tendering;
- The entire curriculum and assessment system, ie GCSE, TVEI and TVEX, the National Curriculum and TGAT;
- The whole approach to children with special needs, ie enhanced integration and statementing; and
- The enhanced and directed control of curriculum change and teacher INSET through the provision of centrally supported targeted funding — ESGs, TRIST, LEATGS and their successors.

The government has supported this legislation with a consistent attack on the existing attitudes and ideologies. The comfortable and 'soft' ideas of the sixties and the early seventies are to be replaced with the harsher 'realities' of the eighties — the market place (as operated through parental choice), an emphasis on local (i.e., school-based) management, one centrally determined curriculum presented in terms of mandatory attainment targets, the publication of schools' assessment results, performance indicators, inspection, evaluation and accountability. Across all these themes, the rhetoric has been concerned with raising standards through opening up the profession to closer scrutiny and greater parental choice. Caroline Cox sums it up well:

> So, choice and accountability are key concepts of Conservative philosophy which underpin current education policy. They can be the means of giving good schools the opportunity to become even better; but more importantly, they can give greater power and influence to those parents and pupils who are the most vulnerable and whom the present system is failing. Power to the people. Fairer and more democratic policies. These are our concerns. (Cox 1988)

But this arena is very political and words acquire different meanings to suit different occasions — there is really very little evidence to back up many of these statements. For instance, where is the 'fairer democracy' in all this when both local and central government are elected? Where is the real evidence about standards and should we not be cynical when the term 'standards' is rarely supported by either appropriate or valid evidence? And what about the risible statistics that have been used to support the outcome of various new, 'standard-raising' initiatives? Consider, for example, the Government statement in August 1988 that the introduction of the GCSE examination had raised standards by 2 per cent — they forgot, of course, to mention the technicality that the new GCSE grades were norm-related and that the increase in the percentage of 'O' level equivalent grades from 40 to 42 per cent was predetermined and formed the basis for determining the grades that were actually given to the pupils! Furthermore, how much real 'power' do the 'people' get to influence their children's education when we see the government's real enthusiasm is for the centralization of all power? How much enhanced choice is left after the introduction of the National Curriculum and the enhanced Christianisation in our multicultural schools?

The cynic might well suggest that these changes were not really implemented to improve education so much as to increase votes, to effect change without increasing central expenditure and ultimately, to help in bringing about the demise of local government. Overall, education must be seen as part of a wider canvas.

It is against this political backcloth that this paper sets out to explore the education realities behind the rhetoric of parental choice. It starts with a brief résumé of the history of the legislation before drawing upon the parental choice research undertaken by Stillman and Maychell to describe how the new legislation was implemented in the early to mid-1980s. The paper concludes by tentatively considering how the 1986 and 1988 Acts are now changing the ideas of choice within education.

Throughout the paper I consider the parental choice rhetoric and legislation from a very pragmatic educational perspective. This approach gives rise to four thematic questions which perhaps offer the best introduction:

1. What are the essential ingredients of choice? What has to be done to increase it? What are the limiting factors?
2. Does the term parental choice refer to the global sum of all the choice available to all the parents, or does it refer to the potential amount of choice available to all parents but only taken up by the few?
3. What is the relationship between parental choice and what parents actually want?
4. How effective is the parental choice legislation in bringing about the educational improvements claimed for it?

The Effective Beginnings of Choice: the 1944 Act

Section 76 of the 1944 Act required the Minister of Education and Local Education Authorities (LEAs) to have regard to the general principle that so far as was compatible with the provision of efficient instruction and training, and the avoidance of unreasonable public expenditure, pupils were to be educated in accordance with the wishes of their parents. Over the years this section has been used by many parents to get their children into their preferred school.

However, although this statement has often been taken on its face value, there was never any intention for it to offer choice between *like* schools, i.e., between two or more schools which in major respects might be similar. According to Lord Butler, the minister who effectively steered the original Act through Parliament, 'The objective of that settlement and of section 76 was to give Roman Catholic and Anglican parents a choice of school' (House of Lords Debate, Vol. 353: Col 590, 10 July 1974). Part of the 1944 Education Act was designed to bring Anglican and Catholic Schools into the state system and this was the section that attempted to guarantee Anglican and Catholic parents the right to send their children to the appropriate religious school within the state system if they wished. In the context of the 1944 Act and its parliamentary debate there was no need for the religious element of choice in Section 76 to be other than implicit: away from that context, however, it has gained this far broader interpretation.

Various parts of the 1944 Act allowed parents to appeal to the Minister of Education against LEA decisions if they wished. In 1946, within two years of the Act being passed, the then Labour Government's Ministry of Education became sufficiently concerned about the nature of these appeals that it published Circular 83, Choice of Schools, a circular that with only slight amendments stayed in operation until 1980. This circular offered LEAs guidance on how the Minister would consider the arguments in these appeals. The intention was that LEAs might like to adopt these guidelines for their own initial usage and thus rationalise the whole process. For the first time, this 1946 circular opened up the range of what may be chosen, and whilst it commenced with the qualification: 'At the onset it should be noted that section 76 does not confer on the parent complete freedom of choice', on the very next page it offered, 'Section 76 is not limited to choices made on denominational grounds. Nor does it apply merely to the initial choice of school.'

The circular listed eight reasons LEAs might like to consider for accepting parents' wishes in the choice of school. Of these three were deemed 'strong': the school's denomination, the provision of specific types of work, and the linguistic medium used, i.e. Welsh or English. Whilst increasing the number of acceptable reasons for choosing a school, or at least, whilst publishing an increased list of reasons the Minister would be likely to accede to in the case of an appeal, the Minister also saw fit to strengthen the LEAs' administrative arguments against accepting choice. Here, in effect, we encounter the first references to their being a need to balance the potentially conflicting outcomes of parental choice with the LEA's need to manage education. The circular suggested that the arguments for each side should be 'weighed' against each other.

But the idea of there being a 'balance' between the needs of the LEA in providing education for all and the wishes of the parent in respect of the individual child is very difficult since implicit in this is the view that one can evaluate the relative strengths of the two sides' arguments. This cannot be easy. Consider, for example, just one of the 1944 Act's 'approved' reasons for rejecting a parent's choice, that is, the grounds of 'avoidance of unreasonable public expenditure.' Just how is financial 'unreasonableness' to be determined, and is it the same for all LEAs, all schools and all time? How well would parents take criteria that changed from one year to the next? Patently, the factors in the circular and legislation lent themselves to local interpretation, and indeed, this was a principle that has been endorsed throughout — the government was keen that local issues should be resolved locally. But in allowing a channel for parents to appeal to central government against their LEA's decision, a channel for hearing local appeals centrally, central goverment gave itself the difficulty of attempting to apply a consistent and common set of judgements to appropriately local considerations. And here the degree of 'localness' should not be underestimated, for the NFER research showed that the balance between how the arguments were weighed varied not only from one local authority to the next and even from one division to the next within the LEA, but also, from one group of schools to the next.

Political problems and solutions from the 1970s onwards

For all the publication of this circular, activity with central appeals remained low until sometime in the early to mid-1970s when numbers and publicity began to increase (see Fowler, 1986). The DES and LEAs were sufficiently embarrassed with the increasing numbers for them to feel that some form of action was necessary: a mechanism was needed for central appeals to be stopped at source or at least diverted back to the local authorities from whence they came. From this feeling of a need to act it has been argued that had the 1944 Act not allowed parents this right of appeal to the Minister, the 1980 Act would never have come about since it seems that the concept of there being a demand for parental choice basically stems solely from this embarrassing but relatively small number of central appeals (*ibid.*). We should note, in passing, that for all the political significance ascribed to these central appeals, they were rarely effective from the parents' point of view — the number of successful appeals was consistently low. In 1977, for instance, only 2 out of 1124 section 68 complaints and 24 out of 40 section 37 complaints were upheld!

By 1976–7 there were three recognizable pressures bearing upon the Labour Government: (1) there was this embarrassing problem of the large number of central appeals; (2) this gave rise to the government *perceiving* there had to be a demand for parental choice; and (3) falling rolls were just beginning. It should also be recalled that these three pressures all arose at a time of very real economic constraint.

The then Secretary of State for Education and Science, Shirley Williams, offered potential solutions to all these points in the 1977 Consultation Paper, 'Admission of Children to Schools of Their Parents' Choice' (DES, 1977). Amongst other things the Paper suggested that parental preference should be regarded as having a degree of intrinsic validity and that it should be given some thought in the allocation procedure; that LEAs should be able to plan the operating capacity of their schools and be able to refuse a child a place at a particular school if the school was 'full'; and that each authority's arrangements should also include a procedure for local appeals such that questions of admissions to schools would be specifically excluded from central consideration under Section 68. Although Shirley Williams has latterly suggested that these proposals would have strengthened the parents' case (Williams, 1985), they appear much more likely to have emphasised and strengthened the LEA's management role — and indeed, given the economic problems and the pressure on LEAs to reduce the numbers of spare places, this does not seem at all unreasonable. For the most part, these recommendations appeared a year later as the 1978 Education Bill, but with the parliamentary delays and the government's weaknesses at the time, and with the general election in 1979 when the Tories returned to power, this Bill never reached the statute books.

Notwithstanding the change in government in 1979, the incoming Conservative Secretary of State for Education was still faced with the same three problems. However, the Conservative party viewed parental choice in a different light. Members of the party had argued that not only was choice a good thing in its own right, but that through the process of parents being allowed to make choices, popular schools would grow and prosper while unpopular schools would either have to recognize what was good and mend their ways or eventually close due to lack of custom. The issue of diversity of provision has also been raised, with some arguing that choice between good and bad is no choice at all and that if 'real' choice was to exist then it must be between different styles and characteristics. In line with this came discussion on the provision of the information parents would need to make these choices — how, after all, could parents make informed choices if they knew little about the schools concerned?

Less attention seems to have been given to the issues of transport, the minimum number of schools required to constitute a choice, the idea of there being a reduction in choice if some parents wanted schools that were forced to close because of the action of others, the processes by which schools were supposed to learn of the parents' wishes, and the issues of how parents might influence a school once their child was in attendance (although in many ways this was later rectified by legislative moves to increase parent representation on governing bodies).

But when the Act came into force in the Autumn of 1982, for all the theoretical extra choice, some education officers argued that it increased very little, and indeed, in some LEAs choice was thought to have been reduced because of it (Stillman and Maychell, 1986). This is not perhaps surprising though, since however strong the political and philosophical considerations, the country was still reacting to a financial crisis. The Conservative government was encouraging LEAs to manage their schools more 'economically', to take out many of the spare (falling rolls) places, to reduce surplus staffing and to minimise costs as much as possible. (For evidence on falling rolls see National Audit Office 1986, and on the issue of the reduction in county hall staff, see Stillman and Grant, 1989). All in all, many of these facets would seem more likely to reduce parental choice than enhance it and in practice we can see that the government afforded less priority to the actual enactment of parental choice, as opposed to the frequent statement of intention, than to the quest to reduce expenditure. Various ambiguities in the legislation appeared to allow this to happen quite easily.

Ever since then, however, there has been constant pressure from the centre to strengthen the individual parents' arguments for having their choice accepted. As a result, the government has reduced the strength of the LEA's argument for the economic and efficient use of resources, but these pressures have hardly disappeared. Whilst offering little publicity to this aspect, the government has continued forcing harsher and harsher cuts on LEA expenditure and in effect, on the resources that reach the school places the parents have chosen! The authorities and to a lesser extent, the parents, are caught in a trap.

Since 1982 it is possible to plot the various developments which appear to have strengthened the parents' arguments for choice. The first of these was a judicial review of a statutory appeal in May 1984 (*Regina* vs *the South Glamorgan Appeals Committee*). This review suggested the need for major changes in the way educational appeal committees interpreted cases and in the way evidence was presented — it suggested that the onus of proof be changed such that in future LEAs would have to establish that there would be deleterious effects before the parents were required to establish that they had a need. The outcome of the review put parents in a much stronger position and gave all parents the same rights as just a few had had under section 37 appeals to the Secretary of State prior to the 1980 Act.

The second development occurred when the 1986 Education (No.2) Act stated that LEAs' admissions procedures should be put onto the agenda of the newly-constituted school governing bodies' (Section 33(2) of the 1986 Act). On its own it is difficult to see what was meant to happen, since no action appeared to be required as a result of the consultation, but when seen as part of the package that brought more parents onto governing bodies and gave governors far greater powers than before, it appears as yet another way shifting the emphasis away from the LEA towards the school — and at the time of falling rolls most school-governing bodies might be thought keen to protect and enhance their school's numbers with perhaps less thought for the consequences on neighbouring schools.

A third development epitomizes the inherent conflict between promoting the 'health' of the individual school and looking after the needs of all schools *and pupils* in the district. This is the appearance in the 1988 Act of the long-dead idea from Kent LEA for Open Enrolment. The 1980 Act made no reference or distinction between the efficient provision of education *in the area* and *in the school*, though with falling rolls this was a distinction many LEAs felt compelled to make to protect individual schools within clusters. Under the 1980 Act LEAs were allowed to use 'the efficient use of resources in the district' argument and to argue at appeal that to allow one school in a group to take in more children would produce deleterious results (financially or educationally) in one or more of the neighbouring schools.

In a separate part of the Act LEAs were also 'allowed' to reduce the 1979 size of their schools by up to 20 per cent without specific permission being sought from the Secretary of State. That is, in the face of economic constraints and falling rolls they were able to reduce the intended intake figures for any or all of their schools and by doing this, save money and protect the provision of education across an area or LEA. But the combination of these two facilities stopped individual children getting places in schools which on the face of it had empty places. Where LEAs 'protected' the other schools (or the rights of the other parents), the government felt they were restricting both choice and the effects of market forces. Cox, of the Centre for Policy Studies, commented that:

> Open enrolment prevents LEAs from cutting back pupil intakes at popular schools to bolster schools to which parents do not want to send their children. Of course choice is not infinite; some parents may still not get their first choice. But more choice is still preferable to less, and is a democratic way to achieve rationalization caused by falling rolls. (Cox, 1988)

Open enrolment has thus apparently been brought in to stop LEAs refusing admission before a school reaches its full 1979 roll — a figure that harks back to the days of very full schools. We should also note that LMS requires each LEA to develop a formula which will determine the allocation of resources to schools. Since this formula must be primarily based upon pupil numbers, we can see the government is also preventing LEAs from providing extra support for small or unpopular schools — the market forces model is being pushed very hard. Initially, as Cox suggests, this all might sound like a positive move in favour of choice, but perhaps one should also ask:

Just how effective will Open Enrolment be in providing extra places?
Who is it that gets the increased choice? Is it really democratic?
What factors influence who can make the choices?
What are the costs involved to those already in the school and to those attending declining schools?
What happens to the amount of choice in the long term, for instance, once the extra 20 per cent has been filled and one or more of the neighbourhood schools has closed?

The first of these questions relates to the issue of whether the legislation has increased the global amount of choice for all. But here we might first refer to what has been happening to the numbers of school places since 1979, since the availability of choice must be connected to schools' ability to take in more pupils and this in turn will be related to the number of spare places available. Between 1979 and 1985 over a quarter of a million school places were taken out of circulation at the government's behest (National Audit Office, 1986), and further reduction is still being sought with the government asking for another 430,000 places to be removed between 1987 and 1990 (Surkes, 1988). Patently with falling rolls there are now fewer pupils to teach (though numbers are on the increase in primary schools). But even with the reduction in children, the reduction in places will inevitably have reduced the amount of choice available, and it may well be that the rhetoric of Open Enrolment from one government department has done no more than to redress the reduction in choice caused by another. In other words, as the government talks of extra choice, it has failed to mention that it has achieved no resolution of the inherent conflict between choice and economy.

What it has done, however, is to blame LEAs for a lack of both these elements and then portray them as 'ogres', based on the (government's) analysis of the situation that they have neither given parents enough choice nor made enough savings. With LEAs being cast in this role, (in parallel to the roles the government has painted for other local authority departments) the government has moved in a number of ways: firstly it has brought in a series of ways to circumvent existing LEA choice procedures, secondly, it has introduced machinery to increase the amount of information schools are required to publish to parents, and thirdly, it has brought in legislation for LMS. All in all, the old vouchers system has been introduced by the backdoor (as Hywel Thomas argues in Chapter 5 in this volume). But it is the first of these two moves that effect us here: the Government's moves to increase choice through circumventing existing LEA procedures and the requirements for enhanced information to be provided to parents.

The most recent of the circumvention moves is seen in the introduction of Grant Maintained Status under which schools which can 'opt out' of the LEA system and be directly funded *and controlled* by the DES. But the educational arguments for this are basically as unsound and specious as those used by the

Secretary of State when opposing LEAs' planned reorganizations — who else, for instance, could defend single-sex, half-form entry grammar schools in shabby buildings on the grounds of proven merit? (The Grant Maintained arguments have also been described as 'misleading, meretricious and mendacious!' — Surkes, 1988). But more often we see the arguments for opting out being phrased in terms of release from the spectre of LEA control, but rarely do these arguments dwell on the long-term merits and ability of the new masters to maintain the standards the schools and LEAs have achieved together.

The financial arguments are arguably similarly thin — see, for instance, the arguments by Dennison (1988) which in promoting GMS wholly ignore the need for, and the expense of, the support LEAs currently provide schools. (Note that Dennison also ignores the central administrative cost of the DES administering and inspecting schools). However, the reply from Houlden and Tipple (1988) redresses the balance, gives a more accurate analysis and basically gives the lie to the financial arguments. Of course, what one should also be aware of, is that opting out reduces the strength of the authority.

But opting out is only one of several similar moves which have appeared over the years under the guise of choice which appear to have had more to do with subverting the LEA role than increasing educational standards. For instance, the 1980 Act offered the Assisted Places Scheme; the 1986 Act offered Open Enrolment and City Technology Colleges (CTCs); and now from the 1988 Act, Grant Maintained Status. But when we examine what is meant by choice in these cases, as the research later shows, we will come up against the two same issues — how can we equate the choice for some when we are also responsible for the choice for all, and in all but the Open Enrolment case, how can we balance the cost of choice when the government offers it at a price they will not allow the LEAs to pay — consider the handouts being offered for CTCs.

The second development, that of increasing the amount of information available to parents, appears however to be more useful to the parent. Whilst not actually increasing choice *per se*, it encourages the development of informed choice and as such is one of the few parts of this legislation that might be seen as being positive. But it is also one that philosophically must be taken carefully — who, for instance, determines what information is provided? And furthermore, with the 1988 Act bringing in a National Curriculum, National Testing and Performance Indicators, it might appear that the required information and indeed the National Curriculum itself, are all leading us all down a very closed avenue, an avenue that might be restricting choice at the same time as giving us more information about it!

The NFER research into parental choice of school

So far we have only been concerned with the politics, legislation and, to a lesser extent, the philosophy of choice. In seeking to understand what it all means in practice it also makes sense to look at how LEAs, schools and parents react to 'choice', and this was exactly the task given to the 'Information for Parental Choice' project at the National Foundation for Educational Research in 1983. (For full details of this research see Stillman and Maychell, 1986).

The research started by addressing the question of just what was meant by choice and what were the prerequisites for it to be available. It formulated the working premise that for educational choice to operate there needed to be two or more schools within reach, a diversity of provision, and no restrictions on parents' rights of access, e.g. transport costs, enforced catchment areas or difficult adminstrative hurdles. But beyond this, if choice was to have the potential to bring about educational benefits, then it seemed that some other features would also have to be taken into account.

First, if the process was to increase the parents' involvement in their children's schooling, the choice procedures themselves would need to initiate and/or encourage the parents' involvement. In some way or other they would need to encourage parents to actively respond to the issues of what they wanted for their child and which school she or he should attend — passive acceptance of a predetermined LEA decision was thought unlikely to draw parents into the issues.

Second, if choice was to improve the match between the specific needs of the child (and/or parents) and the specific expertise of the school, then the procedures would require accurate and relevant information about both the child and the school so that the parents could make appropriate and informed choices. Similar levels of information about the school would be needed if greater accountability was to be achieved and if the stimulation and improvement of schools was to be encouraged through the operation of market-forces effects. For their part, if schools were to be able to respond to parents' wishes in more subtle ways than just counting heads, then there must be the appropriate channels of communication which would allow them to become aware of the parents' views and to react to them if they wished.

In stating these premises it was accepted that they were contentious and that the effects of choice and its processes were open to debate. However, from the research point of view, the premises served to give a framework to the research and to structure many of its questions.

There were three main elements to the research:

1. Four case studies, each in a discrete geographic area, which involved between them 18 secondary schools and the majority of their contributory primary schools. Work on these case studies continued over the entire duration of the project.
2. A questionnaire survey to over 3000 'intake' parents in the case-study areas based upon the responses gained from interviews with over 100 parents at these schools.
3. A set of brief questionnaires to all LEAs seeking information on how they had implemented the parental choice legislation and seeking an individual statement for each area of the LEA which had different choice arrangements — many LEAs still had differences stemming from the pre-1974 arrangement.

The enormous variation in practice

In looking at how LEAs had implemented the 1980 Act the project team identified and described the many different procedures used by LEAs in allowing parents to choose schools. Two of the team's main findings related to the degree of variety in systems used and to the large differences in the amount of choice available to parents. However, to the team's surprise, these differences were rarely determined by the schools themselves. Within small geographic areas, perhaps involving several secondary schools, the choice procedures appeared to be basically similar. The differences we found lay between the areas and as such it appeared that the causes lay with the LEA or with echoes from their pre-1974 precursors. Overall, as regards choice, LEAs differed considerably one from another both in their stated educational policies and in their administration of school allocation. Furthermore, the match between an LEA's stated policy and its implementation was not always particularly coherent.

Part of the variation between LEAs lay with social and geographic factors such as size, whether they were urban or rural and whether they used divisions or were centrally administered. The research also detected the strong influence of the LEA's pre-1980 practices and how enthusiastically and coherently the subsequent 1980 legislation had then been superimposed onto what they had already been doing.

Various practices were identified as being instrumental in determining the type and amount of choice available. The most influential of these included the provision of transport, the difference between a school's actual physical capacity to seat and teach children and the LEA's intended intake figure for that school, the LEA's policy for reducing surplus places, the specific published admissions criteria and how readily they seemed 'user friendly', the LEA's outward attitude towards parents' wishes, and finally, its encouragement of uniformity or diversity between its schools. Overall it seemed as if the amount of choice on offer by different LEAs could be viewed as a continuum with unhindered free choice at the one end and minimum choice brought about by tightly controlled catchment-area policies at the other.

Within those authorities operating catchment-area policies there was still a fair variation in the amount of choice on offer. Factors such as the requirement for a reply from all parents as opposed to just from those who wished to state a preference for an alternative school; the sending of a pro forma for stating preference rather than the requirement of a formal letter of application to be written by the parents; and the assurance to parents of a reserved place at the catchment-area school whatever other school they might apply for — instead of the 'threat' of the withdrawal of the right of a place at the local school if the parent should request another — all had the potential to increase the apparent amount of choice.

By the same token, in those authorities that operated without catchment areas, choice could still be limited, even to the extent of there being potentially less than might be available in an average catchment-area system. The major factors here included the viable number of schools a parent could choose from and whether transport was paid, or even available, to all, some or just the one 'local' school. Similarly, even in a 'free-choice' area, the actual criteria used for assessing children's rights of access to a popular school could reduce the amount of choice to that of a rigid catchment-area approach. If the main selecting criterion was distance from home to school, then choice, as regards popular schools, could be seen to be catchment-area based.

If the effects of the admissions and information procedures for all LEAs were compared, then the authorities appeared well spread out along the continuum of choice described earlier. However, along this continuum a certain amount of clustering was visible and three distinct though not necessarily discrete groups were recognizable. The first group appeared to offer parents a genuine choice between all the schools in the division or area and this group we labelled the 'optimal-choice' group. At the opposite extreme another group of LEAs held that the ideal of community schools and community education was more important than parental choice and that if necessary, it should override the needs of parental choice. This might be termed the 'minimal-choice' group. The last cluster of LEAs combined elements of choice and community education and was perhaps best identified as the 'hybrid' group. It was notable that although geographic features influenced these divisions, they were by no means overriding: the project encountered minimal-choice LEAs in totally urban settings as well as optimal-choice LEAs in rural situations. Somewhere off the minimum end of the choice scale there were one or two geographic regions where the distances between schools were sufficiently large as to deny any possibility of parents being offered any really viable choice, but these cases were unusual.

The provision of information for choice

Differences in how LEAs approached choice could also be seen in the quantity and quality of the information they and their schools published for parents. The legally required provision of printed information fell into two categories: (1) that provided by the LEA, usually in the form of a booklet, which described amongst other things the admission procedures across the division or LEA and gave lists of schools and the addresses of neighbouring LEA offices; and (2) that put out by the LEA or the school in the form of a brochure which served to describe the school and provide certain mandatory information — examination results, uniform costs, curriculum details and so forth.

The distribution of the LEA booklets was fairly uniform across the country and most parents of transferring pupils would have received their copy. This is not to say, however, that either the content or quality was as uniform, since these booklets were seen to range from being friendly and informative to being terse, legalistic and minimalistic. Some of them seemed designed to put parents off the idea of choosing any school other than the one which the authority had already recommended.

In many cases parents would have experienced difficulties understanding what was written either because the language was difficult or because it was not presented in the parents' mother tongue. In terms of readability, Beck in 1986 commented on the accessibility of the English in the LEA booklets given out by London Boroughs. With all the necessary caveats about the difficulty of interpreting the results of readability tests, he showed the London Boroughs' booklets to require reading ages which varied from 12 to somewhere in excess of 22 years (Beck, 1986). And in respect of publishing in languages other than English, although Smith had shown in 1982 that most LEAs should produce translations for those parents whose first language was not English, the NFER research found very few translations to be available and Beck, in his 1984 study of the choice procedures operating in London Boroughs, only found three London Boroughs involved in this work.

The provision and distribution of the school information and brochures again differed between LEAs and in practice was found to relate closely to the amount of choice on offer. In areas of minimal choice, school brochures were usually available only upon request and open evenings or talks were rarely held prior to the date for expressing preference. Even when these occasions were held, the invitations were often only passed on to catchment-area parents — but then many schools took the view that they should not actively try to attract (poach) other schools' pupils. This attitude clearly supported a view that schools have certain territorial rights over their 'local' parents. By contrast, in optimal-choice LEAs pre-choice open evenings were more common, though by no means universal, and different schools' information was much more readily available.

Unfortunately, whatever the provision, the quality and usefulness of the information in the school brochures was frequently marred by poor presentation, difficult language and a fairly common LEA requirement for all its schools' brochures to be presented with uniform formats which concentrated solely upon the common elements. Whilst one can understand an LEA's desire that its schools should not be chosen (or rejected) solely on the differences in their brochures, where the common format was linked to maximum economy the brochures did appear to become unnecessarily unattractive and difficult to use.

For all the arguments about how useful it might or might not be, the project found the legally required publication of school examination results to be sporadic and there appeared to be a reluctance amongst many heads and education officers to publish this information. It is worth noting, however, that the 1986 Act seems to have taken up this latter point and these same sets of exam results now have also to be published annually to *all* parents with children in the school by the school's governors in their annual report. Furthermore, the 1988 Act will require the publication of the Levels of Attainment achieved by various age groups within schools. What the 1980 Act started, the 1986 and 1988 Acts have furthered, though we still have no answer to the vexed question of the educational value of any of this information.

The parents' responses

The observations so far have related to the policies and administrative procedures employed by schools and LEAs. The research also sought the complementary information from parents and used interviews and questionnaires in the four case-study areas where the team already knew what the schools and LEAs offered.

One of the most striking features was the degree to which the parents endorsed the idea of there being varying amounts of choice in different LEAs. In the case-study area which offered the least choice according to the criteria already described the parents were in no doubt: when asked if they felt they had been offered a choice of school, 66 per cent (543) answered 'no' with only 27 per cent saying 'yes'. At the opposite extreme, in the case-study area which best fitted the 'optimal choice' characteristics, 84 per cent (538) of the parents answered 'yes' to this question with only 12 per cent saying 'no'.

The parents were asked what things they considered important when choosing a school. Across the 2740 responding parents whose children had just entered, or were about to enter, the 18 secondary schools in the case study areas there was a tendency to attach most importance to 'educational standards' and 'academic record'. Not surprisingly, the respective popularity of these reasons varied considerably from school to school, but not always in line with the school's relative academic standing. There seemed to be a possibility that parents were not actually choosing schools in a rank order of 'high standards' so much as having to satisfy themselves that their respective choice had 'high standards'. In fact it would be difficult for any parent to rank the schools' standards and anyway, if they could, the ranking would have little reliability over the time the child would be in the school. However, it is reasonable to assume, and indeed a number of parents stated this in interview, that they could not choose a school which did not have sufficient standards. In other words, they had to be assured that the school had good enough standards before they could choose it on other grounds: 'high standards' became the first gate rather than the most important goal. Other reasons parents gave were mostly varied, localized and often reflected a specific image or aspect promoted by the individual school.

One feature which emerged was the apparent link between the amount of perceived choice and the level of the parents' activity in the choice procedures, i.e., in their attendance at open meetings, the number of brochures they read and the number of people with whom they discussed the possible choices. It seems that the more choice parents perceived they had, the more they engaged in this type of pre-choice activity.

The child's sex and its position in the family exerted a small influence on the parents' activity in the choice procedures and the eventual choices they made, with the parents of girls and first children reporting using marginally more information than the parents of other children. Parents of first children also appeared slightly more likely to send their child to a school which was not the nearest, an aspect which suggested that they were being more selective; they also felt there to be marginally less choice available than did other parents.

Although these position and sex factors bore only a small influence, in the majority of cases the individual child was reported as exerting a considerable impact upon the choice of school. Sixty-five per cent of responding parents reported that their child felt strongly about the prospective secondary school. Seventy-eight per cent of these 1,792 parents felt their child's opinion was 'very important' in the choice of school and a further 20 per cent felt it to be 'fairly important'. Given the size of these figures and the enormous influence and importance of the child's feelings in this matter, one cannot help but wonder whether the information for parents might have been equally addressed to children — an aspect that does not yet appear in the legislation (see National Consumer Council, 1986). The child's sex and position in the family had little impact on how important the parents felt the child's feelings to be.

The parents' own education and employment were also found to be influential. The longer they were in full-time education and the higher their job classification the more information they used and the more likely they were to choose a more distant school. Although the data showed certain social class groups to be more active than others, it also showed members of all classes to be participating — if there were choices to be made, there were no groups which wholly ignored the process.

The outcome of the choice procedures was also of interest. From the questionnaire to LEAs it would seem that in both 1983 and 1984 some 91 to 92 per cent of all parents gained access to an acceptable school at the initial allocation. On the other hand, for about seven to eight per cent of parents the initial outcome of their interaction with the LEA was one of conflict — the parents wanted a place in a school that the LEA was unwilling to concede. Once this state had been reached there normally followed a period of discussion, review and/or quasi-appeal. Whilst the first two of these might be endorsed as being eminently sensible ways of seeking solutions and understanding each other's positions, the third is more difficult to accept. If an internal appeal sets out to do anything more than review whether the LEA has operated its criteria properly there is the risk it will change the admission criteria for specific parents and therefore operate double standards. If, however, it sets out to do no more than review its procedures, then the idea of it being an 'appeal' hearing is perhaps misguiding to parents.

One way or another, the outcome of these procedures was that the next 6 per cent or so of parents were then offered acceptable places. This left about one and a half per cent of parents at loggerheads with their LEA.

Under the 1980 Act if a parent was unhappy about the place offered by the LEA they could take up their right of a statutory education appeal. For each of 1983 and 1984 the project estimated there to be approximately 10,000 such appeals, though for a variety of reasons these numbers were, and still are, difficult to determine accurately. One way of considering the number of appeals is to view it as involving just about one-and-a-half per cent of all transferring pupils. (It has been estimated that the 10,000 appeals in 1984 had a cost of about two million pounds).

Although space forbids a more detailed examination of these appeals, there are three particular issues worth mentioning. First, there appeared to be some confusion as to whether or not the appeal was an integral part of the LEA's normal allocation procedures. If the appeals committee saw its role as being involved in the LEA's allocation procedure, then from time to time we would see the chair of the appeal committee asking the officer in charge of admissions for a wide range of cases to be put forward so that some could be 'successful' and some could 'fail'. Patently some committees wished to be seen as both human and fair and thus wished to be able to 'give in' to some cases. Furthermore they would ask for a number of school places to be left vacant, again so that they could be seen to be fair and to 'give' places to a number of parents. There seemed to be a tendency for the appeal committee to become the last stage in the LEA's process and thus to decide who got what in the difficult cases.

However, if the committee were to operate independently and outside the system, the LEA would initially have to fill all its places according to its published criteria and the appeal committee would exist solely to place those parents whose cases were sufficiently extreme to fall outside the normal LEA procedures. Although it is easy to understand why appeal committees might find it easier to operate as part of the LEA's system, this fitted uncomfortably with both their 'independent' role and with the LEA's statutory duty to accede to any parental request while they still had vacancies. The LEA cannot refuse a choice if there is space available and the pupil fits the school's denominational, ability and sex criteria.

The second issue concerns the idea that the number of appeals was directly related to the demand for choice. In reporting Kenneth Baker's speech on May 1, Meikle described him as wanting more places to be freed for choice, with one of the grounds for this being the large number of appeals (1987). Similarly, one of the early drafts for performance indicators suggested that the number of appeals would be a suitable measure for determining a good school. But contrary to the thinking behind both these ideas, in practice it appears that the number of appeals will increase where parents are more involved in the choice procedures. We can thus see that the more choice that is offered, the more parents will be involved and in absolute terms, the more school place choices that will have to be refused. Far from reducing the number of appeals, if Mr Baker's GM schools and Open Enrolment are to increase choice, they are also likely to increase the number of appeals.

The third issue takes us back to the beginning of this chapter where it was argued that one reason for the legislation being brought in was that politicians were very sensitive to the number of central appeals prior to the implementation of the 1980 Act. In many ways it was felt that the demands of just a few people had influenced the procedures for the rest. *Plus ça change!* The statutory local education appeal can now be seen to be just as influential, for although it only applies to a small number of parents, probably just about one and a half per cent overall, LEAs are still very sensitive to their appeal committees' thinking and we were very much aware of officers trying very hard to avoid having decisions made against them for the same reason two years running.

A tentative conclusion

Throughout this paper there has been a consistant questioning of whether any of the legislation has managed to increase parental choice either through making more school places available (the 1980 Act and Open Enrolment) or through increasing the variety of school characteristics available (the Assisted Places Scheme, CTCs, and Grant Maintained Status). The discussions have also sought to understand how such changes might improve education in any fashion, since this is the rhetoric we are offered for their introduction.

Furthermore, there has been the idea that we should look at the issue over the long term as well as the short, an idea that raises a number of serious questions about the case for the Assisted Places Scheme, CTCs, and GM schools, since one might suspect that none of them will have any significant long-term effect on the real number of places available or on the real variety of choice available. As each scheme is encouraged to take in more places, an equivalent number of places will have to be taken out of the existing system.

In effect, the main influence of much of this legislation will be to have changed the procedures for deciding which parents have access to which schools and to change the body which controls that access, perhaps moving it from an LEA officer to an appeals committee member or, in the case of CTCs and GM schools, perhaps a DES official in Elizabeth House. What is sure is that access to a more or less fixed number of places has to be decided by someone under some particular set of criteria. Thus if one system is changed for another, a different set of parents gains the priority access — perhaps it is those with children already at the school, perhaps those who live the nearest to the school, or perhaps those prepared to argue longest. Within the LEA system one can understand why the majority of LEAs have in the past used 'distance from home to school' as the major deciding criterion since it is easy to measure and offers an easy and objective way to rank requests. (It has also been encouraged by successive governments). The fact that it also encourages local involvement in the school and reduces transport bills is of secondary importance in this context though not in educational terms as a whole. In this light it will be interesting to see what criteria will finally be used with the CTCs and GM schools.

Of course, where there are spare places, where there are several schools with different characteristics and where distances are not too large, then the legislation appears to have given parents a number of extra rights. Where these conditions persist we can see that the global amount of choice in an LEA or division may well have increased, especially if the LEA was not already offering choice before the Act, but then, many LEAs were doing just that.

Where there is more choice, we might then look for evidence of school improvement, but it could well be that we are asking too much of the procedures. For instance, when stating their preferred school one might expect parents to express their educational requirements and for schools to listen to these views. But for very practical reasons LEAs have chosen to emphasise non-educational grounds as the criteria for ranking admission to school — criteria such as distance, health, siblings, and so forth — and have asked parents to express their reasons in these terms alone as only these reasons will carry any weight. The use of these criteria is supported by the requirements of DES, Circular 8/86, which, like the original 1946 document 'Choice of Schools', sets out to make the criteria more clear cut and easier to produce incontrovertible rank orders. Unfortunately it is difficult to see how a school might be sensitive to the parents' educational wishes when they are required to use non-educational criteria to simplify the ranking procedures. Furthermore, since most admissions procedures are dealt with at divisional or county office level, most schools never see their application forms anyway.

So far it would seem that the legislation has failed to offer any method to encourage school improvement within the finances available to LEAs other than in a rather gross and unreliable head-counting way. This is not to say that parental choice cannot bring about improvement so much as that as yet, there are few methods and processes apparently being used which could allow improvements to happen.

Where LEAs have followed government guidelines and taken spare places out of the system and where popular schools are as full as they ever were, then it is difficult to see how the three Acts give more choice either in global or individual terms unless the LEA changes from a catchment-area system to one of open or free choice, but this was not what the research revealed. In fact, a number of LEAs argued that with the introduction of the 1980 Act they had had to change from a relaxed approach to an enforced catchment-area system in order to cope with the more stringent arrangements and the necessary planning of the published intake limits. It is easy to see how the 1980 Act was able to reduce choice!

It seems appropriate to end this discussion by looking at the last of the three questions raised in the introduction, that of the relationship between parental choice legislation and what parents actually wanted. In terms of 'choice' itself, one way of looking at this is to ask whether the legislation has allowed more parents to get the schools they wanted, or alternatively, are there now fewer 'unhappy' parents? Given that the research found about 60 per cent of the annual 10,000 appeals were awarded in the LEAs' favour, we may deduce that some 6,000 or more parents per annum were unsatisfied with the school to which their children were sent. This is over three times the number of central appeals we saw in the mid- to late 1970s, but of course this sort of statistic tells us little since the context has changed, there are fewer pupils and places now available and we may well expect the legislation and media attention to have raised parents' expectations of their entitlement. Unfortunately, these expectations have become increasingly difficult for authorities to meet without spending extra money, and this goes directly against the government's other wishes.

Acknowledgements

This chapter is a revised version of a paper written by the author and first published in Bastiani (ed.) (1988), 'Parents and Education II: Policy to Practice', NFER-Nelson, under the title *Parents and Politics, Choice and Education.*

The author acknowledges the funding and support provided for this project by the National Foundation for Educational Research. The author would also like to express his gratitude to all those teachers, heads, education officers and parents who so willingly helped the project, to the Steering Committee and Margaret I. Reid who guided the research so carefully and to the author's colleague and co-researcher, Karen Maychell.

Note

'Choice' and 'Preference'. It is acknowledged that the 1980 Act and subsequent legislation only entitles parents to the expression of preference, and not choice *per se*.

References

BECK, I. M., (1986) 'Response to the 1980 Education Act relating to parental preferences: a survey of the Outer London Boroughs 1984/1985', Unpublished M.Ed Thesis, Liverpool University.

BOSELEY, S. (1987) Article on front page, *Guardian,* 7 May 1987.

CONSERVATIVE PARTY (1974) *Putting Britain First: A National Policy From the Conservatives,* London, Conservative Central Office.

COX, C. (1988) 'What makes people like us tick' *Times Educational Supplement,* 16 September.

DENNISON, W. (1988) 'No need to sugar the pill', *Times Educational Supplement*, 25 November.

DES (Department of Education and Science) (1977) 'Consultation Paper: Admission of Children to Schools of Their Parents' Choice', (October) London.

DES (1986), Circular No. 8/86; 'Education (No. 2) Act 1986', 19 December, London.

FOWLER, G. (1986) 'A reply to Jack Tweedie', in Stillman A. B. *The Balancing Act of 1980*, NFER, Slough.

HOULDEN, R and TIPPLE, C. (1988) 'The bitter pill', *Times Educational Supplement,* 16 December.

MEIKLE, J. (1987) 'Parent power promises to open up debate on quality', *Times Educational Supplement,* 8 May (The article refers to the Speech by the Secretary of State for Education regarding the removal of 'artificial limits' on school size.) See also Boseley S. (1987) 'Parent power is the watchword', *Guardian,* 25 May 1987.

MINISTRY OF EDUCATION (1946), 'Choice of Schools: Circular 83', London.

MINISTRY OF EDUCATION (1950), Manual of Guidance, Schools No. 1; 'Choice of Schools', (23 August), London.

NATIONAL AUDIT OFFICE (1986) 'Department of Education and Science: Falling School Rolls'. Report by the Comptroller and Auditor General, HMSO, London.

NATIONAL CONSUMER COUNCIL (NCC) (1986) *The Missing Links Between Home and School: A Consumer View,* National Consumer Council, London.

SMITH, G. (1982) 'The Geography and Demography of South Asian Languages in England', Linguistic Minorities Project: Working Paper No. 2., London, Institute of Education — as mentioned in Beck (1986).

SOUTH GLAMORGAN HIGH COURT, (May 10th 1984) *Regina vs. the South Glamorgan Appeals Committee, ex-parte* Dafydd Evans. Transcript available from Marten Walsh Cherer Ltd., London.

STILLMAN, A. B. and GRANT, M, (1989) *The LEA Adviser — A Changing Role*, NFER-Nelson, Windsor.

STILLMAN, A. B and MAYCHELL, K. (1986) *Choosing Schools: Parents, LEAs and the 1980 Education Act,* NFER-Nelson, Windsor.

STILLMAN, A.B. (1986) (Ed.) *The Balancing Act of 1980: Parents Politics and Education*, NFER, Slough.

SURKES, S. (1988) 'Authorities postpone surplus places plans', *Times Educational Supplement* 25 November.

WILLIAMS, S. (1985) Unpublished interview with Jack Tweedie and Andy Stillman.

7
Neither Ryhme nor Reason: Primary Schooling and The National Curriculum

Kevin J. Brehony

Rather than try to discuss in this chapter the likely impact upon primary schools of all the relevant measures contained within the Education Reform Act, I have chosen instead to try to situate or contextualize only the three main elements of the National Curriculum and to discuss their possible effects upon primary schooling. These elements consist of: the programmes of study, the attainment targets, and the provisions for testing at the ages of seven and eleven or, as they are rather coyly referred to in the Act, the assessment arrangements. The National Curriculum has been selected for consideration on the grounds that, because it is subject based and because it introduces testing in order to divide schools and set them in competition against each other, it appears to run against the grain of what has in the past been regarded as the ideal model of curriculum and pedagogy for our primary schools. Inescapably, the selection for discussion of only one of the many facets of the Act carries with it hazards which are almost always associated with the act of abstraction. Most of the Act's major innovations, like the local management of schools for example, contain implications for the curriculum and pedagogy of all schools but such considerations are beyond the scope of this chapter. Hence, the bracketing out of many of the other provisions of the Act and the concentration upon the National Curriculum means that in much of what follows I will present a partial, as opposed to a comprehensive, view of the Act and primary schooling. Furthermore, because it is about rapidly changing contemporary events, my discussion will also inevitably be of a speculative nature. Not unfettered speculation, however, but of a kind which is grounded in a particular analysis of the recent history of the politics of primary schooling.

I shall begin my analysis by making a few general points about educational politics and the theoretical framework which I have adopted. I shall also pose some questions about what the National Curriculum is intended to achieve in primary schools and by questioning its rationality. After that I shall commence my discussion of the National Curriculum and primary schooling by trying to plot the route that got us to the Education Reform Act. I shall begin by looking briefly at the 1960s and early 1970s, the apogee of child-centred ideology in the primary sector. I shall also consider the reaction to the child-centred ideology which marked the beginning of the New Right's upward trajectory in education and its domination of the subsequent debates about curriculum and pedagogy. In the following section I shall examine some of the other social groups involved in these debates which, when they addressed the primary school at all, were fundamentally concerned with its nature and purposes. Inevitably, the airing of these issues led to the formation of educational policy. This, I shall assume, following Harman (1984), is a fairly rational process which consists of a number of clearly identifiable stages which begin with the identification of problems. This preliminary work is then followed by the formulation of policy solutions, which take account of the means available for the implementation of policies and the resources which are at the disposal of those charged with their implementation. Following attempts to implement the policies a final stage in the process is begun in which evaluation of their effectiveness in producing their intended effects takes place. Applying this model I shall describe the responses of some of the key social groups involved in the determination of educational policies to the question of what is wrong with primary schooling. After this, I shall question, from the perspective of the model just outlined, the rationality of the National Curriculum, as applied to primary schools. As part of that process of questioning I shall look at the availability of the resources necessary for the implementation of the national curriculum. Foremost among these resources must be included the primary school teachers whose reactions to the National Curriculum I shall consider along with the question of their availability, supply and their competencies. In the final section, I shall examine the fears of many primary school teachers that the National Curriculum will be assessment led and that this will produce, from their point of view, many unwelcome effects.

The politics of primary schooling

The idea that there may be a politics of primary schooling is not a familiar one and, due to the particularistic political culture of primary school teachers (Lee, 1987; Ross, 1984), it is probably not one that would be readily accepted by many of them. By politics I mean conflicts and debates which involve and are resolved by the deployment of power. Power, in the sense used here, ranges from the overt power mobilized by the state to secure its aims by means of legislation which, ultimately, is backed by force to the less visible form of conditioned power. This is power which is exercized through persuasion and the winning of consent and which brings about the submission of those who are subject to it without them recognizing the fact of their submission. This latter usage of the concept of power may be connected to that of ideology as it is partly through ideology, conceived in its widest sense as beliefs and ideas, that consent is engineered. Both power and ideology are concepts central to conflict theories of schooling which hold that education policy is a field characterized by, often, intense ideological divisions and clashes between opposing interests. Around policies to do with primary schooling, those clashes have often been seen, at a high level of generality, as mainly taking place between, on the one hand, supporters of child-centred ideologies and, on the other, the supporters of traditional ones. By adopting these labels and taking them seriously as identifiable, opposing positions on primary schooling I am not suggesting that they can necessarily be translated into easily identifiable teaching styles or measured in surveys of teachers' attitudes. On the contrary, these are not the levels at which the analysis of educational ideology works best. The level on which that analysis is most effective is that of discourse about education which, more often than not, takes place at some distance from the classroom and involves not only teachers but other interested parties as well.

What is the National Curriculum for?

My approach to the likely effects of the National Curriculum is deliberately tentative because for every announcement of what schools are now intended to do there is a growing body of evidence to suggest that, for a variety of reasons, many schools are not going to do it or at least not in the way that it was intended. In the case of the National Curriculum, as with other provisions of the Act, the unintended consequences may well far outweigh what appear to be its intended ones. It might be objected that this is so with all programmes and that to say that some of the effects of the Act are likely to be unintended is only to reiterate Weber's point about the indeterminacy of social action. That is to say that there is often a disjuncture between intention and effect because we can never plan our actions with sufficient knowledge to predict all their consequences (Smart, 1983). This problem is a prominent, as well as an enduring, one in the analysis of social policy but an adequate discussion of it is beyond the scope of this chapter. Nevertheless, a consideration of what the intended effects of the Act upon primary schools are, and whether or not they have a rational basis, is desirable for the following reasons. First, there has been little debate about the desirability or value of the intended effects of the National Curriculum. This may be explained, in part at least, because what those intended effects are has not been made all that explicit. In addition, the discussion of what the National Curriculum was meant to achieve was soon overtaken, due to the break-neck pace of its introduction, by a debate about its content and as a consequence that discussion was curtailed.

Another source of confusion about the intended effects of the National Curriculum is the way in which, as a massive extension of state power over schools, it appears to be contradicted by other provisions of the Act, particularly those, like opting-out, which, in the rhetoric of the government, are intended to increase choice and competition and to roll back the state in education. Furthermore, the imposition of its attainment targets and its programmes of study do not appear to be the solution to any particular problem within primary schooling which has been identified in the last ten years or so of debate and inquiry. But because the National Curriculum appears to lack rationality on educational grounds that should not lead to the conclusion that it is totally irrational. The assessment arrangements, for example, may not appear to be rational on educational grounds but if the intention behind them is to increase social class, gender and racial divisions in education and to strengthen the selective work of schools then their rationale can be more easily inferred; particularly when set within an analysis of the politics of primary education over the last twenty years.

The child at the heart of the educational process: Plowden revisited

I shall begin that analysis by noting that English primary schools were once the envy of the educators of young children throughout the English speaking world. Their growing international reputation was largely due to the efforts of educators from the United States who were in the forefront of those publicizing child-centred, English primary school practice in the late 1960's. Their enthusiasm, as some openly admitted, was not entirely disinterested. In many instances, the observers from the United States were more than a little concerned to describe a model of primary schooling against which to measure the short-comings of their own elementary school systems (Simon, 1980; Silberman, 1973). This overriding interest in the restructuring of elementary schools in the United States sometimes gave to their accounts the tunnel vision characteristic of educational tourists (Brehony, 1987) but many of the features of the 'open education' which these observers admired (Silberman, 1973) were also treated approvingly by the Central Advisory Council for Education. In 1967, this body produced what became widely known, after its chairperson, as the Plowden Report. Significantly, and in line with the two previous major reports on the primary sector (Board of Education, 1931; Board of Education, 1933), Plowden presented a cautious, and sometimes contradictory, endorsement of child-centred ideas and practices.

Child-centredness is a fairly imprecise notion which is most often used in educational discourse to indicate an educational practice which starts from the interests of the child and the developmental stage which the child has reached rather than from the notion that there are fixed bodies of knowledge which it is the duty of teachers and schools to impart or 'deliver' as the vocabulary of the new brutalism has it. This was the ideology which was used to legitimate the primary school, the birth of which was induced by the reorganization of secondary schooling which followed the Hadow report of 1926 (Brehony, 1989). The use of child-centred ideology to legitimate the new primary school is most noticeable in the Hadow report of 1931, the publication of which was analagous to the primary school's christening ceremony. In this report, it was announced that the primary school would be an institution radically different from the secondary school; in a key statement the report declared that the criterion of the primary school 'must above all be the requirements of its pupils during the years when they are in its charge, not the exigencies of examinations or the demands of the schools and occupations which they will eventually enter' (Board of Education, 1931). For most schools, this wish remained largely unfulfilled until the 1960s when, consequent upon the move to comprehensivization, the 11+ was abolished and the primary school began to adopt, in practice, some of the recommendations and suggestions contained in its founding document (Cunningham, 1988). Nevertheless, despite the support of Plowden, the acceptance of child-centred ideas was far from universal although they did secure an institutional base in many primary schools, particularly in infants' schools and departments, as well as in a few well-known secondary schools. As has been well documented (Musgrove, 1987), these developments soon attracted the hostile attention of a small section of the right and not long after the appearance of the Plowden report a small grouping with a passing — almost accidental — interest in schooling (Cunningham, 1988) launched an attack, in the form of the Black Papers, upon child-centred or progressive practices in primary schools and the ideas associated with them.

The rise of the New Right and its attack on child-centredness

During the 1970s, rapid and far reaching changes in the conditions in which primary schools operated, among which falling rolls, financial crisis and the ending of the social democratic consensus were prominent, provided an opportunity for the critique of a part of what eventually became known as the New Right to gain a wider audience. The fortunes of the right in education paralleled those of the political right generally, so much so that it is possible to read the history of primary schooling from around 1973 to the Education Reform Act as a story of the decline of child-centred progressivism and the inexorable rise of the ideas of the Black Paperites and their successors, the various tendencies and currents of the New Right. In this reading, one of the New Right's most significant achievements has been to orchestrate the view that something is radically wrong with schooling. In terms of the model of educational policy adopted here, what the New Right did was not so much uncover or identify a problem in primary schooling as to manufacture one. Thus, owing to the New Right's position as the ascendant ideological tendency in the Tory party, the educational concerns and social engineering preoccupations of a marginal right-wing group prospered as the Tory party prospered electorally to the extent that many of those concerns have now found expression in the law of the land. It is, therefore, perhaps no accident that much which appears in the National Curriculum was prefigured, to a considerable extent, in the Black Papers. In them, for example, may be found demands that primary schools adopt 'specific standards of attainment', testing at specified ages and 'basic syllabuses' (Cox and Boyson, 1975). Similar demands appear in the pamphlets of the Hillgate Group, a component of the New Right.

However, it should be noted that the Black Paperites, in calling for tests and syllabuses, were only articulating well worn themes associated with traditional educational ideology and the opponents of public education. Thus, rather than formulating radical new proposals on the curriculum, the New Right's role has been to revive in the Tory party prescriptions which in the years of Butskellism had been suppressed but nevertheless remained the educational common sense of most sections of the Tory constituency. Faced by, what is to them, the mysterious and unknown world of primary schooling, the right, lacking a theory of this stage of education, generally reverts to commonsense or popular nostrums about the efficacy of pencil and paper tests and discipline which have a history at least as old as Robert Lowe's revised code of 1862. This being the case, the temptation to regard those parts of the National Curriculum which are likely to have the effect of fundamentally changing primary school practices as having been engineered by this small grouping of 'outsiders' is one that is hard to resist. Nevertheless, such a view needs to be qualified on a number of grounds. While prominent former Black Paperites and New Right ideologues, like Baroness Cox, have had a direct influence upon the content of the Education Reform Act some of what has emerged, like the statutory programmes of study, does not find favour with either Cox and her allies in the Hillgate Group, nor with the right-wing Institute of Economic Affairs and the Centre for Policy Studies, owing to their often expressed distrust of *dirigiste* measures (Hillgate Group, 1987; in Haviland, 1988; Centre for Policy Studies, 1988). But a more important reason for not over-estimating the role of the New Right is that, while in its various guises and metamorphoses it undoubtedly helped pave the way for a National Curriculum which is likely to push primary schools in a direction diametrically opposite to that of Plowden, other significant individual and corporate players were also instrumental in its formulation.

Other significant players

Among the corporate players whose activities have been influential in the field of educational politics and who should be singled out for attention are the Department of Education and Science and Her Majesty's Inspectorate. Evidence abounds to show convincingly that on many issues the officials of the Department of Education and Science have been at variance with HMI (Lawton, 1984; Chitty, 1988; Maw, 1988; Salter and Tapper, 1988). Nevertheless, in its prescriptions regarding the curriculum, HMI provided support for the bid by the Department of Education and Science to establish more central control over the education system (Maw, 1988). Another important grouping which has played a leading role in the struggle to alter the direction that the education system has been taking is the industrial training tendency represented by Lord Young. However, while the industrial trainers have managed to raise the temperature regarding vocationalism, science and technology in primary schools, in many respects most of the prescriptions which emanated from this quarter have not been about primary schools at all. In this, the industrial trainers were at one with the Department of Education and Science officials whose early excursions into the curriculum field were mainly restricted to the secondary school curriculum.

This initial concentration on the secondary school curriculum, and the consequent neglect of primary, is best explained in terms of one of the elements in the new consensus about what was wrong with the education system as a whole which began to form in the mid-1970s. From the time of Callaghan's speech at Ruskin, and as youth unemployment began to rise, a central emphasis has been placed by successive governments upon the need to restructure the relation between school and work. This emphasis rests upon the arguable assumption that there is a direct relationship between the kind of schooling provided and the performance of the economy. As was so often the case in the past, this argument, which is invariably based upon references to economically successful foreign countries (Department of Education and Science/Welsh Office, 1988) in which it is assumed that schooling is better organized and more suited to the needs of the capitalist economy, is rarely challenged. As they are the furthest from the labour market, primary schools have tended to have been bypassed, in its initial stages at least, in this the latest manifestation of the long-running school industry debate. Armoured by a deep rooted belief that the main purpose of primary education was to secure for their pupils individual self-development, and by the experience of their own formation isolated from the world of industrial production, primary teachers have tended to ignore the pressure to make schooling more 'relevant' to the requirements of the labour market.

What is wrong with primary schools?

Having looked at some of the players involved in the formation of educational policy, and in the formation of policy affecting primary schools in particular, I shall now examine some of their respective answers to the question of what is wrong with primary schools. The inclusion of the word 'reform' in the title of the 1988 Education Reform Act distinguishes it from those of the major education acts, commencing in 1870, which have increasingly regulated the development of the state system of education. In the context of political history the term reform resonates with a sense of amelioration and of progress conceived of as the widening and extension of citizenship rights. But the use of reform in the title of the Education Act may best be seen simply as a hollow, rhetorical gesture intended to emphasize the radicalism of the Thatcherite approach to education and at the same time to signal that something is being done about the supposed mess that education is in. What the govenment considered to be wrong with primary schooling when framing the Education Reform Act, however, is not entirely clear.

The debate on the Bill, in contrast to the great debates on the Acts of 1870, 1902 and 1944, was often more notable for its vacuousness than for informed debate on the issues. A case in point was former Education Minister, Sir Rhodes Boyson's contention that if a school had not got a hall big enough for assembly there was 'plenty of room outside, even if umbrellas are needed' (Hansard, 23 March 1988). There was also little elucidation of the government's rationale for and vision of how the National Curriculum was to work in school. Undoubtedly the fact that the official opposition belatedly announced that its conversion to a national core curriculum and to testing predated that of the Tories and then attempted to distance itself from its former allies in the main teaching unions, has left little disagreement between it and the government in these areas (*Education,* 17 February 1989). The need for reform in education has gained general acceptance; as Kenneth Baker put it, 'the need for reform is now urgent. All the evidence shows this — international comparisons, the reports of Her Majesty's inspectors and, most recently, the depressing findings on adult literacy' (Hansard, 1 December 1987).

Leaving aside the major methodological questions which are begged about the validity of each one of the three sources of evidence cited, what seemed to matter most to the Secretary of State was the use to which the findings could be put rather than to the substance of what each one revealed. Thus the evidence on adult literacy was deployed by him to blame the unemployed for much of the current level of unemployment on the grounds that they were unemployed because they lacked communication skills and not because of government policies. A classic case of blame the victim and a move which for the umpteenth time links the purpose of state schooling firmly to employment while the private school sector is left free to pursue the long established liberal aim of individual self-development or whatever else the schools within it might wish. Apart from this statement of the Secretary of State little else was revealed in the Parliamentary debates about what it was the Bill was intended to put right.

What is wrong: the HMI version

Of the three sources of evidence cited by Kenneth Baker, that of HMI is the one which has informed most the debate about, and national policy towards, primary schooling in recent years. The primary branch of HMI may legitimately be regarded as a part, albeit a semi-detached one due to its much vaunted independence, of the primary school professional establishment. It is certainly regarded by the New Right as such (Hillgate Group, 1986) and, among other things, it is actively involved in the promotion of groups concerned with professional issues in primary education (Bayliss, 1989). As a result, the voice of HMI has been an important one within the primary sector in the formulation and propagation of its official ideology. However, on the basis of its stance in recent years it may also be inferred that the primary HMI has had to temper its professional role to take account of changed political requirements many of which are antipathetic to the child-centred notions it once promoted. In a stream of surveys which have covered the primary age range (Department of Education and Science, 1978; Department of Education, Northern Ireland, 1981; DES 1982, 1985b) HMI have confirmed what much classroom research has also revealed and that is that far from primary schools having fallen to the progressives, as the Black Papers asserted, they were populated by teachers who were often didactic in their methods and overwhelmingly concerned with teaching the basics of reading, writing and mathematics. In response to what it regarded as the narrow curriculum pursued in primary schools the inspectorate hammered home the message that the class teacher system whereby one teacher is responsible for teaching the whole curriculum to her class is in need of modification. This was because HMI felt that the subject knowledge of generalist class teachers was insufficient, especially for the older pupils in the primary age range (DES, 1978). Curiously, given that many of the teachers in the schools surveyed were trained as subject specialists and given the diverse nature of the schools, the conclusions of the surveys on this issue were so similar as to raise the suspicion that what was found was that which was looked for. While HMI, led by senior chief Eric Bolton, offended child-centred sensibilities by beginning to talk about the need to introduce subject teaching into primary schools (Thomson, 1985; Richardson, 1987), an attempt to tackle what the inspectorate perceived as the problem of weak subject knowledge appeared in 1983 in the White Paper, *Teaching Quality* (DES, 1983a). This laid down that the time devoted to subject study in the BEd., the degree taken by intending primary school teachers, should be at least equivalent to two years (Hallett, 1987; Proctor, 1987). The subject study requirement was then enforced through the criteria drawn up for the accreditation of teacher training courses, which were given by the Secretaries of State to the Council for the Accreditation of Teacher Education (CATE), the formation of which was announced in Circular 3/84 (DES, 1984). In future, students on CATE approved courses were to be trained to be subject specialists who, in addition to teaching other classes would act as curriculum consultants, a model which corresponded more to that of the secondary teacher rather than to the previously existing one of the generalist primary school teacher. That the primary school curriculum, in this respect, should become more like that of secondary or possibly even preparatory schools appears to be a conclusion which HMI had reached.

One of the first indications of HMI support for the trend towards convergence appeared in 1985 when it signalled a major change of direction by publishing *The Curriculum from 5 to 16* (DES, 1985a). Instead of the line, which had been promoted from Hadow to Plowden, that primary schools should differ from secondary schools in what and how they taught, because of the physical, emotional and learning needs of the child specific to the age range, HMI announced the need for 'coherence and progression' in the 5 to 16 curriculum (DES, 1985a). Almost over night, HMI had abandoned the child-centred view of the primary school as a place unique to the educational needs of pupils in that phase of childhood in favour of one which inevitably subordinates the aims and practices of the primary school to that of the secondary school and, by extension, to the requirements of the labour market. What is noticeable, in this respect, about *The Curriculum from 5 to 16*, compared to the child-centred approach of Plowden, is that the question of how children learn is virtually ignored in favour of an approach which focuses almost entirely upon knowledge and skills. Thus, at a stroke, learning becomes simply a matter of being taught or being exposed to what is considered to be appropriate knowledge and no space is given to the possibility that pupils may not always learn or even want to learn what teachers have tried to teach them.

By the time the consultation document *The National Curriculum 5–16* appeared the aim of this curriculum had been pared down to the bald utilitarianism of, 'the aim is to equip every pupil with the knowledge, skills, understanding and aptitudes to meet the responsibilities of adult life and employment' (DES, 1987a). Now, the chief inspector for primary education, Jim Rose, propounds the view that the gap between primary and secondary schools has grown too large and, in opposition to the child-centred position, he embraces the view that primary schooling should be preparatory for that which is to follow (quoted in *Junior Education,* Vol. 12, No. 11, 1988). The spectacle of the independent inspectorate adopting this line on primary schooling is no doubt a tribute to the conditioned power of the industrial trainers within and outside the government.

Associated with the move towards more subject teaching has been the increasing tendency in official discourse to discuss the primary school curriculum in subject terms, a practice which, because of the prevalence of integrated topic or project work in primary schools together with the objections of curriculum theorists (Blenkin and Kelly, 1981), had been largely abandoned. The use, by the Department of Education and Science, of subject categories to describe the primary curriculum (DES, 1980) was a trend which, at first, was resisted by HMI, which proposed the alternative of nine 'areas of learning and experience' (Department of Education and Science, 1985a). In this HMI proved to be more 'progressive' than Plowden which had clung to traditional subject divisions when it discussed the primary school curriculum. But as is by now well known, the National Curriculum ignored the approach of HMI and also the fact that, in infant and first schools particularly, many of the learning activities defy description by means of traditional subject categories (DES, 1982; Mortimore *et al.*, 1988). From this episode it might be seen that the primary HMI, the part of the primary school professional establishment closest to the government, in terms of its ability to give advice, has had its power severely curtailed despite its attempts to accommodate the political demands made upon it.

A lack of balance

By way of contrast, one aspect of the curriculum work of HMI that has not been ignored by the Act is the use of the term 'balance'. The Act states that the curriculum of a maintained school satisfies the requirements of the Act's first section if it is 'balanced and broadly based' (Education Reform Act, section 1). The use of balance as a criteria by means of which to assess curricula was utilized by HMI in the survey of middle schools published in 1983 (DES, 1983b). In this survey the definition of the term was rather vague but in the survey of Combined and Middle schools balance was clearly related to the time allocated in the curriculum to different 'areas of learning' (DES, 1985a). In the White Paper, *Better Schools,* balance was once again used to refer to time allocation as it also was in the HMI publication *The Curriculum from 5–16* (DES, 1985a). Used in this way to refer to time spent on each area of knowledge the primary school curriculum was found by HMI to be unbalanced. But this judgement is extremely difficult to sustain when the curriculum is not divided into neatly packaged subjects. Reading, for example, is not confined to English lessons or science to lessons labelled as such. Moreover, any notion of curriculum balance must depend upon what the ends of schooling are held to be. If the purpose of schooling is to produce computer technicians then the curriculum designed to achieve that end will be balanced differently from that to produce musicians. The specification of aims is, strictly speaking, not the province of HMI, but the attempt to measure the primary curriculum in terms of the time spent on different learning activities is and when HMI came to survey the primary curriculum it did so in subject terms. On this basis, HMI found, among other things, that too little time was spent on science and that which was observed was weak and poorly organized (DES, 1978). More recently the senior chief HMI Eric Bolton, in the course of a speech in September 1988, reportedly said that science topic work in primary schools was 'an almighty mess' (*Times Educational Supplement,* 7 October 1988). Thus it would not be too inaccurate to suggest that, in its most coherent usage in official discourse, balance in the primary curriculum refers to the time spent teaching science. It therefore follows that calls for balance are in fact calls for more science teaching in primary schools which Kenneth Baker has described as 'vital' if the number of science and technology graduates is to increase (*Education*, 3 February 1989). What evidence he and the DES have that this end would necessarily follow has not been revealed.

The problem of match

A third weakness in primary schools identified by HMI was the gap between the standard of work that children were seen to be doing and the standard HMI considered them capable of. This gap is referred to by HMI as the problem of 'match' and for both the 'less able groups' and 'the more able groups' the lack of match was held by HMI to be greatest in science (DES, 1978, tables 31 and 32). As with the other criticisms made by HMI, the principal target of this was the primary teacher. There is a sense in which this is almost inevitable because if the material resources and conditions are ignored then all there is left in the equation to work on are the human resources. Even so, as Jim Rose, the chief inspector for primary education, admitted recently, 'we may have to admit that complete matching is an unobtainable ideal and that conditions are so difficult and demands so great on teachers that it can't be otherwise' (quoted in *Teachers' Weekly,* 10 October 1988).

The attempt to make good what HMI regarded was wrong with primary schooling by means of the central regulation of what should be included in the BEd. degree, has not yet had enough time to work for an evaluation of it to be made. The research for the HMI report *The New Teacher in School* (DES, 1988), which found that 'poor' lessons were often ones in which work was 'ill-matched' and that some teachers in primary schools had an insufficient 'mastery of the subjects' they were teaching, was completed before teachers trained under the CATE criteria were in post. Nevertheless, HMI criticism of primary teachers' practices continues. The senior chief HMI Eric Bolton, for example, in the course of the speech cited above, was reported to have said that primary maths lessons were 'generally awful' (*Times Educational Supplement,* 7 October 1988). At the same time, the senior chief HMI for primary education continues to press the case for subject consultants (*Teachers' Weekly,* 10 November 1988).

What is wrong: the New Right's version

Teachers are also held to be responsible for what is wrong with primary schooling by the New Right. From this wing of Conservatism there has emanated, alongside what under the leadership of HMI has largely been a technical debate about subjects or integrated work, specialist or generalist teachers and the question of match, another more public, headline-grabbing one in which the ideological themes of choice and competition are paramount. The New Right in education, unlike HMI, is dominated by figures who have little knowledge, understanding or experience of state primary schools and it frequently shows. Their refrain since the appearance of the first Black Paper is a familiar one: that primary schools are in the grip of progressive teachers who are wreaking havoc with the nation's children and undermining the fabric of society (Musgrove, 1987). This theme was taken up, in part, by Callaghan at Ruskin College and, together with a number of associated nostrums, is now sufficiently well entrenched among the powerful in the Tory party for Kenneth Baker to make frequent genuflections and concessions to it. It is in this context that his, 'I want children to learn their tables' speech to the Tory party conference in 1988 may best be understood and also his claim that in the 1960s, 'far too many teachers were reluctant to impart traditional moral values to those pupils who are single young mothers or divorced young parents of the 1980s' (*Times Educational Supplement,* 11 November 1988). While the public display of political machismo is to be expected in the current climate from any Tory politician who wishes to succeed Mrs Thatcher as party leader, its translation into dictats about the content of the primary school curriculum is almost without historical precedent. Such was the case when Kenneth Baker responded to the English working party report (the Cox report) by insisting that he wanted more attention to be paid to grammar and that there should be a higher weighting given to the reading and writing components, as opposed to the speaking and listening components, by the time children were about to finish primary school (*Times Educational Supplement,* 18 November 1988). This 'tough' posture of the Secretary of State was made essential by the necessity to appease the New Right. The story of the conflicts between the Cox committee, the National Curriculum Council and Kenneth Baker has yet to be fully revealed but there is no doubting that the Secretary of State was subjected to immense pressures from the New Right to reject the relatively liberal proposals set out in the Cox report. An indication of this was given by the right-wing paper *The Mail on Sunday* which ran a headline over a story on the Secretary of State's response to the National Curriculum Council's final report on English which read, 'It ain't on, Baker tells the trendies' (Lightfoot, 1989). The trendies in question were the members of the National

Curriculum Council whose rewriting of the Cox report was so objectionable to Cox that he threatened to resign (Nash, 1989b). Kenneth Baker's responses to the report of the Mathematics working party show a similar desire to shape the curriculum in accordance with political requirements brought to the fore by the power of the New Right.

Underlying these authoritarian actions is a belief, which Baker appears to share with the extremists of the New Right, about professional power. As he declared in his speech introducing the second reading of the Bill, the education system has become 'producer-dominated' (Hansard, 1 December 1987). Arguably, this belief was of far greater importance in the formation of the National Curriculum than one in the weakness of the existing school curriculum. Set alongside the Act's other provisions, the National Curriculum may be seen primarily as a device to destroy teachers' workplace autonomy, and from this perspective it appears a perfectly rational solution.

Is the National Curriculum a solution to the faults identified?

For the New Right it clearly is not. The Hillgate Group, for example, is quite content to bring teachers to heel through testing, the publication of the results and then allowing market forces or what is paradoxically referred to as choice to do the rest (Hillgate Group, 1987). If this is an accurate representation of the Hillgate Group's position and if it does have power and influence within the government then it may well be, as Chitty has argued, that the National Curriculum is an irrelevant 'fig leaf' which masks the hidden agenda of the Act which is that of vouchers (Chitty, 1988). The analysis of HMI, on the other hand, at some point meshes with the National Curriculum though not at others. It is clear, for example, that a nine-subject National Curriculum in primary schools will hasten the trend towards the subject specialization which it desires. Already, in schools large enough for it to be meaningful, the designation of specialist curriculum co-ordinators is going ahead. In practice, however, the integrated approaches which are characteristic of primary school work might be strengthened simply because the attainment targets cannot be met in a curriculum organized on a subject basis because there is not sufficient time to teach all the subjects required. With respect to 'balance', that other objective of HMI, the likelihood is that in the short term at least it cannot be achieved. Of course much depends upon how such a loose term is defined. However, if, as I have argued, one of its principal meanings has to do with getting primary schools to grant to science and technology the same amount of time as the other two core subjects of English and Maths, then it is unlikely that this will occur — at least not without a massive increase in in-service training which, as it would require extra resources, is not acceptable to the government.

The lack of suitably qualified teachers

At the heart of the matter of the absence of science is the fact that the overwhelming majority of primary school teachers are women and as is well known women are not encouraged to study science and neither do they do so in great numbers. The official evidence regarding the number of primary teachers who have a qualification in science beyond A-level in England and Wales is incomplete as only the Welsh Office has published the results of the primary school staffing survey which was conducted in 1987. This survey reported that 'Women were less likely than men to hold qualifications in Mathematics, Science, Geography, History and Physical Education' and more likely to hold qualifications in 'English, Religious education, Music and Art/light craft' (Welsh Office, 1988). The background of the teachers and their feelings of 'vulnerability' regarding science teaching (Barnes and Shinn-Taylor, 1988) might be held to account for the fact that the Welsh survey found that while English and Maths accounted on average for 48 per cent of class time, Science and Nature Study only took up 7 per cent (Welsh Office, 1988). It is possible that Welsh primary schools are not typical of those in England but data released from the, as yet unpublished, Department of Education and Science 1987 Primary Staffing Survey shows that English and Maths take up 49 per cent of average class time whereas Science and Nature Study take up only 6.5 per cent (*Education,* 9 December, 1988). Further evidence that primary school teachers lack a scientific background comes from research conducted in the north-east of England which found that just over half of the teachers interviewed in a survey of five primary schools rated their competence low in science (Barnes and Shinn-Taylor, 1988). More confirmation of primary teachers' lack of a science background comes from the International Council of Associations for Science Education's research which found that 'only one in ten of those teaching science to ten-year olds had science as a main subject in their teacher training and that fewer than half of all the primary teachers had studied science at all beyond the age of 13' (*Times Educational Supplement,* 13 January 1989). The Department of Education and Science must have been aware of this lack of suitably qualified teachers of science in primary schools before the plans for the National Curriculum were finalized and yet there is to be no phasing in of science. To embark on such a project with the knowledge that the means for its implementation were not available and that the political will to secure those means was absent calls into question the rationality of the National Curriculum. Once again, only if the paramount political requirement is merely to be seen to be doing something about, rather than actually dealing with, shortages of skill in key areas of employment can the National Curriculum be seen as a means to that end and a rational measure.

The missing teachers and the missing non-contact time

The lack of teachers in an absolute sense, presents a formidable obstacle to the introduction of the National Curriculum. Unfilled posts in English and Welsh primary schools, according to Department of Education and Science figures presented to Lord Chilver's Interim Advisory Committee on teachers' pay, stood at 1.5 per cent of primary teachers in 1988. This percentage hides some significant variations. In Greater London, for example, one in every twenty-four primary posts were unfilled *(Times Educational Supplement,* 4 November 1988). In practice this leads to a situation in which it is difficult to sustain any kind of continuity and sometimes even the basic conditions for learning. Evidence of the effects of teacher shortages was presented to the Commons Select Committee for Education, Science and Arts inquiry on teacher shortages by Harriet Harman MP for Peckham. Her report to the committee contained case studies of primary schools in her constituency in which there were children who had been taught by as many as four or more teachers per year. Evidence was also presented of senior teachers leaving the service worn out after months of covering for absences *(Times Educational Supplement,* 11 November 1988). In Waltham Forest, parents are suing the council because in two primary schools there were not enough staff to open for more than four days per week. A similar situation exists in Tower Hamlets where, owing to teacher shortages, 500 mainly Bangladeshi children are currently without a place in primary school (Hugill, 1989). Even if these shortages could be resolved, and their resolution must surely require extra resources as a minimum condition, it is still uncertain as to how the National Curriculum could be implemented in primary schools as intended. This is because the time for teachers to act as subject consultants and co-ordinators as well as to moderate tests is simply not available. According to Jim Rose, the chief inspector for primary schools, average primary class contact time is 90 per cent *(Times Educational Supplement,* 9 December 1988). In small primary schools the actual contact time is likely to be higher than average as in those schools headteachers must also teach. On the general issue of primary school teachers' contact time HMI concluded that 'in practice, most teachers teach for 100 per cent of the time available' (DES, 1989a; Thomas, 1989). Allied to the lack of contact time and compounding the difficulties faced by primary teachers charged with the task of implementing the National Curriculum is the unavailability of supply cover. Such supply cover that there is, is in demand by all schools at the same time due to the need to prepare for the introduction of the National Curriculum.

For the ideologues of the New Right the lack of teachers with a science or technology background does not constitute a major problem as their acceptance of the need for such teaching is somewhat half-hearted (Hillgate Group, 1987). Moreover, the only response of the Hillgate Group to the problem of teacher shortages thus far has been to back government plans to allow people to teach without formal qualifications (*ibid.*). Recent New Right propaganda regarding primary teachers has in any event stressed that they do not require much training (Boyson, quoted in *Times Educational Supplement*, 23 October 1987). In this they are at variance with the CATE policy, initiated by Sir Keith Joseph when Secretary of State for Education, which regarded the nature of teacher training as sufficiently serious as to specify what teacher training for primary teaching should consist of. They are also, in their proposals that an apprenticeship model should be adopted for teacher training (Hillgate Group, 1989), at odds with Kenneth Baker's plans to secure even more control over how universities, colleges and polytechnics train teachers (DES, 1989b). Baroness Cox, in her interventions on this issue (Cox, 1989), appears to desire the restoration of something akin to the Article 68s. These were women — 'motherly girls' in the parlance of the late nineteenth century — who were over 18, who had been vaccinated and could satisfy an inspector that they could teach. Particularly in rural areas, unqualified labour like this was in great demand as it was much cheaper than the trained, certificated variety. This, no doubt, is what the New Right would like despite the fact that such untrained labour was universally held to have been unsuitable.

The attitude of primary school teachers: panic or complacency?

For the New Right, and likewise for the Secretary of State, the success of their policies in education depends largely upon the teachers who have to carry them out. This is not just a question of teacher supply, and what in Department of Education and Science-speak is called 'teaching quality', it is also one which centrally involves the attitude of teachers towards the new measures. It is probably extremely trying for the New Right that its plans have to depend upon those that one of their leading propagandists has labelled a 'parasitic stratum' (O'Keefe, 1981). The constant denigration of the work of primary teachers by figures like Education Minister, Angela Rumbold (Wilton, 1986), is not likely to do much to win their consent for the new turn and neither was the imposition of a new pay and conditions settlement by the Secretary of State likely to achieve that end either. Primary school teachers' reactions to the national curriculum can be divided into two: those expressed through professional associations including the unions and those expressed by individuals. Among the unions, the National Union of Teachers has traditionally represented the majority of primary school teachers. It was brought into being in order, among other things, to oppose government control over the elementary school curriculum. Its opposition to the imposition of the National Curriculum on primary schools has been largely couched in the language of child-centred ideology (NUT, 1987; NUT, 1988). The threat to the unique nature of primary schooling was also referred to at the annual conference of the National Association of Schoolmasters/Union of Women Teachers in 1988. There the debate on a motion opposing the imposition of the National Curriculum included contributions from speakers expressing the fear that the National Curriculum would change radically the practices of primary education (NAS/UWT, 1988). This rush to the defence of child-centred education by the unions is a little late and given their previous stances towards it not entirely convincing (Cunningham, 1988). Nevertheless, the fact that the unions were prepared to restate the child-centred case is significant given the relative lack of enthusiasm or support for it from within the primary professional establishment. That the child-centred alternative to the National Curriculum is alive and capable of mobilizing support was demonstrated by the interest shown in the views of a primary school teacher, Mary Poole, whose television appearance in 1989 attracted much interest (Poole, 1989).

While the views of teachers' organizations are relatively easy to discover, the general attitude, Mary Poole excepted, of primary school teachers towards the National Curriculum is not. The Secretary of State claimed at the beginning of 1989 that teachers had got 'confidence' in the National Curriculum but Fred Jarvis of the NUT responded by arguing that the National Curriculum had lowered further the morale of teachers (reported in *Junior Education,* Vol. 13, No. 2 1989). The view that primary teachers' morale is low is supported by research conducted before the passage of the Act at Birmingham (Teaching Research Unit Birmingham University, 1987) and by a Times Educational Supplement/MORI poll (Hugill, 1987). Since the Act was passed the Interim Advisory Committee on teachers pay has also spoken of its concern for the level of teachers' motivation and morale *(Times Educational Supplement,* 24 February 1989). Letters to the education press and articles on primary teachers' opinions provide both evidence of support for the National Curriculum as well as hostility towards it (Saunders, 1988). Significantly, the *Times Educational Supplement*/MORI poll conducted in 1987 found that 80 per cent of the teachers polled favoured a core curriculum for all pupils from 5 to 16 (Hugill, 1987). Because, however, there was general assent to the idea of a core curriculum it does not mean that there is the same level of support among teachers for the form that it has taken in the National Curriculum. Confronted by the new demands, there is evidence that primary teachers feel either that they cannot understand the National Curriculum or that it is nothing new (Nash, 1989a). The latter attitude virtually amounts to a belief that by changing the labels given to current practices, the National Curriculum can be absorbed, 'modified' and 'incorporated' (Moyle, 1988). This feeling has been strengthened by the positive messages which have emanated from within the primary, professional establishment. Initially, many felt that topic or project work would have to give way to subject teaching but this impression has been criticized by Norman Thomas, the former senior HMI for primary education, who has argued that topic work should be 'absolutely safe' (O'Connor, 1988). The approach of Thomas typifies a certain professional reaction to the new conditions brought about by the Act. While the main unions, for example, have adopted an oppositional stance and have continued to raise the issue of resources, those, whom Richards has labelled the liberal pragmatists, convey the new realist line. This consists mainly of the view that the full version of the child-centred position is untenable and that the only way to combat the traditionalist assault of the New Right is to promote the opinion that there is a silver lining discernible in the National Curriculum cloud (Richards, 1987; Pollard, 1989). Undoubtedly there is some substance to this view and the strategy which flows from it. Ultimately, however, it rests upon the calculation that the primary professional establishment is strong enough, if not to subvert the National Curriculum then at least bend it to what are regarded as desirable ends. As Campbell, who without doing too much violence to the evidence can be identified as a liberal pragmatist, has so appositely noted, the working party on science and technology in its first report constructed 'a Trojan horse of progressivism and discovery learning' right at the centre of the National Curriculum (Campbell, 1988). Similarly, the English working party's first report lifted many spirits by its general support for progressive practices and because of the paradox that in the report of a group chaired by Professor Cox, an editor of the first Black Paper, Plowden's ringing declaration of the centrality of the child to the primary school curriculum was quoted (DES/Welsh Office, 1988). Nevertheless, the liberal pragmatist view is fundamentally flawed on a number of grounds if its intention is to subvert the more unappealing aspects of the National Curriculum. Not the least of these is its inability to probe the level of appearances. In the present conjuncture the professional establishment may be of little consequence as political not educational considerations are paramount. Thus political not educational means are required if the least desirable aspects of the National Curriculum are to be resisted. In addition, progressive slogans and verbal support for progressive practices cannot hold much water in the face of the obdurate refusal of central government to address seriously the resource implications of the National Curriculum. While the working parties write into their reports programmes of study which require, on one estimate, an expenditure on new technology next year of at least £170 million, the government spent only £30 million in 1988 (Nash, 1989c). Finally, as Kenneth Baker's responses to the reports of the working parties have demonstrated, their progressivism can be modified if the Secretary of State so wishes and, furthermore, optimistic receptions of the reports published so far have tended to avoid confronting the likelihood that the assessment tail will wag the curriculum dog (*Times Educational Supplement*, 7 October 1988).

Testing

In the light of this prediction it is clear that speculation about what will and what will not be saved of current primary school 'good practice' cannot be confined to a consideration of the programmes of study alone; all will hinge on which of two emerging approaches to testing predominates. The first of these is what might be called the professional response enshrined in the TGAT report (DES, 1987b). This report met head-on primary teachers' fears of being plunged back into the bad old days of the 11+ and the Revised Code when the curriculum of primary and elementary schools was subordinate to the needs of the examination and inspection. The task group chaired by Professor Black declared that 'the assessment process itself should not determine what is to be taught and learned. It should be the servant, not the master, of the curriculum' (DES, 1987b). In so far as the standard assessment tasks will be related to the work that an individual pupil has done, then the model of assessment constructed by TGAT has clear advantages over the norm-referenced tests now widely used. These often bear little relation to the curriculum presented in primary schools, their methodology is regarded as suspect and hence, teachers pay little attention to the results provided by them (DES, 1989a). Nevertheless, the model of assessment may still have deleterious effects upon primary schools for the following reasons. First of all, the need to meet the requirement for differentiation, laid down in the remit sent by the Secretary of State to the working party, led TGAT to build into its model a series of criterion-referenced, age-independent levels. Differentiation in HMI-speak refers to the need for teachers to take into account the differing abilities of children (DES, 1985a). More differentiation, in this view, is necessary in order to achieve better match, the holy grail of the HMI Primary Survey. Underlying this notion is the recognition that teaching children of a wide range of ability in a way that takes account of their different needs and interests is very difficult (Mortimore *et al.*, 1988). In mixed age classes, which as a result of demographic changes are now to be found in 70 per cent of primary schools, the difficulties are further compounded (Nash, 1988). Historically, particularly when faced with the requirements of nationwide assessment, primary school teachers have responded to mixed attainment classes by streaming or setting. The former practice declined rapidly alongside the demise of the 11+ , but setting by attainment, particularly in maths lessons, is quite common (DES, 1978; Galton *et al.*, 1980; Barker Lunn, 1984). Given that this is the case it is necessary to pose the question, what is so peculiar about maths that teachers increasingly find it advantageous to set by attainment? Part of the answer lies in the fact that most maths lessons rely upon the use of highly-graded schemes and consequently the maths curriculum is quite highly differentiated. It is also the case that the TGAT report envisages the provision in each class of a highly differentiated curriculum because at the age of 11 it assumes that 80 per cent of the children, and hence 80 per cent of children in a normal class, will be somewhere between levels 3, 4 and 5 (DES, 1987b, figure 1). If each level corresponds roughly to two years, the range of attainment at that age may be at least equivalent to a 6-year range. As Gipps has pointed out, the most likely response of schools to this knowledge is that they will set and stream more (Gipps, 1988). As the content and form of the National Curriculum has been progressively revealed it is becoming more clear that the Department of Education and Science endorses this solution to the problem of implementing a highly differentiated curriculum and has actually published guidance to this effect as has the National Curriculum Council (Weston, 1989). Streaming, as is well known from the experience of the fifties, is socially divisive as well as educationally indefensible.

A second likely effect of testing is that teachers will teach the test. In one sense this is inescapable as the programmes of study and attainment targets are what the Standard Assessment Tasks (SATs) will be based upon. There is, however, another sense in which teachers are likely to teach the test and that is that they will focus their work upon the content of the SATs. The power of the SATs to determine what is taught was hinted at by the chairperson of the School Examination and Assessment Council, Philip Halsey, when he implied that in-service work on assessment should wait until the publication of a few SATs (Makins, 1988). The SATs have not yet been produced and so speculation in this area is hazardous but one of the groups, awarded a contract to develop them, forecast that they will take up a considerable amount of time to administer. Tom

Christie, the leader of the STAIR consortium which gained the largest amount of money from the School Examination and Assessment Council to develop SATs is reported to have said that a set of three SATs for 7-year-olds will represent a major part of the formal work of the third term of the top infant year' *(Times Educational Supplement,* 23 December 1988). If the SATs do become as dominant as existing evidence suggests then they are likely to lend support to a move towards didactic teaching methods and subject based organization. This would be especially regretful if, as under the Revised Code, the schooling of children below the first key stage were to be unduly influenced by the need to prepare them for the requirements of assessment at the age of 7. Drawing upon experience in the United States, Nuttall has suggested that in order to enhance their standing in local assessment league tables some schools might even introduce a form of selection at the age of five (Nash, 1989b).

Leaving aside the formidable problems faced by primary teachers which flow from their lack of non-contact time and which make it likely that they will have no time for adequate training in the required methods of assessment or for the necessary moderation meetings, and leaving aside the potential for sexual and racial bias in the teacher ratings, virtually all of the deleterious effects of assessment that have been noted here could be avoided if it were not for the requirement that the aggregated results be published. It is this which will encourage and foster those aspects such as streaming and formal teaching which proved so inimicable to the facilitation of the learning of the majority of primary school children in the past. While the mode of assessment associated with the National Curriculum may go some way towards the achievement of match, what is gained in that direction is likely to be overwhelmed by the kind of didactic teaching and unimaginative work which has so often been deprecated by HMI. This double-edged nature of the TGAT model of assessment has been noted by Gipps who has perceptively observed that, 'TGAT's real trick has been to adopt educative forms of assessments . . . in which the student competes against his or her self . . . and to harness them to the highly competitive arrangements required by GERBIL' (Gipps, 1988). Once again, the irrationality of another aspect of the Education Reform Act is exposed for if, as Professor Black insists, the purpose of the assessment arrangements is to provide teachers with diagnostic evidence why then the stress on the publication of aggregated results? Conversely, if the principal end desired was the fostering of competition then the means of assessment should have been harnessed solely to that end.

Testing: the New Right's case

Testing is what the neo-liberal sections of the New Right seemed to have wanted most. On many occasions, figures associated with the New Right have articulated the view that testing is principally a means both of disciplining teachers and of fostering competition. Hence most of the pronouncements of its adherents on testing have been subordinated to those ends. In his attack upon the 'educational establishment', which he also referred to as an 'in-bred, decadent cognoscenti', Letwin, formerly an adviser to Mrs Thatcher, made the point that universal tests would reveal that children were not acquiring basic skills and, by implication, that the 'educational establishment' needed disciplining (Letwin, 1987). But the argument in his article which drew the most responses and which was the most hostile to the child-centred primary tradition, was not the attack upon teachers but his view that children ought to learn to accept failure, by coming 'to terms with their own capabilities', at an early age if they are to become 'decent, upright adults'.

These polemical shafts would be of little consequence if it were not for the fact that the New Right, as I have argued throughout, are able to exert considerable influence and pressure within the Tory Party. Within the government Mrs Angela Rumbold, Minister of State for Education, has struck some of the more unyielding poses with regard to the competitive features of the model of assessment adopted (*Education,* 2 October 1987). The consultation document *The National Curriculum 5–16* (DES, 1987a) was quite clear that one of the main purposes of assessment was to indicate to the public at large how a particular school was performing; this information would then, it was assumed, inform parents' choice of school. Popular schools would then thrive and unpopular ones would go to the wall. This is a law of the market and one which proved so inadequate in meeting the nation's needs in the nineteenth century that the state was compelled to step in and impose some kind of order on the chaos produced. Nevertheless, New Right figures like Dr Sheila Lawlor are already exerting pressure for a more rigorous form of testing than has been proposed by TGAT. She believes that the assessment procedures for 7-year-olds, proposed by the Schools Examination and Assessment Council, which are intended to rely mainly on teachers' own assessments, will not produce what was intended with regard to fostering competition (Gow, 1988). In response to such reaction and possibly to the danger of being seen to be too close to the educational establishment, Kenneth Baker produced a statement to the effect that he was determined to ensure that the tests for 7-year-olds would be 'rigorous'. Once again, political requirements and considerations take precedence over the formulation of appropriate educational ends and their intelligent pursuit.

Conclusion

For many years the primary school curriculum has been one of the most hidden corners of the secret garden. Now its future, and that of primary school pedagogy, will also be decided by the outcome of the struggle between the political right and the primary educational establishment. At the moment the jury is still out and the verdict may go either way despite the appearance that the right has the lead by a fine margin. While the professionals lack experience of political conflict and have been disarmed from within by the criticisms of HMI, the ideologues of the right are lacking in knowledge of primary schools and the means to win the approval for their aims from primary teachers whose reactions range from resignation to resentment. As I have tried to demonstrate, the New Right does, however, have political power and without a political upheaval of seismic proportions there appears to be no obstacle to its plans to divide the state education system into two parts. One part of the divided system will provide a basic education for the disadvantaged and the other, a wide and well resourced experience for the selected few. With the support of well-heeled parents such schools will be able to attract the staff to teach the shortage subjects by paying them salaries which are locally negotiated. They will also be able to afford the huge demands made by the National Curriculum for equipment and other resources. Other primary schools, especially those in inner city areas, will revert to the status of the old elementary schools and provide an impoverished service which will provide an absolute minimum in sink school conditions. As an antidote to this vision of the future it is as well to remember that political landscapes have been transformed overnight in the past and they may well be so again.

There is much that is wrong with our primary schools, and even if most problems can be laid at the door of inadequate resources not all can. It is also a matter of some regret that all pupils are not given access to some areas of the curriculum, especially to science and technology during their primary years. Not so that they will become scientists and technologists necessarily but so that they can observe and record their discoveries about the physical world. There is much also that is deficient in child-centred ideology, particularly in its total subordination of societal requirements to those of the individual. The child-centred position has also helped to sustain a professional self-image that was frequently hostile to accountability and one that was arrogant towards and uncomprehending towards disadvantaged social groups. Above all, the primary professional establishment has singularly failed to explain and to justify to the public at large what it regards as good practice. It strains credibility to breaking point, however, to imagine that a subject based curriculum accompanied by tests whose intention is to sort the weakest schools from the fittest, imposed upon teachers whose work has been consistently devalued and whose negotiating rights have been summarily taken away, can even begin to address those things that are wrong, let alone raise standards of attainment. Taking the shortage of primary teachers who feel competent to teach science as an example, the kind of policies required in this instance are ones which address the gender divisions which affect the way that all knowledge is produced and distributed. The shortage of teachers overall could be resolved by the application of market principles; if it is desirable to increase the supply of a commodity the most effective way to do it is for the purchaser to raise the amount that they need to pay until it reaches the level at which demand is satisfied.

My argument has been that in overall educational terms the National Curriculum lacks rationality as a policy response to educational problems and that its most likely effect is that primary schools will lose much of their distinctive character for which they were once internationally renowned. That is to say that they will no longer be places where young children are encouraged to develop socially and cognitively in a supportive environment guided by enthusiastic and committed teachers who empathize with children. In their place, driven by the logic of a mixture of political opportunism and ideological necessity there will emerge crammers for the CTCs and GM schools and, on the other side of the tracks, 'sink' schools within which teachers will be impelled to press recalcitrant children into the nine-subject mould and mourn the absence of any pupils on levels 4 and 5. For Plowden's child at the heart of the educational process, there should now be substituted the Standard Attainment Test.

References

BARKER LUNN, J. (1984) 'Junior school teachers: their methods and practices', *Educational Research*, Vol. 26, No. 3, pp. 178–88.

BARNES, L. R. and SHINN-TAYLOR, C. (1988) 'Teacher competence and the primary school curriculum: a survey of five schools in north-east England', *British Educational Research Journal,* Vol. 14, No. 3, pp. 283–95.

BAYLISS, S. (1989) 'New networks', *The Times Educational Supplement,* 17 February.

BOARD OF EDUCATION (1981) *Report of the Consultative Committee on the Primary School.* London, HMSO.

BOARD OF EDUCATION (1988) *Report of the Consultative Committee on the Infant and Nursery Schools*, London, HMSO.

BLENKIN, G. and KELLY, A. V. (1981) *The Primary Curriculum.* London, Harper & Row.

BREHONY, K. J. (1987) 'The Froebel Movement and state schooling 1880–1984'. Unpublished Ph.D. thesis, The Open University.

BREHONY, K. J. (1989) *Primary Issues*, Unit 20, E208 *Exploring Educational Issues.* Milton Keynes, The Open University.

CAMPBELL, J. (1988) 'Reform Bill update', *Junior Education, 12,* 2, pp. 6–7.

CENTRAL ADVISORY COUNCIL FOR EDUCATION (1967) *Children and Their Primary Schools, Vol. 1.* London, HMSO.

CENTRE FOR POLICY STUDIES (1988) *Correct Core: Simple curricula in English, Maths and Science.* London, Centre for Policy Studies.

CHITTY, C. (1988) 'Two models of a national curriculum: origins and interpretations', in Lawton, D. and Chitty, C. (Eds) *The National Curriculum,* Bedford Way Papers 33, London, University of London Institute of Education, pp. 34–48.

COX, C. (1989) 'Unqualified approval', *The Times Educational Supplement.* 6 January.

COX, C. B. and BOYSON, R. (1975) (Eds) *Black Papers 1975,* London, Dent.

CUNNINGHAM, P. (1988) *Curriculum change in the primary school since 1945*. Lewes. Falmer Press.

DES (Department of Education and Science) (1978) *Primary Education in England: A survey by HM Inspectors of Schools,* London, HMSO.

DES (1980) *A Framework for the School Curriculum,* London, HMSO.

DES (1982) *Education 5–9: An Illustrative Survey of Eighty First Schools in England.* London, HMSO.

DES (1983a) *Teaching Quality,* London, HMSO.

DES (1983b) *9–13 Middle Schools: an illustrative survey,* London, HMSO.

DES (1984) *Circular 3/84 Initial Teacher Training: approval of courses,* London, DES.

DES (1985a) *The Curriculum From 5 to 16,* London, HMSO.

DES (1985b) *Education 8–12 in Combined and Middle Schools,* London, HMSO.

DES (1987a) *The National Curriculum 5–16,* London, DES.

DES (1987b) *National Curriculum: Task Group on Assessment and Testing,* London.

DES (1988) *The New Teacher in School,* London, HMSO.

DES (1989a) *Standards in Education 1987–8,* London, DES.

DES (1989b) *Future Arrangements for the Accreditation of Courses of Initial Teacher Training: a consultation document,* London.

DES/WELSH OFFICE (1988) *English for Ages 5–11,* London.

DES/NORTHERN IRELAND (1981) *Primary Education: Report of an Inspectorate Survey in Northern Ireland,* Belfast, HMSO.

GALTON, M., SIMON, B. and CROLL, P. (1980) *Inside the Primary Classroom,* London, Routledge & Kegan Paul.

GIPPS, C. (1988) 'The TGAT report: trick or treat', *Forum,* Vol. 31, No. 1, pp. 4–7.

GOW, D. (1988) 'Baker insists 7-year-olds will be tested rigorously', *The Guardian,* 20 December.

HALLETT, J. (1987) 'What CATE is doing to schools'. *Forum,* Vol. 29, No. 2, pp. 36–8.

HARMAN, G. (1984) 'Conceptual and theoretical issues', in Hough, J. R. (Ed.) *Educational Policy,* London, Croom Helm, pp. 13–27.

HAVILAND, J. (Ed.) (1988) *Take Care, Mr Baker! A selection from the advice on the Government's Education Reform Bill which the Secretary of State for Education invited but decided not to publish,* London, Fourth Estate.

HILLGATE GROUP (1986) *Whose Schools?* London.

HILLGATE GROUP (1987) *The Reform of British Education,* London, The Claridge Press.

HILLGATE GROUP (1989) *Learning to Teach,* London, The Claridge Press.

HUGILL, B. (1987) 'A sharp kick in the shins for Mr Baker', *The Times Educational Supplement,* 12 June.

HUGILL, B. (1989) 'Parents sue borough over four-day week'. *The Times Educational Supplement,* 10 February.

LAWTON, D. (1984) *The Tightening Grip: growth of central control of the school curriculum.* Bedford Way Papers 21, London, University of London, Institute of Education.

LEE, J. (1987) 'Pride and prejudice: teachers, class and an inner-city infants school', in Lawn, M. and Grace, G. (Eds) *Teachers: The Culture and Politics of Work,* Lewes, Falmer Press, pp. 90–116.

LETWIN, O. (1987) 'Testing issues', *The Times Educational Supplement,* 18 September.

LIGHTFOOT, L. (1989) 'It ain't on, Baker tells the trendies', *The Mail on Sunday,* 12 March.

MAKINS, V. (1988) 'Delegates fear assessment will overshadow national curriculum', *The Times Educational Supplement,* 25 November.

MAW, J. (1988) 'National curriculum policy: coherence and progression?' in Lawton, D. and Chitty, C. (Eds) *The National Curriculum,* Bedford Way Papers 33, London, University of London, Institute of Education, pp. 49–64.

MORTIMER, P., SAMMONS, P., STOLL, L., LEWIS, D., and ECOB, R. (1988) *School Matters,* Wells, Open Books.

MOYLE, J. (1988) 'In my view', *Child Education,* Vol. 85, No. 11, p. 17.

MUSGROVE, F. (1987) 'The Black Paper Movement', in Lowe, R. (Ed). *The Changing Primary School,* Lewes, Falmer Press, pp. 106–28.

NASH, I (1988) 'Mixed-age groups worry inspectors', *The Times Educational Supplement,* 9 December.

NASH, I. (1989a) 'Fears are assuaged as heads take the plunge', *The Times Educational Supplement,* 20 January.

NASH, I. (1989b) 'Cox "threatened to resign" ', *The Times Educational Supplement,* 21 April.

NASH, I. (1989c) 'Technology needs "at least" £170 million', *The Times Educational Supplement,* 27 January.

NATIONAL UNION OF SCHOOLMASTERS/UNION OF WOMEN TEACHERS (1988) 'Conference Report Supplement', *NASUWT Career Teacher Journal,* Summer.

NATIONAL UNION OF TEACHERS (1987) *Future of the Curriculum,* London.

NATIONAL UNION OF TEACHERS (1988) 'Primary education could be set back 30 years', *The Teacher,* Vol. 7, p. 18.

O'CONNOR, M. (1988) 'Calm down at the front', *The Guardian,* 26 January.

O'KEEFE, D. (1981) 'Labour in vain: truancy, industry and the school curriculum', in Flew, A., Marks, J., Cox, C., Honey, J., O'Keefe, D., Dawson, G. and Anderson, D. (Eds) *The Pied Pipers of Education,* London, Social Affairs Unit.

POLLARD, A. (1989) 'Can teachers cope?', *Junior Education,* Vol. 13, No.4, pp. 10–12.

POOLE, M. (1989) 'Saboteur in the classroom', *The Listener,* Vol. 122, pp. 4–6.

PROCTOR, N. (1987) 'Academic subjects in the BEd primary course: some worrying evidence', *Journal of Further and Higher Education,* Vol. 11, No.3, pp. 35–44.

RICHARDS, C. (1987) 'Primary education in England: an analysis of some recent issues and developments', in Delamont, S. (Ed.) *The Primary School Teacher,* Lewes, Falmer Press, pp. 186–7.

RICHARDSON, J. (1987) 'Subject to subjects', *Forum,* Vol. 29, No.2, pp. 32–3.

ROSS, A. (1984) 'Developing political concepts and skills in the primary school', *Educational Review,* Vol. 36, No.2, pp. 131–9.

SALTER, B. and TAPPER, E. R. (1988) 'The politics of reversing the ratchet in secondary education. 1969–86', *Journal of Educational Administration and History,* Vol. 20, No.2, pp. 57–70.

SAUNDERS, T. (1988) 'What we think', *Junior Education,* Vol. 12, No. 1, pp. 14–15.

SILBERMAN, C. E. (Ed.) (1973) *The Open Classroom Reader,* New York, Vintage Books.

SIMON, B. (1980) 'The primary school revolution: myth or reality', in Fearn, E. and Simon, B.(Eds) *Education in the Sixties,* Leicester, History of Education Society.

SMART, B. (1983) *Foucault, Marxism and Critique,* London, Routledge & Kegan Paul.

TEACHING RESEARCH UNIT, Faculty of Education, University of Birmingham (1987) *The Primary School Teacher: a profession in distress,* Birmingham, Faculty of Education University of Birmingham.

THOMAS, N. (1989) 'Time, teachers and the national curriculum', *Education Today, 39,* 1, pp. 11–18.

THOMSON, L. (1985) 'Connecting patterns', *Forum,* Vol. 27, No.2, pp. 57–9.

WELSH OFFICE (1988) *Welsh Education Statistics Bulletin: No 5 Primary school staffing survey,* Cardiff, Welsh Office.

WESTON, C. (1989) 'Streaming prospect for primary schools', *The Guardian,* 14 April.

WILTON, G. (1986) 'Minister's line on primaries', *Child Education,* Vol. 66, No.12, p. 8.

8
TVEI, Vocationalism and the Crisis of Liberal Education

Mike Hickox and Rob Moore

It is not our intention, here, to simply look at the possible implications of the Act for vocationalism as it is expressed in the particular shape of TVEI (Technical and Vocational Initiative). Rather, we see the 'vocationalization' of education as providing the broader context within which the Act and associated reforms should be understood. Until very recently the distinctive feature of English education has been its capacity to successfully resist vocationalism and to preserve a distinctively liberal-humanist form of education. This was so despite, on the one hand, numerous attempts by various governments (of Left and Right) to make education more responsive to 'the needs of industry', and on the other, a widespread popular instrumentalism in the use which pupils, students and parents made of education. The real peculiarity of English liberal education has been its ability to sustain itself despite the lack of a major social base for its principles and ideals.

In part this phenomenon reflects the traditional prestige enjoyed by academic elitist versions of liberal-humanism: the public school/Oxbridge tradition and the grammar school. But more significantly and more generally, liberal education (in its progressive Plowden/Newsom forms as well as its traditional ones) has survived by virtue of the degree of autonomy enjoyed by the teaching profession under the conditions of the locally administered, maintained educational system. If we might now be witnessing the demise of liberal education, it is because, after decades of exhortation, Thatcherism has attacked directly, and with scant regard for the opinions and feelings of professional educationalists, its *institutional* base. What Callaghan attempted to do through his invitation to a 'Great Debate' (what could be more expressive of liberal values and practices than that), Thatcherism is achieving with its characteristic contempt for 'the chattering classes'.

The Act is part of a more general movement to reformulate educational institutions in such a way that central control can be effective without the prior necessity of referring to professional opinion, let alone constructing a consensus around change.

Although the form of these changes is consistent with the more general strong state/free-market strategy of Thatcherism, they draw also upon a more specific set of exigencies peculiar to education and which have been intensifying over the past decade. We will characterize these as constituting 'the crisis of liberal education' and will argue that it is this crisis which provides the condition for the vocationalization of education.

We shall examine the economic and social forces which have produced the current crisis of liberal education and argue that, although these cannot be dismissed out of hand, the explanations normally given for the success of vocational education initiatives in terms of the 'needs of industry' are not wholly convincing (despite this being the way in which they are normally legitimated). We shall argue that, in a sense, the roots of liberal-humanism's present difficulties can be traced to its very *successes* over the past century and in particular in the post war period.

Thus, liberal-humanist education has expanded beyond a narrow social elite to encompass a far wider and more socially diverse constituency. One result of this, exacerbated during a period of high unemployment, has been the phenomenon of education inflation whereby more and higher credentials are required over time to gain access to the *same* job. This in turn has created what Randall Collins has termed the 'crisis of the credential' (Collins, 1981). As the liberal-humanist credential loses its buying power, so it suffers a loss of credibility and attempts are made to replace it by an alternative educational currency. At a more general political level, the crisis of liberal-humanism reflects the new political constituency of Thatcherism which embraces social groups, especially the affluent southern working class, which have been largely alienated from the liberal cultural establishment.

The Technical and Vocational Education Initiative

The Technical and Vocational Education Initiative, in its progression from pilot to extension phases, has proved to be a complex development in British education. The very terms, *technical, vocational, educational,* create a juxtaposition which touches sensitive places in the liberal-humanist tradition which has dominated our educational thinking. In key respects, TVEI can be seen as a type of solution to problems in education of which such sensitivies themselves are perceived as a symptom. The series of reforms for which the Education Reform Act provides the general context, arose from a strongly felt sense that our educational system and classroom practices require radical change. Reforms present themselves as solutions to *problems*. The objectives of TVEI implicitly contain a diagnosis of education's ills.

TVEI can be seen as addressing the following concerns. First, it is an attempt to 're-centre' the secondary curriculum around science and technology and to shift it away from the post-Newsom base in the Humanities. Secondly, to facilitate a change in fundamental educational attitudes and values towards positive support for commerce and industry and the practical application of knowledge. This reflects the view that both traditional and progressive liberal educationalists have tended to exhibit an active disdain or outright hostility towards 'enterprise' and industry and have, on the one hand, failed to meet the needs of non-academic pupils and, on the other, failed to meet the needs of the economy by encouraging the high-fliers to seek careers elsewhere (mainly in academia). Thirdly, it attempts to represent these shifts in a pedagogy which more accurately reflects the character of 'real-world' problem solving processes.

Given the radical character of these objectives, it was inevitable that educationalists should have originally approached TVEI with suspicion and hostility. LEAs and Head teachers resented the challenge to their traditional authority and autonomy represented by The Manpower Services Commission (MSC) and its delivery model. Teacher's in general tended to have strong reservations about MSC's behaviouristic skills training approach and the narrowly occupationalist form of its vocationalism. However, it is probably true to say that today many of those same liberal teachers are expressing considerable support for TVEI and fear the possible consequences which the National Curriculum and the GCSE might pose for it.

This enthusiasm may well represent the degree to which teachers have found ways to subvert the original MSC model and translate TVEI back into a more familiar form of secondary progressivism. If this is the case, then for supporters of the 'hard occupationalist' version of TVEI, it represents a failure to bring liberal education to heel. At the same time, yet others (such as the Training Agency's Ann Jones) see the National Curriculum as representing across the board precisely the things that TVEI is all about. From this point of view, TVEI has so successfully permeated secondary practice that even if it were formally abolished tomorrow, it would still have achieved its effect. Hence, there is no simple assessment of TVEI or common perception of its form or of its impact upon and future within secondary education in this country.

This situation can be related to a more general set of tensions between the various camps which broadly support the ERA. Whitty (Chapter 2 in this volume) has addressed the issue of the relationship between the neo-conservative and neo-liberal tendencies within the New Right. Whatever contradictions there might be between those who support the strong State as the means of sustaining 'traditional values' and 'the British Way of Life' and those who support the market as the medium through which the 'consumers' (parents, not pupils) of education exercise their choice, the common presumption is that a traditionalist and narrowly didactic form of academic education is what any sensible person (whether defined as 'citizen' or 'consumer') would want.

The Manpower Services Commission can be seen as representing an alternative approach, one which is characterized by a general hostility to *liberal* education in *any* form. Both neo-conservative and neo-liberals are essentially using different devices (the state and the market) to achieve the same effect: a return to a traditional version of liberal-humanist education which they see as having been undermined by a progressivism which reflected the power of educational 'theorists' in colleges and universities to determine teacher education and the power of the teaching profession to assert an expertise derived from an *educationalist* definition of the needs of pupils. In both instances, 'the problem' was that of institutional and professional autonomy. Both teacher trainers and teachers themselves are seen as having had an unjustifiable freedom to construct a professional self interest in opposition to that of both parents and the nation. Much of what is contained in or associated with the ERA is concerned with reversing that condition, with subjecting educationalists to the twin disciplines of state and market.

The distinctive feature of the MSC approach is the way in which it constructed a model of skills training from sources which were independent of mainstream educational thinking. Its original inspiration was in American and Canadian experiences with behaviouristic psychological approaches most usually associated with 'scientific management' in industry and the training of armed services personnel and with the original, narrowly therapeutic uses of social and life skills training. This tradition stands in stark contrast to the developmental approaches in child psychology which are associated with 'child-centred' progressivism. These developmental approaches resonate, at the more affective levels of progressive teaching ideologies, with the organic growth metaphors of the Romantic tradition with which progressivism is associated. In the eighties, the MSC training paradigm was further extended through the development of a model of the labour market reflected in notions such as job component inventories, occupational training families, generic and transferable skills, etc., MSC declared the explicit aim of relating these methodologies to the school curriculum.

This approach took 'the needs of industry' or 'the national economy' as its starting point. It differs fundamentally from the neo-conservative and neo-liberal tendencies of the New Right by defining Britain's basic problems in terms of the debilitating effects of the classic liberal-humanist tradition in English education, especially its effects upon the social elite which it rendered ineffectual as the ruling class of an advanced industrial society. Hence, it is precisely those 'traditional values' and conservative educational forms which the neo-conservative and market New Right seeks to resurrect which this 'technicist' tendency wishes to expunge.

Interestingly, and significantly as far as TVEI is concerned, the 'technicist' approach can be seen as having more sympathy for aspects of *progressivism* than for traditional liberal-humanism. This is particularly so in terms of the progressive interest in experiential and process learning. In attempting to shift the discipline base of progressivism away from developmental child psychology to behaviourism, the technicist paradigm can be seen as an attempt to reconstruct progressive pedagogy in a form which makes it more amenable to external control in terms of the definition of aims and objectives. Hence the contrast is between using an experiential pedagogy in the service of 'child-centred' needs with expressive and diffuse aims ('personal fulfilment', 'realization of potential', 'personal autonomy', etc.) defined by educational professionals and using it in the service of 'the needs of industry' with discrete, instrumental aims (skills, competencies, performance indicators, etc) determined by non-educational interest groups.

However much the neo-conservatives and neo-liberals might have contributed to the rhetoric and legitimations of the ERA reforms, at a substantive level, it is MSC which can be seen as contributing most to the distinctive changes in the forms of *control* over education which the ERA is formalising. This is true for the more general disciplines such as contract bidding and the emerging regime for teacher training as well as for the more specific features of assessment of performance–profiles, performance indicators, etc. It is in constructing *methodologies of control* that the behaviourism of the technicist paradigm excells.

In its 'progressive' aspects, TVEI fits awkardly into the broader New Right call for a return to traditional education. However, the MSC model of delivery provides effective mechanisms for constraining the teaching profession, not only institutionally, but at the level of classroom practice. It is in the *limitations* of the delivery system in practice that TVEI provided an opportunity for teachers to repossess the scheme in the name of a liberal progressivism in secondary education which can be traced back to the raising of the school leaving age, the Newsom Report and the Schools Council (Jones, 1989).

The limitations in the delivery system reflect the extent to which MSC had to share the implementation of TVEI with the LEAs. Under these conditions, TVEI became an instrument for curriculum development which many teachers of 'the ROSLA generation' identify as a continuation of the spirit of that time. Despite its origins in behaviourist psychology, MSC's form of experiential learning was retranslated into a more familiar, progressive *liberal* form of process learning. In this sense, TVEI can be seen as reinstating the desire for 'relevance' in the curriculum which characterized developments in the upper secondary school in the early 1970s. Ironically, it was precisely these things which, though overshadowed by events at the primary level (exemplified by the Tyndale affair), fueled the Great Debate and initiated the change of climate of which the Education Reform Act (ERA) can be seen as the culmination.

What we are witnessing today, and what TVEI exemplifies, is a characteristic process whereby liberal-humanist education in Britain episodically experiences crises of its established forms. What has been distinctive of this process in the past has been liberal-humanism's capacity to reassert itself in a new form. Whether this will be true today is an open question. ERA attacks the *institutional* arrangements which have in the past supported liberal education. The current combination of state and market strategies are subjecting the educational system to a discipline quite different from the tripartite dispersion of power between the DES, the LEAs and the teaching profession which sustained liberal education in the past. It is also the case that Thatcherism, politically, is characterized by an alliance of forces extremely hostile to the liberal establishment. However, it could be that the lesson of TVEI is the continuing capacity of teachers to subvert government strategies and retain a liberal form to education.

The crisis of liberal education

A basic, qualitative distinction between education and training has been fundamental to educational thinking in this country. 'Education', or 'liberal-humanist education' as we shall term it, seeks to impart certain general moral and cultural qualities while an education based on 'training' sets out to transmit certain discrete skills without attempting to mould the general character of the individual concerned. The influential liberal philospher R. S. Peters, for instance has written:

> We do not call a person 'educated' who has simply mastered a skill even though the skill may be very highly prized such as pottery. For a man to be educated it is insufficient that he should possess a mere know-how or knack. He must have also some body of knowledge and some kind of conceptual scheme to raise this above the level of a collection of disjointed facts. (Peters, 1970: 30)

Such 'schemes' are not purely cognitive, essentially they are to do with what is thought to be 'worthwhile' and imply a distinctive moral dimension. This is not to say that liberal-humanist education does not transmit skills, but these are always seen as subordinate to a higher educational end.

It is important to note that the distinction between these two types of education does not directly correspond to the familiar distinction between 'traditional' and 'progressive' styles of teaching. In the main 'training' will be accompanied by a relatively didactic teaching style, although its emphasis upon quantifiable results may also make the teacher more directly accountable. On the other hand, the educational progressivism which became an important educational philosophy in the 1960s, with its stress upon an equal relationship between teachers and taught, can be seen, in terms of the present argument, as a variant of liberal-humanism since it ultimately set out to educate 'the whole person'.

Recent years have seen a crisis of liberal humanist education accompanied by growing demands for the introduction of a more vocational type of education *at every level.* This has been reflected in the expansion and growing influence within education of the Manpower Services Commission (now the Training Agency). What is perhaps most significant is the aggressive stance taken by the MSC towards the liberal-humanist tradition. Thus the educational ideology of the MSC, with its stress on transmitting discrete, measurable and assessable skills, is more or less directly antithetical to the central values of liberal-humanism. In the Youth Training Scheme (YTS) the MSC has typically set out to recruit its trainers from outside the ranks of qualified teachers. Thus one aspect of the current drive for a more vocational education is the attempt to supplant rather than merely supplement liberal-humanist education. What is seen to be needed is a root and branch reform of the existing educational system.

Education and the Economy

Were the needs of the *economy* the crucial factor in determining the content of education, then *liberal* education would certainly have been on the retreat for the past century. On the contrary, despite periodic calls (as in the aftermath of the Boer War) for a more vocational education, to stem England's relative economic decline, the reverse has proved to be true. Liberal education has not only been able to beat off the challenge from vocationalism, but has become increasingly strongly entrenched over time. Crucial to this process, as Brian Simon (1987) has argued, was the defeat of the middle-class vocational tradition by the public school 'gentleman' concept of education centred around the teaching of Classics (Muller, Ringer and Simon, 1987). Indeed, the historian Martin Wiener, in an influential work (Wiener, 1981), sees this process as a key factor in producing an 'anti-industrial spirit' which has helped to accelerate Britain's relative industrial decline.

From Oxbridge and the public schools the classics-based liberal education was disseminated downwards to mould the curriculum of the grammar schools. Thus the 1902 Education Act confirmed the victory of the liberal grammar school curriculum over the more vocational curriculum of the Higher Elementary School. One additional effect of this was the way in which the Classics-trained generalists came to predominate over the educational 'expert' within the DES. The growing predominence of Oxbridge within British education in the later decades of the nineteenth century in turn had the effect of increasing the hold of liberal education over both the Civil Service and sections of private industry. Thus by the late 1890s the newly-created Oxford and Cambridge Appointments Boards were successfully persuading large firms such as Shell and ICI to recruit Oxbridge classics graduates rather than, as previously, non-Oxbridge scientists and engineers (*op.cit.*).

Essentially, the post-1945 period saw the reinforcement of this trend, reflected, for example, in the failure of the technical schools after the 1944 Act. By the same token, the post Robbins expansion of Higher Education in the 1960s did nothing to shake the hold of liberal-education, although this now took the form of new types of courses differing from the traditional Classics curriculum (e.g., Social Sciences, English Literature).

The success of liberal education and the relative failure of its vocational rival within the context of an advanced industrial society is ostensively peculiar given the tendency of both orthodox (e.g., technological functionalism) and radical (e.g., correspondence theory) theories to link the rise of mass education with the economic needs of such societies. It would be wrong, however, to see the national example as simply another 'peculiarity of the English'. Historical and comparative evidence equally demonstrates a similar tendency in other industrial societies (*ibid.*). Although this cannot be developed in any detail, here, we must observe that this tendency to prioritise the education/*economy* linkage is most probably wrong. Indeed, this assumption underpins our position.

Very briefly, the following points can be made. In the early phase of industrialization, industry tended to be small scale and based on relatively simple technology. Consequently it made few demands on the educational system. Such skills as were required were typically acquired 'on the job', while recruitment to the few elite positions was on the basis of family membership or connections.

Consequently, as is the case in many contemporary, developing countries, the first demand for graduates from both the secondary and higher sectors of education came from the expanding civil service. Later this was augmented by the demand for white-collar personnel to staff expanding bureaucracies of the private sector. Thus the demand for education did not typically derive from the industrial sector.

Also, although for a long period the industrial middle-class remained relatively excluded from the social and educational world of the Southern professional middle-class, it is clear that in late nineteenth and twentieth century England, the expansion of liberal education and its associated concept of the 'gentleman' enabled a social fusion to occur between sections of the landed class and sections of the industrial and professional middle classes. This process is complex and still remains to be fully explored. It became possible on the basis of some version of public school education (if not recruitment to the elite schools) becoming increasingly accessible to larger and larger sections of the middle class as a whole and provided access to higher and middle management positions within the expanding bureaucracies of the private and public sectors.

In many respects, twentieth-century England has seen an increasing social homogenisation between different sections of the middle class on the basis of a shared educational experience (whether this be public or grammar school or a Wilsonian view of the comprehensive as 'grammar schools for all'), although this process is far from complete. Central to this has been the associated expansion of a liberal curriculum based on transmitting general leadership or management qualities rather than 'vocational skills'.

The degree to which liberal education has been successful is reflected in the fact that there is no unambiguous evidence that current demands for a more vocational or industry based education actually represents the attitudes of industrialists themselves. Indeed, it would seem that, if anything industry's preference is often for a 'traditional' (i.e. liberal-humanist) education. At the very least, there is a considerable gap between the rhetoric of industrialists and their actual recruitment practices. Thus a recent survey of graduate recruitment concludes that despite a public emphasis on the desirability of work experience, industrialists tend in practice to favour university trained generalists over the graduates of polytechnic based vocational degrees (Brennan and McGeevor, 1988).

If the pressures towards vocational education cannot be simply linked to the needs of industry, what are their origins? As we have suggested, the crisis of liberal education should rather be linked to processes which derive at least partly from the very success of this form of education. The two which will receive special emphasis are those of *educational inflation,* on the one hand, and *educational differentiation* (in terms of both the curriculum and institutions) on the other.

Credential inflation

The process of *credential inflation* is that whereby, over a period of time, increasingly *higher* levels of qualification are required to gain entry to the *same* level of employment. This generally reflects the fact that, typically, employment opportunities increase, if at all, far more slowly than the supply of education personnel. In turn, the tendency to produce more educated personnel reflects public pressure for access to educational qualifications. The relative cheapness of generalist or liberal education courses (at least relative to subjects such as engineering) is a further factor leading to expansion in these areas.

It is important to recognize that 'public demand' for more education was much more a response to increasing credentialisation in the labour market than a demand for education *per se* — least of all on liberal terms as a 'good thing' in its own right. The demand was predominantly instrumental in character. As Boudon has clearly demonstrated (Boudon, 1974) the process brings no net advantages to individuals. In general, the decision by any individual to get marginally more education is, in the first place, a response to the condition created by the aggregate effect of similar decisions by other individuals. This aggregation effect simultaneously provides the pressure for individuals to extend their education *and* wipes out any net advantages a similar decision might have gained at some earlier time.

Credential inflation *devalues* qualifications in the labour market in such a way that extended educational aspirations are associated with declining occupational expectations. Hence individuals have to bear the costs (economic, psychological and social) of 'staying-on' without any particular gains in terms of occupational opportunities and without a liberal commitment to education for its own sake. Given the instrumental attitude towards education, this situation seriously undermines the credibility of the liberal credential. For instance, as data from the General Household Survey (1982) demonstrated the 1970s in particular saw a significant narrowing of median earnings differentials between different levels of qualification.

A number of factors combined to fuel credential inflation. The period of post-war economic expansion provided the material resources for developing the educational system and the widespread influence of human-capital theory provided a theoretical rationale for doing so. According to this approach, education itself was a major force for economic development. Hence investment in education was an investment in future growth and prosperity. However, as Gareth Williams (1985) has pointed out, this utilitarian justification for spending did not seriously conflict with *liberal* education because it focused upon the *level* of education rather than its *content* as the significant factor. Hence educational expansion could still be left to the direction of academics and educationalists.

Despite this fortuitous feature of human capital theory, a problem, nevertheless, existed for liberal education under these circumstances. The theory provided a strong, political imperative to expand the numbers in education and improve the general educational level of the population. This was associated with the 'pool of ability' type of argument which seriously questioned the established selection processes (the 11 +) and the tripartite system. (For a classic statement of this position, Floud and Halsey, 1961).

It was argued that not only were the *institutional structures* of the educational system restrictive and inefficient but that the received *form* of academic, liberal education was narrowly exclusive and alienating. Hence the pressure to expand numbers led to a questioning of the received forms of liberal educational institutions, curriculum and pedagogy. The major Reports of this period — Robbins, Crowther, Newsom — can each be seen as attempting to reconcile a liberal model of education with the requirement to accommodate both national economic objectives and the interests of groups previously excluded from continuing education.

One effect of this at the school level was to shift influence away from *academics* (defining, through University examination syllabuses, appropriate *knowledge*) to *educationalists* (particularly in the expanding Colleges of Education) charged with the task of developing new types of curriculum and pedagogy appropriate to new types of pupil in the upper secondary school. It is quite clear in Newsom, for instance, how *vocationalism* is essentially a device for making schooling appear more 'relevant' to non-academic pupils. The pressures from expansion favoured the 'progressive' end of the liberal educational spectrum which started from the needs of children rather than the nature of knowledge — 'we teach children, not subjects'.

Hence the need to accommodate large numbers of pupils who were either 'first generation' of their families in selective schools (see Halsey, *et al.*, 1980, ch. 5) or 'staying-on' in secondary modern or comprehensive fifth-forms created pressures to radically reformulate the *character* of liberal education.

However, the process of credential inflation is clearly one that can only carry on to a certain point and must halt long before it reaches the ultimate absurdity of the Ph.D. street cleaner. Before this, the net effect, as Collins suggests, is to increasingly discredit the whole currency of liberal education itself. This is exacerbated by the fact that, as we have seen, typically the ideology of liberal education does not claim to transmit useful or relevant skills. Indeed, it may even make a virtue of its apparent lack of practical relevance. However, even if covertly, its status and popularity has always been linked with its ability to provide employment opportunities. Once this ceases it has, as it were, no fall back position, except, perhaps, to argue, unconvincingly, that education should be seen as an end in itself or to present some compromised variant such as 'education for leisure' or 'social education'.

Differentiation — the new liberal education

The process of differentiating the forms of liberal education as a way of accommodating expanding numbers is a second factor that has led to the undermining of the currency of liberal humanism. Its increasing differentiation in the post-war period in terms of the creation of new courses and subject areas has been aided by the decentralization of the British education system and the way in which the curriculum was left very much to the innovative interests of professional educationalists.

The way in which this process was managed is symptomatic of the condition which the current Act is aiming to reverse. The expansion of education incorporated an expansion of both *educators* and *educationalists*. The latter in particular can be seen as experts in the *educational process* rather than, as R. S. Peters would say, *authorities in a subject*. Starting still from liberal-humanist precepts, their concern was to address the developmental needs of 'the whole child' and to forge a curriculum and pedagogy which would be 'relevant' to children from all types of social background.

This approach was generally hostile to traditional, subject-based 'academic' liberal education. It attempted to extend the 'benefits' of Plowden-style progressivism at the primary level into the secondary school (the middle-school movement explicitly used such an argument in support of the middle-school system). This type of thinking is clearly seen in Schools Council projects aimed at the so-called Newsom Child in the ROSLA period and in the CSE exam (especially the Mode 3) which enabled teachers to work to these ends outside of the restrictive influence of university entrance requirements.

Crucially, the expansion of the educational system posed the problem of *how* new groups were to be accommodated within extended educational careers. Until the late 1970s this problem was defined and almost exclusively discussed in terms of the dilemmas of liberal-humanism. Controversies ranged around issues such as the survival of the grammar school, humanities vs science, pure vs applied, traditionalism vs progressivism. The dualisms of these debates were generated by the fundamental principals of liberal-humanism.

One of the most highly symptomatic features of the current situation is that these issues are simply not perceived *as issues*. The question of the relationship between pure and applied knowledge, for instance, is not acknowledged as a serious issue by MSC. New research funding principles in higher education are, despite the strenuous efforts of the scientific community to protect theoretical work, effectively imposing instrumentalism regardless of professional objections.

What were perceived at the time as *fundamentally* opposed positions can now be seen as tensions between the opposite poles of liberal-humanism — between a 'classic' concern with the purity of educational knowledge (prioritizing the *curriculum*) and a progressive preoccupation with 'the whole child' (prioritizing *pedagogy*). Essentially, whereas the 'classic' position held that individuals were *civilized* through initiation into worthwhile forms of knowledge, the progressive view was that knowledge was sanctified experientially through the *cultivation* of inner potential.

The post-Newsom concept of 'relevance' was thus defined in *educationalist* terms derived from liberal-humanist principles and was sustained by the expansion of teacher education and the institutional autonomy of the teaching profession. The character of this autonomy significantly affected the accommodation of expansion. Liberal constructs of 'relevance', whilst making sense in terms of 'child-centred' liberal-humanism, had little to do with the instrumentalist motivations behind either the political expansion of education (national economic interest) or the popular pursuit of credentials (getting a job).

This created a number of problems for the liberal credential and liberal-humanist values as such. First, it created (or exacerbated) a split within the liberal camp between 'traditionalists' and 'progressives' (exemplified in the Black Papers debates). Secondly, because of credential inflation, extended educational careers brought no real returns to those forced by circumstances to 'stay-on'. Thirdly, the differentiation of courses and approaches was developed according to liberal, progressive criteria by professional educationalists whose concerns were fundamentally at variance with the instrumentalism of the popular pursuit of credentials.

Whilst, at the lower level, extended education brought no improvement in occupational opportunity, at the higher level the increasing numbers of graduates could not be accommodated within jobs which traditionally met graduate expectations. These problems have been intensified by recession which has not only affected the supply of jobs overall, but has led specifically to a contraction of education and public service posts which in the past provided an ethos more commensurate with liberal values than the industrial and commercial worlds. At the higher level, the expansion of liberal-humanist education ran up against the problem of extending a liberal *cultural* form beyond the traditional confines of the ruling elite.

Arguably, for liberal education to fulfil its function of reproducing a culturally homegenous elite, it must retain a unitary nature. What counts as constituting liberal humanist culture, although it may change over a period of time (as exemplified by the loss of status of Classics), must not vary too greatly at any *particular* time. Thus the rise of new subject areas, essentially extensions of the liberal tradition, such as Sociology in the 1960s, has arguably created some confusion regarding the definition of the 'educated person', as has, also, the development of new institutions of higher education, e.g. the new universities and polytechnics.

Thus it is interesting to note in this context that employers display a marked preference for the university over the polytechnic 'generalist' (see Brennan and McGeevor, 1988). They also appear to have greater confidence in 'A' level scores as against performance at degree level – possibly because 'A' levels reflect a nationally based and generally accepted educational currency.

The problems created by the tensions implicit in accommodating expansion, plunged liberal-humanist education into an increasingly destructive, downward spiral accelerated by a recession which radicaly reversed the conditions which had sustained the original expansion.

Responses to the crisis

At one level, the tensions outlined above have to do with the ways in which liberal education attempted to accommodate a more diverse constituency. At another level, one has had the alienation of the Conservative government from sections of the traditional liberal cultural establishment (e.g. the Church, civil service, universities). Undoubtedly a major factor in this has been the new political constituency of Thatcherism which since the 1979 election has come to include large sections of the affluent working-class, linked to the Conservative Party on an instrumental rather than a deferential basis. Arguably, it is this very social group which has been largely excluded from the benefits of the post-war expansion of liberal education. Certainly the pages of the *Sun* display little respect for those whom the *Daily Mail* journalist, Paul Johnson, refers to as 'the chattering classes'.

The social basis of opposition to the liberal credential can be linked both to its growing failure to meet the occupational expectations of its traditional middle-class consumers together with the conservative government's electoral dependence on social groups which have few traditional links with this form of education. At the same time there are clearly powerful interest groups within education, e.g. the MSC itself, which have a material vested interest in a transformation of the present educational curriculum. Despite the general tendency of current reforms to increase central control over education, the most striking feature of the attendent debates is the lack of consistency or agreement. This is reflected, for instance, in the controversies surrounding curriculum reform proposals, assessment and testing and *right-wing* attacks on the new GCSE. This fragmentation on the right can be seen as reflecting what is, in fact, the diversity of its constituency and the tensions within it.

Indeed, it is indicative of the wide variety of social groups within the new Thatcherite political constituency that this includes not only, as has been argued, social groups largely alienated from liberal culture, but also a right wing intelligensia (often claimed to represent the *first* British right wing intelligensia) whose social status largely depends upon its possession of a cultural capital derived from traditional, liberal education. Certainly, few conservative political tracts can have contained so much discussion of education as Scruton's *The Meaning of Conservatism*. This cultural capital it sees threatened by both educational progressivism and the subject areas associated with TVEI and the growing demands for vocationalism (thus Scruton is opposed to both forms of 'relevance').

This diversity within Thatcherism tends to make nonsense of any assumption that there is a unified New Right approach to the curriculum and education. The heterogeneous groups concerned are perhaps only united by a common hostility to a 1960s inspired 'educational progressivism' and to the socialist controlled LEA. Hence the disagreements can be seen as reflecting, on the one hand, a 'traditionalist' group seeking a return to some purified form of liberal-humanism and, on the other a thoroughly instrumental demand for practical (especially *vocational*) relevance which has little sympathy for liberal appeals of *any* kind. The latter embodies a form of 'common-sense' impatience reflected in Mrs Thatcher's apparant ceaseless irritation at the inability of 'experts' to simply get us back to 'old-fashioned' basic learning ('facts') and 'top of the class' type tests.

More generally, reaction to the crisis of liberal education has essentially taken two forms. The first is an attempt to replace the liberal credential by a new, apparently vocationalist, form of educational currency purportedly based on the transmission of skills. The second is the diametrically opposite attempt to restore the credibility and purchasing power of traditional, liberal education.

This second strategy is currently most closely associated with that section of the New Right linked with Roger Scruton, sometimes termed the 'neo-conservative' as opposed to the 'market' right. Intellectually this group are heirs to the Black Paper writers of the late 1960s and 1970s with a typical grammar school/Oxbridge educational profile. Crucially this strategy involves an attack on the new 'trendy' liberal humanist disciplines of the 1960s, on both intellectual and political grounds, coupled with a demand for the return of a more traditional form of the liberal curriculum, with the implication that this will also bring about the restoration of traditional 'respectful' moral values. This demand for a 'pruning' of the curriculum associated with a more restricted access to higher education ('more means worse') can be seen as a response to the twin threats noted to the liberal curriculum of educational inflation and differentiation.

Turning to the vocationalist position. From our perspective, the vocationalization of education can be seen as an alternative method of accommodating the expansion of education in the light of the failure of liberal-humanism to 'deliver the goods' in *instrumentalist* terms. Its success in expanding the system during the 1950s and 1960s was matched by its failure either to successfully export its *values* or to extend the covert instrumentalism of its cultural capital beyond the elite sphere within which it had its organic base.

In the ROSLA period, vocationalism in the Newsom mould was essentially a strategy for making education appear more relevant to non-academic pupils. The 'world of work', as well as things such as social education and community and environmental studies, was part of a broader, progressive programme to direct education away from the formal, book-based methods of academic education. The documents of this time (see, for instance, the DES Circular on Work Experience Schemes for Schools, DES 7/74) characteristically stress that work experience, for instance, should be a part of 'general education' and related to broad concerns with personal development. The 1977 Green Paper, following the Great Debate, focused particularly on the issue of 'esteem' for commerce and industry, reflecting employers' feelings that teachers often deflected their brighter pupils from taking up careers in industry. TVEI, and current vocationalism more generally, is specifically concerned with direct preparation *for* work. This type of approach is often distinguished from the other by the term 'occupationalism'.

Occupationalism has radical implications for education. First, it attempts to derive a 'curriculum' directly from what purport to be the actual skill requirements of industry. Hence what is to count as 'educational knowledge' comes to be determined by sources outside of education. Secondly, following from this, groups other than academics or educationalists are empowered to determine educational aims and objectives. MSC's systematic exclusion of teachers from its various boards is indicative of this. Thirdly, the behavioural objectives approach (in combination with profiling) not only further restricts teachers' professional freedom of manoeuvre, it also increases their degree of accountability relative to these educationally impoverished criteria. Fourthly, it is associated with a broader reconstruction of the institutional arrangements of education (the Act, the National Curriculum, etc) through which it becomes possible for the central state to impose its will upon schools and to constrain the professional independence of teachers.

Williams *(op. cit.)* has associated 'occupationalism' with a shift from human capital theory towards a 'manpower planning' approach. Manpower planning is characterized, in this sense, by its policy objective of linking education more directly with the 'needs of industry' through concretely defined skill requirements. This links with the MSC's behaviouristic skills objectives model. The shift to this perspective was facilitated in the mid-1970s by the developing crisis in the nation's economy. The DES, in particular, suffered criticisms from international organizations such as OECD that education was not effectively meeting manpower requirements. Hence the frustration of instrumentalism at the popular level was reinforced by a similar type of criticism of education at the level of the national economy. The Great Debate essentially tried to focus the liberal educational establishment's attention on both sets of demands but the strategy, in itself, reflects the DES's institutional incapacity to directly impose change on a decentralised, maintained education system.

The intervention of MSC can be seen as a necessary consequence of the DES's inherited limitations. As an external agency, MSC was not subject to the complex system of constraints which had been forged historically *precisely* in order to limit central control over the educational system. Both ROSLA and the Great Debate had failed to shift the curriculum in the desired directions. MSC, operating with a radically different set of instruments (contract bidding and compliance, etc.) was able to enforce an entirely new set of conditions for promoting change.

Most significantly, they drastically curtailed the capacity of *educationalists* to manage change. Indeed, *educationalists* hardly figured in the process. MSC delivered its own model constructed from an entirely independent tradition of skills training developed from North American sources and thoroughly researched by MSC personnel in the late 1970s (see MSC, 1977; and Moore, 1987). This approach was further developed for local application by agencies outside the educational establishment (e.g. the Institute of Manpower Studies, 1983). This process involved not only MSC sponsorship of research, but a circulation of personnel between MSC and the organizations in its 'network'. Hence, MSC has been able to present a distinctive and coherent approach, quite independently of mainstream educational agencies, and to enforce its requirements through delivery mechanisms fundamentally different from those of the DES.

However, the MSC was, in effect, playing a trail-blazing role in these developments. It was signposting the way for a more general shift in structures and methods which are clearly visible in the new forms of INSET funding, in CATE and across the entire spectrum of educational institutions. Essentially, these new arrangements both curtail the influence of educationalists and the professional autonomy of teachers and subject education to a wide range of 'lay' pressures from parent dominated governing bodies to 'representatives' of industry.

At one level the success of the MSC can be seen to have rolled back the post-war extension of liberal education, in the form of educational progressivism (e.g. Plowden/Newsom), to the working class. Arguably this extension of liberal education was always weakly based given the relative failure of the working class to benefit from the expanding credential system. In many respects it can simply be seen as a response to the educational vacuum left by ROSLA and the traditional British failure, as compared with other European countries, to provide vocational education for the working class. Ironically, educational progressivism's net effect has been to export the educational ideology of liberal humanism (education as a 'good in itself') without the hidden benefits to be derived from success in the credentials system.

These basic tensions within the New Right constituency can suggest an interpretation of current educational restructuring as an attempt to restore a traditional division between non-academic (working class) and academic (middle class) streams within education. Crucially this interpretation depends on the extent to which the vocationalist ideology is successfully penetrating the levels of further and higher education. Its presence can be clearly seen, for instance, in the attack upon pure research in the sciences and in the new research funding regimes. Evidence here is unclear — whilst there is obvious pressure to preserve 'A' level, there is also the growth of a new network of qualifications (B/Tec etc.) in the sixth forms. Our view, however, is that rather than these restructurings and associated patterns of educational differentiation reflecting a *single* strategy (i.e., to restore a traditional division), they reflect fundamental divisions and conflicts within the New Right.

Credentials and work

Recent studies of graduate employment patterns suggest that new forms of linkage between education and employment might be developing in response to these conflicting pressures (see Brennan and McGeevor, 1988). First, there is the growth of a new system of generalist subjects with apparently vocational/business connotations, e.g., law, business studies or more specific occupational links such as with pharmacy or computer studies. Secondly, there is the development of a pattern whereby a traditional liberal course of study is followed by a vocational qualification such as accountancy. There could well be a conflict between these two types of career pattern, both implying a more vocational educationalist mix.

However, if the past history of education is a sufficient guide, the generalist element within overtly vocational subjects is likely to take precedence over the purely skills training element. This may be particularly true of university graduates relative to public sector ones. Industry will continue to prefer to train its own on the basis of the 'right kind of person', i.e., one having a *generalist* liberal educational background. However, it is possible that 'A' levels rather than degrees could be favoured with companies using them as a way of recruiting good quality candidates for career development programmes aimed at professional rather than academic higher qualifications.

Finally, both responses to the crisis of the liberal credential may be seen to represent a relative loss of status on the part of the *educationalist*. This is most apparent in the case of the vocationalist ideology with its aggressive rejection of the values of liberal humanism, narrow concentration on closely defined and assessible skills and contempt for the teaching profession (a contempt more or less in line with Willis' Lads, to say nothing of figures such as Norman Tebbitt). However, it is also implicit in the attitude of the traditionalist Black Paper position since these writers wish to take the definition of general culture out of the hands of educationalists and restore it to one more congruent with that possessed by the generally educated middle-class person. This involves a double attack on educational progressives who are seen as undermining the hold of the traditional disciplines but also on the jargonized, politically suspect 'non-subjects' (e.g., peace studies, multicultural education, personal and social education) which are depicted as having seized control of the school and higher education curricula.

Indeed, in retrospect the heyday of educationalist control over the curriculum occurred in the 1960s in the context of the massive expansion of the credential system. In the early stage of credential inflation the increased supply of credentials is associated with a massive expansion of job opportunities within education itself which tends to reinforce the educator's definition of what constitutes 'relevant knowledge'. This is further strengthened by the relatively strong buying power of the credential in the wider labour market, the consequence of which is that little attention is paid to the exact nature of the currency in this period. This was reflected in the relatively marginal position of the Black Papers group in this period, even on the right.

Conclusion

The starting point for the argument developed in this paper is that of 'the crisis of liberal education'. We relate this crisis to two major features in the development of the educational system in the post-war period. Both relate to the expansion of the system. The first is that of credential inflation which undermined the currency of the liberal credential and imposed a general requirement for pupils to acquire more education for no net returns in terms of improved chances of occupational and social mobility. The second is that of educational differentiation which reflected the need for liberal education to diversify its forms in order to accommodate groups previously excluded from extended educational careers. This had the effect of weakening the definition of what counted as 'an educated person'. Further, this process was largely managed by professional educationalists in a form which tended towards the more progressive end of the liberal spectrum. The new forms of education became increasingly perceived (throughout the 1970s in particular) as leading to a lowering of academic and social standards — a popularist reaction which the current reforms have effectively played upon — and reflecting the special interests of educationalists rather than those of either parents or 'the nation'.

The expansion of liberal education failed to extend to its wider constituency the benefits of either improved employment or its traditionally prestigious cultural capital. After the mid-1970s and the deepening of the recession (particularly in its effects upon the youth labour market), the educational system no longer enjoyed the expectation that it could deliver either the general social reforms predicted by social democracy or the personal, instrumental advantages which individuals desired. Given the abandoning by the emerging radical right, with its general rejection of Keynsian/social democratic reformism, of the broader social programme, the demand in the 1980s has tended to be simply for an education which delivers identifiable goods in the form of 'standards', jobs and national economic efficiency. These demands have taken the substantive forms of either a more obviously vocational education or a return to familiar, traditional types of schooling. A principle requirement, in both cases, is that of control over the educational profession itself and a radical curtailment of *its* capacity to determine the forms and objectives of schooling. Through the combination of strong state and free market strategies, the ERA aims to achieve this effect.

Although in many respects antithetical, both the vocationalist and traditionalist demands can co-exist around the view that it is a traditional concern for 'standards' which is more likely to secure employment. This co-existence is aided by the fact that the two forms of education can be distributed between different social groups, so reinstating something like the old secondary modern/grammer school division. The major problem which liberal-humanism faced was that its broad support was always instrumental in character rather than reflecting any real commitment to it on its own terms (i.e., the *intrinsic* value of education as a good thing in itself). It was sustained not so much by a major social consituency as by the peculiar institutional arrangements of the maintained education system in this country. Although there have been previous episodes of crisis for liberal education, what is, perhaps, special about the current one is the way in which the ERA is dismantling precisely that institutional structure which sustained it in the absense of a popular base.

Despite these things, however, TVEI illuminates the contradictions and tensions beneath the surface. In the final analysis, the neo-conservatives, neo-liberals and technicists are pulling in different directions. What coherence there is within the reforming programme reflects relatively tenuous contingencies within the wider political context: a shared hostility to teacher autonomy and professionalism, on the one hand, and a failure, on the other, of the opposition to assert an effective counter agenda to Thatcherism. Should the latter emerge, it is not at all obvious that the former alone will be sufficient to hold the various elements of 'the New Right' in education together.

TVEI also illustrates the capacity of teachers, even under present conditions, to repossess an initiative which was virtually custom designed to minimize their freedom of manoeuvre. The translation of TVEI back into a progressive, liberal educational form reflects not just the availability of spaces remaining within the maintained system, but contradictions within the technicist model itself — namely its commitment to the principles of experiential and process learning.

There is, ironically, a further source of optimism for the future of liberal education. A major part of the rhetoric of vocationalization is the need to meet the *new* needs of the economy, to produce a workforce able to accommodate the requirements of new technologies and production processes. Given what appears to be the character of 'post-Fordist' industry, it can be suggested that both the skill training and the neo-conservative approaches are singularly *ill-equipped* to do this. The former because it derives its approach from a form of behavioural psychology which is not only twenty years out of date but can be seen as a quintessential expression of old style 'scientific management', and the latter because of its stress upon the inflexible inculcation of *traditional* values and expectations.

Both these forms can be seen as conflicting with the actual requirements of the new forms of production, especially in terms of the need for flexiblility and adaptability. However, this is not simply a *technical* matter. There are also significant demographic changes, associated with fundamental changes in the character of the labour force, which will demand radical *social* changes in the organization of working life. The most significant of these is the dramatically increasing importance of *female* labour.

The major requirement of post-Fordist industry will be not simply for a *skilled workforce* but for an *educated citizenry* capable of accommodating not just new techniques of production but new arrangements of working and social life. Precisely, in other words, the 'rationally autonomous' products of a general, liberal education. The problem for liberal education is to create a form appropriate to this task. For some, the success of TVEI might suggest how this could be done.

References

BOUDON, R. (1974) *Education, Opportunity and Social Inequality,* New York, John Wiley.

BRENNAN, J. and MCGEEVOR, P. (1988) *Graduates at Work,* Jessica Kingsley, London, and the various publications associated with the CNAA's *Higher Education and the Labour Market* (HELM) project (details of which can be obtained from Phil McGeevor at the Polytechnic of the South Bank).

COLLINS, R. (1981) *The Credential Society,* New York, Academic Press.

FLOUD, J. and HALSEY, A. H. (1961) 'English secondary schools and the supply of labour', in Halsey, A. H. *et al., Education, Economy and Society,* Fress Press, New York.

INSTITUTE OF MANPOWER STUDIES (1983) *Training For Skill Ownership,* IMS, Brighton.

JONES, K. (1989) *Right Turn: The Conservative Revolution in Education*, Hutchinson Radius, London.

MANPOWER SERVICES COMMISSION (1977) *Analytical Techniques for Skill Comparison,* MSC, Sheffield.

MANPOWER SERVICES COMMISSION (1981) *Young People Starting Work,* MSC, Sheffield.

MOORE, R. (1987) 'Education and the ideology of production', *British Journal of Sociology of Education,* Vol. 8, No. 2, pp. 227–42.

MULLER, D. K., RINGER, F. K. and SIMON, B. (1987) *The Rise of the Modern Education System: Structural change and social reproduction*, 1870–1920, Cambridge, University Press.

PETERS, R. S. (1966) *Ethics and Education,* London, Unwin Books.
WIENER, M. (1981) *English Culture and the Decline of the Industrial Spirit, 1850–1980,* London, Cambridge University Press.
WILLIAMS, G. (1985) 'Graduate employment and vocationalism in higher education', *European Journal of Education,* Vol. 20, Nos 2–3, pp. 181–91.

9
The Reform of School-Governing Bodies: The Power of the Consumer over the Producer?

Rosemary Deem

In this chapter I shall be looking at the attempts being made by both the 1986 and the 1988 Education Acts to reform and reshape the governance of schools. It is important to look at the *combined* effects of both pieces of legislation as they have different intentions and consequences for school governors. Furthermore some aspects of the 1988 Education Act contradict or change the provisions of the 1986 Act (for example on responsibilities for the curriculum and staffing). Some commentators, including some of the contributors to this volume, doubt whether the 1988 Act is intended to work (Simon, 1988; Lawton and Chitty, 1988; Deem, 1988), rather it is seen as a way of preparing for a more fundamental privatization of education and perhaps the introduction of vouchers. It is certainly the case that when one looks at the tasks facing school governors from 1989 onwards, it is hard to see how anyone can possibly expect voluntary governing bodies and lay governors using their 'spare' time actually to control and run schools. However, the replacement of producer power (that is, teachers and LEAs) by consumer power (parents, employers, the community) is one of the major planks of the Reform Act and nowhere is this enhanced consumer power more evident, in intention if not in practice, than in the recomposition of governing bodies and the bolstering of their responsibilities. Later I shall question the appropriateness of this producer/consumer analogy in education.

I will begin by saying something about the recent history of school-governing bodies and the relevant provisions of the 1986 and 1988 Acts, before going on to look at the issues raised by these changes and developments, including who the 'new' governors are, which groups are represented and which under-represented, what assumptions lie behind the recomposition of school governance, the politics and dynamics of governing bodies and the coping strategies that new governors are using to manage their reponsibilities. Although I shall draw on existing research and publications about governors, much of this was done before either Act had taken effect. I shall also refer to more recent research, including a Leverhulme project on parents as governors based at the University of Exeter and a continuing study on the politics of the new governing bodies that Kevin Brehony and I are currently conducting, which at the time of writing involves fifteen governing bodies in two LEAs. Any reference to research in progress does of course need to be treated carefully and some of what I have to say is necessarily speculative.

Governing bodies 1944–1986 — a benign lay influence?

Over the past five decades in England and Wales there have been some very significant shifts in the balance of forces between LEAs, teachers, governors and parents. The 1944 Education Act supposedly established a partnership between teachers, central government and local education authorities, although this was never an evenly balanced distribution of power and responsibilities (Bogdanor, 1979). Governors played little or no role in the partnership and nor did parents. LEAs oversaw the implementation of educational policy but central government had little direct involvement (for example, there was no compulsion on LEAs during the early stages of comprehensivization), despite exercising some control over the LEA purse strings. Teachers and heads gradually acquired the status of largely autonomous experts, to whom the running of schools could safely be left. This was despite the fact that overall direction of education policy at a local level, headteacher appointments, advising and inspecting and distribution of staffing and resources to individual schools rested firmly with the local authorities.

The 1944 legislation required all maintained schools to have a body of governors (secondary schools) or managers (primary schools) whose powers would be described in the 'instruments and articles of government'. Whose interests should be represented on the governing or managing bodies was not laid out (for example, parents *could* be represented, but there was no necessity for them to be so), and it was possible for a single governing body to govern many different schools. This situation remained the case for a long time after 1944. In the period 1965–9, for instance, a quarter of English and Welsh LEAs had only one governing body for all their schools. The functions of governing bodies varied widely between different LEAs, but mostly concerned very general oversight of internal organization, financial matters and curriculum, care and upkeep of the premises, a few aspects of staff appointment and dismissal (governors might, for instance be involved in the appointment of a new head or the dismissal of one), involvement in out-catchment pupil admissions and the fixing of occasional day holidays. Governing and managing bodies were often dominated by political nominees of LEAs. But by the early 1970s, as the first concerns in the post-war period began to be raised about educational standards, the running of schools and the costs of education (Ransom, chapter 1 in this volume, discusses this in more detail than there is room for here) questions began to be asked about the professional autonomy of teachers, the role of parents in shaping education and the importance of accountability in education (Cox and Boyson, 1975; Dale, 1981; Boyson, 1981).

In 1975 the Taylor Committee was set up with a brief to examine the arrangements for governing schools and to make appropriate recommendations. The Committee's report (usually referred to as the Taylor Report, DES, 1977), whilst recommending that LEAs should continue to remain responsible for the overseeing of school government, suggested that much more power than previously should be delegated to governing bodies themselves. Ideally each school should have its own separate body, on which would sit equal numbers of LEA representatives, school staff, parents, pupils where appropriate and members of the local community. The powers of the new bodies would include establishing the aims of the school and the ways in which these were to be achieved, although the headteacher would retain ultimate control. Other powers of governors would include submitting of annual estimates of school income and expenditure; consultation with the LEA over buildings and maintenance; joint responsibility with the LEA for appointments of heads and full responsibility for the appointment of other teachers. What Taylor proposed was a full partnership for governors and teachers in conjunction with the LEA, although it did not suggest that parents should outnumber other representatives on the governing bodies. Indeed under these recommendations they would always be a minority. As Whitehead and Aggleton (1986) note, this recommendation was supported by the main teaching union, the NUT, on the basis that it would not threaten teacher control. The Report did not focus to any significant extent on the responsibilities of governors for the curriculum and the organization of the school.

As with many educational Reports, the Taylor recommendations were only partially incorporated into subsequent legislation. Perhaps they were seen at the time as being too radical a change. Or maybe politicians were simply not ready at that point to extend greater involvement to parents and pupils. Whatever the reason, the Taylor recommendations have never been fully acted upon. The 1980 Education Act, whilst allowing for some restructuring of governing bodies by ensuring that each school would usually have its own governing body, did not really impinge much on governors' powers. It did, however, set out new bases for membership, with a minimum of two parents and one or two teachers on each governing body, depending on school size. Prior to the Act itself, some LEAs, notably Sheffield, had already set up separate governing bodies for each school and enabled parents, teachers, heads and older secondary pupils to become members of these alongside the traditional LEA political representatives (Bacon, 1978). In fact, all the 1980 Act did was to clarify what was already legally permissible, without extending the powers of governing bodies or radically altering their composition, although by also setting up mechanisms requiring schools to publish exam results and provide 'information for parent' booklets, the Act did prepare the ground for what was to emerge under the 1986 Act (for example the annual report by governors to parents). Although some governing bodies became much more involved than others in the period after 1980, much of the research shows that governors generally operated in an advisory and supporting capacity, in conjunction with headteachers, even though the potential existed for them to have some considerable influence over schools (Kogan *et al.*, 1984; Taylor, 1983). It is clear that while few governors had the desire to take over the running of schools; many probably did not even have the opportunity. For as Hall, Mackay and Morgan's (1986) study of the work of headteachers found, heads were in a good position to manipulate and direct their governing bodies, should they wish to do so (and many probably did).

The 1986 Education Act — a recomposition of school-governing bodies

The 1986 Education (No. 2) Act began its life in Parliament as a Bill which was intended to clarify and redefine the membership and powers of school and college governing bodies in England and Wales. Bur during the course of the Bill's passage through the Committee stages and whilst before the House of Lords, under pressure from right wing groupings of educationists principally represented by Baroness Cox, various new clauses were added, including those giving governors the right to decide whether their school should provide sex education, the banning of 'partisan politicial activity' by primary school teachers and pupils, and a requirement that school governors should have regard to representation about the curriculum made by local Police Chiefs (O'Connor, 1987; SEO/ACPO, 1986).

One of the key features of the 1986 Act was the introduction of changes in the composition of governing bodies. These included increasing parental governor representation in schools of over 600 pupils from two to five and proportionately in smaller schools, decreasing LEA representation (with minor local authority representation going altogether in secondary schools) and increasing co-opted membership (intended to bring wider community involvement, and more particularly people representing the business community). No governors under 18 were to be allowed thus removing the possibility of pupil governors in secondary schools, as recommended by the Taylor Report in 1977. All Governors would in future serve four years, unless they chose to resign. But Local Authority governors can still be removed by the appointing body under Section 21(1) of the 1944 Education Act; it will be interesting to see whether LEAs choose to use this power to remove defeated councillors from governing bodies after local elections, which in the main no longer coincide with the terms of office for governing bodies. This course of action may be made more difficult by a Court of Appeal decision in February 1989 (Regina v Inner London Education Authority, Ex parte Brunyate and Hunt). The case concerned two LEA governors of Haberdashers' Aske's Hatcham Schools. The governors of these voluntary-aided schools had met in May 1988 to discuss the future status of the two schools, with options including becoming grant-maintained (GM) schools or city technology colleges (CTCs). In November 1988 ILEA sought from each LEA governor an assurance that they would support the ILEA line that the schools should retain their present status; two governors were unwilling to do this, arguing that to do so would mean acting as ILEA's delegates. ILEA then tried to remove the two governors under Section 21 of the 1944 Act and the governors sought judicial review to prevent this happening. The Court of Appeal said in its judgment that ILEA had no right to remove its nominated governors from a governing body, if by doing so it interfered with those governors' exercise of powers within a sphere of independent responsibility, as set out in the 1944 Education Act.

The 1986 Act made special provisions for the election of parent governors; such elections must in future be done by secret ballot, with postal voting for all eligible parents (this was rarely done prior to the Act; more usually only those attending a nominating meeting could vote). Although those who stand for election as parent governor must have a child in school at the time of election, they are elected for a period of four years and may if they wish, remain a governor for that time even if their child leaves the school before then. Previously, parent governors whose children left the school had to resign.

The 1986 Act also significantly adds to the powers and duties of governing bodies. LEAs were required to publish and regularly review a statement of their policy on the secular curriculum for their schools. Within this framework, governors were to consider, in conjunction with the headteacher, the curriculum aims of their school and how, if necessary, to modify the LEA's curriculum policy. The 1988 Act and the National Curriculum, however, reduce the amount of room for curriculum manoeuvre available to governors, although they will still be able to amend LEA curriculum policies within the constraints of the National Curriculum. Governors also share with the head the responsibility for ensuring that the education in their school is not politically biased and that any treatment of political issues is 'balanced'. A further curricular responsibility is that governors must also determine whether or not sex education takes place in their schools, having regard to 'moral considerations and the value of family life'. This particular section was taken further by an amendment to the 1988 Local Government Act which outlaws the promotion of homosexuality in schools. The 1986 Act also gave governing bodies the duty to write an annual report for parents, setting out what the govering body has done over the past year. The report has to be circulated to parents two weeks in advance of an annual meeting between the governors and the parents of all pupils in the school. This meeting is empowered to discuss and vote on any resolutions put forward, providing the parents of at least 20 per cent of the registered pupils are present.

Under the Act LEAs still retain ultimate control over the appointment and dismissal of school staff, although governors must be represented on the interview panels for headship appointments in equal numbers alongside LEA representatives and also get a say in shortlisting (previous practice on this varied; see Morgan, Hall and Mackay, 1983). So far as other teaching and non-teaching staff appointments are concerned, these must be advertized by the LEA but governors have responsibility for selecting and interviewing candidates and making a recommendation to the LEA. However, the 1988 Act quite significantly changes all these provisions except for those schools too small to have Local Management of Schools (LMS). LMS will give effective hiring and firing rights to schools and their governing bodies, although the LEA will remain the nominal employer and will retain some involvement in headteacher selection.

The final section of the 1986 Act required LEAs to make training available for governors (previous practice on this has been very variable, with many LEAs providing none at all) and offered LEAs the empowerment (but not requirement) to pay travel and subsistence allowances to governors. What was not included, perhaps surprisingly in view of the number of extra responsibilities given to governors and the emphasis on involving more parents and members of the wider community in governing schools, was anything requiring employers to give time off work to employees who are governors or any means of providing financial recompense for loss of wages to employed governors who take time off in order to carry out their responsibilities.

The 1988 Education Act

This Act, as we have already seen, is not entirely consistent with the provisions of the 1986 Act, which adds support to the view that the idea of a Reform Act was cobbled together during the 1987 General Election to attempt to deal with perceived parental concern about the workings of the education system, prior to subsequent privatization (Lawton and Chitty, 1988). The main features of the Act which are relevant to school governors are the National Curriculum, open enrolment, LMS, the possibility of opting out and the policy on charging for education. All except the last are the subject of separate chapters in this book. The Reform Act takes much further two strands of educational control — the enhancing of the power of the Secretary of State, even though some of this is in conjunction with other bodies like the National Curriculum Council — and the increase in consumer power over teachers and LEAs, or educational producers as it is becoming fashionable to call them. However, the roles of consumer and producer are more clearly delineated in theory than in reality since, for example, pupils are not considered to be consumers and teachers are still producers even if they are also parents of school-age children.

The Act has been made to look as though it heralds in great changes for education. So Kenneth Baker, Secretary of State, said about the then 1988 Bill at the North of England Education Conference in January 1988: 'It is about enhancing the life chances of young people. It is about devolution of authority and responsibility. It is about competition, choice and freedom . . . it is part of the search for — and achievement of — educational excellence. It is about quality and standards.' He might well have added that the Bill was also about ideology and rhetoric, because the sheer number of changes expected and the speed of their introduction must make anyone seriously interested in the future of state education wonder just how much thought and rational planning and research went into the Bill's preparation. Indeed it is possible to see the strengthening of central and government control over education as an attempt to achieve a radical change in the culture and ethos of state schooling, ultimately ending in a widespread shift to forms of privately funded schools, a move which would satisfy both those members of the Tory party who wanted to be seen to be doing 'something' about education and those who feel that the state should only provide a framework for education, not fund it as well.

The proposals were first set out in the Queen's Speech of June 1987, discussion papers were issued in the school holidays of 1987 and views sought by the early autumn. The short time allowed for consultation on the Bill itself merely prepared the way for what was to follow, although the consultation timescale attracted a good deal of adverse comment from both sides of the political fence (Haviland, 1988). Indeed, giving people little time to implement changes in schools seems to be part of the critique of education implied by the Act — education always moves slowly, unlike industry, so it must be made to hurry up — with little thought apparently having been given to exactly how all the necessary work would get done or its effects on morale when it got done hurriedly. The Bill was well established in its passage through the House by the end of 1987 and was given the Royal Assent at the end of July 1988.

Many of the innovations in the 1988 Act can only work with the help or at least the tacit consent of governors. Governors play a key role in making the initial decision to apply to the Secretary of State to opt out of local authority control. Indeed some parent governors may have stood for election with just this purpose in mind. Governors will have the responsibility of ensuring that their school's curriculum and assessment arrangements conform to the National Curriculum. They will have to work out a way of coping with open admissions policy — which could become a significant problem if their schools are either under or oversubscribed. The complex arrangements for charging for educational activities as set out in a DES circular in January 1989 (DES, 1989) will have to be turned into a workable policy by governors and heads. The whole Local Management of Schools (LMS) policy, once LEAs have worked out their formula funding arrangements and had these approved by the Secretary of State, will stand or fall by the ability and capacity of governors to cope with the heavy responsibilities it will impose on them, including hiring and firing of staff. The Act will allow all secondary schools and primary schools with more than 200 pupils to have full responsibility for managing their own schools and budgets. This will include staffing, resources, heating and lighting and cleaning, although LEAs will retain control over school transport, advisory services and administering pay, tax and pensions.

The notion of LMS has been welcomed by many schools and governing bodies, but the responsibilities it implies are very considerable ones to give to a governing body of untrained volunteers doing the task in their spare time, even though some training will have to be provided. Some people have interpreted LMS as being mainly about finance. But its implications are far wider than that, as Thomas's chapter in this volume demonstrates. Coopers and Lybrands' Report for the DES (Coopers and Lybrand, 1988) also makes this point strongly: 'The changes require a new culture and philosophy of the organization of education at the school level. They are more than purely financial: they need a general shift in management' (Coopers and Lybrand, 1988). Furthermore, Coopers and Lybrand say at the end of their report, 'It is difficult to say whether, in the long run, LMS by itself would lead to net savings or net costs.... On balance we would be surprised if there were net savings. However we have stressed how important it is that LMS should not be seen as a means of cost reduction; its purpose is to produce a more effective and responsive school system, not necessarily a cheaper one' (*ibid.*). Similar messages are writ loud and clear in the other innovations of the 1988 Act too. Reshaping governing bodies is ostensibly supposed to be about transferring power from producers to consumers and about making schools more 'effective'. But there is a need to look critically and sceptically at the producer/consumer analogy as applied to the educational context.

Consumers and producers — nearer the market place?

Underlying the last ten years of discussion and debate about the role of governors has been a desire to increase the participation and involvement of parents and employers (educational consumers), and to a lesser extent other lay members of the community, in the running of schools. In itself such a desire to make the governing of schools more representative of the wider community is commendable. However, as Whitehead and Aggleton (1986) point out, this desire is not quite straightforward as it might appear, since it is possible to point to distinctly different views about the nature of lay participation in the running of schools and about its purposes. One view is the wish, as an end in itself, to create more open and democratic forms of school government. The second view sees more open forms of school government, not as an end itself, or just as a means to greater public accountability of schools, but also as a way of wresting control over the structure and content of education away from the teaching profession and LEAs altogether. There is also a third view, particularly manifested in the 1988 Act, but not mentioned by Whitehead and Aggleton, which pays lip service to parental and community choice and involvement, but which puts forward consumer control of education as a hidden route to the future private funding of state schools. Making people other than teachers and LEAs responsible for running schools is one important step towards this process of privatization. Local management of schools will be a major plank in the attempted transfer of power from producers of education to consumers.

It is important to look carefully at the new rhetoric about producers and consumers in education. It is not necessarily what it seems. Producers in the public sector have had a bad press during the years of Thatcherism, whether they be teachers, social workers or refuse collectors. They are seen to be groups of workers who are in the main, lazy, left wing, inefficient and union-dominated. In addition, such groups are perceived as exercising too much power over their occupation, caring too little about those they serve and are considered poorly trained to do their jobs. Consumers, on the other hand, are individuals (rather than collectivities) who are able to exercise freedom (including voting Conservative), are good at making choices in the market place, know what they want, are in favour of high standards and efficiency and put strong emphasis on value for money. Both conceptions are stereotypes based on a conception of society which says there is no such thing as society but only individuals. Consumers in the public sector are goodies whilst producers are baddies. The stereotypes mask real social differences — gender, age, class, ethnicity — within the two categories consumer and producer. They also mask contradictions and inconsistencies. Why is it *parents* of school pupils who are considered educational consumers rather than the pupils themselves? The categories themselves are not even mutually exclusive, especially in the context of education. Thus a teacher-producer is often also a parent-consumer; an industrial manager (consumer) may teach an evening class (producer). Furthermore, in other contexts (such as the food industry), producers, far from being attacked, are lauded and protected from consumer demands (for safer food, for instance). So the notion of pitting producers against consumers is simplistic in the extreme but it clearly forms an important part of making education more 'market-oriented' and ultimately more likely to be privately funded, so that there is a direct economic link between parent and teacher or employer and teacher.

Consumer power — which consumers and why?

We now need to turn to the question of who consumers actually are. Parental consumers, of course, come in more guises than parent governors. Parental involvement in schools can mean parents attending discussions about their individual children with teacher; it might also include helping in the classroom or giving a talk to a class. But is can also mean a more formal representation of parental interests such as being on the committee of a parent teacher or 'Friends of the School' organization. Being a governor is a very particular form of parental involvement. The Leverhulme study of parent governors in Devon suggests that in some areas during Autumn 1988 standing for election as a governor proved quite popular (*Education*, 23 December 1988). Our own study, however, suggests that this wasn't universal. In our sample some schools had either insufficient candidates or the same number of nominations as vacancies. Co-opted governors are also intended to represent consumer interests, this time in the form of commerce and industry or the local community. Unlike parent governors, co-opted members are not elected but are chosen by the other members of the governing body. In many LEAs considerable efforts were devoted to attracting people who might wish to be considered as possible co-optees. But in our own study four out of fifteen schools had not filled all their co-opted places by their first formal meeting. Just as parent governors may cover a wide spectrum of interests, so too do co-opted governors. The Leverhulme study (*Education*, 23 December 1988) found that in their 23 Devon schools, 66 per cent of the co-opted governors were male (it was highest of all, 88 per cent, in middle schools). But only thirteen of seventy-nine governors were recognizably part of the local business community and only 4 per cent were 'housewives' (Doe, 1988). From the preliminary results of our own research, it seems that boards have mostly gone for a combination of business people, generally those at a fairly senior level, and people who are active in either the voluntary or public sector in the catchment area of the school. The latter group, not unnaturally, includes some teachers (for instance a deputy head of a secondary school being co-opted onto the governing body of a feeder primary school). The functions of these different kinds of co-opted governors and the rationale for their selection of course vary. Whereas industrial governors are valued for their employment contacts (especially in secondary schools) and their financial or business expertise, community governors are more likely already to have some connection with the school and are often closely in touch with the way the school is seen by local residents.

Governor representativeness — whose interests?

For both co-opted and parent governors the issues of whom they represent and how they feed back to those groups are crucially important concerns at the present time, since the 1986 Act and the 1988 Act assume that this will happen. Some parent governors come up through the ranks of Parent-Teacher Associations (PTAs) and claim representativeness on that basis, as well as being able to use their Association to communicate with parents. Other parents represent only their children and although very real efforts are undoubtedly being made to find ways in which other parents can contact and raise issues with parent governors, this is not an easy task. The Kogan (1984) study found that strategies used by parent governors included PTA meetings, attending teacher-run parents evenings and, in primary schools, meeting parents at the school gate. However, the question of how parents communicate with the governing body is potentially a tricky one. A London parent governor at a large comprehensive produced her own newsletter in the autumn of 1988 but was refused permission to distribute it through the school because it was both the work of only one governor and because it was highly critical of the local LEA (Hempel, 1988). Governors are supposed to hold power as a corporate body, not as individuals, so the line between good communication and contravening instruments and articles is a fine one. Attempts by another parent governor, this time from Kent and also a chief executive in a finance company, to use his status as a governor to tout for business, was viewed with concern by both the LEA and the DES (Watson, 1988). The same governor subsequently became prime mover in persuading a group of parents to sign a petition to the governors requesting a ballot on opting out, even though the governing body as a whole was not in favour of moves to opt out and was happy for an LEA-inspired merger with another school to take place.

The middle-class, white background of governors raises very real questions about the inadequate representation of working class and black or Asian groups. Of course no-one is asking that working class parents should be massively represented on the governing bodies of schools where most pupils are middle class or that Asian parents should predominate in an almost all-white school. Yet the converse of this, largely Asian schools with mainly white governing bodies, is not infrequently found and does raise issues about how, in such schools, majority working class and Asian interests are to be represented. Not all previous research has tackled this issue. The Kogan study (1984) had insufficient data about the make-up of particular school populations to say for sure whether parent governors were representative of the school intake as a whole. But Golby, director of the Leverhulme 'parent as school governor' project, has noted from their much more recent study that 'a widening gap in participation may be opening up . . . school government may be yet another instrument of social division' (*Education*, 23 December 1988).

The discussion about representation in relation to parent and co-opted governors is differently perceived from that of the question of who should be an LEA governor. Concern has been shown by the DES, the Department of the Environment and MPs about the political packing of governing bodies with LEA nominations which reflect only one political party, whatever the political composition of the local council (Surkes, 1988). But most of the recent concern about representativeness has been about parent and co-opted governors. The 1986 Act itself has already tackled concerns about political governors by reducing LEA membership of governing bodies, since LEA governors are assumed to represent producer rather than consumer power. Our own research suggests, however, that LEA governors are not always so easily distinguishable from other categories of governor, especially amongst those who are not councillors. 'Business' governors and educational experts, as well as politicians, are to be found amongst the ranks of LEA governors.

Why are the new governors needed?

There are, of course, a number of assumptions other than representativeness underlying the increased numbers of co-opted and parent governors on governing bodies. The same assumptions also underpin the 1986 Act's requirement that each governing body should hold an annual meeting with parents (Earley, 1988). Two of these assumptions stand out, although they are themselves contradictory. The first is the belief that parents and employers are very dissatisfied with their children's schooling and need a forum where they can complain as well as a means by which to impose their view of education. The actual source of this belief is difficult to discover; for example, many industrialists know little about education and employers of school leavers often place little faith in formal qualifications (Brown and Ashton, 1988). Parental views on education do, of course, vary but the 'highly dissatisfied' view is hardly supported by the very low turnouts at annual governors' meetings for parents. The NFER (1988) study on the first year (1987) of these meetings found that the LEA average attendance across all schools was just under 5 per cent of those parents entitled to attend. The second assumption made is that educational consumers are a homogenous group who will act and work in predictable ways in relation to education. This assumption too is difficult to relate to any real body of empirical knowledge. After all, parents and those who work in industry, if we include employees as well as employers, are subject to the same divisions of class, gender, race and ethnicity as the rest of the population.

The lack of representation of disadvantaged social groups on governing bodies has already been mentioned. Other researchers and organizations have noticed it too. An NFER study of governor training published in 1988 (Streatfield, 1988) recommended that more attention be paid in future to recruiting black and Asian governors. The Equal Opportunities Commission is also concerned about the relationship between governing bodies and the pursuit of equal opportunities, both in terms of who becomes a governor and what policies governors adopt (EOC, 1986). The Leverhulme study in Devon has found that although 57 per cent of parent governors were female, this gender trend was reversed for co-opted governors, where 66 per cent were male. No governors in the Devon study were black or Asian. From our own research, which is still at an early stage, it is apparent that there are more men than women on secondary school governing bodies and there are only a handful of black and Asian governors in our fifteen case study schools, which include three largely Asian schools (this is discussed in more detail in Deem, 1989).

Another issue has been about when a parent is not really a 'genuine' parent. This question has been brought to prominence by the belief that there may be a high number of parent governors elected in the autumn of 1988 who are also teachers (but not in the same school, which is disallowed). The evidence for this is limited (Hadfield, 1989; Judd, 1988) and needs to be carefully examined before jumping to conclusions. For example, the Exeter University study of Devon parent-governors found that 57 per cent of their sample came from education-related or professional jobs. But education-related could mean a school secretary, caretaker, welfare assistant or a university administrator, none of whom are school teachers. The National Confederation of Parent-Teacher Associations has expressed concern about the possibility of teacher numerical domination of governing bodies, if teachers are also being elected as parent governors or by being co-opted as well as holding teacher governor positions. The DES has asked NFER to investigate how many teachers are parent or co-opted governors (Hadfield, 1989), presumably with a view to restricting teachers to teacher governor positions only. So whilst it apparently does not matter to the DES that there are very few ethnic minority or working class parent governors it does matter that teachers are parent governors. The latter, of course, results in a cross-cutting of the category of consumer governor with that of producer governor. A teacher is not regarded as a real parent.

Golby, whose Leverhulme project evidence is one source of the information on teachers as parent governors that has alarmed the DES has rightly condemned the view that teachers should only become teacher governors; he said in a letter to the *Times Educational Supplement*: 'The representation of others will not be improved by diminishing the rights of teachers who are also parents and citizens. Rather the efforts of professionals to involve others in the life of schools should be supported' (Golby, 1989). The DES concern about teachers masquerading as parent governors is even more interesting because parent governors, of course, are elected, not appointed; so even democracy doesn't stop producers getting muddled up with consumers. All the evidence so far points to the view that for the DES the ideal parent governor is white and middle class, with a strong, preferably religious moral code, is employed in industry and has a strictly instrumental interest in being a governor (their children's education or controlling teachers) rather than any wider notion of community involvement in schooling. Governing body recomposition, then, has not necessarily produced exactly what the DES wanted, nor has it produced a wider representation of all social groups on governing bodies. But being on a governing body is one thing. What is achieved, once there, is another matter.

Politicization and school-governing bodies

The political or other nature of school-governing bodies has long been argued about, perhaps particularly because party political nominations have for several decades dominated school governing bodies in many areas, despite Kogan's argument that the intention of the 1944 Act was that no single group should occupy a dominant position in the running of the state education system. Indeed Kogan's (1984) study found that the political culture of the LEA itself was a fairly crucial variable in determining whether or not governing bodies were party politicized. However, the whole context of governing bodies has changed quite significantly with the advent of the 1988 Act, coming so soon after the 1986 Act. Kogan's research suggests that in the early 1980s most governing bodies tended to see themselves as supporters of their school and acted as pressure groups in obtaining or trying to obtain more resources for the school from the LEA. Councillors who were also governors were one major channel through which that pressure was applied. Now governors are supposed to apply pressure to schools as well as to LEAs, since both institutions are identified as producers. Furthermore, the need to pressure the LEA will diminish as LMS comes into play, although whilst formula funding is being fought over it will be very important, particularly for schools which stand to lose money from the low weighting of social criteria or because they have higher than average costs.

It is hard to see governing bodies as anything other than political organizations, since what they do, implicitly or explicitly, is to exercise power over the running of schools. This is so whether governors operate by applying pressure to schools, LEAs and the DES, whether they simply support and advise the school or whether they actually take on, as far as practicable, directing and running the establishment. However, the exercise of power and party politics are not synonymous with each other, although in the English and Welsh context, the commonsense notion of something being political implies party politics. Hence any governor who is not an LEA nominee or a member of a political party is widely assumed to be non-political. This assumption underlies the new legislation (ironically, also the work of politicians) and also underpins the interpretation of that legislation by those organizations (for example the National Association of

Governors and Managers) who seek to represent the 'general interest' governor.

Clearly, some governors are more concerned than others about the appearance of party political characteristics in school governing bodies. The Leverhulme study (Exeter Society, 1987) found that parent governors were very concerned about party politics surfacing in governor meetings since they did not regard this as appropriate. Sallis, equally concerned about any such trend, feels that it is unlikely that school governing bodies will become politicized and has commented thus: 'My impression from visiting many schools is that the majority of school parents are frightened of politics in school affairs and very suspicious of anyone who introduces party issues' (Sallis, 1988). The National Confederation of Parent-Teacher Associations (NCPTA) is, however, apparently worried that this politicization has already occurred as a result of the new legislation. Complaining about teachers and politicians standing for election as parent governors and also sliding in as co-optees, an executive member of NCPTA said in October 1988, 'This is the craziest piece of legislation. Here (in Dorset) we used to have governing bodies which were non-political. Now they are extremely politicised' (Judd, 1988). Paradoxically, the legislation to which the NCPTA member referred (the 1986 Act) seems to have been designed with an intention to reduce 'political' nominees, for example by uncoupling the dates for the re-establishment of governing bodies from the dates of relevant local elections. However, what the NCPTA and others seem not to have fully realized is that it is the superimposition of the 1988 Act on the 1986 Act which has led to the politicization, by changing and greatly extending what governors are responsible for. The 1988 Act is a very political piece of legislation, which owes as much to ideology as to rationality. It is precisely the advent of things like local management of schools and the possibilities of opting out that have led groups of all kinds, political parties, teachers unions and governor pressure groups, to try to ensure full representation on governing bodies. A non-political response to such legislation is just not possible, since the Reform Act tackles head-on the exercise of power over schooling.

The concern of parent governors about 'political' governors, however, is also worthy of a little unpacking. Like the 'teachers as parent governors' issue, it is not a straightforward matter. There are some good reasons why some parents and the governor pressure groups feel as they do. Past research on governors has indicated that political governors do not always necessarily behave in an exemplary manner on governing bodies. Indeed, they may alienate other governors by elitist attitudes, the way meetings are conducted and by suggesting to them that mere parents are too insignificant to be of much use (Exeter Society, 1987). Several parents in the Leverhulme study complained of being patronized or 'fobbed off' on issues they felt were deserving of more detailed attention. Parents also made complaints about co-options being rushed through so that new governors hardly understood what was happening (Exeter Society, 1987). In our own research it is clear that in some schools the election of a chairperson was little more than a ritual, with new governors playing little part in it since, unlike previous governors of the school (mostly those from the LEA), they did not know any of the actors.

Hence several bodies re-elected previous LEA nominees as their chair, although this was not true of all our research governing bodies and five of them did elect parent governors as their chairs. However, given the scale of changes that the new governing bodies have needed to cope with, it is understandable that there should be attempts to ensure continuity between old and new governing bodies. Where any voluntary body has new members, it is likely to take time for those members to understand the system. Chairs of governing bodies are in any case subject to annual re-election.

Under the pre-1986 system LEA governors certainly did have a privileged position, if they chose to use it, relative to other governors. This privilege arose because of their more informed knowledge of the political system running education, better access to information, their circle of contacts including LEA officers and their greater experience of running and attending political meetings (Exeter Society, 1987). The methods of running meetings used by experienced politicians used to coping with long and controversial agendas can also disturb new governors and inhibit them from speaking, even if that is not the intention. This finding emerges strongly from the interim report from the Leverhulme study (Exeter Society, 1987). However the impression gained in our study from two terms of attending formal governors' meetings is that often the most efficient and rapid meetings involving decision-making are run by experienced political chairs. A more relaxed approach may have other costs; meetings can take as long as five hours and be rambling occasions in which few decisions are made, even if everyone feels they are valued.

We can then begin to see why parents, wrongly in my view, see politics as having no place in governing bodies. They are wrong precisely because governing schools is irretrievably about the exercise of power. In future, governors will have to fight their corner harder than ever if they are to tackle LMS, the National Curriculum, open admissions, charging and many other things. Education is a profoundly political issue, from who pays for it to what content it has and the 1988 Act has emphasized this in a very pointed way. There is no longer any even loose consensus about education; views do differ quite sharply and governing bodies will find themselves in the midst of heated debates about the way forward, both amongst their own members, between teachers and governors and between governors, teachers and central government.

Will governing bodies be able to cope?

It seems possible that with the new responsibilities of governors, it may be the financial experts and the education experts rather than politicians and heads, who take over the pole positions in governing bodies, although power will not be yielded easily. The whole strategy of giving power to the consumer rather than the producer is a risky one, particularly since as I have shown, one cannot guarantee in advance the social and political affiliations or the world views of governors. Even if governors do manage to wrest power from educational professionals, they may not act in the ways hoped for by the instigators of the 1988 Act. Also, as I have shown, there is a very blurred line between consumer and producer and the whole notion of these two catagories being invoked as the main contestants in the battle for the future shape of education must be problematic for anyone who does not accept the associated efforts to subject education to the laws of the free market economy. But whoever governors are and no matter what interests they represent, there must also be an element of doubt about whether governors will have the time and be able to develop the kind of coping strategies necessary to take power over schools away from professional educators.

It is unclear at present whether headteachers will continue to dominate governing bodies in the way that they did prior to the new legislation. Certainly headteachers have often viewed governors either with disdain or as part of a necessary but relatively unimportant ritual in the past. The Kogan study (1984) suggested that the relationship between the head and the governing body was crucial in determining how governors work. Hall, Mackay and Morgan (1986), in their intensive study of the working lives of headteachers, found a variety of different approaches to the head/governors relationship: one was always at odds with them, another saw them a lot and tried to get their approval for his decisions, a third only used them to express his opposition to aspects of LEA policy and the fourth had a very good rapport with the governing body and encouraged their involvement in the school. The most sceptical of the heads in their study said, 'I can invent a governors' report without having to refer to much, I'm afraid, out of my head. I know that will keep them quiet' (Hall, Mackay and Morgan, 1986). This head was concerned to get through meetings without confrontation and filled the agenda with uncontroversial items. Other studies of secondary heads, for example a DES funded project looking at 40 heads in six LEAs, suggest that some might have difficulty sharing power with governors since even in the terms of their relationship to teachers they are often autocratic and may lack the training and skills necessary to cope with the complex tasks of running large schools (Lodge, 1986, 1987). A recent book by Jones (1988), drawing on a questionnaire survey of 400 members of the Secondary Heads Association, found only four heads who had positive comments about relationships with governors. A review in *School Governor* (March, 1988) noted with dismay some of the comments made by heads in the survey: two examples were, 'I detest justifying my work to ignorant governors'; and 'I dislike writing governors' reports and attending governors' meetings'.

Much of the research on governing bodies, then, suggests that prior to the 1986 Act a skilful head could manipulate governors, feeding them selected bits of information and pushing them into a supportive role whether this was what the governors wanted or not. But the 1986 and 1988 Acts make this more difficult. Governors now not only have wider responsibilities defined in law but may potentially, as LMS and the National Curriculum get under way, be taken to court for failing to exercise those responsibilities in accordance with the law. Heads retain the option under the new legislation of opting not to be a governor and this can allow some distancing from the governing body's decisions. But with substantial authority vested in governors for overseeing the general running of schools, the curriculum and financing, even heads who are not governors will probably find it less feasible to keep the governing body purely as an advisory group. Governors will need to spend more time in schools and in formal, informal and subgroup meetings of the governing body. It will be harder for those heads who wish to do so, to conceal things from governors and continue to manipulate them. But it will still be possible. It is after all the professionals, heads and teachers, and ancillary workers, not the lay governors, who spend all their working days in schools. No governor who is not a teacher, even if they come into school as a voluntary helper, is likely to have the same understanding and knowledge as someone for whom the school is a workplace.

First impressions from our research of the coping strategies which governing bodies are employing to handle their new responsibilities suggest that many of them are busy burying themselves in endless meetings and pieces of paper. Whilst armed with good intentions, such strategies may ultimately be self-defeating — there will be no time or energy left to make decisions or dream up new ideas. The 'consumers' have been given the potential to control; however, in practice they may prove unequal to the task, by being either unable or unwilling to control producers. If governors prove unwilling or unable to take over the day to day running of schools from professional teachers it is likely to expose and question the controversial basis on which consumers are set against producers in an arena which is far removed from the economic market place. It would also point up the folly of expecting voluntary bodies to cope with making crucial decisions about things like charging for education, the National Curriculum and LMS at breakneck speed. If, however, the consumer power over schools strategy succeeds, in conjunction with LMS, it is likely to move us closer to a privatized system of education, which appears to be one of the hidden agendas of the 1988 Act. Governors now have the power, in theory, to run the schools. Whether they can actually do so, however, still remains to be seen.

References

BACON, W. (1978) *Public Accountability and the Schooling System*, London, Harper & Row.

BOGDANOR, V. (1979) 'Power and participation', *Oxford Review of Education*, Vol. 5, No. 2, pp. 157–68.

BOYSON, R. (1981) 'Collapse of confidence', in *The Crisis in Education*, London, Woburn Press.

BROWN, P. and ASHTON, D.N. (1987) *Educational Unemployment and Labour Markets*, Lewes, Falmer Press.

COOPERS & LYBRAND (1988) *Local Management of Schools*, London, HMSO.

COX, C. and BOYSON, R. (1975) *Black Papers*, London, Dent.

DALE, R. (1981) 'Control, accountability and William Tyndale', in Dale, R., Esland, G., Fergusson, R. and MacDonald, M. (Eds), *Education and the State: Politics, Patriarchy and Practice*, Vol. 2, Barcombe, Falmer Press.

DEEM, R. (1988) 'The 1988 Education Bill — some issues and implications' *Journal of Education Policy*, Vol.3, No. 2, pp. 181–89.

DEEM, R. (1989) 'Feminist sociology and educational change — studying the reform of school governing bodies'. Papers presented to British Sociological Association Conference, Plymouth Polytechnic, March.

DEPARTMENT OF EDUCATION AND SCIENCE (DES) (1977) *A New Partnership for Our Schools* (the Taylor Report), London, HMSO.

DES (1988) *Circular 2/89, Education Reform Act 1988: charges for school activities*, London, DES.

DOE, B. (1988) 'Good turnout for the middle classes', *The Times Educational Supplement*, 16 December, p. 15.

EARLEY, P. (1988) *Governors Reports and Annual Parents Meetings*, Slough, NFER.

EQUAL OPPORTUNITIES COMMISSION (1986) *Equal Opportunities and the School Governor*, Manchester, EOC.

EXETER SOCIETY FOR CURRICULUM STUDIES RESEARCH GROUP (1987) *Parents as School Governors: interim report*, Exeter, University of Exeter.

GOLBY, M. (1989) letter to *The Times Educational Supplement*, 3 February, p. A23.

HALL, V., MACKAY, H. and MORGAN, C. (1986) *Headteachers at Work*, Milton Keynes, Open University Press.

HADFIELD, G. (1989) 'Teachers "exploiting parent power laws" ', *Sunday Times*, 22 January.

HAVILAND, J. (1988) *Take Care, Mr. Baker!* London, Fourth Estate.

HEMPEL, S. (1988) 'Through the grapevine', *The Times Educational Supplement*, 13 January p. 25.

JONES, A. (1988) *Leadership for Tomorrow's Schools*, Oxford, Blackwell.

JUDD, J. (1988) 'Parents robbed of school power', *The Observer*, 23 October.

KOGAN, M., JOHNSON, D., PACKWOOD, T., and WHITTAKER, T. (Eds) (1984) *School Governing Bodies*, London, Heinemann.

LAWTON, D. and CHITTY, C. (1988) *The National Curriculum*, Bedford Way Papers 33, London, University of London, Institute of Education.

LODGE, B. (1986) 'Poly researchers say heads are still far too autocratic', *The Times Educational Supplement*, 7 March.

LODGE, B. (1987) 'Struggling to cope with the unfamiliar', *The Times Educational Supplement*, 2 May, p. 7.

MORGAN, C., HALL, V. and MACKAY, H. (1983) *The Selection of Secondary Headteachers*, Milton Keynes, Open University Press.

NFER SCHOOL GOVERNORS' RESEARCH GROUP (1988) 'Governors' reports to parents and annual parents meetings: a national overview', in Earley, P. (1988) *op. cit.*

O'CONNOR, M. (1987) 'Promotion for PC Plod', *The Guardian*, 9 June, p. 17.

SALLIS, J. (1988) *Schools, Parents and Governors*, London, Routledge.

SIMON B. (1988) *Bending the Rules: the Baker 'reform' of education*, London, Lawrence and Wishart.

SOCIETY OF EDUCATION OFFICERS/ASSOCIATION OF CHIEF POLICE OFFICERS (1986) *Liaison between Police and Schools*, London.

STREATFIELD, D. (1988) *School Governor Training and Information for Governors*, Slough, NFER.

SURKES, S. (1988) 'Ministries to discuss governors', *The Times Educational Supplement*, 23 September, p. 15.

TAYLOR, F. (1983) 'Why teacher governors are justifying their seat on the board', *The Times Educational Supplement*, 7 October, p. 4.

WATSON, C. (1988) 'School governor "touted for trade" ', *The Guardian*, 28 October.

WHITEHEAD, J. and AGGLETON, P. (1986) 'Participation and popular control on school governing bodies: the case of the Taylor Report and its aftermath', *British Journal of Sociology of Education*, Vol. 7, No. 4, pp. 433–49.

10
Race, Schooling and The 1988 Education Reform Act

Jan Hardy and Chris Vieler-Porter

On the 2 October 1985 Ray Honeyford, headteacher of Drummond Middle School Bradford, was invited to attend an educational seminar at 10 Downing Street with the Prime Minister, cabinet ministers and a number of right wing educationalists to discuss the long-term direction of the educational system. Ray Honeyford had been for three years the centre of extreme controversy regarding his published views on the multicultural education policies of his employing authority and his racist views of the family backgrounds and origins of black pupils at his school. Thatcher's views on multicultural education have never been signalled more clearly.

The black community remain fundamentally discontent with the educational system in its lack of receptiveness to the needs of black children. Equally many schools which have attempted to implement antiracist initiatives have faced suspicion from white parents and in most LEAs little support from education officials. In a political and media climate which stresses ideals of individual and family above community and society and which depoliticizes, individualizes and pathologises disadvantage, it is difficult for a school or LEA to deliver social justice or even to win the ideological ground necessary to set about doing so. The few LEAs which have attempted to represent black communities and to control service delivery directly towards antiracist ends, with determination, have frequently been the object of media vilification and political attack.

As Whitty and Menter note, the influence of New Right racism can be detected in the 1988 Act in a number of manifestations.

> The very emphasis on 'National' in the National Curriculum, the centrality of a notion of national testing with all the cultural and linguistic bias which that implies, the failure to recognize languages other than Welsh and English as pupils' first language, and the omission in any of the Consultative papers, let alone in the Act, of any reference to the 1985 report of Lord Swann's Committee of Enquiry into the Education of Children from Ethnic Minority groups 'Education for All'. (Whitty and Menter, 1989)

The 1988 Education Reform Act is part of a series of strategies designed to facilitate the restructuring of society in contemporary terms. The characteristics of contemporary society include a shift to the new 'information technologies', greater 'flexibility' and a decentralization of the forms of labour and the organization of work, a decline in the traditional manufacturing industries and the growth of service and computer based industries, the de-regulation of services and functions of the state through privatization or contracting-out, an increase in the range of choices and the differentiation of market products, the reorientation of promotion through marketing and design and packaging. Underpinning these shifts is a narrow conception of the individual as consumer, divorced from those traditional attributes of class, 'race', religion, language and dialect.

The Education Reform Act is the latest and most far reaching in a series of education based legislation: the 1980 and 1986 Education Acts; a shift to vocationalism in education as exemplified by the Technical and Vocational Education Initiative (TVEI) and project funding through the Manpower Services Commission; the 1987 Teachers' Pay and Conditions Act; central government control of teacher in-service training, LEATGS (previously known as GRIST); and new developments in assessing (and therefore labelling) pupils through the use of attainment targets. These assessments will form part of a pupil's 'profile', the purpose of which is to provide potential employers with a detailed description of the characteristics and attributes of a given pupil above and beyond the level of their attainment. As a result of these imposed changes in education, the ERA should not be seen in isolation but as part of a systematic programme of change. The programme on education has occurred within the context of legislation that has sought to return numerous state industries to the private sector, enacting further restrictive changes in Immigration Laws, as well as introducing new laws governing housing, trade unions and local government. The essential ideological thrust of these changes is a shift from public service to private practice.

The failure of social democracy and consensus politics in the 1960s and 1970s has provided the present Conservative Government with the ideological arguments for their present policies. The social-democratic project was founded upon the assumption that the state could legitimately act as the representative and guardian of collective social interests. However the reality became one in which interventions in the economy were increasingly less efficient and welfare policies seemingly necessitated ever larger bureaucracies for a poorer quality of service. The image of the state from the 1960s onwards increasingly became one of a paternalistic landlord over the communities it was intended to serve.

Throughout the 1980s, a period of far-reaching political activity, government policies and the extensive social and economic restructuring of society have not been perceived or experienced evenly, neither have they been met with universal approval. There have been confrontations between the unions and the police, between the unions and certain 'captains' of industry. Property prices in the south-east have risen as have unemployment figures in the North, small private investors have seen their savings drop in the stock market 'crash', the inner city areas have seen civil disorder. Troyna and Williams (1986) show that this economic restructuring and the simultaneous effect of government policies and reductions in funding, particularly in the fields of housing and social services, had their most negative effects in precisely the geo-political spaces occupied by black communities. During this period the 'Falklands War' (sic) provided a dramatic example of the potential of nationalism to unite the nation and to rescue Thatcherism at a time when the government was at its lowest point in the opinion polls.

This image of 'nation' was an important and early part of Conservative Party legislation. The 1981 Nationality Act redefined British nationality but more importantly than the actual boundaries of belonging that were constructed was the whole symbolic and ideological interest invested in the construction of a national identity.

Consequent to this construction of the nation there was also a construction and attack on the alien, those individuals and communities who are perceived as the cause of civil decay and as a threat. This has appeared as a heavily orchestrated political and media attack on the activities, standards and policies of trade unions, political organizations of the left, left-wing teachers, progressive education, certain local authorities, 'illegal immigrants' and 'welfare scroungers' as well as state institutions. Within this generalized attack there has been a consistent, highly selective and specific focus upon 'race' — providing a 'lens' through which the crisis has been articulated. Examples of this political and media attack within the field of education include the issues of parental choice as in the Dewsbury case. Here a group of white parents insisted on their children attending a different school from the school allocated by the LEA because the Church of England primary school had a majority Asian intake. The white parents argued that the school would not be able to support the culture of their children. The central role of the media in articulating the demands of these white parents and selectively focusing on the issue of their right to choose the school for their children, enabled the issue of parental choice, already a key strategy in Tory education reform, to be played out in racial terms.

A further example of the important role of the popular media can be found in the attack on anti-racist policies. The supposed 'failures of anti-racist policies' in Burnage High School, Manchester being the prime example. Here anti-racist policies were presented as the cause of the breakdown of order in the school and implicitly the death of Ahmed Ullah. Little media attention was focused on the previous disciplinary record of Darren Colburn who killed Ahmed Ullah, the management of the school or previous cases of racial harassment and attack within the school. The Macdonald enquiry established to investigate the incident has still to be published in full. Racism killed Ahmed Ullah. Mismanagement, minimal and sectarian involvement and consultation conditioned the environment to make it possible.

Other examples include the role of headteachers with regard to LEA policies as in the case of Honeyford, Drummond Middle School and Bradford LEA; the issues of LEA policies and staffing as in Brent's Development Programme for Racial Equality. In his 1978 article 'Racism and Reaction' Stuart Hall made the point that popular racism has often proved an invaluable ideological position at moments of 'moral panics'.

> This is not a crisis of race. But race punctuates and periodizes the crisis. Race is the lens through which people come to perceive that a crisis is developing. It is the framework through which the crisis is experienced. (Hall, 1978)

The present crisis in British Education is not a crisis of 'race' but 'race' has been used to present and represent the crisis and to legitimate the kinds of 'reform' contained within the Education Reform Act.

The construction of the 'nation' implicit in the Act can be highlighted by reference to two extracts from leading Conservative politicians, spanning Conservative rule in the 1980s. The first piece is spoken by Margaret Thatcher leader of the Conservative Party and about to win the 1979 General Election.

> There was a committee which looked at it [immigration] and said that if we went on as we are then by the end of the century there would be four million people of the New Commonwealth and Pakistan here. Now that's an awful lot and I think it means that people are really rather afraid that the country might be rather swamped by people with a different culture. And you know the British character has done so much for Democracy, for law and done so much throughout the world that if there is any fear that it might be swamped, people are going to react and be rather hostile to those coming in. We are a British Nation with British characteristics, every country can take some small minorities and in many ways they add to the richness and variety of this country. The moment the minority threatens to become a big one people get frightened. (Margaret Thatcher, interviewed on World in Action, Granada TV 1979)

During October 1987 Channel 4 News invited Kenneth Baker to produce his own report on the Education Reform Act for the programme; the newscaster was at pains to remind the audience that the views expressed in the special report were those of Kenneth Baker himself and not those of the programme or channel. The words spoken by Baker anchored a range of images. Firstly (#1) Baker's voice over images of him at work in his office at the DES. Then (#2) he turns and talks directly to camera. Then the image changes (#3) to outside in the grounds of a secondary school with Baker's voice over the images before there is a further image change (#4) showing Baker in a school library sitting around a table with some parents.

> (#1) When Margaret Thatcher made me Education Secretary seven months ago I was delighted. This is the best and most challenging position in Government because our children are the future of the Country. But when I compared the achievements of our schools with several other countries I saw that we were falling behind. (#2) The

> reforms which I'll be introducing over the next twelve months will improve the quality of education for all our children throughout the country. The simple truth is that while much of our education is good, it's not good enough. (#3) There are two fundamental aims behind our reforms. Raising standards and increasing choice. I want parents to have a greater say over which schools their children go to and a greater commitment to those schools. I also want to ensure that when our children leave school they will be ready for work in a very competitive and technically advanced world. At the heart of our reforms is the National Curriculum reinforced by attainment targets for children at the age of 7, 11, 14 and 16. This will help parents, pupils and teachers to know where they stand both locally and nationally. (#4) Many parents at the moment don't know how their children are doing as I found out when I spoke to parents in Northampton. (Kenneth Baker during his Channel 4 News special report transmitted 21 October 1987)

Throughout this section of the report there are no images which affirm the multicultural, multiracial or multiethnic nature of contemporary British Society. Rather, an homogenous image of British children is portrayed, with children dressed in school uniform and being white. It is not till later when the question of education in the inner cities is raised that we see any black children. It is important to stress that the report that Baker produced for Channel 4 was/is his report. Within the extracts offered both by Baker and Thatcher is the invocation of that aspect of the ideology that lay behind the establishment of State Education.

> Civilised communities throughout the world are massing themselves together, each mass being measured by its force; and if we are to hold our position among men of our own race or among the nations of the world we must make up the smallness of our numbers by increasing the intellectual force of the individual. (W.E. Forster speech to the Education Bill 1870 in Hansard)

Thatcher talks about 'British character', Baker about 'our children' and Foster about 'our own race'. The discourse here, presented by Tory politicians past and present, holds as fundamental the interests of all individuals. 'There is no such thing as society. There are individual men and women and there are families' (Margaret Thatcher, February 1989). The language is not just a 'language of unity', it is also a language that seeks to shift political discourse from that which sees the interest of the masses in the institutions of the state, to the interest of the masses in the pursuit of self interest through those institutions. 'I want parents to have a greater say over which schools their children go to'. This language has been repeated on a number of occasions as Government Ministers have sought to encourage us all to buy a part of the institutions and the economy. This under the banner of freedom of choice.

The Education Reform Act aims to provide a 'popular' education within an ideological framework which is individualistic, competitive and racist. The Act aims to increase parental choice through open admissions where so called 'artificial ceilings' on school numbers are removed. It is instructive to examine the way this aspect of the Act is ideologically constructed in the booklet Education Reform published by the DES for parents, teachers and school governors.

> Many parents already get their first choice because the 1980 Education Act gives them the right to name the school they would prefer their child to attend, and ensures that they can be refused their preference only in strictly defined circumstances. But in so many cases, parents are disappointed because artificial ceilings are set on the number of places available at popular schools. That barrier needs to be removed. (DES, 1987a)

Two points are immediately obvious. The notion of individual choice in an unequal society is heavily ideological. In effect, of course, it will provide choice only for those who have the means to transport their children to alternative schools. It will further encourage and enable racist 'white flight' from multiracial schools (the Dewsbury syndrome) and further weaken the position of many such schools which are frequently located in those urban districts most affected by demographic drift and falling rolls. Where local schools close then the links between schools and the communities they serve will be further weakened. The second point about the ideological construction above is that attempts by LEAs to plan service delivery on a social basis where factors such as demographic change, social disadvantage and community needs can be taken into account are dismissed by the term 'artificial ceilings'. The argument for open admissions is of course that the 'best schools' will survive and thrive through the mechanism of consumer choice. In fact the result will be social polarization and racial segregation. Where white parents view multiracial schools as bad-schools no amount of good education will change those choices.

Opting for grant-maintained status has not, at the time of writing, proved as popular as the government would have wanted. In the main it has been precisely those schools threatened by closure or amalgamation through LEA rationalization programmes which have seen this option as an attractive one. If the government can overcome uncertainties about the administrative and bureaucratic consequences of opting out and if, as seems probable, some financial incentives can be offered in direct or indirect forms then grant-maintained status may become an attractive option. Grant-maintained status may appeal particularly to the schools which have resisted attempts to offer comprehensive let alone a multiracial education and particularly to ex-grammar schools in the shires and in the suburbs which have the strong support of the white middle class in preserving their character. The admissions policies of oversubscribed schools have often been highly suspect in the field of race with social selection operating on a strongly discriminatory basis. The prospect of reintroducing academic selection, where assessment procedures contain a social and racial bias, will be highly attractive. Already the politics of closure and amalgamation in many urban areas has brought the politics of race to the surface where popular largely white schools are asked to amalgamate with multiracial schools.

Again it is instructive to examine the ideological construction of this aspect of the legislation through the DES. In addition to the idea of a wider choice between schools the DES invokes notions of concern about standards and implicitly links such concerns with LEA control.

> Where parents are dissatisfied with existing standards they will be able to act so that their schools develop in ways best suited to the needs of their children in accordance with their wishes. (DES, 1987a)

We notice the repeated use of 'their'. *Their* schools, *their* children, and *their* wishes. Education is no longer to be seen as representing any collective, community or social interest — but rather as institutions through which to pursue self interest. For a parent to take an active role in determining the standards that their schools should be achieving, they will need to be a part of that school community. It also demands a certain understanding of the process of schooling and an easy facility with such institutions. In schools where black parents are well represented and organized this is possible. However the majority of schools have small numbers of black parents and in these instances they are dependent upon the support of white parents. The experience of Dewsbury suggests that there will be many situations where the wishes of black parents are frustrated.

The combined effects of grant-maintained status and open admissions in many areas will be to segregate further black children into schools with falling rolls and low staff morale. As the Dewsbury example shows, the parents who will receive the greatest support in their demands for choice will be white parents. Consequently popular schools will have to devise mechanisms by which they will select their intake. Aside from the sibling factor, authorities usually use factors such as geographical location, and a broad category other reasons. Here the onus is on the parents to provide a strong argument usually in a written form to support their application. Such a procedure, because it places at a disadvantage parents who are not literate in the English language or whose command of English language in its written form may influence the degree and level of attention given to it, may be discriminatory. Headteachers will also be aware of competing budgetary demands and may view staffing in the areas of English as a second language, special educational needs and learning support as a drain on staffing for specialist subject areas in the national curriculum.

> Spending decisions are best made by those most closely involved with a school — the governors and headteacher. (DES, 1987a)

The introduction of financial delegation and local management of schools completes the measures by which the Education Reform Act aims to shift the balance of power and decision making from LEAs to school governors. Funding will largely be based on school numbers and the age of pupils. The result will be to reward popular schools and to remove funding from schools with falling rolls. The ability of LEAs to compensate for the effects of demographic change and falling rolls on the curriculum and importantly to use financial mechanisms to support and improve schools with problems is highly constrained. The facts of racial disadvantage and the demography of 'race' in Britain dictate that black pupils and their families will be over represented in those schools which lose out in this process.

> School governors will be responsible for a wide range of issues including the selection of staff and promotions. (DES, 1987a)

The exact extent of these powers not only to hire, but also the power to fire, is made brutally clear in the following extract.

> What if governors at a school with financial delegation wanted to reduce the number of teachers on their staff? The governors would consider a number of possible options. They might want to find out if any teacher in a relevant area of the curriculum were planning to leave, or would be willing to take premature retirement, or would volunteer for redundancy. They could give the Education Authority the names of teachers who were willing to seek employment at another school and whom they were willing to release. If none of these approaches prove succesful, they may consider compulsory redundancy. In that case in schools other than voluntary aided schools they would notify the authority which teacher they propose to make redundant and the authority would have a duty to give that teacher notice of dismissal. (DES, 1987a)

The black community have long been concerned about the effectiveness of LEA equal opportunities policies in the recruitment and promotion of black teachers. The delegation of these processes to governors will have the effect of weakening accountability and the decentralizing of control over procedures and decision making. The same effects will be felt at the level of multicultural/anti-racist policies. While the effectiveness of LEA race policies has always been in doubt, there is little question that the Act will further widen the gap between LEA policies and school policy and practice. Black groups and organizations will find it more difficult to influence individual schools than LEAs — particularly schools in mainly white areas where black governors are scarce. The need to train governors in the field of 'race' and equal opportunities and to ensure the representation of black communities on governing bodies has been seen as a priority response to the Act and rightly so. However outside of metropolitan boroughs where black people constitute a large slice of the population and where anti-racist service delivery is high on the agenda these responses will be difficult to manage.

In considering the National Curriculum, a number of factors need to be considered. Firstly there is the imposition of a 'visible pedagogy', a defined, clearly bounded curriculum, with each area of knowledge having a prescribed place and relationship to each other. The relationship of areas of knowledge in the National Curriculum is one of superordination and subordination. The core of intellectual development is based on English, Mathematics and Science, followed by the foundation subjects and any others. Secondly the curriculum will be 'reinforced by attainment targets for children at the age of 7, 11, 14 and 16'. In the Baker Channel 4 report, referred to above, the Secretary of State for Education discusses with a Secondary Head of Science a test he had done on a previous visit to the school. He asked more generally about testing.

K. Baker: How do children react to tests?

Head of Science: Well for some it can be a motivation. And I think it does tend to obviously focus things very clearly for the pupils and for the teacher but its the quality of the tests which is the biggest deciding factor. And we are trying to spend quite a lot of time working and developing those tests so that they actually tell us something rather than just the child's factual recall.

The comment by the Head of Science clarifies where we are at the present in terms of our understanding about testing and the relationship between testing, assessment and their role in motivating pupils. The TGAT Report stressed that 'As with most assessment, the results of the standard assessments are likely to show difference between groups'. (Task Group on Assessment and Testing, DES, 1987). These differences can be gender or race specific. Although national systems of assessment may take account of item bias, there still remains the question of whether and then how schools will address the issue of item bias in their locally produced assessment tasks. With regard to the question of children whose first language is not English TGAT suggests that 'wherever practicable and necessary' assessment tasks should 'be conducted in the pupil's first language' (DES, 1987b). The document suggests a commitment to addressing item bias and to ensuring that pupils can be assessed in their first language. We believe that it is extremely difficult to detect item bias especially if this is conducted within the confines of a 'national' system of assessment and testing. Such a system would be based on notions that are shared and jointly understood. This in itself denies the various permutations that contribute to any individual's understanding of their ethnicity. Secondly 'wherever practicable and necessary' is an extremely loose statement of commitment. Within the 'cash limits' that a school will be required to operate in, 'practicable' means financially practical. The extent of a school's ability to meet needs will be conditioned by financial factors. Prior to the full implementation of ERA it may be possible for LEAs to centrally provide such support. Such central resources will be under pressure when formula funding is introduced. The possibility of a school being able to hold, in terms of staffing, posts that could provide support in assessment and testing in a number of languages is highly unlikely. Seventy-five per cent of the financial budget that will be delegated to a school through formula funding is to be based on the numbers and ages of pupils. Early results from piloting permutations of the formulae have shown that schools that presently receive extra support because of their socioeconomic and/or their ethnic composition may find that they lose staffing.

However the constraint is not just financial, 'wherever practicable and necessary' also requires a school to have identified the fact that a child may possibly show higher levels of cognitive development and consequently achieve higher attainment ratings if they were to be assessed and tested in their first language. This requires an understanding of the bilingual child and a commitment to recognize what the child is bringing to the school in the same way that we would expect all childrens' contributions to be valued. History does not offer us much optimism. Black and bilingual children still disproportionately appear in the lower bands/sets, are not proportionally represented throughout the option choices and are more likely to be statemented or to be placed in special schools. The likelihood is that headteachers will seek to disapply developing bilingual children in order to ease financial demands and to protect the results that a school, in order to gain a reputation as a good school, will strive to achieve.

A school's national assessment results 'will need to be reported to a variety of audiences' (DES, 1987b). Although TGAT have recommended 'that national assessment results for any individual pupil be confidential' and that 'national assessment results for a class as a whole and a school as a whole should be available to the parents of its pupils' there is still a question as to where this places prospective parents. Headteachers will use their results to attract parents at occasions like prospective parents' evenings, thus rendering such results as public. Authorities when producing their general reports of the area within which a school operates will be able to draw attention to the 'socio-economic and other influences which are known to affect schools' thus drawing attention to and emphasizing the 'problems' that a school has to 'cope with'. In these instances the local media is bound to summarize school results for their readership and this invariably will mean league tables. League tables are already a feature by which publications like the *Times Educational Supplement* compare LEAs and have therefore set a precedent for such forms of comparisons between institutions. It is unlikely that the local media will put results in a social context or provide any critical examination of the effects of financial circumstances on schools' performances.

The outline of the Curriculum for the three core subjects has reached a first draft stage. However these first drafts lead us to question the following. In terms of its philosophy, its aims and its objectives the proposed curriculum does not allow all learners an educational experience, at whatever level they are able, because it is based on a process with definable and testable attainments that all children are expected to achieve at defined ages. This is an extension of the previous discredited system of assessment at 11+ . Further there is little evidence as to how an essentially content led curriculum will be empathetic to both the learner, their ethnic identity and the racist society within which the content of the curriculum is to be delivered.

It is this defined, clearly-bounded curriculum which is seen as the key to 'raising standards'. However the curriculum as defined in the Education Reform Act is not about delivery. Although advocating a broad and balanced National Curriculum, the Act fails to address the question of how to provide a coherent learning experience for each student which will recognize, support and utilize the diversity of experiences, linguistic, cultural, economic, religious, gender and ethnic which provides a basis for each student to question and evaluate the worlds of knowledge and lived experience.

It is precisely these experiences that a student can bring to school which the present legislation is attempting to deny and to marginalize. This is achieved by legislating against the developments in curriculum theory and practice that have occurred throughout the last twenty years. The developments in experiential learning through mode 3 syllabuses, the development of thematic approaches that cross traditional curriculum boundaries such as peace studies, local and environmental studies, social studies and multicultural and anti-racist curriculum initiatives all of which attempt to provide 'new' relations of teaching and learning that place the child at the centre of the educational experience. As Whitty and Mentor (1989) point out the present structure of the National Curriculum takes the traditional subject boundaries of the Secondary School Syllabus first laid down by the Board of Education in 1904.

In their discussion of the emergence of LEA multicultural and anti-racist policies Troyna and Williams (1986) make the point that the direction of change orchestrated by the DES has been in direct opposition to this kind of local policy initiative.

> This perceptible shift in central governments' control over education decision making has been justified largely on the grounds that schools have not been sufficiently responsive to 'national needs' and therefore required strict guidance and direction to ensure that there is greater comparability between what the student experiences and what will be required of her/him in the world of work. (Troyna and Williams, 1986)

The ideology of 'equality of opportunity' which was important in the structural development of comprehensive education and in progressive curriculum reform has been overtaken by a greater emphasis on the economic functions of education in preparing pupils for the world of work in an increasingly unequal society.

> It is vital that schools should always remember that preparation for working life is one of their principle functions. (DES, 1985)

In the debate over history this struggle can be clearly seen. Kenneth Baker has indicated that he wants all pupils to know about the facts of British 'heritage' as they occurred in chronological order. In contrast many people would rather focus on a selection of historical moments and carefully examine them, stressing the variety of experiences of all people at those moments, the conditions of their lives and the events, momentous and momentary, that surround and involve them. Both histories can still tell partial stories but in retelling the 'new history' potentially offers space to contradictory stories, to major characters and minor persons, to women's story, to the black perspective. In contrast Baker's view of history is essentially celebratory — how a free and democratic society has developed over the centuries. This view of history as a progressive development which sees parliamentary democracy as the pinnacle of achievement denies a whole range of 'stories' which would question such a claim. For instance one analysis of parlimentary democracy as it operates within the United Kingdom would argue that rather than offering up greater opportunities for individual freedom this 'state' is the most highly controlling state in the western world and demonstrates clearly that parliamentary democracies in western capitalist societies can coexist with inequalities — class, race and gender — of a high degree.

In addition to the creation of subject boundedness and hierarchy, the narrowly white and English concept of the 'national' in the National Curriculum is clearly noted in Mr Baker's emphasis on British history. Similarly the Reform Act has produced regulations governing the teaching of religious education and school assemblies that they should be 'mainly and broadly' Christian acts of worship. Interestingly it is in the area of assemblies that not only black communities but also some teacher associations and individual headteachers have been most vocal in their recognition of the potential divisiveness of the Act. It has been pointed out that this regulation in particular provides a powerful instrument for some white parents to confront and resist the development of aspects of multicultural/anti-racist work in schools. While the Act provides the opportunity for schools to apply to 'opt-out' of this regulation through application to LEA Standing Advisory Committees for Religious Education, many schools are finding that taking such a step is difficult to sell to largely white governing bodies. It is significant that schools will have to apply to 'opt-out' and are not required to 'opt-in' to the provision of a single faith act of worship in a multi-faith society. A similar message can be found in the DES consultation letter 'Modern Foreign Languages in the National Curriculum' (DES, 3/3/89). We find that while Welsh has been recognized as a core curriculum subject in Wales, the other living languages of Britain, in some schools representing a majority of children, are to be relegated to 'Schedule 2' as options to be offered as an alternative to the required 'Schedule 1' European Community working languages.

In conclusion we argue that an Act based on a political and economic philosophy of individualism and consumerism in a capitalist free-market, an Act which attempts to reconstruct through education a national identity based on a narrowly defined notion of 'Englishness', stands in stark contradiction to the political ideals and aspirations of justice and equality which underlie the antiracist movement. The Act is tightly controlling but there are areas within which those committed to anti-racist perspective can seek to redress the balance imposed by the Education Reform Act. Antiracist teachers within the constraints of the National Curriculum can imaginatively subvert the nationalistic intentions that we have highlighted in this chapter. While the management of schools has been devolved to school governors the control of the curriculum has been taken away from schools to the government heavily mediated by the LEAs. In those few LEAs where antiracist service delivery is central to the agenda it may be easier to direct curriculum development through LEA policy within the National Curriculum than is currently the case. Equally in these areas local management of schools may empower black communities through governor representation. However in most authorities the atomization of management and the bureaucratisation of curriculum development will pose major challenges to the black communities and to antiracists working in the field of education.

References

DES (1985) *Better Schools,* London, HMSO.

DES (1987a) *Education Reform. The Government's Proposals for Schools,* HMSO.

DES (1987b) *Task Group on Assessment and Testing,* HMSO.

DES (1989) *Education Reform 1988: Modern Foreign Languages in the National Curriculum.*

FORSTER, W. E., HANSARD series iii, Vol. 199 cols. 465–6.

HALL, S. (1978) 'Racism and reaction', in *Five Views of Multiracial Britain,* London, Commission for Racial Equality.

TROYNA, B. and WILLIAMS, J. (1987) *Racism Education and the State,* Beckenham, Croom Helm.

WHITTY, G. and MENTER, I. (1989) 'Lessons of Thatcherism — Education Policy in England and Wales 1979–1988', *Journal of Law and Society*, Vol. 16, No. 1, Spring.

11
Girls' Education in the Balance: The ERA and Inequality

Sheila Miles and Chris Middleton

The opening section of the 1988 Education Reform Act (ERA) asserts that 'a balanced and broadly based curriculum' is one which prepares pupils 'for the opportunities, responsibilities and experiences of adult life' (ERA, 1.2). This key statement, however, is open to alternative interpretations. For some (but not all) liberal-feminists the National Curriculum can be seen as a welcome opportunity for promoting girls' education, though even within this perspective there are grounds for caution about some of the Act's implications. From a more sceptical standpoint, however, it might well be observed that the opportunities, responsibilities and experiences facing most girls in adult life are severely constrained, especially if they come from black or working-class backgrounds. An educational reform that disregards this reality, and actually marginalises those parts of the curriculum which aim to develop a critical social awareness in children, will merely help to reproduce existing inequalities.

This chapter will explore such issues in the context of the underlying economic rationale of the Act and the present underachievement of girls in key areas of education. It will examine the argument that the National Curriculum could promote equal opportunities by giving girls access to traditionally masculinized subject areas and occupations, and will suggest grounds for scepticism that the principle of increasing access will be sufficient for meeting even these limited objectives. Some of the factors which might inhibit the implementation of equal opportunities (such as classroom processes, teacher recruitment and training, and pupil attitudes to subject content and testing) will be considered, and it will be argued that in some respects at least the Act will prove deleterious in its effects. Differing strands of Conservative ideology represented in the Act may also have contradictory implications for girls' education. The National Curriculum is the DES's response to employers' demands for an educated workforce that would draw on a wider pool of ability regardless of gender, but the preference for traditional, subject-based forms of education may in fact prove damaging both to training efficiency and equal opportunities. Moreover, the Conservative commitment to 'traditional' family life

(Hiskett, 1988), as reflected in the Act by the call for greater parental 'choice', may conflict with moves that could improve career prospects for girls. Finally, it will be suggested, the liberal-feminist conception of equal opportunities that has informed much of the discussion around the National Curriculum is too limited. There is a need to question the social relationships of adult life into which girls and boys are being inducted, and within this framework to consider afresh what a balanced and broadly based curriculum would entail.

The Education Reform Act, equal opportunities and the economy

The ERA is not about equal opportunities. It is about raising educational standards to meet the needs of the economy and of industry — an objective which, according to social market theory, is best realized by making education more responsive to consumer demand. The Act seeks to reflect this imperative in two ways: by centralizing the curriculum (with the government effectively acting on behalf of employers) and by removing education from the control of teachers and LEAs. Kenneth Baker made this clear when he introduced the Second Reading of the Bill in December, 1987:

> This Bill will create a new framework, which will raise standards, extend choice and produce a better educated Britain . . . We must give the consumers of education a central part in decision making. That means freeing schools and colleges to deliver the standards that parents and employers want. (Hansard, 1 December 1987, c771/2, quoted in David, n.d.)

The clear inference from the legislation is that the government perceives teachers and LEAs as the inhibiting forces from which schools must be freed if they are to be responsive to consumer demand. Parents, frequently held to be responsible for their children's achievement and underachievement, are now to be reconstituted as consumers; the rhetoric has shifted from parental involvement to parental choice. The needs of employers are to be catered for by the National Curriculum's emphasis on core subjects, with regular assessment to ensure improved standards of literacy and numeracy. Centralization of the curriculum would not be inconsistent with the decentralization of control if, as the Government expects, the demands of parents were to converge with their own view of what employers need.

It should be noted that not all industrialists agree with the Government's prescription for meeting their training needs. Many believe that the enterprise culture, with its demand for transferable skills, is best fostered through an interdisciplinary curriculum 'focused on *doing* rather than simply on *knowing*', and they have been critical of the National Curriculum's return to traditional subject-based learning (as advocated by the right-wing Hillgate Group). These divisions are reflected in the divergent strategies advocated by different government departments, particularly by the DTI and the DES. and it appears that the 'traditionalists' have been notably successful in influencing the direction that the ERA has taken (Jamieson and Watts, 1987). Whitty (Chapter 2 in this volume) sees the National Curriculum as a short-term measure 'to ensure that the pervasive collectivist and universalistic welfare ideology of the postwar era is restrained' and to promote 'the development of an appropriate sense of self and nation on the part of citizens who will be making their choices in the market'. However, the education of girls may turn out to be one area where the choices of citizens are not always congruent with the needs of the market economy.

There is a broad political consensus in the UK that future national prosperity depends on increasing the supply of highly qualified recruits to the labour force, especially in the fields of science and technology (Hough, 1987). The educational system has long been criticized for failing to meet this demand and thus of wasting the abilities of many young people. Leading industrialists have accused it of failing to 'provide a general training which adequately prepares young people for work' and for training teachers in a way that is 'remote from industry' (NEDC, 1982). The National Curriculum's provision of a core education emphasizing maths, science and technology is seen by the Government as a vital move in securing the future of the British economy.

Since the end of the war the recurring theme of wasted talent has served as a link between the needs of the capitalist economy and social democratic demands for the provision of wider educational opportunities for all pupils. In 1959, the Crowther Report argued that,

> Primacy must be given to the human rights of the individual boy or girl. But we do not believe that the pursuit of national efficiency can be ranked much lower . . . there seems to us to be no social injustice in our community at the present time more loudly crying out for reform than the condition in which scores of thousands of our children are released onto the labour market. (Quoted in Hough, 1987)

Until the 1960s attention was focused mainly on the waste of working class talent, although the underachievement of girls did receive some comment — the Robbins Report, for instance, referring to 'reserves of untapped ability' among girls. But in the 1970s equal educational opportunities for girls were to become a prominent public issue as enshrined, for example, in the Sex Discrimination Act. The intellectual and political framework for the growing concern with equal opportunities is usually described as liberal-feminist, which we may define as an attempt to remove or compensate for the ascriptive and social impediments that prevent women from competing on equal terms with men, without otherwise challenging the hierarchical structures within which both sexes operate. However, this term does tend to obscure the presence of two rather different perspectives within the equal opportunities tradition. Firstly, there are those who, in keeping with the liberal and individualistic traditions of Western culture, wish to ensure that pupils' ascribed characteristics do not serve as the basis for discriminatory and exclusionary practices against them. In this context the National Curriculum can be defended as offering considerable leverage for implementing equal opportunities as an entitlement curriculum, prioritising those very areas where girls are known to be underrepresented and to underachieve, and making them compulsory for all pupils. But, secondly, there are those who, in accordance with social democratic traditions of thought, lay more emphasis on the complex *social* bases of disadvantage and the necessity of overcoming them if equal opportunities are to be effectively implemented. From this point of view the formal structural reforms instituted by the National Curriculum seem unlikely to herald any drastic changes. The liberal-feminist arguments for and against the ERA are set out in the remainder of this section.

The national curriculum: girls into science and technology?

In 1986–7 there were almost 25,000 full-time undergraduatess in the UK studying engineering and technology, of whom only 2,741 were women (Association for Science Education, 1988). In view of the falling birth rate there are likely to be fewer entrants to these subject areas during the next decade and this is causing concern among scientific and engineering employers. Women are an obvious source of recruitment for making good the shortfall. According to the latest DES Statistical Bulletin twice as many boys as girls gain an A-level pass in mathematics, and three times as many do so in physics (DES, 1988b). Among those leaving school at 16, twice as many boys as girls have a higher grade O-level/CSE qualification in physics, and the proportion of boys with higher grade passes is also greater in mathematics, chemistry and, particularly, CDT subjects (ibid).

Table 11.1 School leavers in England: Leavers with higher[1] grade passes at 'O' level or CSE in selected subjects — percentage of all leavers

	1976–7			1986–7			Percentage change 1976–7 to 1986–7		
	Boys	Girls	Total	Boys	Girls	Total	Boys	Girls	Total
Any subject	49.5	53.3	51.4	51.3	57.9	54.5	+ 4	+ 9	+ 6
English	31.9	42.0	36.9	34.3	45.5	39.7	+ 8	+ 8	+ 8
Mathematics	28.0	20.5	24.3	32.6	27.7	30.2	+ 16	+35	+24
Physics	18.1	5.0	11.7	21.9	9.2	15.7	+ 21	+84	+34
Chemistry	12.7	6.1	9.5	15.8	11.5	13.7	+ 24	+89	+44
Biological sciences	11.9	17.7	14.8	12.3	18.6	15.4	+ 3	+ 5	+ 4
Craft design, technology and other sciences	17.5	2.5	10.1	17.1	4.5	10.9	− 2	+80	+ 8
French	10.8	16.6	13.6	10.9	18.2	14.5	+ 1	+10	+ 7
History	13.7	15.3	14.5	13.3	14.9	14.1	− 3	− 3	− 3
Geography	17.7	13.7	15.7	18.1	14.2	16.2	+ 2	+ 4	+ 3
Creative arts	10.8	15.1	12.9	11.0	18.1	14.5	+ 2	+20	+12
Commercial and domestic studies	1.8	17.1	9.3	4.1	17.4	10.6	+128	+ 2	+14
General studies	2.2	1.9	2.1	2.6	2.6	2.6	+ 18	+37	+24

[1]O level grades A–C, CSE grade 1.
Source: DES Statistical Bulletin, 1988, Table 8.

Unfortunately, we have no indication of how ethnic minority or working class girls fare in these subjects, as the Bulletin does not provide the relevant statistical breakdowns. This is an important omission to which we shall return later.

The table shows that in the decade to 1987 there were substantial rises in the proportion of girls achieving higher grade O-level/CSE passes in physics, chemistry, and craft, design and technology (84, 89, and 80 per cent respectively), but it must be borne in mind that, given the minute number of girls studying these subjects in the late 1970s, small gains make a falsely dramatic impact. Despite the improvement, fewer than 1 in 10 girls are now achieving higher grades in physics (compared with more than 1 in 5 boys), and fewer than 1 in 20 girls gain these grades in CDT (compared with more than 1 in 6 boys).

Under the National Curriculum, it could be argued, girls will no longer be able to opt out of traditionally male areas of the curriculum and will therefore have the chance to gain qualifications equipping them for a much wider range of prestigious and highly-paid jobs. Boudon argues that the provision of unlimited subject-choice and 'branching off' points in the school system can foster inequality by allowing differential cultural expectations to structure achievement along lines of class, gender and race, so that paradoxically a reduction in choice may enhance equal opportunities (Green, 1988). Moreover, it is not only pupils' expectations that may be neutralised by this means. The specification of a core curriculum and content for each subject, the setting of attainment targets, and a national system of testing with published results might also conceivably help to overcome the effects of low teacher-expectations as an important factor in working class, black and female underachievement. A working party set up by the Association for Science Education seems to have concluded that a common core curriculum in which science and technology figure prominently would be a step in the right direction:

> There are indications that the change towards double award balanced science will increase the numbers of girls studying science in the sixth form. The HMI Girls and Science Report (1980) found that SCISP (Schools Council Integrated Science Project) had this effect and preliminary reports from the Suffolk Science Project point to a similar trend. (ASE, 1988)

The limitations of 'compulsory access'

The argument in favour of the National Curriculum concentrates on the *formal* provision of equal access, but takes insufficient account of the kinds of issue that have been raised within the social democratic tradition of liberal-feminism. In a society permeated by gender divisions and inequalities, it is implausible to suppose that the treatment of girls and boys as though they were already equal will result in the creation of genuine equality of opportunity. Gender is well established as an organizing principle of the practices and power structures embedded within educational institutions and these will need to be fully addressed if access is to be made meaningful. Management hierarchies within most schools are dominated by male teachers especially in most of the subject areas given prominence by the National Curriculum. Within the classroom there is evidence that both male and female teachers give more of their time and attention to boys, ask them more questions, give them more praise and generally find them more interesting. Boys monopolise formal interaction, classroom workspace and resources especially in lessons on science and technology (Licht and Dweck, 1987; Buswell, 1981; Stanworth, 1983; Mahoney, 1985; Kelly, 1987; Arnot and Weiner, 1987; Wolpe, 1988).

Pupil attitudes are also important. Research by the Assessment of Performance Unit has shown that 15-year-old boys enjoy maths and science subjects (with the exception of biology) more than their female peers, find these subjects less difficult and achieve better results. But it stresses that these findings must be interpreted with care. Boys fare better in applying concepts in physics and chemistry and in tests of physics *knowledge*, but do less well than girls in observational tests. Competence in the use of measuring instruments seems to be influenced by out-of-school familiarity with their use, girls and boys performing equally well on instruments used for measuring time, temperature, volume, mass and weight. The differences observed at age 15 do not appear to reflect *natural* aptitudes. Boys and girls have similar attitudes towards maths at age 11 — both sexes recognize its usefulness, find it equally difficult, and girls actually enjoy it slightly more than boys. Variations in attitudes towards maths emerge at a later stage. Performance and attitude differences in physics, however, are established at a much earlier age and may plausibly be interpreted as 'arising from differences in the science relevant out-of-school activities and interests of boys and girls as young children' (APU, 1988; see also Johnson and Murphy, 1986; Joffe and Foxman, 1988).

In part, girls' disaffection from science appears to be a response to science's masculine and impersonal image. Whereas boys are interested in controlling the material world, girls consistently show greater interest in subjects they regard as having more to do with 'people' than 'things' (Gilligan, 1982). There is a danger, then, that in forcing girls to study, for such a substantial part of their school lives, subject areas to which they have a real aversion, the National Curriculum could end up by transforming disaffection from certain subjects into a rejection of schooling itself. We referred earlier to evidence suggesting that double award balanced science would lead to an increase in the number of girls studying science in the sixth form (though whether this will give them equal access to prestigious and well-paid jobs is another matter entirely). However, it is surely unwarranted to conclude from this evidence that 'science for all to 16 does not appear to turn girls away from physical science' (NCC, 1988). It is quite possible that the experiences of girls who continue with science into the sixth form will diverge sharply from those who do not. A TVEI co-ordinator felt that, 'One might be creating, at least in the short term, a number of highly dissatisfied girls who feel they have been forced into quite unwanted territory — a reservoir of disaffection and indiscipline' (quoted in Millman and Weiner, 1987).

Low achievement on the assessment tests (see below) may aggravate this problem. A recent investigation into truancy among girls found that, apart from problems at home or with health, fear of failure was the main reason given by interviewees for absenting themselves from school. Girls 'bunked' individual lessons because they disliked the subject or the teacher (Le Riche, 1988).

The possibility of an increased number of disaffected girl pupils should not lead us to abandon the 'science for all' policy. Rather, attention should be paid to the structure and content of the science curriculum and to the way in which it is taught. Many science educators have proposed the development of a 'girl-friendly' science which would aim to teach traditional scientific principles, but would do so initially through topics that are likely to interest girls (Kelly, 1988; Harding, 1983; Smail, 1984). It would also work towards a more contextualized approach that would include a consideration of 'the implications and applications of the subject as a fundamental part of the syllabus' (Kelly, 1988: 169). Other approaches emphasise the importance of encouraging co-operation rather than competition within the classroom and developing a concern for social, moral and ethical issues (Bentley and Watts, 1986), or of challenging the nature of science itself by questioning its claims to objectivity and disinterestedness.

The retreat from compulsory 'science for all'

Letter from Mr Kenneth Baker to Professor J. J. Thompson, Chair of the Science Working Group, dated 21 August 1987:

> It will also be important to bear in mind that the curriculum should provide equal opportunities for boys and girls; and to consider, in this context, the expectations and attitudes of girls to science. (DES, 1988a)

In its report to the Secretary of State the NCC Science Working Group acknowledged the significance of this body of social and psychological research and concluded that much needed to be done if the concept of 'science for all' was to be realised. But the Government's response to the Group's preliminary recommendations illustrates the tenuous or contingent nature of the link forged between the needs of the economy and equal opportunities policy. In August 1988 Kenneth Baker insisted upon several important amendments to the Working Group's proposals which were likely to undermine much of what they were trying to achieve. The most critical change required was the withdrawal of the proposal that *all* fourth and fifth-year pupils (Key Stage 4) should spend about 20 per cent of the week studying a broad and balanced science programme leading to a double GCSE award. Instead the Group had to produce a two-tier scheme which would allow pupils a choice of an alternative 12.5 per cent programme leading to a single award. According to the subsequent Consulation Report (NCC, 1988) this alternative model will provide an insufficient basis for A-level work and, in practice, will mean that many pupils' career routes will be determined at 13. The Report believes that the most serious consequence of this change is likely to be a 'gender imbalance between those choosing the single and double science route . . . the SCISP study confirms that the proportion of girls doing A-level physical sciences is dramatically increased by the deferral of choice' (*ibid.*). Furthermore, the single option will not give a qualification in any branch of science which equips a student to go on to A-levels. A *Times Educational Supplement* editorial pointed out that:

> a girl . . . who now takes biology in GCSE, may not receive a 'broad and balanced' science education, but for occupations such as nursing she can, at least, get a basic qualification on which further studies can be built. This will not be the case for girls who take the 12.5 per cent option in the national curriculum. To continue with science to an A-level they would have to take a crash conversion course. (*TES*, 9 December 1988)

The 12.5 per cent route necessarily leaves out significant elements of the full science syllabus, and the model recommended by the Report would exclude certain Attainment Targets such as the scientific aspects of information technology (AT 12). Thus pupils taking this option, the majority of whom will undoubtedly be girls, will face severe constraints on their choice of jobs.

The Consulation Report has also been modified in other respects in response to Baker's criticisms. The 20 per cent syllabus is now to lay greater emphasis on scientific knowledge and understanding (i.e., those aspects in which boys perform best) as against other components such as exploration and investigation, communication and science in action. Aspects of science which might appeal most strongly to girls, such as the 'consideration of the power and limitations of science in solving industrial, social and environmental problems' and the use of technology for birth control and contraception, have been withdrawn. The retreat from the policy of 'science for all' and the downgrading of those aspects of the curriculum which girls tend to find attractive, reveals the Government's lack of real commitment to equal opportunities.

Equal opportunities initiatives under threat?

If this were the whole story one might simply conclude that the ERA represents a missed opportunity — an organisational and curricular reform unlikely to make much impact on equal opportunities one way or the other. Alarmingly, however, certain aspects of the legislation seem destined to place in jeopardy the small number of positive equal opportunity initiatives that have been undertaken in recent years.

The main institutional base for systematic equal opportunities work (and for more radical anti-sexist and anti-racist interventions) has been located in a minority of committed LEAs and groups of progressive teachers. Several LEAs have produced equal opportunities policy statements, while some have appointed

Equal Opportunities Advisors or advisory teachers and have organized In-Service Training (INSET), including the use of Baker Days, to raise these issues. Schools within these authorities have also been encouraged to produce their own 'whole school' policies in which every aspect of the curriculum and school organisation is subjected to scrutiny. At least two projects have been jointly funded by the School Curriculum Development Committee (SCDC), the Equal Opportunities Commission (EOC) and participating LEAs to produce materials for teachers and develop equal opportunities work in primary and secondary schools. (Genderwatch, and the Greater London Consortium on Gender in which eight boroughs were involved). The continuation of this kind of work must now be seen as under threat as control of educational policy-making is shifted away from the LEAs and teachers. The SCDC has been closed down, while the abolition of the Inner London Educational Authority (ERA, Part III) may be seen as an additional blow since ILEA had an outstanding record of equal opportunities work on gender, class and race and, through its Research and Statistics Branch, was responsible for generating an impressive body of relevent research. In fact, Government hostility to these 'producers' of education has been due, in no small measure, to the widely publicised endeavours of those tackling sexist and racist attitudes and discriminatory practices. Right-wing lobbies such as the Adam Smith Institute and the Hillgate Group argue that education has suffered the hallmarks of 'producer capture' and that it has come to serve the interests of teachers and administrators, leading to the study of subjects which promote egalitarian principles and thus 'distract the child's attention away from serious forms of learning' (Omega Report, quoted in Demaine, 1988; Hillgate Group, 1986).

In reducing the power of LEAs and teachers, the Government claims it will make education more responsive to consumer demand. 'Parents' are to be given more choice and influence through open enrolment, participation as governors, opting out and Local Management of Schools (LMS). But the formally neutral categories conceal a sharply inegalitarian reality. As Rosemary Deem has observed, 'parent power may turn out merely to add to the power of those parents who already have access to mechanisms of power rather than those who have little or no access at present' (Deem, 1988: 186).

A 'balanced and broadly-based' board of governors (if we may borrow the phrase) depends on the willingness and confidence of parents to put themselves forward, but a recent NFER survey commissioned by the DES reveals concern among LEAs that not enough governors come from underprivileged backgrounds or from black or Asian communities (Jefferies and Streatfield, 1989). Yet, as governing bodies take up their new responsibilities under the Act, pressures will arise that could make them even less representative of their communities than they are now. Their enhanced role means that they will need to recruit individuals with particular administrative and financial skills, and members will also be required to devote much more of their time to governing activities. Lack of relevant expertise and domestic commitments may discourage many women from coming forward, especially if they are from working class or some ethnic backgrounds, while those members (mostly professional males?) who possess the relevant skills may acquire a disproportionate influence in the government of schools.

Under local management of schools the extension of governors' powers in relation to staffing will be considerable, including the selection of headteacher. In this connection, the EOC's education officer fears a serious deterioration in career development for women teachers through 'a re-introduction of traditional employment practices with reduced opportunities for part time work and job sharing' unless information on sex discrimination is included in governors' training (Lynda Carr, quoted in Pandya, 1989). The importance of such training is indicated by the fact that in 1988 the EOC received 288 complaints from teachers alleging sex discrimination in selection and appointment procedures, and a number of successful industrial tribunal cases have identified unlawful discriminatory practices by governing bodies and employers (EOC, 1989). The Government has rejected the EOC's recommendaion that training should be compulsory. Governors will not be required to adhere to equal opportunities in terms of employment or the curriculum beyond the requirements of the Sex Discrimination Act, and even then it will be the LEA rather than the governors themselves who will be legally liable for any discrimination that takes place (Pandya, 1989).

In-Service Training (INSET) on equal opportunities is another key area of work which must be considered under threat from the new legislation. A National Curriculum briefing document *From Policy to Practice*, distributed to all teachers, states that there should be 'coverage across the curriculum of gender and multi-cultural issues' (DES, 1989a), whilst also acknowledging that the commitment of individual teachers will be crucial in making the National Curriculum work. Yet research into teachers' attitudes suggests that, in the absence of appropriate INSET, many remain far from convinced of the need for or even the desirability of equal opportunities. A study undertaken by the EOC found that nearly half the secondary school teachers surveyed were 'overall, unsympathetic to equal opportunities in school'. Among male teachers 50 per cent expressed opposition, and more than half of these fell into the most hostile category. When classified by subject area, teachers in maths, physical sciences, technical crafts and languages were found to predominate among those least in favour (Pratt, 1985, Pratt, Bloomfield and Seale, 1984). Secondary school teachers also seem to rate technical education as more important for boys than for girls, and it is among science teachers themselves that this opinion is held most strongly (Spear, 1987). An action-research project designed 'to explicate the reasons for girls' under-achievement in physical science and technical subjects . . . and (the) effectiveness of interventions aimed at improving the situation' found that most teachers involved in the research were neutral or only mildly supportive of the intervention. A few, mostly male teachers, were distinctly hostile, expressing their belief that sex differences were natural and that sex equality was not an educational problem. These teachers feared that any positive action for girls would lead to unacceptable discrimination against boys (Whyte, 1986). Other surveys, according to Acker, 'find that there is support for equal opportunities in principle, but that teachers are disinclined to believe schools actually favour boys and wary about interfering in the processes whereby girls make traditional career choices' (Acker, 1988). If access under the National Curriculum is to be made at all meaningful, it will evidently require extensive support from carefully designed and sensitive programmes of INSET on equal opportunities. How confident can we be that such programmes will be forthcoming?

The ERA has been introduced at a time of chronic teacher shortage, especially in those areas of the curriculum which the DES deems vital for national economic recovery. According to an editorial in *The Independent* (1 March 1989) recent estimates suggest that the state system could be short of 12,000 maths teachers, 2,300 physics teachers and 3,000 language teachers by 1995, and the latest HMI Report observes that primary schools are 'critically short of teachers with expertise in science, technology and mathematics' (DES, 1989b). Since teachers in favoured subject areas (which tend to be male-dominated) are more likely to be eligible for discretionary and incentive payments, the teacher shortage seems bound to have the effect of widening still further those considerable differentials in pay that currently divide men and women teachers. Schools will need to recruit many more science teachers if the demands of the National Curriculum are to be met, yet applications for undergraduate courses starting in 1989 are 28 per cent down in physics and 16 per cent down in chemistry. (Such immediate and pragmatic considerations, which will be seen by many in the profession as the bitter harvest of persistent underfunding by the Government, must have been uppermost in Kenneth Baker's mind when he criticised the 20 per cent 'science for all' proposal as 'over-ambitious'.) *From Policy to Practice* sees a need for INSET to back up the introduction of the National Curriculum, but in view of the teacher shortage, limited funds and lack of supply cover, it is difficult to see how adequate preparation and training can be provided. In these circumstances it must be expected that work on equal opportunities and anti-sexism will be viewed by many authorities as a luxury and consequently squeezed out. Equal opportunities have never been a National Priority Area under Grant Related In-Service Training (GRIST) and, given the lack of government commitment, there is no reason to believe that priorities will be any different in relation to the National Curriculum.

The Secretary of State's most recent solution to the looming crisis in staffing levels is to suggest the introduction of untrained graduates into schools as licensed teachers. The DES may experience great difficulty in getting this proposal off the ground, but if it does 'take off' it is likely to have a detrimental effect on girls' education, especially in those subjects where they lack confidence or which they are reluctant to enter. The details of how these recruits will be trained and acquire qualified teacher status are unknown at the time of writing, but if as is anticipated, training will be done 'on the job', the danger arises with 'teachers training teachers' that existing inegalitarian practices will simply be reproduced (Miles and Furlong, 1988). Unlike students undergoing Initial Training, they will not be exposed to educational disciplines which address equal opportunities issues, nor is it likely that they will benefit from a systematic training in classroom management and control, both areas where the hidden curriculum of gender differentiation operates. As a result licensed teachers are likely to be particularly unaware of the difficulties girls face. There must also be concern that most science, maths and CDT teachers recruited under this scheme will be men (especially if, as we anticipate, incentive allowances are offered to attract recruits away from industry), and they are likely to import from industry firmly masculinised models of their subject areas.

A testing time for girls

Finally, there must be concern that the National Curriculum will exacerbate existing inequalities of gender by giving a more prominent role to assessment procedures. According to the teachers' briefing document, assessment is held to lie 'at the heart of the process of promoting children's learning' (TGAT quoted in *From Policy to Practice*). An unprecedented decision has been made to test the performance of 7-year-old children against centrally determined Attainment Targets, as well as to introduce additional stages of testing in later years. The target-related Assessments are intended to be formative, summative, evaluative and informative; that is, they are supposed not only to evaluate the child's development to date, but to influence decisions affecting her or his subsequent educational experience.

Assessment will be by a combination of national external tests and assessment by teachers. The kind of external testing envisaged for the National Curriculum entails a departure from the principle (established by GCSE) that assessment procedures should be designed to examine what the pupil knows rather than what she or he does not know. Since evidence suggests that girls tend to be more frightened of making mistakes and hence more cautious about attempting answers, particularly in areas already known to provoke anxiety, they may be less likely than boys to function to the best of their ability in such a formal testing situation.

Research by Goldstein and others has shown that there are important gender differences in the test performances of boys and girls which stem as much from the design of the tests as from the characteristics of individual children (Goldstein, 1987). Several of these findings were noted in a document submitted by the EOC to the Task Group on Assessment and Testing (TGAT), but were only included as an Appendix to their Report (DES, 1988c). It appears, in particular, that the format of a test is of crucial significance. There is evidence, for instance, that although girls perform better on more open-ended tasks requiring extended writing, they fare worse than boys on multiple choice questions and (from age 13) non-verbal tests. Gender differences in skill and conceptual ability may well be open to social modification and we are certainly not suggesting that they are 'natural' in any deterministic sense. But, for so long as they do persist, test performances of girls and boys will vary according to the relative proportions of different kinds of item included in the assessment. For a combination of practical and philosophical reasons it seems likely that the system of external testing will rely heavily on the multiple choice format; the size of the operation, the time and effort that assessment will involve, and the formalistic assumptions that inform the setting of national Attainment Targets all favour this kind of approach. Will it prove expedient, in these circumstances, to overlook the fact that this format appears biased in favour of boys?

The part to be played by teachers is hardly more reassuring. Caroline Gipps believes that this could potentially be the most discriminatory area of national assessment. 'We have plenty of evidence to show that teachers' judgements of children are deeply affected by stereotypes. There will be plenty of scope for the score of boys and girls who perform marginally at a particular level of maths and science to be edged up and down' (*Times Educational Supplement*, 24 March 1989). Gipps emphasizes the importance of addressing the problem of gender stereotyping in in-service training on teacher assessment, but in view of our earlier comments on INSET we cannot be confident that the problem will be tackled thoroughly.

There is clearly a need for stringent monitoring of gender differences in relation to assessment and testing. Tests and assessment procedures which avoid gender-bias need to be carefully designed and sensitively administered. Yet, as the DES admit, the TGAT's suggestions on moderation 'appear complicated and costly' (DES, 1988d). If past experience of public testing can be taken as a guide, the proposals on assessment will introduce new rigidities into the educational careers of children, and these rigidities will tend to discriminate against girls.

Of words and deeds

The impression that the Government's commitment to equal opportunities is less than wholehearted is reinforced by its use of sexist language in the wording of the Act. The world encompassed by the legislation is consistently masculine: pupils, parents, teachers and governors (not to mention the Secretary of State!) all being referred to as if they were invariably male.

Even more crucially, perhaps, the process of implementation has shown that this language is not some legal anachronism, irrelevant to the world we live in, but continues to reflect political and administrative relations to a significant degree. The number of women appointed to the National Curriculum Council's Working Groups has been disgracefully small — roughly three women to every thirteen men according to the EOC's Education Officer, Lynda Carr. The Working Groups provided a rare opportunity for a systematic review of teaching content and the creation of curricula that were free from gender bias and appealing to girls. Yet the Secretary of State failed to ensure the widespread involvement of those equal opportunities researchers responsible for devising programmes of intervention in schools, and the documentation so far produced has done little more than pay lip-service to these ideals.

The NCC has established several Task Groups to explore cross-curricular links including personal and social education, Special Educational Needs and multicultural issues. A further Task Group on gender had originally been proposed, but this plan has now been abandoned. Speaking at the Cambridge Institute of Education in May 1989, Duncan Graham, Chair of the NCC, defended this omission by claiming that 'gender is too subtle' and permeates the discussions of all the Subject Working Groups. This is surely too sanguine. The influence of all the Task Groups will be attenuated by their belated start, but the principle 'better late than never' certainly applies here. The lack of a Task Group on gender means there will now be no institutional basis for ensuring that permeation is achieved or progress monitored.

Beyond equal opportunities

We have devoted the best part of this chapter to a consideration of the ERA's implications for equal opportunities as these might be debated by different strands within the liberal-feminist tradition. They are important debates, but their horizons are strictly limited. We could, of course, have adopted a different approach. We could, with some justification, have set out to demonstrate the irrelevance of the ERA to most of the issues that have concerned socialist-feminists over the past two decades, but this would have been to eliminate nearly all substantive comment on the Act itself. On this occasion, the limits of the analysis must be set by the boundaries of our terms of reference. The ERA offers no radical departures for girls' education. If its strategies are often unfamiliar within the context of British educational policy, its central objective — the gearing of education more closely towards the perceived needs of industry — is remarkably traditional. Its rhetoric is that of creating a balanced and broad curriculum to prepare pupils for adult life, yet it fails to acknowledge that in reality adult life varies for different groups in the population.

In this final section, however, we do want to extend the parameters of our discussion. We shall note the limitations and weaknesses of liberal-feminist approaches, focusing especially on their marginalisation of the concerns of working-class and ethnic minority girls, and then go on to consider how a focus on equal opportunities may divert critical attention away from the gender-linked value systems that underpin the educational process and the ERA's tendency to reinforce them.

The limits of equal opportunities

We do not wish to underestimate the value of equal opportunities work. If a group is denied full rights of social citizenship, remedial action should not be postponed until a more profound transformation of social relations can be accomplished. (Nor would many progressive teachers find such a stance helpful.) In Juliet Mitchell's words, 'a new society that is built on an old society that, within its limits, has reached a certain level of equality clearly is a better starting point than one that must build on a society predicated on privilege and unchallenged oppression' (Mitchell, 1976). Nevertheless, it is important to recognize what those limits are.

We have described the liberal-feminist project, and the equal opportunities work that reflects its concerns, as an attempt to remove or compensate for the ascriptive and social impediments that prevent women from competing on equal terms with men. But the language of equal opportunities is deceptively neutral. While it appears to embrace all women within its objectives, it does so only by overlooking the social realities of class and ethnic division. It is significant, in this context, that nearly all the research on equal opportunities treats girls as a homogenous category, failing to acknowledge the variety of their other social characteristics. Recent ILEA statistics on ethnic background and examination results provide an honourable, if still partial, exception (ILEA, 1987). In all the material on girls and science, for example, we could find no figures analysing the class and ethnic origins of girls who go on to do sixth form science, though it would indeed be surprising if these were not significant variables.

But a girl's experience of gender cannot be abstracted so neatly from any other aspects of her life. Girls from different social backgrounds will not experience patriarchal culture in identical ways, and the adult lives they anticipate will promise different kinds of opportunity, responsibility and experience. Their priorities as girls will reflect those disparities. (Thus, for example, opening up access to specialized science, even if successfully implemented, is not a programme that will be relevant to all.) The ERA will not be neutral in its effects on different classes and ethnic groups, and these consequences may prove more significant for many girls than some of those we have been discussing. How, to take one example, will increasing access via the National Curriculum improve the life-chances of girls trapped in under-resourced, struggling inner-city schools? The implications of the clauses on opting out, open enrolment and devolved management will have significant and divisive effects on large numbers of pupils, both girls and boys.

Even if we could somehow set aside issues of class and ethnic *origins*, a liberal-feminist reform of education would benefit only a minority of girls. Equal opportunities perspectives are circumscribed by the fact that they offer only the prospect that some individuals will advance in an unequal world. The framework within which men and women, as social equals, are intended to pursue success remains a meritocratic and competitive one. We have seen, indeed, that this openly inegalitarian government is not averse to equal opportunities measures insofar as these may enlarge the pool of talent from which employers may draw. But highly-paid and prestigious jobs are, by definition within such an order, relatively scarce, so that the achievement of parity between the sexes will still leave the inequalities *between* women (as well as those between men) unimpaired. It is always important to ask what happens, under such circumstances, to the majority population that inevitably falls behind.

Parents are promised by Government ministers that their children will be able to escape from schools that are 'failing'. This is hardly the language of a said, is an equal opportunities policy which, by glossing over the social differences between girls, can be consummated when some manage to escape to better things.

The reinforcement of gender hierarchies

If we ignore the rhetoric and consider the substance of the National Curriculum proposals, including the guidelines that Kenneth Baker has been issuing to the subject Working Groups, we can see that they are informed by a set of linked assumptions and priorities concerning the economy, technology and education. It is assumed, in the first instance, that the British economy can prosper in the world markets only by pursuing a vigorous policy of *growth* based on investment in high-technology industries; secondly, that the market is the only mechanism for efficient economic expansion, and that business must therefore be set free from all forms of collective constraint; and, thirdly, that the main function of education is to serve the needs of the 'enterprise culture', even if this can only be achieved at the expense of other educational objectives.

The pedagogic implications are captured by the word 'training' rather than education. The issue involved is not whether scientific and technological subjects should have a place within the core curriculum, but how these and other subjects should be taught and in what context. The government's commitment to a regime of high-tech economic growth is not to be deflected by encouraging debate about the social context and limits of technology, or centering issues of social control and responsibility in science. The kind of education apparently favoured by the Secretary of State is non-reflexive in character, essentially encouraging the learning of 'facts' rather than skills of interpretation, critical enquiry or aesthetic appreciation. (His guidelines to the History Working Group, stressing pupils' acquisition of their national culture, are another example of this outlook.) Values are not excluded from the educational process, but they enter as the inculcation of a *particular* set of viewpoints rather than in a spirit of open enquiry and with a due sense of relativity. As the Minister wrote to Lady Parkes, Chair of the Design and Technology Working Group: 'We want you to show how real world contexts for technological problem-solving can help to develop economic and careers awareness and business understanding' (DES, 1988e). Meanwhile, social and political education as a separate area of study is relegated to the margins of the curriculum and although, late in the day, a Task Group is to report on its status as a cross-curricular issue, any recommendations that the Group makes will, if accepted, be grafted on to subject curricula whose main outlines and content have already been decided.

The ERA's privileging of maths, science and technology incorporates a hidden curriculum on gender. It has been widely observed that the values and procedures of Western science tend to be gender-specific, reflecting distinctly masculine modes of thought and understanding (e.g., Easlea, 1981; Keller, 1982). These differences, we would contend, are social and historical in origin, not innate, but their effective presence in contemporary culture is hardly in dispute.

Under the Act, male-dominated areas of achievement and masculine styles of learning will be accorded even higher status than before, while feminine intellectual qualities and those subjects which girls currently find most attractive and accessible will be correspondingly devalued. We would not suggest that the gender contouring of this hierarchy of knowledge is intended, but the message that it will convey to girls and boys will be none the less powerful for that. (It is an ironic feature of equal opportunities perspectives that, far from challenging this principle of 'male-as-norm', they tend to endorse it by focusing so heavily on gaining entry for women into masculinised areas of life.)

The reverse side of this coin is the marginalization of that special curriculum for girls, organized around preparation for family life and motherhood, which has informed British education since Victorian times (Wolpe, 1974; Purvis 1984). Although Home Economics may still be taken as an option, it will have to compete in a restricted timetable with other subjects outside the core curriculum. From an equal opportunities perspective this could be interpreted favourably as representing a defeat for those conservative policy groups advocating separate adult roles for men and women and an appropriately differentiated curriculum for boys and girls (Anderson, 1988). But this would be to take a restricted view of the possibilities. The most likely outcome of excluding the personal and caring components of the curriculum from the core will be to preserve them as girls-only enclaves taken mainly by pupils with low career prospects (which means, of course that the tension between 'industry-led' conservatives and 'family traditionalists' will be substantially reconciled). If the government was concerned to foster sexual equality in adult life, it would accord these subject areas high status and, following the example of some LEAs, would seek to make them relevant for both sexes. HMI Patrick Orr has commented that 'many boys lack experience in the personal and caring areas of the curriculum' and that 'such initiatives may in the long term, help to establish the desirability of a broader curriculum for boys in the later secondary years' (Orr, 1985). Equal opportunities policies pursued in isolation tend to lead only to the phenomenon of the 'double working day' for women, or else to an increase in personal and domestic service as professional couples employ young or working class women to look after their children or do the housework. Persuading men to take on the routine responsibilities of caring, whether inside or outside the home, is quite as important for sexual equality as the conventional concerns of liberal-feminism. A curriculum that fails to acknowledge this can be considered neither balanced nor broad.

Finally, however, a vision of girls' education that goes beyond equal opportunities cannot be satisfied with adjustments in the sexual division of labour. 'Who does what?' is an important issue, but one that has to be transcended (not displaced) by questions concerning the social organisation of caring, reproduction, production and welfare. The preparation of children for adult life cannot be indifferent to the nature of a society in which women are systematically subordinated to men, yet divided in their experiences of inequality by dint of class and race. In some ways women's appreciation of the world is distinct from that of men. Perhaps it is by virtue of the fact that they 'straddle public and private worlds in different ways from men (that) they cannot so readily conceive of themselves in public terms alone' (Phillips, 1987), and so, as girls, are more interested in subjects having to do with 'people' rather than 'things'. But if all this is true, education to make children aware of their social and political environment, including anti-sexist and anti-racist work, has to be built into the foundations of the curriculum, not added on as an afterthought. The greatest threat to girls' education posed by the ERA may have nothing to do with its immediate implications for equal opportunities. The threat will come from its contribution to government efforts to stifle dissent and to exert control over the way we think.

References

ACKER, S. (1988) 'Teachers, gender and resistance', *British Journal of Sociology of Education*, 9, 3, pp. 307–22.

ANDERSON, D. (Ed.) (1988) *Full Circle*, Social Affairs Unit.

ARNOT, M. and WEINER, G. (Eds) (1987) *Gender and the Politics of Schooling*, London, Hutchinson.

ASSESSMENT AND PERFORMANCE UNIT (1988) *Science at Age 15*, HMSO.

ASSOCIATION FOR SCIENCE EDUCATION (1988) *Gender Issues in Science Education*, Working Party Draft Statement of Policy, Hatfield, ASE.

BENTLEY, D. and WATTS, M. (1986) 'Courting the positive virtues: a case for feminist science', *European Journal of Science Education*, 8, pp. 121–34. Reprinted in Kelly, A. (1987) *Science for Girls?*, Milton Keynes, Open University Press, pp. 89–99.

BUSWELL, C. (1981) 'Sexism in school routines and classroom practices', *Durham and Newcastle Research Review*, IX, pp. 195–200.

DAVID, M. (n.d.) 'A new ERA for education', unpublished paper.

DEEM, R. (1988) 'The great Education Reform Bill 1988 — some issues and implications', *Journal of Education Policy*, 3, 2, pp. 181–9.

DEMAINE, J. (1988) 'Teachers' work, curriculum and the New Right', *British Journal of Sociology of Education*, 3, pp. 247–64.

DES (1988a) *Science for Ages 5 to 16*, August.

DES (1988b) *Statistical Bulletin*, December.

DES (1988c) *National Curriculum Task Group on Assessment and Testing: A Report.*

DES (1988d) *DES News*, No. 175/88, 7 June.

DES (1988e) *National Curriculum Design and Technology Working Group Interim Report.*

DES (1989a) *National Curriculum: From Policy to Practice.*

DES (1989b) *Standards in Education 1987–8. A Report by H. M. Inspectorate.*

EASLEA, B. (1981) *Science and Sexual Oppression*, London, Weidenfeld and Nicholson.

EOC (1989) *Gender Issues: The Implications for Schools of the Education Reform Act 1988*, EOC Education Section.

GILLIGAN, C. (1982) *In a Different Voice*, Boston, Harvard University Press.

GOLDSTEIN, H. (1987) 'Gender bias and test norms in educational selection' in Arnot, M. and Weiner, G. (Eds) *Gender and the Politics of Schooling*, London, Hutchinson, pp. 122–6.

GREEN, A. (1988) 'Lessons in Standards', *Marxism Today*, January, pp. 24–31.

HARDING, J. (1983) *Switched Off: The Science Education of Girls*, Longman for the Schools Council.

HARDING, J. (Ed.) (1986) *Perspectives on Gender and Science*, Lewes, Falmer Press.

HILLGATE GROUP (1986) *Whose Schools? A Radical Manifesto*, London, Hillgate Group.

HISKETT, M. (1988) 'Should sons and daughters be brought up differently? Radical feminism in schools', in Anderson, D. (Ed.) *Full Circle*, Social Affairs Unit, pp. 153–168.

HOUGH, J. R. (1987) *Education and the National Economy*, London, Croom Helm.

ILEA (1987) *Ethnic Background and Examination Results, 1985 and 1986*, RS 1120/87

JAMIESON, I. and WATTS, T. (1987) 'Squeezing out enterprise' in *The Times Educational Supplement*, 18 December.

JEFFERIES, G. and STREATFIELD, (1989) *Reconstitution of School Governors*, Slough, NFER.

JOFFE, L. and FOXMAN, D. (1988) *Attitudes and Gender Differences: Mathematics at Age 11 and 15*, APU, Windsor, NFER–Nelson.

JOHNSON, S. and MURPHY, P. (1986) *Girls and Physics*, APU Occasional Paper 4, DES.

KELLER, E. F. (1982) Feminism and Science' in Keohane, N. O. *et al* (Eds.) *Feminist Theory: A Critique of Ideology*, Brighton, Harvester Press, pp. 113–26.

KELLY, A. (1987) 'Why girls don't do science', in Kelly, A. (Ed.) *Science For Girls*, Milton Keynes, Open University Press.

KELLY, A. (1988) 'Towards a democratic science education' in Lauder, H. and Brown, P. (Eds) *Education in Search of a Future*, Lewes, Falmer Press, pp. 150–73.

LE RICHE, E. (1988) *Why do teenage girls truant?*, London, Roehampton Institute of Higher Education, Department of Sociology and Social Administration.

LICHT, B. G. and DWECK, C. S. (1987) 'Sex differences in achievement orientations', in Arnot, M. and Weiner, G. *Gender and the Politics of Schooling*, London, Hutchinson, pp. 95–107.

MAHONEY, P. (1985) *Schools for the Boys? Co-education Re-assessed*, London, Hutchinson in association with the Explorations in Feminism Collective.

MILES, S. and FURLONG, J. (1988) 'Teachers training teachers: an opportunity for a sociological break in education transmission?', in Woods, P. and Pollard, A. (Eds) *Sociology and Teaching*, London, Croom Helm, pp. 76–91.

MILLMAN, V. and WEINER, G. (1987) 'Engendering equal opportunities: the case of TVEI and secondary education', in Gleeson, D. (Ed.) *TVEI and Secondary Education*, Milton Keynes, Open University Press, pp. 165–76.

MITCHELL, J. (1976) 'Women and equality' in Mitchell, J. and Oakley, A. (Eds) *The Rights and Wrongs of Women*, London, Penguin, pp. 379–99. Reprinted in Phillips, A. (Ed.) (1978) *Feminism and Equality*, Oxford, Blackwell, pp. 24–43.

NATIONAL CURRICULUM COUNCIL (1988) Consultation Report, Science, December, York.

NATIONAL ECONOMIC DEVELOPMENT COUNCIL (1982) *Education and Industry*, Memorandum by the Director General, ref. NEDC (82) 85.

ORR, P. (1985) 'Sex bias in schools: national perspectives', in Whyte, T. *et al.* (Eds) *Girl Friendly Schooling*, London, Methuen, pp. 7–23.

PANDYA, A. (1989) 'Equal but different', *Education*, 24 March.

PHILLIPS, A. (Ed.) (1987) *Feminism and Equality*, Oxford, Blackwell.

PRATT, J. (1985) 'The attitudes of teachers' in Whyte, J. et al. (Eds.) *Girl Friendly Schooling*, London, Methuen.

PRATT, J., BLOOMFIELD, J. and SEALE, C. (1984) *Option Choice: A Question of Equal Opportunity*, Windsor, NFER–Nelson.

PURVIS, J. (1984), *Women's Education*, Open University Course E205, Block 6, Unit 25, Milton Keynes, Open University Press.

SMAIL, B. (1984) *Girl Friendly Science: Avoiding Sex-Bias in the Classroom*, London, Longman.

SPEAR, M. (1987) 'Teachers' views about the inportance of science for boys and girls' in Kelly, A. (Ed.) *Science for Girls*, Milton Keynes, Open University Press, pp. 52–57.

STANWORTH, M. (1983) *Gender and Schooling: A Study of Sexual Divisions in the Classroom*, London, Hutchinson in association with the Explorations in Feminism Collective.

WHYTE, J. (1986) *Girls Into Science and Technology*, London, Routledge and Kegan Paul.

WOLPE, A. M. (1974) 'The official ideology of education for girls' in Flude, M. and Ahier, J. (Eds.) *Educability, Schools and Ideology*, London, Croom Helm, pp. 139–159.

WOLPE, A. M. (1988) *Within School Walls*, London, Routledge.

12
The Education Reform Act — The Implications for Special Educational Needs

Philippa Russell

> The 1988 Act aims to raise the expectations of all pupils, including those with statements. Built into that Act are provisions to ensure that these expectations are appropriate so that all children, including those with special educational needs, can benefit to the best of their ability. Irrespective of the type of school placement, appropriateness and quality of provision are vital. (DES, 1988)

The Education Reform Act sets the scene for educational advancement (or decline) for decades to come. One of the most complex pieces of legislation in recent years, it aims to 'promote the spiritual, moral, cultural, mental and physical development of pupils' — aspirations with which all of us who are parents would have sympathy. But the strategies for achieving these global aims are less clear, more centralized and imply a new competitiveness within a 'market place' approach to education in the UK.

The 1981 Act gave LEAs new strategic roles in orchestrating a complex range of services in meeting *individual* special educational needs, acknowledging the changing context and concepts of disability and learning difficulties. But the Education Reform Act weakens the powers of LEAs and many parents and professionals fear that children with special needs may seem less attractive to ordinary schools without the advocacy and support of coherent whole-authority policies and the relevant support and advisory services. Kenneth Baker, in an interview with Margaret Peter, editor of *Special Education*, forecast a small group of very specialized special schools by the end of the century (with integration increasing) (Baker, 1988). Some would fear the opposite and see a return to special schools as sanctuaries for resources and serious back-tracking in ordinary schools where children with special needs may seem too expensive and complicated to manage. However, all new legislation is initially perplexing and, fortunately, UK legislation has always been enabling rather than minutely prescriptive — even when laying down the components of a National Curriculum! Before resigning ourselves to permanent depression and a feeling that special needs have slipped from the political agenda, it may be useful to look again at some of the implications for change *for the better* (as well as for the worse) within the new legislation and to identify in particular where the 1981 and 1988 Acts prove incompatible. One minor consolation may be the realization by parents and LEAs (both officers and elected members) that they are going to need each other as they never did before and that partnership in the Warnock mode must be cherished and actively developed over the coming decade.

The cornerstone of the 1988 Act — towards the National Curriculum

The National Curriculum will be introduced progressively from the start of the Autumn Term 1989. Draft guidance notes that 'the Curriculum is expected to be balanced and broadly based and relevant to the full range of pupils' needs' (DES, 1988). The same guidance (a revision of Circular 1/83 setting out arrangements for assessment and statements of special educational needs in the context of the 1988 Act) emphasizes that 'the Secretary of State believes that *all* pupils, including those with special educational needs, should have the opportunity to obtain the maximum benefit possible from it' (my emphasis). Some consumer organizations have suggested that the Act might offer *entitlement* which could be capable of legal endorsement. Some special schools, like the independent sector, recognize that they may be exempted from the constraints of such a curriculum, but feel that it should be followed for comparability with all schools and pupils. Encouragingly some of the curriculum consultation papers (including Maths and English) have fully endorsed the importance of having curriculum arrangements which do include all pupils and which offer a progression of skills which will be applicable to all pupils.

However, Sheila Browne, a former Senior Chief Inspector, expressed the genuine concern — and aspirations — of parents and professionals when she spoke at the North of England Education Conference:

> If only one could be sure that in the Bill, the overriding sub-clause, 1[2] would dominate. This reads: 'The curriculum for a maintained school satisfies the requirements of this section if it is a balanced and broadly based curriculum which (a) promotes the spiritual, moral, cultural, mental and physical development of pupils at the school and of society; and (b) prepares such pupils for the opportunities, responsibilities and experience of adult life.' That is light years away from clause 2 with its itemized requirements for attainment targets, programmes of study and assessments arrangements . . . (Brown, 1988).

The debate over the need for a National Curriculum is an old one. Most of our neighbouring EEC countries have some form of national curricular framework within their schools. But there are inherent dangers in 'borrowing' other education systems without examining their potential fallibility and looking to the needs and aspirations of *all* children within the present system. There have always been two voices about the introduction of any such National Curriculum in the

UK. Lord Eccles in the 1970s described the National Curriculum as a 'secret garden' within which children would flourish. In 1988 Lord Joseph forecast in the House of Lords that a National Curriculum would be a 'straight jacket upon our schools'. Certainly the idea of a broad but differentiated curriculum being part of the entitlement of all children would gain general support. For children with *special* needs, the concepts of 'access to the curriculum' and 'curriculum entitlement' have been long-term objectives of those who have admired the curricular requirements of Public Law 94:143 in the USA. But there will not be 'equal access' to the curriculum for children with special needs under the present arrangements. Independent schools will not be required to follow such a curriculum — although the vast majority of children in independent *special* schools are sponsored by LEAs who will have general duties within their own schools to implement a centrally determined curriculum. Children with Statements may have parts of the curriculum modified or may be exempted altogether. Whilst flexibility is important (essential in the light of Lord Joseph's fears about 'straightjackets'), modification and disapplication of parts of the National Curriculum may be too easy for special needs. In the new market place with financial delegation and theoretically greater power for parents as managers in schools, access to the full curriculum will require resources. For children with special needs, it will also require understanding and protection of support services to ensure equal opportunities for all.

The Warnock Report (DES, 1978) introduced a wider concept of special educational needs. The abolition of the old categories of disability reflected a new era of thinking about not only *educability* (the 1970 Education Act having established that principle with regard to all children even those with severe learning difficulties) but also about the purposes of education for all children. Warnock emphasized the importance of acknowledging a continuum of special needs, noting that 'it is . . . impossible to establish precise criteria for defining what constitutes handicap' (*ibid.*). The Committee envisaged up to 20 per cent of the school population having some kind of special need during their school lifetime. In terms of a National Curriculum, formally implemented and regularly tested, such a flexible approach, based on the recognition of a broad continuity of special needs rather than specific definitions of disability, seems unlikely for a substantial proportion of the population. It also raises the question of what a National Curriculum is *for*. There can be little doubt that parents and politicians alike want *quality* in education. But how do we define an 'effective education'?. The Fish Committee, appointed by the ILEA to review special educational provision in the ILEA (ILEA, 1985), emphasized the importance of seeing the aims of education as being substantially the same for *all* children, noting that:

> the long-term aims of education for children and young people include the achievement of responsible personal autonomy and full participation in the communities within which they live . . . *The aims of education for children and young people with disabilities and significant difficulties are the same as those for all children and young people* (ILEA, 1985).

The Fish Committee emphasized the need for schools to have a clear idea of progression in all aspects of the curriculum and to use it in evaluating individual progress. It emphasized that it was only possible to become aware of children who have special educational needs if the progress of *all* children was adequately monitored.

Arrangements for assessment and testing

Assessment and testing have always been integral parts of the education system. The motivation for assessment arrangements has been varied. Early identification is essential for effective intervention and parents are bitterly resentful of time lost when a learning difficulty has beeen overlooked or disregarded over a period of time. Assessment may also be a corporate activity in order to ensure that the teacher has an overview of how the whole class is learning, of any children who need special help to make progress and the efficacy (or otherwise) of teaching methods and materials. Assessment may also serve as surveillance for other non-educational problems such as family or health needs.

The Fish Committee (ILEA, 1985) saw continuous assessment and 'progress' as being clearly linked to a process which acknowledged that the sequence of goals in different curriculum areas would vary in respect of individuals and groups. The notions of continuous assessment and progress do indeed exist within the National Curriculum and the proposed assessment and testing arrangements. But, as the DES curriculum consultation document noted:

> At the heart of the assessment process there will be nationally prescribed tests done by all pupils to supplement the individual teachers' assessments. Teachers will administer and mark these, but their marking — and their assessments overall — will be externally moderated. (DES, 1987a)

For any parent of a child with special needs, the notion of 'nationally prescribed tests' and 'externally moderated assessments' could appear entirely retrogressive and quite contrary to a broader definition of special needs. Circular 1/83 on the assessment procedures of the 1981 Education Act rightly noted that: 'Assessment should be seen as a partnership between teacher, other professionals and parents in a *joint* endeavour to discover and understand the nature and different needs of individual children' (DES and DHSS, 1983).

Although the 1981 Act has been criticized by the House of Commons Select Committee (1987) and the University of London Institute of Education research (Goacher *et al.*, 1988) for bureaucracy and an escalation of paper work and associated delays, most parents would acknowledge that things are getting better. Parental involvement in assessment is becoming a reality. Statistics on the numbers of children integrated into mainstream schools are difficult to obtain (particularly where such children are nominally on the roll of a special school but spend all or part of their school week in a mainstream school). However, DES figures suggest a steady, albeit slow, increase in numbers. Parents' organizations confirm growing demand from younger parents in particular for mainstream placements for their children, with correspondingly higher expectations of the education system. As the House of Commons Select Committee (1987) stressed: 'There is very general support for the comprehensiveness of the assessment procedures set out in the Act, particularly their multiprofessional nature and the participation of parents'. But a major cause for concern in the new climate of 'testing' and monitoring children's academic progress must be the tension between such specific time-related monitoring and the more dynamic and multiprofessional approach to assessment processes begun by the 1981 Education Act and endorsed by the Select Committee. The complexity of formal assessment under the 1981 Act has been much criticized. Yet some of this bureaucracy has been inevitable because of the requirement for the first time in UK legislation that health, social services and *parents* should be seen as equal stakeholders in assessing needs and making the subsequent provision work.

How the National Curriculum will work for children with special educational needs

Section 2 of the 1988 Act requires the curriculum in every maintained school to comprise (a) a basic curriculum which includes religious education for all pupils regardless of age (except those in a maintained special school), and (b) the National Curriculum for pupils of compulsory school age. The National Curriculum consists of core and foundation subjects, for each of which there will be established:

1. *Attainment Targets,* defined as the knowledge, skills and understanding pupils are expected to have by the end of each key stage. They will provide targets for what is to be learned in each subject during that stage.
2. *Programmes of Study,* defined as the matters, skills and processes which must be taught to pupils during each key stage. These programmes will set out the ground to be covered in order to meet the *attainment targets* in 1 above.
3. *Assessment arrangements,* defined as the arrangements for assessing pupils at or near the end of key stages for the purpose of finding out what they have achieved in relation to the attainment targets set for that stage.

The *core* subjects of the National Curriculum are mathematics, English and science, the *foundation* subjects are history, geography, technology, music, art, physical education at all stages, and for secondary pupils a modern foreign language. All the attainment targets, programmes of study and assessment arrangements are to be specified in relation to four *key stages* covering the period of compulsory schooling. These key stages will be approximately ages 5–7, 7–11, 11–14 and 14–16, although some variation is possible for individual pupils.

DES guidance on the implementation of the curriculum and assessment notes that 'both attainment targets and programmes of study must be appropriate to pupils of different abilities and maturities' (DES, 1988). A Task Group on Assessment and Testing was appointed under the chairmanship of Professor Black and has reported on how children's progress might be assessed — including those children who have special educational needs. The Task Group (DES, 1987b) recommended that wherever possible, such children should undertake national tests if they were able to do so, and, by implication, that children should follow the National Curriculum wherever possible. The Task Group acknowledged, however, that a special unit should produce test material and devise testing and assessment procedures appropriate to the needs of such children. It concluded that national tests should wherever possible be appropriate to children across the whole ability range and modified as necessary for children with particular problems, including those with communication difficulties. The Task Group recommended also that *exemption* from the national testing programme should be at the discretion of the head teacher if testing would be likely to produce such stress that a medical or emotional condition would be exacerbated. To avoid the possibility of children seeing themselves as 'failures', the national tests should be designed in such a way as to permit the teacher to curtail the test discretely without the child being conscious that this was being done.

The notion of *entitlement* to a National Curriculum could be to the advantage of children with special needs, who have been too readily excluded in the past. But the concept of exclusion and disapplication from the National Curriculum poses a range of problems. The National Curriculum *will* apply to all children with special educational needs, but taking into account their particular cases or circumstances. Draft guidance suggests how this might be done:

1. By orders or regulations, for example where attainment targets, programmes of study or assessment arrangements involve practical or demonstration work which might be impossible for a child with a disability.
2. In a Statement of special educational needs made under the 1981 Education Act. Any or all of the requirements of the National Curriculum may be modified or disapplied if they are inappropriate for the pupil concerned (Clauses 17 and 18 of the 1988 Act).
3. By regulations which will enable a head teacher to disapply or modify the application of the National Curriculum temporarily in specified circumstances. Such instances could include the time during which a child was being assessed under the 1981 Act or in periods of family difficulty, ill health or other *temporary* reasons. Clause 19 of the Act sets out the temporary exemptions in greater detail. Such exemptions should not last for longer than six months in the first instance (extendable on review) and are primarily the decision of the head teacher. The head teacher has no duty, as under the 1981 Act, to take advice from a range of professionals nor from the local authority, although she or he could do so voluntarily.

Some of the greatest fears have been expressed about temporary exemptions, where the parent is *told* rather than consulted, where the appeal process is less rigorous than under the 1981 Act and where a child could find it very difficult to return to the full curriculum without immediate intervention and proper support in the exemption period.

The DES (1989) gives practical consideration as to how the basic requirements of the National Curriculum can be adapted so that children with special educational needs can benefit so far as they are able. The DES envisages such adaptation as being achievable by:

1. Enabling pupils to progress through the ten levels covering compulsory schooling at a slower speed than their contemporaries.
2. Avoiding over-prescription in programmes of study in each foundation subject, so that teachers are free to determine their own teaching approaches and ways of delivering the programmes. The consultation documents on English, Mathematics and Science published by the National Curriculum Council (1988) indicate some different methods of adapting the curriculum to special needs, for example for physical or sensory handicaps.
3. By enabling individual pupils to work with a class of older or younger pupils for some or all subjects, since each key stage is defined by reference to the age of the majority of pupils in a class or teaching group. The DES states that there is no intention that pupils should have to be kept down or moved up on the grounds of how they do in formal assessments alone (as happens in West Germany).
4. Using the overlap of levels of attainment and of programmes of study between the four key stages in each foundation subject so that pupils can work according to their own abilities and needs at each stage.

However, the four approaches to meeting special needs flexibly within a classroom setting may be inadequate and, if so, there may be considerable pressure to disapply the National Curriculum.

The greatest anxiety about pupils with special needs will almost certainly lie with those who do not have Statements (which must in the future indicate precisely how the National Curriculum will be modified for the individual pupil) and the accompanying resources for any special educational provision to be made. The arrangements for temporary modifications and disapplications of parts of the curriculum could pose threats to children for whom no adequate substitute arrangements were made. Appeal rights against temporary modifications are limited, with the governors who hear such appeals probably being reluctant to query a head teacher's decision. Additionally, whilst the 1981 Act assessment procedures require consultation with school psychological, health and education services and with parents, temporary modifications only require that parents are *informed*. Whilst protracted and bureaucratic assessment procedures would clearly be unworkable with temporary modifications, the procedures must be seen as potentially damaging to children and likely to precipitate self-fulfilling prophecies when children with temporary exemptions are quite unable to re-enter the National Curriculum after six months absence from it.

If *assessment* is the key to progress and achievement, what are parents of children with special needs to make of these new arrangements for assessment and testing? Of course, schools have always tested. A survey by the University of London (Gipps *et al.*, 1983) found that testing at ages seven and eight was fairly common in LEAs and that 86 per cent of schools used tests with whole age groups on top of those required by their LEA. But the tests most currently used were standardized group reading and reasoning tests — not related to the curriculum in primary schools and used as a process for recording progress in a child and also identifying incipient special needs. The new tests, with their prescribed 'levels', will be there to ensure that the curriculum is *taught.* Even if flexibility in the *age* at which children take particular tests is assured, how long will we wait before we hear children described as 'level one' or 'level two' with all the implications of failing to keep pace with their peers? Inevitably, testing will introduce a degree of competition into classes. Formal and structured teaching will become more significant. Parents as well as teachers will be anxious for school to 'perform well'. Already one London borough is proposing to keep children 'down' a year if they fall behind. The concept of a truly comprehensive system must be threatened by the sometimes arbitrary introduction of 'performance indicators' which affect a child's chronological progress through the school system.

An obsession with competition and 'success' (however defined) in any service of life bodes ill for minority groups. It is part of a much wider ethos, forecast in the White Paper *Working Together — Education and Training* (DES, 1986), which clearly links the lack of competition and motivation for achievement in schools with Britain's serious economic difficulties. The city technology colleges in turn aspire to attract premium funding from industry and capture top teachers by luring them with enhanced terms and conditions — and will extract 'contracts' of a kind with successful pupils and parents to ensure that they maintain commitment to an enriched education programme. It is interesting to speculate how may *disabled* children will have access to the accelerated curriculum and undoubtedly greater employability opportunities of the city technology colleges. It is to be hoped that competitiveness does not spill over into further education, where so much progress has been made in developing programmes for students with a range of disabilities. At the back of any parent's mind is the thought that we do need expectations (if not competition). We should expect that young people with special needs should acquire skills which make them employable. We must monitor how children progress and ensure that schools are accountable, effective and meeting local community needs. But we also need to remember that success can be described in different ways for different children. The *attainable* targets of Professor Black and TGAT must be the way forward, for they will ensure realistic goals, targeted educational resources and respect for differences in individual abilities. One of the most encouraging developments is the announcement in January 1989 that *records of achievement* will be generally introduced and that, tests notwithstanding, all children will have relevant and positive personal profiles which emphasize *success.*

Implications for integration

The 1981 Act was intended to set the framework for increased integration in schools. Although the conditions for integration could have been used to ensure that it never happened, general consensus is that there is a widespread (albeit slow) increase in mainstream placements for some groups of children with special needs. But despite the Government's firm avowals in both Houses of Parliament that the Education Reform Act would not reverse this trend, most parents would argue that a reversal in integration is almost inevitable. As the University of London research showed:

> It was apparent that professionals and administrators in education, health and social services held a wide range of views concerning what constitutes integration. It also became clear that diametrically opposed opinions of and attitudes to integration were often found within one LEA. (Goacher *et al.*, 1988)

The Fish Committee (ILEA, 1985) described integration as 'planned interaction' and emphasized the importance of perceiving integration as a process not a state. The Committee perceived the dangers of regarding integration as placement only and the need to see it as a process by which the school, relevant professionals, pupils, parents and the child worked together to achieve maximum co-operation and genuine integration in all aspects of school and community life. But such 'planned interaction' will have resource implications and it will affect the way in which a school views its own responsibility to *all* members of a local community. Many parents fear that open enrolment will make popular schools less willing to commit themselves to children with special needs. Financial delegation to schools (even if there is some form of 'premium funding' accompanying a special needs child) will challenge the new breed of governors who are actually required to govern with uncomfortable truths to face in their own budgeting if they fail to take account of the special requirements of such children. Many of us are already cynical about the emphasis given to disability even within schools which have an 'equal opportunities' policy. The consequences of the new legislation for children with special educational needs who do *not* have a statement could be considerable. Some LEAs have traditionally opted for 'low statementing' policies. Some, like Oxfordshire, felt a minimalist policy was right because they could provide support services without recourse to formal assessment procedures — in themselves consumers of expensive resources in terms of staffing. But the LEAs will have very limited resources for such a centralist policy under the 1988 Act. Not only is there likely to be increased pressure for statements from anxious parents and from schools. Schools will also have to make important 'in house' decisions about how they prioritize the needs of larger groups of children with special needs without a statement and the extra resources they require from within the school budget. The temptation to modify and disapply parts of the national curriculum could seem a tempting solution when there are competing priorities (such as the need for extra science or maths teachers).

Integration has been a process of evolution rather than revolution in the United Kingdom. Many integration programmes have, perhaps ironically, developed from the special schools themselves which have frequently fought hard to develop at least part-time integration programmes with local mainstream schools. The advantage of what has been called 'incremental' integration is that it demonstrates the art of the possible to doubting mainstream schools and offers direct experienced and available support from the staff of the special school to support a mainstream placement. The numbers of such schemes are not recorded (some indeed operating entirely on an informal basis). But Seamus Hegarty (1988) noted that 'there is wisdom in flexibility when there are no absolute truths . . . diversity permits experiment and can encourage creative responses to individual needs'. He recognized that such diversity could be arbitrary in practice and lead to over-dependence upon 'individual enthusiasm and happenstance' rather than the development of clear frameworks with accountability and a policy thrust. But unfortunately the Education Reform Act seems unlikely to permit the existence of at least some degree of 'happenstance' within individual schools facing integration for the first time. Hegarty (1988) found that three-quarters of the special schools in the NFER study of support in ordinary schools had links with local ordinary schools. Other schools were planning such arrangements. About a third of schools also sent *staff* out into mainstream schools. At least a quarter of the teachers spent at least a full day a week in ordinary schools. Whilst the LEA retains the strategic overview, such arrangements can flourish and indeed develop into larger LEA-wide policies for integration. But without such an LEA perspective (and many of us fear the gradual erosion of the commitment and parent and professional solidarity which has been a feature of the special needs sector even during the recent hard years of undervalued education services and demoralized staff), it is difficult to see the growth of the 'whole school policy' advocated by Fish and Hegarty as a condition of effective integration. One potential barrier to integration in the 1981 Act was the requirement that integration should represent 'an efficient use of resources'. In the more competitive open market, with a declining birth rate and threats of school closures in some authorities, integration could be seen to be exactly the opposite of efficient use of resources unless there is a strong national and local authority view that it is right and, as Ronald Davie said at the North of England Education Conference in 1988, 'the onus is now upon LEAs to demonstrate why a child should not be admitted to ordinary schools with appropriate support rather than arguing the reverse'. But the LEAs may not be doing the arguing and the new generation of parent governor-managers may have a sharper view about what constitutes quality in education and the optimum targets for their budgets in order to achieve such goals.

The role of the LEA — the implications of local financial management and grant-maintained schools

Provision for special educational needs requires continuous negotiation between a range of LEA schools and support and advisory services. But the Coopers and Lybrand Associates Report (1987) notes 'a new culture and philosophy', of how education is organized at school level. The shift away from local administration to local *management* by schools has major implications for children with special educational needs. Guidance on the 1981 Act endorses the concept of effective multi-professional work (requiring co-operation, collaboration and mutual support on the part of all the contributors) as a means of identification of learning difficulties. But the skills, perceptions and insights of professionals in different disciplines will be more difficult to bring together when more responsibilities are devolved to schools. Although the same guidance emphasizes the need for clearly identified channels of communication to gain access to outside specialized support and advice between schools and child health, social services and the school psychological service, many schools will have little experience in managing such resources, or indeed in resourcing multi-professional record-keeping and assessment procedures.

The Coopers and Lybrand Report proposed that LEA advisory and inspectorate services should be 'bought in' on a customer/contractor basis by the grant-maintained schools (and, presumably, by other schools under local financial management). At present an *LEA* can orchestrate its own advisory, inspectorate, psychological, education welfare and school medical services. But, as Coopers and Lybrand noted:

> If *schools* had the responsibility to 'buy in' psychological, welfare or medical services, such resource decisions would need to be balanced against their other demands for resources. This might encourage a tendency in schools to under-purchase such services and seek to make do with staff less professionally qualified, perhaps at the expense of the pupil(s) concerned. (*ibid.*)

The Report goes on to confirm many parents' worst fears, namely that 'there might be an unfortunate tendency for schools to be more reluctant to accept pupils who might need such services — in so far as schools were in a position to influence entry' (*ibid.*). Although an 'insurance' approach could theoretically be adopted (rather than a complex and burdensome fee-per-item approach in buying special services), the end product could be the loss of an overall LEA plan and enormous problems for the grant-maintained schools. If resource allocation is too low, then pupils with special needs might indeed be excluded. But the reverse could be true if 'premium funding' is very generous. In that instance schools might bid for pupils whose needs they could not address because of the associated revenue consequences and in order to maximize resources in a particular establishment. In either case, arrangements would tend to be *ad hoc* and the basis for calculation complicated. With random demand and debates about accountability for costs, it is hard to envisage LEA support services escaping disruption and fragmentation within the new arrangements. Additionally pupils without statements, which can carry extra resources, might well be disadvantaged and possibly viewed more unfavourably by popular schools already over-subscribed under open enrolment.

Parents as partners?

The Warnock Report heralded the advent of an era of 'parents as partners'. The concept of parent participation was written into the 1981 Education Act, with its emphasis on collaboration and informed consent. If the rhetoric did not always match the reality, the failure lay not in intent but in the timescale of acknowledging that both voluntary and statutory services must work together to provide parents with advice, training, support and respect in order to become 'partners'. The work of Sheila Wolfendale (1986) in developing 'parent profiles' as a means of enabling parents to use their genuine expertise and observations on their child during assessment reflected what Warnock had called a 'sea change' in attitudes and expectations not just about disability and special needs, but about the concept of *families* as contributors to the assessment process. The new partnership did not only extend to assessment. The 1986 and 1988 Education Acts have been hailed as 'empowering' parents in other directions. Research from Plowden onwards has shown the importance of involving parents in schools. But the new arrangements, as Tomlinson (1988) noted, mean that 'parents are being asked to adopt the role of inquisitor and monitor of teachers and schools, and to use the new complaints procedures, all in the exercise of consumer sovereignty'.

The DES White Paper, *Better Schools* (1985), emphasized that the quality of education concerned *everyone*. The report set out a number of policies for education in schools which had been 'reviewed by the Government and its partners'. But the Education Reform Act redistributes old and allocates new powers — estimated at over 180 — to the present and future Secretary of State. The tension between centrally-directed education policy and devolution to individual schools (which may be less benevolent and harder to challenge on policy issues than LEAs) must have repercussions on *parents* whether or not they are exercising their new powers under the legislation. Many parent organizations wonder whether parents will wish to assume new responsibilities in governing and managing schools, when the tasks will be heavy and the decisions difficult with partnership assuming the role of a business exercise. Revised Draft Circular 1/83 (DES, 1988), examining assessment procedures under the 1981 Act, comments on *participation* by parents. 'Frankness and openness' are recommended, together with the need for parent advocates and accurate information in 'straightforward plain language'. But guidance for parents on the 1988 Act is less clear, despite the likely anxiety of parents whose children have temporary exemptions. Parents of children with special needs will also worry about the willingness of all parents to accept equal responsibility for less advantaged children.

Most importantly, as noted below, the ability of the LEA to advise and orchestrate a range of support and advisory services may be greatly limited. Attainment targets, programmes of study and assessment are intended to offer parents, schools, LEAs and the government clearer and comparable information about the achievements of pupils and schools in ways that can improve performance individually and generally. However, the new arrangements appear to see such assessment as essentially 'in school' and there is little mention in the draft guidance of the wider range of professional advisers who might contribute to such clearer understanding when a child is experiencing difficulties. The draft revised circular on assessment and the 1981 Act (DES, 1988) conversely (when discussing special educational needs and *statemented* children) proposes that modification or disapplication of the national curriculum will be decided by an LEA in the light of educational, medical, psychological and other evidence, including the views of the child's parents. The procedure will be subject to the parents being consulted. Although Section 55 of the Circular suggests that modification or disapplication should 'be applied sensitively and positively', in the case of temporary exemptions parents need only be *informed.* Hence parents of children with special educational needs *without* statements will have less protection and their children could have significant changes in curriculum made without wider professional consultation.

Implications for governors

The DES pamphlet (1988), *School Govenors — A New Role,* states that the 1986 Act has created a new statutory framework for school government. The redefinition of the respective roles of governors, local authority and head teacher will enable each to make their own distinctive contribution to a school's 'success'. 'Success' is the key word, for both the 1986 and 1988 Acts, in theory at least, represent moves towards a pursuit of excellence in education. The 1988 Act has the overall objective of promoting 'higher standards of education' in all maintained schools. Governors will share responsibility for the first time equally with the head teacher and LEA for implementing the new procedures. Financial delegation will impose major new duties with regard to forward planning and prioritizing of available resources in schools.

All these arrangements could be of advantage to children with special educational needs. The increased numbers of *community* governors could produce more caring schools. Some parents of disabled children have argued that the Education Reform Act might give a new *entitlement* to access to the full curriculum for those children who had previously missed out because of their special needs. But the majority of parents fear exactly the opposite. Compatibility between the philosophy of the 1981 Act (which relies on an LEA strategy for orchestrating the various professional resources needed to meet special educational needs), and the 'market forces' approach of the 1988 Act which places major responsibilities upon individual schools, may be hard to achieve.

Governors will have major new duties as well as powers, the National Foundation for Educational Research in a recent report suggested that some 400,000 school governors would be needed in England and Wales (Roberts, 1988). The National Confederation of Parent Teacher Associations, at its Spring Conference 1988, echoed the alarms expressed by many LEAs that there would be real difficulties in finding sufficient parents and local community members to participate in governing schools. A survey by the Labour Party in July 1988 (*The*

Times Educational Supplement, 28 October 1988) found that 63 per cent of LEAs contacted had problems in recruiting *parent* governors. In practice, however, most LEAs appear to have recruited their full complement of *parent* governors. But representatives from *voluntary* organizations have proved much more difficult to find. The new duties will be time-consuming. Without out-of-pocket expenses (as are already paid to Community Health Council members and magistrates) and child-minding and loss of earnings compensation if appropriate, parents of children with special needs and disabled people will be penalized in seeking to become governors. Equally worrying, NFER (Roberts, 1988) found that only 11,000 governors received any training in 1987. Conversely, all new magistrates (who are also lay people) now have compulsory initial training and ample opportunity for further training throughout their careers.

Problems in recruitment and training are particularly serious when considering the implications of the new legislation for special educational needs. Local financial management, for example, will test the new governing bodies. Prior to the 1988 Act, LEAs had primary responsibility for the orchestration of the rich network of services which children with special needs might require. The 'whole authority' approach made sense when special needs were randomly distributed and where some authorities (such as the ILEA at the time of the Fish Report) might have 65 per cent or more of their special needs pupils identified where they were already in mainstream schools and not conveniently identified at the beginning of a financial year. In these circumstances, planning on a *school* basis will be almost impossible without the LEA's strategic role. The temptation for governors not to fund remedial preventive services may be very great when the generous resourcing of a mathematics or geography department will show easily observable results and may appear to please the majority of the parents.

Perhaps the keynote to success under the new arrangements is training. Training will include accurate information and the Welsh Consumer Council has already taken a major initiative in preparing an information resource for parents and governors. As the DES White Paper, *Better Schools,* emphasized, quality in education concerns *everyone.* But consumer responsibility will not come easily.

Conclusion

In July 1988, Bob Dunn in the House of Commons stated:

> A striking feature of the passage of the Bill has been the concern shown for pupils with special needs not merely by Members in both Houses but by Members of both sides of each House. I am glad to observe that the welfare of children with special needs is one subject that can be guaranteed to transcend party divisions and to unite both sides of the House. (Hansard, 3 July, 1988)

The unanimity across party, professional and disability boundaries was indeed a characteristic of the debate as the Education Reform Bill trundled through

Parliament. It was entirely due to this genuine cross-bench support that some concessions were indeed won for children with special educational needs in a complex and massive piece of legislation which set out to reform UK education more radically than the 1944 Act had done and in a fifth of the time. But consumers, professionals and local authorities alike all considered that awareness of special educational needs came much too late in a piece of legislation which, in the words of Kenneth Baker (press release on the 'Education Reform Bill', November 1987), set out to provide 'a better education — relevant to the late twentieth century and beyond — for *all* our children, whatever their ability, wherever they live, whatever type of school their parents choose for them'. Those of us concerned about special educational needs share those aspirations. For parents of children and young people with special needs, they represent a philosophical basis to our educational system. As Mary Warnock has observed:

> An educational policy that is for *everyone* is not necessarily one that is incompatible with competition . . . schools may compete with one another to do better *for* their pupils. But we must remember that competition can best and most fruitfully take place in a condition of justice where everyone may enter the race and do his [sic] best . . . no-one has the authority to impose form on the educational system but parliament itself. It is crucial, therefore, that Parliament should base its decisions not on prejudice or ignorance but on a democratic belief in the possibility of educating *all* children. (Warnock, 1988)

But what about the 1981 Education Act, which has had profound effects upon the thinking and expectations of parents, local authorities and indeed on local communities in meeting the needs of 'all children'? Incompatibility with the Education Reform Act seems a real possibility unless the issues of a national curriculum and assessment and testing are firmly addressed. Grant-maintained schools, local financial management, open enrolment and a more powerful local voice on governing bodies *may* energize the system and keep education relevant to local and national needs. But some of us fear that special educational needs may have slipped off the educational agenda just when progress was being made and the 1981 Act was beginning to produce change. American evaluation of Public Law 94:142 has emphasized the slow process of educational reform and the timescale for ensuring that all the stakeholders (in particular elected members and administrators) fully understand and endorse the new practices. The Education Reform Act may have halted such a 'drip and trickle' effect in terms of implementation of the 1981 Act. And, leaving special needs apart, educational reform is not a matter of one piece of legislation. It requires a climatic change which challenges us all. The Plowden Report developed the concept of a 'horticultural model' of education, because the Committee wished to enable individual children to flourish and develop. If we extend the analogy to the 1980s (and the concept of horticultural models of education is not incompatible with quality and effectiveness in schools), those of us who are consumers of the system will be asking in some anxiety whether the 'slow developers' will be seen as important 'plants' to be nurtured, supported and valued for themselves. Or will they be 'weeds' within Lord Eccles's vision of a 'secret garden' of a national curriculum where beds are well tended but uniformity prized and difficulties eradicated? We have to be optimistic but we must also accept that the price of educational reform for all children will be vigilance, constant restating of priorities and a powerful advocacy for children with special needs — and the 1981 Act.

A final cause for concern — and a thought for the future — has to be the total lack of reference to services for children under five within the Education Reform Act. The 1981 Education Act introduced the concept of education literally from birth as an important preventive measure for children with disabilities and special needs. In terms of the introduction of testing at age seven, the experiences of children in their pre-school years will be of supreme importance in measuring and assessing past and present progress. Yet these important years have been totally omitted from the 1988 Act. As T. S. Elliot said in 'East Coker', 'Our end is where we started from'. Without an all-age, all-children perspective, the aspirations of the Education Reform Act will be thwarted and the National Curriculum will not be so much a 'secret garden' as a wilderness neglecting the potential and aspirations of children less able to succeed.

References

BAKER, K. (1988) 'More replies from the Education Secretary', *British Journal of Special Education,* Vol. 15 No. 1, pp. 6–7.

BROWNE, S. (1988) Presidential Address to the North of England Education Conference, Nottingham, January.

COOPERS & LYBRAND (1988) *Local Management of Schools*, A report prepared by Coopers and Lybrand for the DES, London, DES.

DAVIE, R. (1988) 'In pursuit of excellence', Address to North of England Conference, Nottingham, January.

DEPARTMENT OF EDUCATION AND SCIENCE (DES) (1978) *Special Educational Needs,* London, HMSO (the Warnock Report).

DES (1985) *Better Schools*, London, HMSO.

DES (1986) *Working Together — Education and Training*, London, HMSO.

DES (1987a) *The National Curriculum 5–16: a consultation document,* London, HMSO.

DES (1987b) *National Curriculum: Task Group on Assessment and Testing: A Report,* London, DES.

DES (1988) *Draft Circular* [*1/89*] *Revisions of Circular 1/83. Assessments and Statements of Special Educational Needs: Procedures within the Education, Health and Social Services,* London, DES.

DES (1988) *Draft Circular, The Education Reform Act: the School Curriculum and Assessment,* London, DES.

DES (1988) *School Governors — A New Role,* London, DES.

DES (1989) *National Curriculum: From Policy to Practice,* London, HMSO.

DES and DEPARTMENT OF HEALTH AND SOCIAL SECURITY (1983) *Assessment and Statements of Special Educational Needs, Circular 1/83* (DES) *Health Circular HC (83)3/Local Authority Circular LAC (83)2* (DHSS), London, DES and DHSS.

GIPPS, C., STEADMAN, S. D., BLACKSTONE, T., and STIERER, B. (1983) *Testing Children: Standardised Testing in Local Education Authorities and Schools.* London, Heinemann Educational Books.

GOACHER, B., EVANS, J. WELTON, J. and WEDELL, K. (1988) *Policy and Provision for Special Educational Needs: Implementing the 1981 Education Act,* London, Cassell.

HEGARTY, S. (1988) 'Supporting the ordinary school', *British Journal of Special Education,* Vol. 15, No. 2. pp. 50–3.

HOUSE OF COMMONS (1987) *Third Report from the Education, Science and Arts Committee, Session 1986–87, Special Educational Needs: implementation of the Education Act 1981,* Vol. 1, London, HMSO.

INNER LONDON EDUCATION AUTHORITY (ILEA) (1985) *Educational Opportunities for All?,* London, ILEA.

ROBERTS, B. (1988) *School Governors: Training and Information,* Slough, NFER.

TOMLINSON, J. (1988) 'Curriculum and market: are they compatible?' in Haviland, J. (Ed.) *Take Care, Mr Baker! A selection from the advice on the Government's Education Reform Bill which the Secretary of State invited but decided not to publish,* London, Fourth Estate.

WARNOCK, M. (1988) *A Common Policy for Education,* Oxford, Oxford University Press.

WOLFENDALE, S. (1986) *Primary Schools and Special Needs, Policy, Planning and Provision,* London, Cassell.

13
The Act and Local Authorities

Ron Wallace

It is tempting, but mistaken, when considering the Education Reform Act from a local authority perspective, to despise it because of the obvious increase in central government power. The Act, together with local government legislation which requires local authorities to shed services, is achieving both centralization — the acquisition by central government of powers formerly exercised by others, and decentralization — the loss of powers by local government to institutions (local management of schools and colleges) and to private contractors. The key to understanding the local education authorities' new roles is to concentrate on the essential purposes of local authorities in relation to education. They are to plan strategically a comprehensive education service and to be assured that children and young people have access to high quality education.

There is undoubtedly a new balance of power, with central government now involved in the curriculum as never before in Britain. The debate about whether the government should have involvement in the curriculum is unusual except in Britain. In countries as diverse as Canada and West Germany, the curriculum is controlled by provincial governments covering much larger areas than the largest English and Welsh local education authorities and serving as a regional tier of government which does not exist in Britain. In other countries noted for their liberal and democratic traditions, such as Sweden, the national government is in control. Whatever the motive of the British government which designed the Act, it cannot be regarded as anything other than usual in a world context that national or regional governments should have a view on what is taught in schools, and there seems to be no difference between the British political parties on the desirability of that. This is not, in any case, a seizure of power by central from local government, since local authorities have not had a statutory role or exercised much influence on the curriculum in the past.

The real seizure of power is not by central from local governments, but centrally by politicians from professionals. Although it has been possible to blame that seizure on a concern about low standards — an issue raised most prominently by James Callaghan, a Labour prime minister — the reason for it has nothing to do with quality. There are some grounds for concern about standards, and the teaching profession's vulnerability to fashionable trends (eg the widespread adoption and then abandonment of the Initial Teaching Alphabet in the early 1960s) denies it the right convincingly to proclaim its own innocence. The significance of those concerns is not that they justify or indeed relate in any way to some of the current changes. It is that they allowed the educational right to influence the political debate and to capture the thinking of the party in power. Some of the legislation is concerned with right-wing ideology, most evident in competitive tendering for school meals and cleaning, not with the relationship of central and local government, and it is not possible to have an educational debate on such matters. There are also more tensions in the Act than clear statements about where the power of decision lies. These tensions reflect a division within the Conservative government between those who favour a reformed state education system and those who favour a market-dominated largely or wholly private system. Local authorities have both lost and gained control over schools and colleges of further education. The main losses are administrative and financial. The main gains are curricular and concerned with the promotion and monitoring of quality.

Lost LEA administrative powers: consideration of an example

It is necessary first to consider the lost administrative powers. Some of the powers thought to have been lost by local authorities were illusory and the changes may not be as great as their proponents claim or their opponents fear. The ability of local authorities to take strategic decisions in relation to the organisation of secondary education will serve as an example. The need is to reduce the number of secondary school places to match a very big fall in the number of pupils, which is not again expected to reach the high number of the 1970s despite later increases in the number of children being born. The final decision on the closure of schools was the Secretary of State's before the Act and remains his. It is held that local authorities will be in a weaker position to propose closures as a result of three new features of the Act — the ability of schools to seek grant maintained status, the creation of city technology colleges and what has been called open enrolment.

The first of these certainly substitutes a relationship with the DES and HMI for that with local authorities. That may be why GM status initially proved much less attractive than its originators had hoped. At the time of writing (April 1989) the parents of only 51 schools in the whole of England and Wales had held ballots on this matter, and only 38 had voted to apply for this closer relationship with the government. Of those, 15 were seeking to leave Conservative local authorities, and 25 had fewer (some substantially fewer) than 750 on roll; indeed many were the subject of closure or amalgamation proposals.[1] There is an anxiety about the domino effect in that GM status might be thought in some cases to confer status and cachet. (That a closer relationship with Whitehall should be so regarded is one of the paradoxes of the political climate in Britain in the late 1980s.) The fear is that, if a locally-prestigious school (probably a single-sex former grammar school, preferably founded no later than the sixteenth century) were to acquire GM status, the next most prestigious school would feel the need so to do, and so on, leaving the local authority only with undersubscribed and unpopular schools which it might then have to close. If that were to happen throughout Britain, the Act would have created a centrally-run national schools system at secondary level, with no local authority involvement. The phenomenon of the Gadarene swine, which in this case would mean school after school following the initial irrational decision of a few to seek illusory independence by putting themselves in a relationship with national government, is not, of course, unknown.

Unless the government were to abandon all responsibility for standards, such a system would have to be the most centralized in the world with a vast Whitehall bureaucracy, management systems which transferred information by computer direct from schools to the DES and centralized 'inspection in all its forms'.[2] The government's interest in attainment targets, testing, inspection and performance indicators suggests that it does not have such an abandonment in mind. The Labour Party's interest in such matters is no less than the government's. There is, of course, a school of thought in the Conservative Party that the market alone will maintain and raise standards, and that no other controls are necessary, but its views have not prevailed in the Act. Indeed, such a view would not require there to be an Act or a Department of Education at all, let alone local authorities. That is not to say that such views will not triumph in the future, and it is possible to see the Act as a modest first step down the road to a wholly private education system. That, however, is conjecture. The Act as it stands enables a small number of thoughtless schools to begin the deluge, but it does not make that inevitable, and so far schools, their governing bodies and their staffs have shown considerable shrewdness in recognizing a Greek bearing gifts.

The offer by government of GM status should have little effect on the ability of local authorities to reduce the number of secondary schools. This has never been easy, and local authorities have rarely tried to close popular schools and even more rarely succeeded. There have been three principal ways of reducing the number of secondary schools. The first is to have a whole authority re-organization plan. This is not necessary and usually has a reduction in the number of schools as a subsidiary aim, the main purpose being to set up a different kind of secondary system, eg to change from selection to comprehensive, or from 11–18 schools to 11–16 schools with a tertiary college. The second is to close schools, but usually schools which are unpopular, since the DES, irrespective of its political control at any particular time, does not like to close popular schools. The ability to cause delay and inconvenience is available to parents of threatened schools as a result of the GM status option, but the Secretary of State has made it clear that he does not intend to clutch non-viable unpopular schools to his bosom.

The third is to amalgamate two schools. In this case the local authorities may find it more difficult to amalgamate a popular with an unpopular school, for the former could resist, if it so decided, using the opting out (GM status) threat. There are, however, as many reasons against the amalgamation method of reducing the number of schools as there are in its favour, and its loss will not be universally regretted. The fact is that, whatever the quasi-judicial procedures associated with closing schools, before and after the Act, there is always a strong political element in both local and national decisions. Secretaries of State have routinely taken 6 to 12 months to reach decisions on contested cases, so delay will not be new and the results may not be very different.

The City Technology Colleges' story is something of a farce. They were to be new institutions, privately-financed by industrial sponsors, dedicated to curriculum with a technological bias, and sited in areas of inner city squalor. The magnet schools of New York contributed to the thinking. The first one has been established in Solihull, Warwickshire. Another one is to be partly sponsored by a record-maker, is to emphasize the performing arts and was launched by the Secretary of State, posing as a Beatle on the famous Abbey Road pedestrian crossing. A case can be made against them. Farce could descend, as always, into tragedy. In most local authorities they do not exist and are unlikely to exist. The idea may be silly and objectionable but is unlikely to worry most local authorities.

The Secretary of State has not given to schools the right to recruit as many pupils as they like. Open enrolment is an inaccurate term. Standard admission number is more accurate, although less politically attractive if you are wishing to convey the impression that you are setting schools free to operate in the market place. It was held in the 1960s and 1970s that a comprehensive school could not succeed unless it had 180 new pupils a year. Some went further and said that such a low figure was possible only if the intake was balanced by ability. When faced with rapidly falling rolls, some local authorities, knowing the difficulties involved in closing schools and having had experience of ministerial cowardice in such matters, tried to avoid closing schools and to spread the woe evenly amongst schools by setting intake limits which were lower than schools could admit and indeed had always admitted. The aim was to force pupils to go to schools which they did not want when it was known that there was space for them in schools which they did want. It was not a sensible policy because it could not be justified as reasonable to parents that their wishes were denied in order to keep numbers up at another school. It also involved, for some people, the total abandonment of their earlier definition of a comprehensive school. The new regulations determine a school's roll at intake by reference to its admissions in 1979–80 or any subsequent levels agreed under re-organization plans approved by the Secretary of State. If the 1989–90 levels were above either of those figures, the higher figure could be followed. Local authorities may apply to the Secretary of State to increase the admission number and the number could vary in future re-organization proposals. To that extent the government has a new power over local authorities, but he/she could not exercise that power without regard to the total number of places available in an area or to the capital cost.[3]

Taking this example, therefore, of a local authority's ability to carry out its strategic function of providing the right number of pupil places in the right areas, it may be concluded that previous local powers were not as great or effective as sometimes supposed. The possibility of change sometimes makes the past and the present seem more attractive than they are.

Political control of the curriculum

Whilst we have all been watching or participating in what has been portrayed as a struggle for local democracy against central bureaucracy, and what might be seen in retrospect as a side-show, the real change has been the wresting of curricular control from the professionals by the politicians. In particular the universities, the examination boards, and the teaching profession have lost ground.

The universities have for long been the controllers of the school curriculum, which has had the purpose of filtering and educating a small number of people in an increasingly specialized curriculum, so that they may be available at the age of 18 in the condition which the universities seek. It is difficult to argue that the ending of this hegemony is a matter of much regret.

The examination boards, more particularly those which controlled the General Certificate of Education examinations for the ablest pupils at the ages of 16 and 18, were also the defenders of a stultifying system which dominated the secondary curriculum. It is rather hard to take the view that any curricular freedom will be lost by the Secretaries of State using the powers which they have always had to require the subordination of examination boards to the needs of a more coherent national view of the curriculum 5–18.

As for the teaching profession, its control of the curriculum was illusory at the secondary level. The secondary curriculum was controlled by the examination boards, themselves dancing to the universities' tune. At the primary level the teaching profession has been charged erroneously with succumbing to 'free expression', which the mythology suggests has been a widespread change from narrow disciplined rote-learning to an emphasis on personal pupil determination of both content and method (as gross a calumny against primary education in the 1950s as it is against that of the 1980s). The more justifiable and dangerous charge is lack of professional rigour in determining the most effective methods of learning. Despite much excellent practice, it is difficult to reject the impression gained by many parents that methodology has been determined from time to time in part by trial and error. Such is not the basis for mounting a professional high horse. In any case, syndicalism, by which groups of workers control the production or service which they provide, looks back to the medieval guild rather than forward to a participating democracy. The danger for the teaching profession is that, having kept too much to itself in the past, it may have invited governors and politicians, national and local, to push too far the boundary which must exist between the professional and the lay controller.

Power has moved from the professionals, whichever of the above groups is concerned, to the politicians. The desirability of that does not now seem to be a matter of disagreement between the political parties. It is now the case that all political parties want to have more influence over the education service and more accountability from it. There does not seem to be much to argue about there. It is called democracy. The point is a constitutional one, and does not depend for its validity on the intentions or worthiness of parties in power at any particular time.

What the Act says on the curriculum is on the whole good, which makes it particularly difficult for professionals to find objectionable the political power which has achieved it. The same political power has simultaneously put an emphasis on periodic testing with the publication of aggregated school results, which serve no educational purpose. The argument is not, of course, that the use of political authority to bring about educational change must inevitably be beneficial; that would be absurd. It is that, in regard to the curriculum, it has on this occasion achieved something better that that which preceded it. The Act begins with the curriculum. It is true that there are traces of that right-wing influence noted earlier. The overwhelming message, however, is one that only a government, with the power to give it, could give. The National Curriculum represents the abandonment of pupil and teacher choice, which means in practice the premature abandonment of essential knowledge and experience, in favour of an entitlement curriculum. Entitlement does, of course, depend on resources, and it may be that budgetary decisions to turn legislative aspirations into classroom reality will not be taken, but the Act is to be welcomed for its curricular signposts. Those owe little to the present government's thinking and much to a consensus which has been emerging over a period of fifteen years and in which Her Majesty's Inspectors and other curricular thinkers have played the leading part.[4]

The new partnership

The issue for local authorities is how power is to be shared between the centre, themselves and the schools, for all three have increased powers. That is the paradox. The new powers of the Secretary of State are well known. They relate mainly to the National Curriculum and are recognized by all teachers, whose work has been enormously influenced by them.

Some people see this acquisition of ministerial power as a breach in a 40-year post-war partnership between central and local government and the teaching profession, based upon a consensus about liberal education. The observations already made about the true controllers of the secondary curriculum suggest that some scepticism is needed about that view. It is very difficult for those who participated during the 1960s and 1970s in the struggle for comprehensive education — nothing if not a battle between ministerial and local authority power — to believe the myth that a partnership has recently collapsed. Believers in a liberal education consensus, which it was claimed was under attack by the Technical and Vocational Education Initiative (TVEI) of the 1980s, have generally conceded, whilst holding to their ideals, that there has been very little liberal education in Britain to which one can point.[5]

Local authorities may have less control over spending levels and less budgetary control through local financial management of schools and colleges (although it will be suggested later that this is a marginal matter), but they have been given a much more powerful role in relation to the promotion of the curriculum and monitoring the work done in schools and colleges. The new relationship between local authorities and their schools and colleges will be based on the need for the latter to prepare development plans annually, showing how staff are to be deployed, revenue is being spent, in-service training for staff is being planned, and academic standards are being monitored and raised. This gives the local authority a much more interventionist and influential role in relation to schools and colleges than they have previously had.

The DES has emphasized the crucial role of each school's National Curriculum development plan, to be discussed and agreed with the local authority, albeit in the context of local authority procedures for annual school reviews.[6] For further education colleges, local authorities have been given an explicit strategic planning role. In many authorities local financial management of further education colleges is giving the local authority much more of a controlling and monitoring role than before the Act. The delegation scheme gives the local authority, unambiguously, the function of strategic planner. The authority determines each college's budget. Each college has a statutory obligation to provide it with information. The DES has stated by circular that, 'The supply of information by the college to the LEA is an essential mechanism for ensuring accountability and proper monitoring, particularly when a college has delegated powers'. The DES, by letter, has emphasised the LEA's inspectoral role in the colleges. These changes are proving something of a surprise to colleges which had thought that they were to be 'set free'. In practice the local authorities' role as a strategic planner, determiner of institutional budgets and inspector gives them more influence than some of them have previously exercised.[7]

For all institutions they have been made monitors and therefore, to a degree, controllers. They will be acting in part as agents of central government, but the role represents a significant shift of responsibility from heads and principals to local authorities in these particular matters.

The tension in the new relationships will be felt initially at local level — between authorities and their schools and colleges — not between central and local government. That is because the government, having forced upon local authorities the devolution of powers to schools and colleges (and their governors) which the authorities themselves previously held, (mainly in relation to budgets and appointments) has then charged the authorities to promote and monitor quality. Put another way, governors and heads/principals have been given new powers, but the local authority has been given the responsibility to ensure that they are wisely used.

There are several aspects of this tripartite relationship between government, local authorities, schools/colleges which need to be examined.

The National Curriculum

The most potent instrument available to bring about change in schools is the National Curriculum. Increased powers for governors, the local management of schools and appraisal schemes for teachers are all important but of secondary importance. It has been suggested above that there is nothing constitutionally objectionable and, outside Britain, nothing unusual about the government, as the nationally-elected body, determining in broad terms the curriculum of schools. There are grounds for concern, however, about the balance between the political and professional contributions. The Secretary of State for Education and Science does not decide matters alone. There are statutory bodies and consultation procedures to be followed. The National Curriculum Council, (NCC) unlike its predecessors the Schools Council and the School Curriculum Development Council, exists by statute. It advises the Secretary of State who has by statute to consult local authorities and many other interested parties. He appoints the NCC. They 'advise' him. The final decision on all matters is his.

The starkest examples nationally of the predominance of the political over the professional view are to be found in the exchanges between the NCC and the Secretary of State over the content of subjects — what is to be taught. The NCC has to tread a difficult path, trying to present recommendations which the Secretary of State will find acceptable, and limiting the occasions when it takes a stand on principle. The difficulty of its position is not always understood. Whilst one of its roles is to assemble the best professional advice for the Secretary of State, the fact remains that statute gives the Secretary of State the power to accept or reject professional advice.

The NCC was criticized strongly for not standing by its own Mathematics recommendations.[8] The working party proposed three profile components (clusters of attainment targets), the third of which was concerned with the practical applications and communication of mathematical skills. The Secretary of State rejected this third profile component. The statutory consultation indicated that most respondents favoured its retention. The NCC then recommended to the Secretary of State its abandonment, i.e., they turned their back on their own initial recommendations, ignored the results of their own consultations and accepted the Secretary of State's view. Some arguments were advanced by the NCC for their change of view, most importantly that it had proved difficult in practice to find sufficient attainment levels for these particular targets and that the same emphasis had been achieved by their absorption into the other two profile components. It can therefore be concluded that the NCC found cogent reasons for modifying their own proposals and for achieving them by different means, risking, as they did so, the charge of being the Secretary of State's poodle. It is a matter of judgement whether one so castigates the NCC or admires them for a clever manoeuvre with a tolerable outcome. What one cannot ignore is the strength of the political force. We are no longer in the age of politicians accepting professional advice on pedagogical matters as being of at least equal importance to their own views.

On the English report, the NCC decided on both compromise and confrontation. Since the working party which had produced the report was chaired by Professor Cox, a man of previously impeccable right-wing preferences and a former Black Paper editor, they may have felt on stronger ground. Here the arguments were about the significance of formal grammar and about the relative importance of writing, reading, listening and speaking. On both, the Secretary of State took the view that the working party's report needed significant modification and in general his views were based on a preference for greater formality. He largely had his way. One clearly personal addition which he made was to require 7-year-olds to be able to learn a piece of poetry by heart and recite it — not a matter of great moment, but a curious insertion by a politician in the final stage before the laying of Orders before Parliament, especially since only the Chairman of the NCC and not the Council itself was even aware of the change.[9]

The role of the local authority is to promote and, if necessary, enforce the National Curriculum. As the agent of central government, it has to use its resources, in particular its advisory/inspectoral staff and its in-service training budget, to prepare teachers for a new curriculum, assessment of pupil performance, recording pupil achievement, testing and reporting. Local authorities have in the past varied in the amount of political attention given to these matters, but few local authorities have chosen until recently to recommend, still less to attempt to enforce, a detailed view of the curriculum. It is only in recent years that a few local authorities have put forward curricular plans. On the Labour side, ILEA in the mid-1980s commissioned David Hargreaves to prepare a report, *Improving Secondary Schools* and then promoted the curricular views which he had outlined. On the Conservative side Croydon followed the lead of its then Director of Education, Donald Naismith, and introduced in the second half of the 1980s a rudimentary curriculum statement, which became more detailed in English and Mathematics and acquired attainment targets and tests which clearly influenced Conservative Party thinking. These and a few others were, however, exceptions and they all date from the mid-late 1980s. No local authority can claim that the national government has seized that which formerly belonged to it. For most local authorities most of these activities are new, although some authorities saw more quickly than others the national trend which had been building up through HMI reports and DES publications for more than a decade and had recently entered this territory, although on the basis of persuasion, not statute.

Schools which decide that they prefer a more direct relationship with the Secretary of State can seek GM status, whereupon they will be taken down the same road by Her Majesty's Inspectors whose boss, the Secretary of State, will expect them to show at least as much virility on his behalf as their local authority counterparts.

The subject programmes of study so far published[10] are outlines and much work has to be done to turn them into syllabuses or schemes of work. The speed at which the National Curriculum is being introduced makes it impossible for schools to do this on an individual basis. Their first response has been to seek local authority help, with writing groups, often led by advisors or advisory teachers, being established to do the initial work for all schools or groups of schools. This is in any case good practice. Thus three levels are emerging: the National Curriculum in outline is prepared by the National Curriculum Council and approved by the Secretary of State; the local authority takes the lead, at the request of frantic heads and teachers, in working this up into schemes of work; the head and teacher plan lessons.

The tension is in the 1986 Education (No.2) Act and the 1988 Education Reform Act. By the former Act the local authority must determine and state its curriculum policy, which must, by virtue of the latter Act, begin with an endorsement of the National Curriculum. Governors of county schools are to consider the local authority's curriculum policy and 'how, if at all' it should be modified. They are required 'to consult the authority before making or varying' their statement. Governors of aided schools are to 'have regard' to the local authority's statement when preparing their own.[11]

Whilst the local authority will be on unassailable ground when promoting the National Curriculum, it might be considered to be on weaker ground when promoting its own curricular policies. The fact is that we do not know, and there may be a rich seam here for lawyers to mine. But laywers only come into the picture when tension becomes warfare. Both the government and the local authority have the instruments to promote curricular policies other than those of the National Curriculum. For example they may use targeted funding which is still possible to a limited degree under local financial management.[12] The in-service training programme is largely in national and government control. A local authority with a strong commitment to multicultural education, equal opportunities, nursery education,etc. will use that part of its own in-service training budget which is within its own discretion to promote those policies, i.e., it will use its part of the training budget in the same way that the government uses its own part.

Local Financial Management/Local Management of Schools

The transfer of financial responsibilities from local authorities to institutions, although causing much anxiety, is a marginal matter in the context of power-sharing. It is based on the belief that schools can be run like small companies, with the parents as shareholders who receive a report at an annual meeting from the governors who are the board of directors. Schools are not like companies. They do not produce and sell. They cannot make a profit or a loss for their shareholders. They cannot take over smaller and more efficient rivals in order to become monopolies or near monopolies. If the local authority does not achieve a balance between the number of school places and the number of pupils, some schools will be less than full and some may be almost empty and may have to close. To that extent the market place is a factor, but there is nothing new about that and it is certainly not the creation of LMS. There are likely to be only three consequences of this change.

First, schools and colleges may initially husband their resources more carefully in the hope of producing surpluses. Heating will be turned down, windows kept closed, telephone calls made more cheaply in the afternoon, entry systems applied to photocopying machines and chains to teaspoons, on the principle of looking after the pennies. The evidence suggests that this hair-shirt approach is difficult to sustain. In any case there is already more of it in most schools than in most commercial organizations.

Second, having thought at first that the appointment of bursars would see them through, heads will realize that they themselves have to take on LFM and that, with the other local management powers available to them, it is a useful but limited instrument for changing their schools. There is a strong case for giving heads greater managerial responsibilities, but the expectations of improvement should not be pitched too high.

Third, schools will put all income together, whether from the local authority, parents or local businesses, and regard them as one. It will be only on the private fund-raising side that increases can be 'earned', so that such activities will become more important. Fund-raising is likely to become a major activity. Existing variations in provision between schools, which are already dependent on the affluence of parents or the fund-raising energies of teachers, are likely to be exacerbated. Some schools already raise more money privately than they receive from public funds for books, stationery and small equipment. It is likely that such activities will grow and that the private as a proportion of the total will increase. This is not, however, a new feature and local authorities do not at present use their financial powers significantly to counter-balance such variations. The publically-funded aspects of school budgets, which for the sake of most schools we must hope will continue to be the larger, will be made available in accordance with a formula, related for the most part to pupil numbers and ages, and only marginally to other needs criteria, and will be unrelated to quality of performance, except in so far as that attracts or loses pupils.

Heads will have to work on fund-raising and pupil recruitment to boost private and public income. The analogy with private schools before the war and now is worrying. It is not generally held that the leadership of private schools is strong at the moment, and a diversion of heads' energies from education to fund-raising and public relations is often cited as the reason. When the major private schools were in financial difficulties in the late 1930s, the consequences of their heads' pre-occupations with the market place were observed with sorrow by two of their leaders. Canon Spencer Leeson, Headmaster of Winchester and soon to be Chairman of the Headmasters' Conference wrote, 'I foresee that practically every school in England will be faced with the problem of falling numbers. I foresee a period of years during which governing bodies will commit themselves to expenditure upon equipment and general window-dressing, in the hope of attracting parents. A new atmosphere will come into English education with serious effects upon the morale of it and upon the values which we try to uphold.' Sir Cyril Norwood, former Headmaster of Marlborough but by now President of St John's College, Oxford, lamented 'the progressive lowering of professional standards' amongst headteachers which he was already witnessing, with heads 'spending half their time in commercial travelling and touting on preparatory school doorsteps.' He saw a lowering of educational standards because, 'the effect is that the worse drives out the better currency: the advertising headmaster succeeds, the headmaster who minds his proper business, and puts education first, fails.'[13] Those ancient private schools were, of course, saved by the war and a post-war Labour government which allowed local authorities to buy places at private schools. The same pressure of competition for pupils has now been invented and applied to local authority schools. Who will save public education in the 1990s?

Performance indicators

The reason why the bigger inspectoral role of local authorities did not immediately impinge on the consciousness of heads is that it was unexpected. LMS and competitive tests with published results at 11, 14 and 16, and putting the customers (or their parents) on the board of directors were intended to raise standards in the same way that competition in business is thought to do. As we might be persuaded that a choice of toothpastes has allowed us to have the most effective at the lowest price, so we might believe that schools competing for customers will raise their standards. Why, then, should it be necessary to require other monitoring instruments? If the market will sort out the good from the bad and the bad will go to the wall, why should local authorities have to devise these other means of checking standards? The answer seems to be that the government is not wholly convinced by the effectiveness of the market place. Other political parties are certainly not.

Local authorities have therefore been charged to develop other controls. First, there will be the annual National Curriculum development plan, to be discussed between the head and a local authority adviser/inspector as a basis for the head's planning. Second, there is to be a very big increase in inspection. Third, the search is on for performance indicators. Fourth, examination results (crude or weighted according to one of the several methods now being produced by this academic sunrise industry)[14] and test results at 11, 14 and 16 will be used to judge schools publicly. Fifth, those who enjoy sophisticated simplicity, will continue with their efforts to develop Data Envelopment Analysis. (A lack of space and belief precludes further explanation of this last technique.)[15]

These are all ways in which local authorities have to be far more obtrusive, on average, than they have been in the past. It is one of the ironies of recent changes, that the Inner London Education Authority, despised and abolished by the government, was much further down this road than most county authorities. Whereas it was at one with the government in a concern for standards and the need for accountability from schools to their local authority, ILEA did not believe that market forces in education would raise standards, but then, as has been suggested above, neither does the government wholly.

Tension will arise because schools and further education colleges, which have been led to believe that they have been set free from largely unoppressive local authorities, will be seeing more of those authorities' advisers or inspectors, who will be seeking more information and giving firmer guidance than hitherto. The other source of tension is that popularity and effectiveness in raising pupils' standards do not always go hand in hand. What is to happen when a popular school is known by local inspectors, on the basis of their performance indicators etc., to be performing poorly?

The DES and local authorities occupy the high ground

A further difficulty for schools and colleges, if they had believed that devolution and delegation meant the freedom to take policy decisions, is that the DES and the local authorities (in part, but certainly not wholly, as the agents of the DES) have in fact taken more of the high ground. It is only the management of institutions which has been delegated. The main 'freedom'gained by schools and colleges is to be efficient. What they have to do, in terms of both policies and procedures, is to be determined by others. Here the key relationship with regard to policy is that between central government and local authorities, with the latter in a subordinate position but nonetheless, in many cases, in a more influential position than in the past.

The model which has been developed by the DES, heavily influenced by the lead of the Manpower Services Commission, is that central government makes a national allocation of money, with criteria for its distribution and monitoring of its use, and then invites local authority bids which represent a wide variety of local authority aspirations. Examples seen so far are Education Support Grants, in which specific curricular and other aims are promoted, eg information technology across the curriculum, primary science and technology; the MSC's (now Training Agency's) Technical and Vocational Education Initiative, with its promotion of a national curriculum for 14–18 year olds before the DES trod that road, and its far-reaching effect on the promotion of school/college consortia, but with a very wide variation of local practice; computer hardware and software offers from the Department of Trade and Industry; the appointment of enterprise advisers through local authorities but with DTI funds, to promote business involvement in education; the various Training Agency's controls of further education policies such as Work-Related Non-Advanced Further Education; and probably the most influential of all, the LEA Training Grants Scheme.

The last of these will serve as an example. Each Summer the DES informs local authorities of the in-service training budget which it is willing to support with national grant. Local authorities can spend more, without grant, or less and forgo grant. The grant-aided budget is divided into national priorities, which are determined annually by the DES and attract a higher level of grant, and local priorities. The local authority does have to satisfy stringent DES criteria, but there is considerable scope for local decision-making, even within the national priority categories. It is likely that local authorities will require, if they have not already done so, each school and college to prepare an annual in-service training programme, to be discussed with and approved by a local inspector or adviser as part of the annual curriculum development plan. Just as the DES releases the grant to the local authority, provided the criteria have been satisfied, so the local authority will release the grant to the school or college, provided criteria have been satisfied. These criteria will include the achievement of local authority as well as national objectives.

Difficulties for local authorities

There are two factors which may reduce the ability of local authorities to discharge their strategic functions and these need to be acknowledged. The first of these is GM status. It has been argued above that the significance of this in determining the number of secondary schools in an area — one of the most important strategic decisions to be taken by a local authority — may be slight. The ability to threaten the local authority with an application for GM status could, however, give the popular over-subscribed school excessive influence in an area. It is a more subtle matter than it seems. The availability of the weapon depends on the nature of the fire which is preferred to the frying pan, ie on whether a school considers the national to be less oppressive and potentially more helpful than the local government. As with all threats, there is a risk, for, once a school has opted out of local authority control, it cannot opt back again. It could opt out of what it considers to be an oppressive local authority, only to find, a general and a local election later, that it has foresaken a local authority which has now become benevolent for a national government which has now become oppressive. The game between schools which choose to play and their local authorities will be cat and mouse. When a capital programme, which is still within local authority control is being discussed, the strong school may drop hints about opting out. If a local authority has a curricular policy, energetically pursued but unwelcome to a strong school, e.g. on streaming or multicultural education, the school may resist with hints of seeking GM status. The schools will need to play a shrewd hand and avoid overplaying it, but it is a game which some may choose to play.

The second is the appointing aspect of the local management of schools will make it much more difficult, perhaps impossible, for local authorities to reach re-deployment agreements with teachers' unions. This may make school re-organizations more difficult than in the past when an element of teacher goodwill was a factor in winning acceptance for school closures or amalgamation.

Conclusions

There are three conclusions to be drawn from this analysis. First, new relationships need to be formed. This has been obvious for a long time as between central and local government. The new relationship between local authorities and schools/colleges may have been misunderstood because of the propaganda emphasis on parent power and devolution to institutions. In reality the government has put most local authorities in a much more influential and interventionist role than they have previously held in relation to curricular and inspectoral activities. Second, the devolution of power to institutions, insofar as it is happening, requires strong local policy-making (albeit in a framework of national policies) and strong and efficient inspection/advisory services.

Third, centralized curriculum control is the price to be paid for the Local Management of Schools. Governments are not in practice willing to give up control of education to parents. The curriculum — what is learned and how it is taught — is the central purpose of schools and colleges. The effective management of institutions has always depended on able leadership from within institutions themselves. It is a *sine qua non* of good learning, but it is the means not the end. As heads and principals are given more budgetary and administrative powers, central and local government have taken control of that for which schools and colleges exist. Greater parental and professional power in the administrative aspects of running institutions is being balanced by greater control of learning. The most important question for the future is the boundary both nationally and locally between the political and the professional, i.e., to what extent the government listens to the NCC and local authority councillors listen to officers, advisers/inspectors, heads and others on the curriculum?

This key fact is at the heart of the relationship between local authorities and their schools and colleges. So far the emphasis has been on what Mr Baker giveth, not on what he taketh away. When the full impact of the latter is understood will be the time for steady nerves in city and county halls and in the heads' and principals' studies.

If any head reading this considers that it is all too awful and that s/he would prefer to leave the local authority and become grant-maintained, s/he should re-read the chapter, substituting the government for the local authority throughout.[16]

Notes

1. J. McLeod, *Education*, 14 April 1989.
2. The Secretary of State's desire that all schools should be regularly subjected to 'inspection in all its forms' has been made known frequently, eg speech to Society of Education Officers, 22.1.88. The phrase implies sample full inspections of schools and colleges, more numerous shorter inspections, and thematic inspections across several institutions, as is already the practice of Her Majesty's Inspectorate.
3. Education Reform Act, Section 27 (1–3) and DES Circular 11/88.
4. The notion of a pupil's curriculum entitlement was first cogently advanced, although not on a subject basis, in a collection of HMI publications, known as the 'Red Books'. The notion of entitlement has been re-worked since 1984 on a subject basis in an HMSO series, *Curriculum Matters*. HMSO, 1984 and continuing.
5. For a rehearsal of the arguments in the debate, see R. Gibson 1986.
6. Letter from J. Bacon, DES, to Chief Education Officers, 17.2.89 confirmed that future success in bidding for Education Support Grants and LEA Training Grants would depend upon the preparation by schools of National Curriculum Development Plans for the LEA's approval.
7. Education Reform Act, Sections 139, 143 (3a) 144 (12), and 152 (5); DES Circular 9/88; Letter from R.D. Hull, DES, to Chief Education Officers, 28.3.89. A good indication of the new partnership to be forged between local authorities and their colleges is given in Birch, Latcham and Spencer, 1988. The duality of planning and delegation is important.
8. DES. *Mathematics for ages 5–16*, August 1988 and subsequent NCC, *Consultation Report*, December 1989 and Orders.
9. DES, *English for ages 5–11*, November 1988 and subsequent NCC, *Consultation Report*, March 1989 and Orders. *Education*, 24.3.89, p. 272.
10. Those on Mathematics and English, referred to above, and equivalent for *Science, 5–16*.

11. Education (No. 2) Act, 1986, Sections 17–19.
12. Local authorities may retain 10 per cent (reducing to 7 per cent) of their total schools' budget for purposes determined by themselves.
13. Public Record Office, *Ed 136/129*, memorandum by Leeson, 14 October 1938; letter by Norwood, 19 October 1938.
14. For example, Gray and Jesson, 'Exam Results and Local Authority League Tables', in *Education and Training UK*, 1987.
15. Data Envelopment Analysis is a statistical technique for measuring the effectiveness of 'decision-making units', based on the hypothesis that a unit is inefficient if another unit can produce the same quality of output at less cost. The London Borough of Croydon commissioned Spicer and Peglar Associates to consider how this technique could be applied to schools and their report was published in 1987.

References

BIRCH, D., LATCHMAN, J., and SPENCER, A., (1988) *Planning and delegation in further education*, Bristol, Further Education Staff College (Coombe Lodge).

GRAY, J., and JESSON, D., (1987) 'Exam Results and Local Authority League Tables', in *Education and Training UK*, Newbury Policy Journals.

GIBSON, R., (1986) *Liberal Education Today*, Cambridge, Cambridge Institute of Education.

HARGREAVES, D., (1984) *Improving Secondary Schools*, London, ILEA.

HMI (1983) *Curriculum 11–16, Towards a Statement of Entitlement*, London, HMSO. (The most important of the 'Red Books').

14
Learning to Live Under Water: The 1988 Education Reform Act and its Implications for Further and Adult Education

Lorna Unwin

Introduction

As with most across the board policy initiatives related to education, publicity surrounding the Education Reform Act has tended to concentrate attention on its implications for primary and secondary schooling. The Act, however, will have a significant impact on the further and adult education sector (FE/AE) whose staff and students have already witnessed considerable change during the 1980s. Coping with a decade of change and now assimilating the requirements of the Education Reform Act has led further and adult education colleagues to compare their plight with a group of desert islanders awaiting a tidal wave. Some colleagues are thinking of building a raft in the hope of escaping the wave, while others have moved to higher ground. The more stoical colleagues, though, have begun learning to live under water. And in discovering this new lifestyle, the biggest adaptation that teaching, support and managerial staff will continue to have to make is to the traditional orientation of the roles they play within their institutions and to the changing face of those institutions.

The decision to deal with further and adult education together in this article requires some explanation. In the first place, the decision was a pragmatic one as it follows the lead of the Act itself which uses Further Education as an umbrella term for:

1. Full-time and part-time education for persons over compulsory school age (including vocational, social, physical and recreational training); and
2. Organized leisure-time occupation provided in connection with the provision of such education.[1]

Adult education is not directly referred to in the Act but at least one-third of its sections have direct relevance to adult learners and educators as much of the provision of adult education relies heavily on the institutions providing further education in general. How to develop a field of education which aims to cater for everyone over 16 has taxed the imagination of educationalists and policy makers alike for generations. Labels such as Lifelong Learning, Continuing Education, Recurrent Education, Community Education, Tertiary Education and so on abound, all suggesting a similar audience, yet each claiming to have a different emphasis in approach and philosophy. In a speech to the House of Lords during the Third Reading of Gerbil, Baroness Hooper indicated where the Government stood over this battle for nomenclature when she said, 'Further education is not defined as being only for 16–19 year olds, or only for those up to the age of 21. It is for all of those over the age of 16' (Hansard (Lords), 7 July 1988). This could be seen as simply the quickest solution to defining the complex and highly diverse area of post-compulsory education. As this paper seeks to show, however, further education has been given a definite functional role to play in the economic restructuring of the country and, hence, a narrowing of how further education might be defined is part of the government's strategy. By separating out the concept of adult education, steeped as it is in the social and cultural development of Britain and, in particular, working-class Britain, the Act would have opened the floodgates to demands from a range of national and community-based interest groups who have always had to seek out an existence at the margins of public sector education.

Such groups may be temporarily encouraged by the fact that the 1988 Act has clarified the much disputed sections of the 1944 Act which led to many local education authorities (LEAs) technically operating illegally in their provision of further and adult education and in the absence of any strategic policy for FE/AE (Cantor and Roberts, 1986). The basis of the clarification is that LEAs are charged directly with securing rather than providing '*adequate* facilities for further education' and to 'have regard for provision made by other agencies' (Education Reform Act, Section 120(2), my emphasis). This places a duty on every LEA to prepare for the Secretary of State a plan for local provision with details of how the budget for that provision will be delegated to newly-elected and employer-dominated governing bodies of individual colleges. It is up to individual LEAs to define the concept of adequacy. The Act, therefore, changes substantially the relationship between an LEA and its associated colleges as the former moves into a strategic role leaving the latter to operate much more independently. The Department of Education and Science (DES) has argued that, under the Act, colleges will be able to respond much more quickly and flexibly to the needs of their customers, be they employers, community groups or individual students (see Libby and Hull, 1988). Yet the climate in which LEAs will plan their provision and in which colleges will respond is one that is more conducive than ever before to the needs of industry rather than wider community interests.

Returning to basics — realigning the FE/AE curriculum

Further education colleges, evolving as they did from mechanics' institutes, were, of course, established to meet industry's needs and until the mid-1960s they were filled largely with young male apprentices taking courses that generations of tradesmen and technicians had followed. But an FE college in the late 1980s is a very different place offering as it does a plethora of courses including GCSE, Higher National Diploma, adult basic skills, social work and the traditional evening class diet of flower arranging and conversational French. The broadening of the FE curriculum has been discussed at length elsewhere (Cantor and Roberts, 1986; Parkes, 1985) but it is important here to establish why the current FE curriculum, spanning as it does both 'liberal' adult education and vocational training, will be realigned towards the vocational end of the continuum. The 1988 Act is a key mechanism for helping colleges and LEAs make that realignment and will also affect adult education provided outside mainstream FE colleges. Although LEAs are only required to delegate financial responsibility to the governing bodies of institutions with an enrolment of 200 or more full-time equivalent students, they can, if they wish, apply the delegation to smaller institutions who typically provide a base for the Workers' Educational Association, REPLAN educational projects for unemployed adults and a range of courses inspired by the community. As FE colleges concentrate their attention on meeting the needs of employers, the space currently occupied by the non-vocational curriculum will become smaller and its supporters may be forced to retreat to the fringe institutions only to find that they too have acquired a more entrepreneurial face.

The contemporary environment into which the Act has been received is described vividly in the White Paper, *Employment for the 1990s,* published in December, 1988:

> Above all, we must invest in the skills and knowledge of our people and build up industry's skill base, through a strategy of training through life, to enable Britain to continue to grow and generate jobs. The prime responsibility for this investment lies with employers.
>
> It is up to employers and individuals, by their actions, to ensure that the jobs come about; and in reskilling the labour force there are new partnerships to be created between enterprise, vocational education and training, between delivery at local level and policies and priorities at national level, and between employers and Government, customers and providers. (Department of Employment, 1988)

The call for Britain to address its poor record in skill training and the need to foster lifelong learning among employees has echoes back to the Crystal Palace International Exhibition of 1852 when concern was expressed about Britain's ability to maintain its lead over its industrial competitors. In 1977, the Great Debate revived the arguments that education be for industry's sake at a time when FE was witnessing a dramatic decline in its bread and butter supply of apprentices. In the wake of growing unemployment and a decided lack of initiative from the Department of Education and Science as to how FE might respond, the then Manpower Services Commission (MSC), reporting to the Department of Employment, began to consolidate its position as a major player in the post-compulsory field. The MSC was supported in its march across the FE landscape not only by both Labour and Conservative Governments, but also by groups of trades unionists, college staff and some academics (see in particular Gleeson, 1985). This support was encouraged by the way in which MSC-funded programmes increased the opportunity for many young people and adults previously denied access to the highly selective world of FE. Through a series of policy statements including *A New Training Initiative* (1981), *Training for Jobs* (1984) and *Working Together* (1986), the MSC forced a contracting FE to examine its non-advanced vocational education and training provision and now, through the non-advanced FE budget (NAFE), controls one quarter of the money allocated to this part of FE's work. With the introduction of the Technical and Vocational Education Initiative (TVEI) in 1983 for schools and the announcement of substantial funds for the promotion of 'enterprise' in higher education, the MSC could be seen to be reaching all parts of public sector education.

Staff in schools, colleges and universities on the receiving end of the MSC's progression have had to adapt to an approach to learning which challenges the perceived wisdom that the teacher stands at the centre and that knowledge rules. There has been an extraordinary consistency of purpose in all of this. Most colleges benefit from Youth Training Scheme (YTS) funding either as approved Managing Agents or as providers of off-the-job training for other YTS agencies, and many are now running TVEI and Employment Training (ET) programmes. Some of the money generated by MSC programmes has been used to fund non-MSC activities. By directly funding initiatives, the MSC and now through its grandchild, the Training Agency, has wooed FE to the point where seeking to disentangle itself from the relationship would result in it feeling seriously undernourished and some institutions directly starving to death. But the agenda for action is not yet complete.

To help facilitate the 'new partnerships' mentioned in the White Paper, *Employment for the 1990s,* provision has been made for the establisment of Training and Enterprise Councils (TECs) throughout the country. These will initially fund and administer YTS and ET on behalf of the Training Agency. The TECs have to draw at least two-thirds of their members from local employers and will have budgets of between £15 million and £50 million depending on the size of the programmes they run. In addition to YTS and ET, TECs can also devise and support locally devised training schemes which might be specific to the needs of one or more companies. Unlike LEAs, TECs will be based on travel-to-work areas and so will cut across LEA boundaries. The first TEC will be approved in June, 1989, two months after the deadline for this paper, so I cannot usefully predict how successful these new agencies will be. It is already apparent, however, that employers welcome the chance that TECs offer to gain a major controlling interest in the planning, design and delivery of vocational education and training. In Staffordshire, for example, the Training Agency's local area office staff have been holding breakfast briefing meetings for employers virtually since the White Paper was published and are involved in negotiations with various consortia seeking to form a Midland-based TEC.

Clearly, employers are not simply attracted by the opportunity to run YTS and ET programmes which, in the more affluent parts of the country, are scarcely now visible. The real potential for the TECs lies in the battle for ownership of the NAFE budget which, from July 1989, passes from local to regional Training Agency (TA) control. Currently, the NAFE budget is allocated to individual colleges following negotiations between an LEA and its equivalent TA area office, and the preparation by the LEA of a three-year rolling plan. When the regional TA offices take over from their local colleagues, each LEA will have to submit its plan to the region which in turn will seek final approval from the appropriate TECs. An LEA like Staffordshire could find itself having to seek approval for its NAFE plans from at least two TECs, one in the north of the county and one in the south. Employers are already saying it would make more sense for the TECs to handle the NAFE budget and so negotiate directly with their local colleges.

For the colleges, newly empowered with delegated financial management through the Act, the TECs may prove to be more attractive masters than the often bureaucratic and school-centred LEAs. The LEA role in relation to NAFE is likely to quickly disappear, but this could also be followed eventually by an emasculated version of the role it currently plays in relation to the FE/AE provision outside NAFE.

Education in the marketplace

To retain their traditional role as the major deliverers of vocational education and training, colleges will need to court the TECs and, at the same time, fight off competition from private training organizations, the in-house training departments of local companies, and neighbouring colleges. These private sector providers are now in a much stronger position to challenge colleges through new accreditation arrangements made possible by the introduction of employment-led National Vocational Qualifications (NVQs) which are discussed in more detail later in this paper. It is not surprising, then, that the section of the Education Reform Act relating to FE/AE matches the tone of the Employment White Paper and gives employers, for the first time, the majority representation on the governing bodies of colleges. It is to these reformed governing bodies that LEAs are required to delegate much of their previous responsibility, a move which could ultimately lead to colleges becoming corporate institutions. As they are dragged, sometimes screaming, towards the 'enterprise culture', colleges and, by association, the LEA departments which deal with FE/AE can expect to go through a period of substantial reorganization.

As long ago as 1963 in the Robbins Report (Committee on Higher Education, 1963) and as recently as 1987 in a Joint Efficiency Study report (DES/Welsh Office, 1987) people have been recommending that FE governors should take control of their finances. The Secretary of State for Education has accepted that advice and clearly sees FE/AE in business terms as he pointed out in a speech to the Association of Colleges of Further and Higher Education in February, 1989:

> Over 1,750,000 people attend further education classes — and that excludes the only slightly smaller number who attend classes at adult education centres. They are taught by the equivalent of 63,000 full-time lecturers. There are some 400 LEA-maintained colleges. But you also have adult and community centres and training workshops. In addition, you teach in firms' premises and in students' homes. The whole thing costs over £1 billion a year. It is a big, big enterprise. (Baker, 1989)

In the same speech, which broadcast the enormous scale of the FE/AE sector, however, Mr Baker also told colleges to dispel their 'dowdy image' and 'low profile' through better marketing and added:

> From next year, your colleges will become much more independent. They will have much greater power over their own finances, staffing and courses.
>
> College principals will have the greater responsibilities for which you have pressed for so long. Your money will depend on planned student numbers — but you can add to this by selling your services to local business and industry. (*Ibid.*)

After hearing this speech and reading the Act, one group of FE/AE lecturers constructed a profile of the typical college principal required for the 1990s: power-dressed, clutching a Filofax, portable phone and computer, the principal moves from one business advisory committee to the next, stopping briefly to consider the new designs for his staff's uniform bearing the college's logo and sponsorship details.

It is not only the colleges that are being advised to be more enterprising. The LEAs, too, are being asked to look to their local business population as they attempt to fulfil the Act's requirements. When the DES considers an LEA's scheme detailing its intentions for providing 'adequate facilities for further education', the criteria to be used include the following:

- That each scheme gives colleges as much freedom as possible to manage their affairs and allocate their resources as they think best within the strategic framework set by the LEA.
- That each scheme promotes responsiveness by colleges to the changing needs of students, *employers* and the local community.
- That each scheme gives colleges appropriate incentives to earn additional revenue by providing courses and other services and facilities for the local community including, *in particular, the business community*. (DES, 1988, my emphasis)

A recent article discussing the Act by two DES civil servants continues in the same vein:

> The key to the LEA's role is planning and co-ordination.
>
> Strategic planning is needed in FE to keep provision abreast of the needs

> of students and employers, and to eliminate gaps and wasteful duplication. Only LEAs are in a position to draw together the necessary information and dovetail provision between colleges and other sectors . . . Within the broad framework set by the LEA, the model is of an entrepreneurial college looking out for opportunities to meet employer and student needs as it perceives them. (Libby and Hull, 1988)

LEAs and colleges are not newcomers, of course, to resource management and have, for some time, been expanding the funding of FE/AE by tapping into various pots of money such as the European Social Fund and, in particular, as has been mentioned earlier, the considerable NAFE pot supervised by the Training Agency. Significantly, for many LEAs, the formal planning and review regulations for NAFE and YTS imposed on them by the MSC and now by the Training Agency, presented them with a mechanism they had previously lacked through which all their post-school provision could be planned.

Given that LEAs are tending to use their NAFE development plans to encompass their post-school provision in general, there is concern that their subsequent interpretation of the Act will be too narrowly focused. In preparing their NAFE plans, LEAs have to use the Training Agency's 17-point, occupation-related TOC(FE) classification.[2] Clear objectives are also given to LEAs wishing to obtain further money from the Training Agency through the Work-Related Further Education Development Fund. Any projects which an LEA wishes to pursue under this fund must seek to improve:

- The responsiveness of the further education service to the needs of the labour market; and/or
- The effectiveness and efficiency of work-related further education.

In its advice to LEAs, however, the DES has stated that it does not wish to prescribe the programme areas around which plans for overall college provision are to be made: 'Colleges and LEAs vary greatly, and will need to work out for themselves what classification best suits existing and prospective patterns of work' (DES, 1988). Obviously recognizing that LEAs might need a little more guidance, the DES circular adds that in assessing their plans, it will consider: whether the groupings are coherent academically, and can be used to reflect appropriately the resource implications of different subject areas for the purpose of setting college budgets; and whether the groupings are more finely divided than they need be (*ibid.*).

Perhaps in order to seek further clarity, LEAs will turn to the Secretary of State's pronouncements on a core curriculum for further education, which, unlike the National Curriculum designed for the school sector, is not mentioned in the Act. Mr Baker has said that there can be 'no single 16–19 curriculum' yet adds 'But I think we do know broadly what we are trying to achieve . . . As I see it, there are a number of skills . . . which young people and adults in future will need' (Baker, 1989). He goes on to list those skills which he sees being translated into individual learning programmes or action plans:

- Communication — written or oral. How to explain a complicated working procedure, or deal with a tricky customer.
- Numeracy. Not simply adding a column of figures, but understanding cores of magnitude.
- Personal relations — team working and leadership.
- Familiarity with technology — especially information technology. Everyone will need this. Very soon there will be a computer on every desk.
- Familiarity with systems — office and workshop procedures, and employment hierarchies.
- Familiarity with changing working and social contexts. In particular, given 1992, the wider overseas dimension — especially foreign language knowledge — to take advantage of the much greater mobility of skilled labour in both directions (*ibid.*).

Anyone familiar with the YTS and ET design frameworks, the Certificate of Pre-Vocational Education (CPVE) core and the philosophy of TVEI is likely to experience *deja vu* when reading Mr Baker's list. He is right to say there can be 'no single 16–19 curriculum' but if his menu for an FE core is placed alongside the competence-based qualifications emerging from the awarding bodies, it is clear that a definite narrowing of the choices open to FE students, of whatever age, is now a reality. Mr Baker not only endorses the mission of the National Council for Vocational Qualifications (NCVQ) to rationalize the nation's plethora of vocational qualifications but urges colleges to link school records of achievement with NCVQ's National Record of Vocational Achievement (NROVA) and so bring 'the whole system of education and training into a single framework, tailored to the individual's changing needs' (*ibid.*). This suggests some startling changes for the way in which the subject-centred National Curriculum in schools is expressed. The NROVA records a person's ability to perform functions, expressed as statements of competence, to specific standards under work-related conditions. Those statements of competence which linked together form NVQs have been created by Industry Lead Bodies in conjunction with the Occupational Standards Branch of the Training Agency. For locally designed school records of achievement to fall in line with the nationally derived and administered NROVA it would mean all subjects being expressed in competence terms and the accompanying tenets of NCVQ's framework being put into place. Briefly those tenets are that a person's prior achievements must be recognized in order for an individual training programme to be drawn up in which the person works towards the remaining competences at their own pace. There are precedents. TVEI and CPVE both offer school pupils the chance to gain experience in the workplace and it is possible that some pupils might achieve competence in a small number of activities during their time on work placement. They also, along with GCSE, place the individual learner at the centre of a learning process which seeks to shift the learner from the role of a passive receiver of knowledge to a much more active role in which he or she can follow a personal agenda. Yet those initiatives have been attacked by parents, some headteachers and contributors to the thinking of the New Right, as attempts to dilute the solidity of a curriculum which has the transmission of knowledge at its heart. Mr Baker has shown a strong tendency to listen to the New Right, as discussed in detail by Whitty elsewhere in this volume, so his plans for bringing 'the whole system of education into a single framework' may have a difficult future.

In areas where tertiary systems are in place, Mr Baker's pronouncements must seem paradoxical. In March 1989, Mr Baker's own inspectors reported that their survey of ten of the fifty-five tertiary colleges in England and Wales found they were providing 'high quality teaching in an attractive environment offering a wide range of recreational and cultural activities' (HMI, 1989). There are as many students over the age of 25 attending tertiary colleges as there are aged 16–19 and they have access to a varied FE/AE menu. If such colleges are to be governed by employers, what will happen to that range of recreational and cultural activities praised by the HMI inspectors? Interestingly, many Labour-controlled local authorities favour the tertiary model for their post-16 provision but under the regulations imposed by the Act the ideals of the tertiary movement, including a dedication to 'meet flexibly the needs of everyone over the age of sixteen in its locality',[3] may be difficult to maintain.

Facing a corporate future — meet the new governors

Some commentators have suggested that the Act itself will have very little impact on the curriculum of FE/AE, but given Mr Baker's notion of core skills for young people and adults, the work of NCVQ, the boundaries within which NAFE planning is carried out and the Act's own moves to delegate college control to employer-dominated governing bodies, it is clear that the Act further embeds a vocationally-orientated view of education. Indeed, since the Act was passed, the Secretary of State has attempted to increase that employer domination by advising LEAs and colleges about the most effective size of governing bodies. The Act states that governing bodies should not have more than 25 members of whom at least half must be representatives of employment interests or co-optees and that not more than 20 per cent should represent the LEA. The Act does not specify where the remaining 30 per cent should come from but the DES did suggest in a circular in September 1988 (DES, 1988) that, based on a governing body of 20, two places could go to college staff and one each to students, a neighbouring educational institution, a community group and the college principal. In April 1989, however, Mr Baker, in a letter to Chief Education Officers, said that he would not normally approve bodies with more than 20 members and would prefer to see bodies rather smaller than this (quoted in *The Times Educational Supplement,* 14 April, 1989). The letter adds that he 'accepts the view of many from industry and commerce that smaller governing bodies are more effective for decision making and more likely to attract the governors' (*ibid.*). John McLeod, of the Association of Metropolitan Authorities, reflected the mood of many LEAs when he said:

> I think the Secretary of State has been got at by some businessmen and has been persuaded that small governing bodies are more effective. It's this idea that the college is a business and that the board of governors should be seen as a board of directors. We think it should be seen as a coalition of interests. (*Ibid.*)

Despite DES assurances that LEAs will still have a leading role to play as regards FE/AE, colleges could, through the delegated powers of their governing bodies, take more of the lead themselves. Within certain constraints (for example, specific grants), the Act gives governing bodies a single sum of money over which they have full powers of virement and the ability to carry forward certain surpluses. Despite the fact that the LEA remains technically the employer, governing bodies have the power to appoint and remove all staff, determine staff grades, duties and conduct, and for part-time staff set the hours they will work. Governors will also be responsible for any academic boards that are established. Michael McAllister, Principal of Blackpool and Fylde College, believes the new governors can meet the challenge:

> Provided the college has an effective management team, these duties ought not to be too enormous. It may well be that the most important job of the new governing bodies will be to assist college senior managements to face up to their new responsibilities. The new governing bodies will need to develop with the senior management team, the kind of relationship that exists between the Board and the senior management team of a successful company. In particular, the chair will need to establish the kind of relationship a company chair has with the chief executive or between the board of trustees of a USA community college and the college president. (McAllister, 1988)

As individual governing bodies formulate their internal college plans based on their view of local need and interest, they will necessarily seek to influence the LEA's scheme and so begin, to use an appropriately North American term, to call the shots. There is obviously room for conflict, as described here by Farley:

> Local education authorities will use their strategic plans to control their colleges. But, will the budget quantum and its distribution in the following year be sufficient to deter colleges — and more crucially, their governing bodies — from moving away from the LEA's intentions? This tension — and potential for conflict — between LEAs and colleges' governing bodies is likely to be exacerbated by the changes in the latter's composition . . . the key question is, do LEAs have the capacity and resources to strategically plan and manage? (Farley, 1988)

There are governors and governors, of course, as every school and college will testify. The increased representation of employer interests on college governing bodies may serve to breathe a new and more dynamic spirit into institutions which have previously been concerned to bolster outdated craft training on the one hand

and the entrance requirements of higher education on the other. This presumes, however, that such dynamic employers with time to spare currently exist and, if they do exist, are available to become governors. Mr Baker believes they do exist but, significantly, has suggested that they will only come forward if colleges promote the right image:

> I hope you will be looking for senior people of ability and experience to commit their time and expertise. I believe you can attract these people . . . We now have the best chance ever of attracting able and enthusiastic business men and women. (Baker, 1989)

There is great concern among some lecturers that this approach could backfire on the Secretary of State for the following reasons. Firstly, many successful business people, certainly at local level, take a very conservative attitude towards education and training, an attitude which is at odds with the competence-based, learner-centred design of NVQs. Local employers, on the whole, feel safer with the sort of qualifications they took at night school or as apprentices and find the concept of competence-based qualifications difficult to contemplate, even though, ironically, they are being introduced as employment-led initiatives. Secondly, an 'old-boy network' exists in most towns and cities which college principals use in different ways. By nominating employers who are known to be sympathetic to a principal's ways of working, or who will simply turn up to meetings to satisfy their need to show a community involvement, a principal, regardless of his/her competency in running the college and standing with staff, could increase his or her personal power over the college. Thirdly, the commercial and industrial make-up of local communities differs enormously. Some towns provide the base for national and multi-national companies who have little involvement with the community as a whole. These companies may decide, for public relations reasons, that having one of their directors on the governing body of the local college would be a smart move, but such directors may have little real empathy with the college's community role. Lecturers at one Midlands college surrounded by large companies and a recently built Japanese factory are anxious that the smaller businesses in the area maintain a voice on the governing body and are not squeezed out by their larger and potentially transitory neighbours.

In the increasingly competitive climate in which they find themselves, and whatever the competence rating of their governors, college management will need to ensure that close working links are maintained with the Training Agency both nationally and locally through the TECs, with Regional Advisory Councils, with LEAs, and with existing employer and community groups. Winning friends and influencing people is an advisable motto for colleges, but old friends and any goodwill generated in the past should certainly be nurtured. Freeing colleges to run their own affairs is vital, however, to allow them the degree of flexibility they need to respond adequately to a curriculum not only increasingly shaped by employers but also by the individual learner, newly empowered by the NCVQ framework (NCVQ, 1988).

Privatizing vocational qualifications — the role of NVQs

The introduction of NVQs demands a complete restructuring for colleges to allow them to facilitate such requirements as open access, credit accumulation, assessment of prior achievement, workplace liaison and student-centred learning programmes. In essence, NVQs demand a shift from courses to competences and, because they are assessment driven, they can be delivered via any organization that registers with a relevant awarding body (e.g., City and Guilds, RSA, BTEC, Hotel and Catering Training Board). Marks and Spencer, British Rail and a host of smaller companies and private training agencies are already approved to deliver NVQs. Vocational qualifications have, in essence, been privatized.

To meet the requirements of the NCVQ framework, colleges will need to establish mechanisms for assessing prior achievement and provide career guidance to help adults plan for the future. Some LEAs are already considering setting up authority-wide assessment centres rather than having them based in individual colleges. Whichever way the assessment is carried out, lecturers will find themselves having to respond to individual needs of students arriving and leaving at different times during the year. Those colleges which have taken the lead in the assessment of prior achievement are offering consultancy services to their local employers to help them identify the further training needs of existing staff. And that need for a working relationship with employers becomes crucial for all colleges as NVQs are introduced, for many of the specified competences can be assessed in the workplace. This consequence of NVQs has led some lecturers to translate the acronym NCVQ as 'Numerous Colleges Vanish Quickly'. To keep pace, all college staff will need to be skilled in promotion and to be able to take decisions quickly when employers and individual members of the public call on the college's services. For college management, NVQs demand new structures and definitions. Long-held practices such as setting cross-college targets for staff-student ratios, defining lecturers' hours in terms of class-contact and charging fees based on the notion of students studying every part of a course have little meaning where NVQs are concerned.

There is a widespread belief among academics and employers alike that NCVQ needs to adjust its initial, largely functional, definition of occupational competence to allow more scope for the assessment of a wider range of skills, knowledge and understanding. There is also, however, acceptance from lecturers that the framework offers many people a realistic opportunity to prove their abilities which previous theory-based qualifications would have ignored. By delegating powers down to colleges, the Act enables colleges to tackle the challenges of NVQs at their own individual pace and provides control over a budget which will need to be handled in a much more imaginative and skilful way than ever before. Any college governors who think FE/AE still contains classes of students following the City and Guilds syllabuses they followed at night school and that lecturers spend all their time in the classroom will require intensive updating if they are to manage their budgets effectively.

Hoping to be heard — adult education makes its case

For adult educators, it is unclear whether the new breed of governors will concentrate their attention solely on the vocational rather than the wider needs of adult learners. It is also too early to know whether LEAs will choose to include adult education institutions with less than 200 full-time equivalent students in their delegated schemes and so bring them under the power of the new governing bodies. In its comments on the Act, the Unit for the Development of Adult Continuing Education (UDACE) has urged LEAs not to stop at simply producing schemes outlining their provision for further education but to see the Act as offering a greater opportunity. UDACE wants LEAs to publish a policy statements which sets out their commitment to an adult service, to include all further education institutions in their strategic planning and to redefine their notions of adult education:

> In many places the term 'adult education' has been traditionally used to describe a particular kind of part-time 'non-vocational' education for adults. As adults become a larger proportion of the student population of the further education system this definition becomes increasingly unhelpful. It is clear that adults follow complex paths through education and training, and distinctions between 'vocational' and 'non-vocational', and between 'adult' and 'further' education are confusing to users and not, in general, relevant to their needs. Such distinctions can also lead to marginalisation and neglect of some of the most accessible further education provision — the gateway through which many adults first return to learning. In view of this it is unhelpful to produce policy statements which consider adults in 'adult education' (in the traditional sense) separately from adults elsewhere in further education. (UDACE, 1988)

Given the curriculum changes imposed by NVQs, the increased accreditation of prior achievement, the freer movement between employers and college staff, and the renaissance of adult basic education through increases in funds available to LEAs, adults should find colleges more attractive places in which to study. Adults will also begin to realize that, given the demographic implications of the falling birthrate, they are vital to many colleges' survival and should, therefore, play a much bigger role in the planning and organization of FE in general.[4] FE/AE has always been the demand-led sector of education, but adults and their educators will have to make sure that in implementing the Act, LEAs give equal attention to their demands.

Conclusion

This article began with a picture of staff in FE/AE learning to live under water. In their efforts to cope with the introduction of NVQs, a switch to an adult rather than teenage body of students and the changing nature of their duties and responsibilities, it is no wonder that staff have tended to see the Act as simply another factor that will keep them submerged for years to come. The 1988 Act is different, however, from previous Education Acts in that it addresses the organizations delivering further and adult education directly. Those organizations that have already formulated a coherent strategy for the future and have paid close attention to their staff development needs could find the Act provides precisely the sort of survival kit they require for their new lifestyle. By increasing its revenue through profitable consultancy work and individually costed training programmes, an FE college could subsidize a range of courses outside the main vocational curriculum. Adult education centres too might be able to increase funds through business-related short courses, for example in foreign languages, and EEC trade regulations, in order to maintain their traditional 'liberal' programme. But this presumes that all educationalists have a broad vision about the service they provide and that the new governing bodies allow for such diversity. At its worst, the Act will herald the dawn of a corporate approach to FE/AE in which, as in the school sector, the concept of customer choice is, for most people, illusory. In such a world staff and students alike may decide, instead of learning to live under water, they should have built that raft after all.

Notes

1. Education Reform Act, 1988, Section 120 (2). The Act abolishes the LEA's duty to provide Higher Education but LEAs will still have responsibility for the strategic planning and funding of certain categories of higher education in colleges, e.g. BTEC, HNC and HND courses.
2. The 17 major groupings are: Administrative and clerical; creative; educational and recreational; health; community and personal service; selling; storage; scientific, hotel and catering; food preparation; agriculture and related; fishing; transport operating; construction and civil engineering; mining, oil extraction and quarrying; motor vehicle repair and maintenance; printing; security; general education; processing; engineering.
3. Proposal of the Tertiary Colleges Association quoted in Terry, D. (1987) *The Tertiary College, Milton Keynes*, Open University Press.
4. By 1994 the number of 16-year-olds in the population is estimated to fall from its 1981 figure of 802,000 to 532,000. See DES Student Number Projections for FE: Projected Numbers of Students in Maintained Colleges Studying on Non-Advanced Courses, 1986–2000. This is already forcing employers to consider retraining their existing workforces in order to maximise human resources.

References

Baker, K. (1989) 'Further Education: a new strategy', speech given to the annual conference of the Association of Colleges of Further and Higher Education, February.

Cantor, L. M. and Roberts, I. F. (1986) *Further Education Today*, 3rd ed., London, Routledge & Kegan Paul.

Committee on Higher Education (1963) *Higher Education: a report,* Cmnd 2154, London, HMSO (Robbins Report).

Department of Education and Science (1988) *Circular 9/88 Education Reform Act 1988:*

Local Management of Further and Higher Education Colleges: Planning and delegation schemes and articles of government, London, DES.

DEPARTMENT OF EDUCATION AND SCIENCE/WELSH OFFICE (1987) *Managing Colleges Efficiently,* Report of a study of efficiency in non-advanced further education for the Government and the Local Authority Associations, London, HMSO.

DEPARTMENT OF EMPLOYMENT (1988) *Employment in the 1990s,* London, HMSO.

FARLEY, M. (1988) 'The core mission of LEAs' in *Education,* 5 August, p.133.

GLEESON, D. (1985) 'Privatisation of industry and the nationalisation of youth', in Dale, R. (Ed.) *Education, Training and Employment,* Oxford, Pergamon Press, pp. 57–73.

HER MAJESTY'S INSPECTORATE (1989) *Tertiary Colleges,* London, HMSO.

LIBBY, D. and HULL, R. (1988) 'The LEA, the college and the community', in Further Education Unit, *Planning the FE Curriculum,* London, DES, pp. 8–18.

MANPOWER SERVICES COMMISSION (1981) *A New Training Initiative,* Sheffield, MSC.

MANPOWER SERVICES COMMISSION (1984) *Training for Jobs,* Sheffield, MSC.

MANPOWER SERVICES COMMISSION (1986) *Working Together,* Sheffield, MSC.

MCALLISTER, M. (1988) 'College governance', in Further Education Unit, *Planning the FE Curriculum,* London, DES, p. 43.

NATIONAL COUNCIL FOR VOCATIONAL QUALIFICATIONS (1988) *The NVQ Criteria and Related Guidance,* London, NCVQ.

PARKES, D. L. (1985) 'Competition . . . and competence?', in McNay I. and Ozga, J. (Eds) *Policy Making in Education,* Oxford, Pergamon Press, pp. 159–73.

TRAINING AGENCY (1989) *Work-Related Further Education Development Fund, Guidance for LEA Applicants,* published guidelines, Sheffield Training Agency.

UNIT FOR THE DEVELOPMENT OF ADULT CONTINUING EDUCATION (1988) *Securing Adequate Facilities* (*Planning for the Education of Adults*), Leicester, UDACE.

15
Higher Education

Gareth Williams

Demographic Imperatives

The Education Reform Act contains four provisions that directly affect higher education: the abolition of life time tenure for new university appointments; the replacement of the University Grants Committee by a Universities Funding Council; the replacement of the National Advisory Body for public sector higher education by a Polytechnics and Colleges Funding Council; and the transformation of the English Polytechnics and about 50 other colleges into independent statutory corporations outside local authority control. Student grants and loans are not mentioned in the Act but the government has since issued a White Paper announcing its intention of gradually replacing a large part of students' current grant entitlement with loans. Between them, these five measures amount to a substantial programme of reform which will shape the pattern of British higher education as it enters the twenty-first century.

However, the most important influence on the higher education debate during the 1990s is not legislation or government regulation. Rather it is the complex effects of the massive drop in births between 1965 and 1978 and the resultant fall in the number of school leavers which will continue until the late 1990s. There has been no such decrease since the 1930s, when participation rates were very much lower.

The extent to which the fall in the number of school leavers will be matched by a fall in the demand for higher education has been the subject of much controversy since the DES published its Discussion Paper, *Higher Education into the 1990s*. The main concern of that paper was that 'the fall in the birthrate since 1964 has already caused primary school rolls to fall sharply; over the next few years our secondary schools will face a similar decline; and our higher education institutions will begin to feel the effects in the early 1980s. This paper is about the development of Britain's higher education in the face of this prospect. Its main focus is the period between 1981 and 1994 (DES, 1978).[1] This paper gave rise to several years of intense discussion about future numbers of students in higher education and the Leverhulme reports on the future of higher education (SRHE,

1983). It is now apparent that the critics who claimed that the demand for higher education would be sustained at least until the end of the 1980s were right. However, the effect that the DES predicted for the early 1980s is likely to occur in the early 1990s. The 18-year-old population is already falling and between 1989 and 1996 the further fall will be of the order of 25 per cent: it is extremely unlikely that increases in participation rates of school leavers will compensate for more than a small part of this fall (see, for example, DES 1987).

Some members of the government will no doubt see the fall in the number of potential clientele as an opportunity to reduce expenditure on higher education still further. Their argument will be strengthened by the fact that at the same time as the school leaving population is falling the proportion of people above normal working age will be increasing rapidly. There will be a rapidly growing demand both for pension benefits and for medical and other services required by the ageing population. Within the education budget there will be increasing competition from the primary and secondary school sector as the rising number of births during the 1980s progresses through the school system. However, the attractiveness to the government of reduced expenditure on higher education will be tempered by fears of shortages of highly-qualified entrants to the labour force. Past experience shows that employers' demands for highly qualified recruits grow at least as fast as output per head. If the economy is to meet even relatively modest growth targets during the 1990s there is likely to be, therefore, a growing shortage of highly qualified entrants to the labour market. These shortages will be felt particularly in some of the public sector occupations; the government is already showing signs of concern about what will inevitably be a massive shortage of school teachers during the first half of the decade, and is prepared to initiate schemes to respond to demand for teachers that by-pass the usual training routes — by licensing graduates after a very short period of formal teacher training. Furthermore, as economic growth comes to depend more and more on high technology goods and services, the standard of education of even the most highly qualified workers will need to improve. The Council for Industry in Higher Education, in its influential policy statement in 1988, pointed out the dangers of an inadequate supply of highly qualified labour force entrants. The statement claims that, 'At present the UK's plans for the development of highly educated people are at odds with its ambitions for national renewal and growth' (CIHE, 1988).

As far as governments are concerned, therefore, there will be two opposing pressures, first to divert some public expenditure away from higher education towards those activities that cater for an aging population, and second to increase both the teaching and research outputs of higher education so as to avoid bottlenecks to continued economic growth and social improvement. The desire for public expenditure restraint accompanied by increased output points to policies that will reduce costs, that will attract funding from sources other than government, that will be selective in their impacts on different higher education activities and that will maintain appropriate standards in an increasingly diversified system. There will also be increased competition between universities, polytechnics and colleges and, inevitably, much more emphasis on 'marketing'. Universities in particular will compete with each other for 'traditional' students and all institutions will try to increase participation from less traditional students. In the polytechnics and colleges sector there will be growing emphasis on 'access' by students from disadvantaged backgrounds and ethnic minority groups and on the continuing education of adults.

The 1980s discovery that research and teaching are essentially different activities exemplified, for example, in the UGC selective funding policies and the Advisory Board for the Research Councils (ABRC) proposals for research universities, will be further accentuated as research-intensive universities will come to appreciate the benefits to them of increasing their share of research and research training rather than competing for students in what they see as low status and poorly-funded teaching of less well qualified school leavers and continuing education students on non-degree courses.

These competitive pressures will generate a growing concern with quality assurance in higher education. Until the mid-1980s, and to a substantial extent even now, British higher education institutions have been largely in the position of offering educational services to students on their own terms. As happens in any market in which demand exceeds supply the interests and priorities of producers have been dominant. In the new era in which supply exceeds demand, producers will need to compete more and more fiercely with each other for customers and students' wishes will tend to dominate as they have for many years in the United States.

In normal commercial activities, producers compete on both price and quality. There is room for both Rolls Royce and popular hatchbacks. In the newspaper market both *The Independent* and *Sunday Sport* are able to secure a niche for themselves. Certainly we can expect the higher education system of the late 1990s to be much more diverse than that of the late 1970s. Even casual observation shows that these trends have already begun. There is much greater diversity of the higher education system in 1989 than there was in 1979. However, a difficulty with education is that quality is not easily discernible by the consumer.

> If markets are to operate properly, consumers must be well informed about the likely outcomes of their purchases, and they must have the opportunity of learning from experience in making subsequent purchases. Decisions about higher education by any individual are usually irreversible and made once only. The ultimate outcomes of a particular choice are not apparent for a considerable length of time, are usually mingled with the effects of many other decisions and are influenced by the decisions that were taken at the same time by large numbers of other students. The essential information feedback of efficient markets is absent. (Williams and Blackstone, 1983)

As in many other activities, including motor car repairs and medical treatment, the client must to a large extent depend upon the professional integrity of those supplying the services. However, professional integrity, when clients are in short supply, is not always the overriding consideration as was shown by some of the responses to the establishment of a free market in the recruitment of overseas students in the early 1980s. There has been much concern, especially in Hong Kong and Malaysia, about what has sometimes seemed unprincipled competition for students from British universities (see, for example, Williams *et al.*, 1987).

Collectively the suppliers of professional services have a strong interest in maintaining, and being seen to maintain, high professional standards. It is inevitable that groups of institutions will take steps to ensure that their market position is not undermined by a few making claims for their services which are not borne out in practice. The present concern with quality assurance will increase. Institutional image building will assume even greater importance.

These developments will be a direct result of demographic pressures and not dependent on the organizational arrangements and financial provision for higher education made by the government. They are the inevitable result of changes in market conditions. However, the form the competition takes and the determination of likely winners and losers depends very much on government policy.

The polytechnics and colleges

In the non-university sector the passage of the 1988 Education Reform Act can be seen as the end of the process which began with Anthony Crosland's Woolwich speech in 1965 announcing the establishment of the binary policy, that is of a separate sector of higher education outside the universities and its concentration into a relatively small number of institutions. The history of the binary policy has been frequently written (one of the best accounts is given in Scott, 1983). It is relevant here only to summarize the main features that bear upon the government's decision to remove polytechnics and major advanced further education colleges from local authority control and to fund them in a way that exactly parallels the universities.

The binary policy converted what were largely local colleges into regional and national institutions but they remained under the control of local authorities and this was supposed to ensure their responsiveness to social needs. However, national institutions funded by local authorities required some mechanism for transferring payments from one local authority to another. This was the Advanced Further Education Pool. The essence of this arrangement was that each local authority paid into the pool according to a formula based upon the size of the school aged population in an area (this was an indicator of potential student demand) and the non-domestic rateable value of the local authority (this reflected the amount of industrial and commercial activity in the area and hence the potential demand by local employers for qualified recruits). Local authorities were able to draw money out of the Pool on the basis of the number of the students they recruited to courses deemed to be eligible by the Secretary of State.

The formulae governing withdrawal of funds from the Advanced Further Education Pool were the dominant influence on the patterns of growth of non-university higher education. There was, for example, an incentive to concentrate on full-time students since, probably in order to help achieve parity of esteem with the universities, the formulae gave more generous treatment to full-time students, particularly to those on degree courses, than it did for part-time students and those on non-degree courses. The overall effect of the arrangement was to encourage local authorities to expand their higher education provision since they could do so at very little cost to their own rate payers. Until the late 1970s the Pool was open-ended and essentially its total size each year depended on the amount local authorities wished to withdraw from it in the previous year. At a time when higher education had high political priority and expansion was considered desirable this was a virtue, and there are many articles of the late 1960s and early 1970s comparing the flexibility of the pooling arrangements favourably with those of the much more dirigiste UGC quinquennial funding system (see, for example, Pratt and Burgess, 1974; and Lewis, 1971). However, when, in the late 1970s, governments wished to restrain expenditure on higher education, the pooling mechanism was seen as a distinct disadvantage and the Labour government set up a Committee of Enquiry (The Oakes Committee) to advise on ways of improving the funding arrangements for Local Authority Higher Education.

A further disadvantage of the arrangements for funding public sector higher education was that the institutions had little autonomy over their use of funds. They had detailed line by line budgets with limited virement between budget heads. Every item of expenditure had to be authorized by the local authority. There was thus little incentive to economize since any money saved by the institutions simply reverted to the local authority. Furthermore, there was little incentive to earn income from other sources because most of what was earned also went to the local authority. This became apparent when full cost fees for overseas students were imposed in the early 1980s. While the universities scrambled for foreign students because of the income they brought with them, most public sector institutions simply acquiesced in dramatic reductions in numbers.

Ultimately, in the early 1980s, the government cash limited the Pool. However, this *increased* rather than diminished the scramble by individual local authorities to expand student numbers in order to increase their share of the cash limited Pool. Thus the public sector response to the swingeing reductions in higher education expenditure announced in the 1981 Public Expenditure White Paper (HMSO, 1981) was to increase student numbers. It has been argued that in part this expansion was a backwash effect of the decision by the University Grants Committee to react to the cuts by reducing student numbers in universities in order to maintain the 'unit of resource' or average expenditure per student. There is some truth in this. The maintenance of 'access' has always had a higher priority in the public sector than in the universities. However, it is also the case that attracting additional students was the best way in which local authorities could obtain the resources necessary to maintain the operating levels of their higher education institutions and hence reduce the need for painful staff redundancies.

Finally, in 1982, the government recognized the need to establish some planning control over the local authority sector and the National Advisory Body for Local Authority Higher Education (subsequently, through the inclusion of the voluntary colleges, for Public Sector Higher Education) was established.

The main function of the NAB was to advise the government on the allocation of the Advanced Further Education Pool. Its functions were thus similar to those of the UGC but its composition and modes of operation were very different. Whereas the UGC was dominated by academics, representatives of local authorities were the dominant force in the NAB. Unlike the UGC, the NAB decided from the outset that formula funding would be its principal mode of operation. It started life in the unpromising atmosphere of expenditure cuts and severe competition for resources between the public sector and the universities and between different institutions and local authorities within the public sector. Despite these difficulties, its open, formula-based approach to resource allocation brought some measure of planning and financial discipline to the sector. The significant achievement of the NAB during its 6 years of existence was to provide for the first time a national voice for public sector institutions in debates both about resources and the aims and purposes of higher education.

There were, however, some weaknesses. One was that the NAB allocated resources not to individual institutions but to local authorities. Local authorities did not necessarily allocate resources to their institutions in the way recommended by the NAB. In some cases they switched funds between institutions, in some they topped up the NAB allocations and, it was widely believed, in some cases they effectively creamed off some of the funds through the mechanisms by which they funded their higher education institutions.

The final government solution was to remove higher education from local authority control altogether. The 1988 Act did this in two ways. First, the institutions were given corporate status, that is they became independent legal entities with the right to manage their own financial affairs. Second, resources are allocated to these institutions by the Polytechnics and Colleges Funding Council (PCFC) whose members are all appointed by the Secretary of State for Education and Science, albeit after consultation with local authority and other interests.

The universities

Just as the creation of the PCFC can be seen as the culmination of a process that began in 1965 so the establishment of the Universities Funding Council (UFC) can be seen as the inevitable result of the public funding of the universities after the Second World War. The procedure whereby very large amounts of public funds were disbursed by a non-statutory agency with very little Parliamentary scrutiny has worried thoughtful observers of British universities since the 1940s and the period since then has seen a progression of incremental change — revised terms of reference to include a planning function in 1948, the transfer to DES control in 1964, the recommendation for a review by the Jarratt Report (1985) and the recommendation for a reconstitution of the Committee by the Croham

Committee (1987). In fact, compared with the radical change in the local authority public sector, the changes in university funding arrangements are not much more than another incremental change. The establishment of the Universities Funding Council can be seen largely as a tidying up operation resulting from the need to have more or less parallel treatment of the two sectors of higher education, partly from a belated realization of possible implications of the fact that the University Grants Committee had no statutory basis and partly, although in practice the change in this respect is fairly marginal, from a desire to reduce academic influence on the allocation of funds to universities.

Suspicions that the UGC would always put academic considerations above what the government saw as national needs were fuelled by the UGC's reactions to the 1981 expenditure cuts. When the government announced its intention of reducing higher education expenditure by 15 per cent the response of the UGC was to reduce student numbers and to defend the unit of resource. Although the UGC's case was that this was intended to protect the traditionally high quality of British university education after nearly a decade of erosion through rising prices, it appeared to outsiders, especially those in the rival public sector institutions, to look very like a vested interest group protecting its privileges. At the same time, because it had to implement the cuts, the UGC was losing the support of many people in its client universities. The strength of the UGC during its heyday in the 1960s was that it represented the university interests to the government without appearing to do so and it carried out government policy towards the universitities without appearing to do so. It was not difficult to foresee that this game would become difficult if universities lost favour with governments or if the UGC had fewer resources to distribute to its client institutions.

The other respect in which the UGC may have contributed to its own downfall was its insistence until the mid-1980s that the funding of research and the funding of teaching were inextricably linked. When student numbers were growing this was, of course, extremely attractive to the universities since research funding grew at the same rate as teaching funding regardless of national scientific priorities. Furthermore, it gave considerable powers to the universities themselves in determining what these national research priorities should be.

The first warnings that the government was not entirely happy with this dual funding system came in the early 1970s following the publication of the Rothschild Report (1972), when funds were transferred from the research councils (the other partner in the 'dual funding' system for university research) to relevant government departments so that it could be dispersed in accordance with government priorities. However, it was in the 1980s that the UGC contribution to university research was really brough into sharp focus. One reason was that the UGC tried to resist government expenditure cuts on the grounds that a substantial part of UGC funds were in fact used for research purposes. This drew attention not only to the very large proportion of UGC funding which was used for research (the rule of thumb figure was about 40 per cent) but also underlined the fact that government had virtually no control over this largest single component in the civil science budget.

The other new factor of the mid-1980s was the creation of the NAB. The NAB saw quite explicitly that one of its functions was to argue for increased resources and an increased share of the available resources for public sector institutions. It focused considerable attention on the disparity in expenditure per student between universities and public sector institutions. The universities' response that this disparity was necessary because of the research activities of university staff not unnaturally caused government to ask what the nation was getting in return for this expenditure. From this it was a short step to the growing emphasis on performance indicators and the attempts by the UGC from 1984 onwards to introduce some selectivity in its research funding. By this time, however, confronted with a government that was determined to root out entrenched privilege, the UGC had lost its image as an impartial disinterested agency acting in accordance with the best long term interests of scholarship in the light of national needs and was increasingly being seen simply as one more interest group that had to be brought to heel. A review committee under the chairmanship of Lord Croham was set up in 1985 and in 1986 recommended that the UGC should be given statutory existence as a University Grants Council with broadly equal academic and non-academic membership. Other major recommendations were that 'selectivity in the funding of research should be continued' and that 'the financial relations between the government and the UGC, and between the UGC and the universities should be governed by financial memoranda' (Croham, 1987). These recommendations were broadly reflected in the arrangements for the establishment of the Universities Funding Council except that the Council is under more explicit ministerial control than Croham recommended. For example, under Section 1.3.4 of the Act, 'the Secretary of State may by order confer or impose on either of the Funding Councils such supplementary functions as he thinks fit . . . ' and 'in exercising their functions under this part of this act each of the Funding Councils shall comply with any directions given to them by the Secretary of State' (1988 Education Reform Act).

The Government's Instructions to the Funding Councils

There is no intrinsic reason why the new Funding Council should act towards individual universities in a fundamentally different way from the University Grants Committee. However, in a letter to the Chairman of the Funding Council in November 1988 (DES, 1988) the Secretary of State made it clear that he does expect fundamental changes. The most important points of that letter are:

> The government intends that funding for research should be more clearly distinguished from funding for teaching, both within the government's grants to the Council and within each university's grant from the Council. I see substantial advantages flowing from the consequent encouragement of universities to think more systematically about the quality of their performance in both teaching and research.

The letter to the polytechnics says that:

> the mission of the polytechnics and colleges in research is properly centred on applied research of relevance to the needs of industry and other end users who pay for it. Along with this some institutions may usefully engage in strategic research in particular fields in which they can establish expertise related to their applied research. The government does not however intend to provide funds for the support of basic research in polytechnics and colleges.

Both letters state that:

> Various views have been put forward about the way in which the purchasing power of students might be given more prominence in the funding of higher education. While some of the possibilities which have been aired would take some time to implement, a more immediate possibility would be a shift in the current balance between the block grant and fees.
>
> In the White Paper the government restated its policy that places should be available to all who have the necessary intellectual competence, motivation and maturity to benefit from higher education and who wish to do so. I will look to the Council to have regard to this principle in its own planning . . . I will also look to the Council to have regard in its allocation in its grant to the government's policies about the balance of places to be provided in the various subject areas in order to produce the balance of skills the nation requires . . . the government looks to the Council to establish mechanisms which ensure that continuing education is taken fully into account in planning at the national and institutional level.

The whole of the section on student numbers, access and balance is identical in the two letters. There is less similarity in the section dealing with quality and efficiency. In both 'the Government believes there is scope for further improvement in the quality and efficiency of higher education'. However, in the universities the main concerns are:

> My predecessor and I agreed a programme of action with the UGC and CVCP in 1986; a series of measures to improve academic staff appraisal, probation and promotion with the CVCP in 1987 as conditions on which the Government made available additional funds, for non-clinical academic pay, and the restructuring programme with the UGC, also in 1987.
>
> The government is also committed to maintaining and enhancing the strength and quality of the science base, including the research activities of the universities. To this end there needs to be greater concentration and selectivity of research work, closer working with industry and other

> users of research, better management to yield greater value for money and increased flexibility enabling faster response to new scientific opportunities.

For the polytechnics and colleges:

> quality is best assured where polytechnics and colleges have substantial responsibility for their own standards . . . I shall look to your Council, in the exercise of its functions to collaborate with the validating bodies and HM Inspectors to develop methods of assessing and monitoring the standards attained by students . . . The number of students entering higher education in the early 1990s is projected to be significantly lower than now . . . I hope that the Council's method of allocating grant will leave institutions themselves to take initiatives towards desirable rationalization . . . Keeping open adequate points of entry into higher education in order to facilitate the expansion of access for part-time students will also be important, although I should expect the Council to give weight to the wider choice and broader educational experience that may be available to students in larger departments and institutions . . . the Government is also committed to the achievement of greater efficiency within institutions. I shall expect the Council to further this objective within its own sector by encouraging polytechnics and colleges to take steps to improve the effectiveness of the internal management and the efficiency with which they use the funds allocated to them.

The section on funding arrangements in general is almost identical in the two letters:

> I shall look to the Council to develop funding arrangements which recognise the general principle that the public funds allocated to universities are in exchange for the provision of teaching and research and are conditional on their delivery . . . The Act requires the Council to have regard to the desirability of not discouraging institutions from maintaining or developing its funding from other sources. I very much hope that it will seek ways of actively encouraging institutions to increase their private earnings so that the state's share of institutions' funding falls and the incentive to respond to the needs of students and employers is increased . . . Within these constraints it will be for the Council itself to devise appropriate means of allocating funds between institutions. I shall however expect to see two key features. The first is a means of specifying clearly what universities are expected to provide for public funds. The second is a systematic method of monitoring institutional performance.

The only difference between the two letters in this section is that the UGC receives a pat on the back: 'The Council inherits a good start made by the UGC in importing judgements of quality into the allocation of funds for research.' The NAB receives no such bouquet.

These extracts have been quoted at some length because it is often claimed that the government's long run intention is for the two sectors of higher education to come together under a common funding Council. Certainly both sectors are expected to do more, both quantitatively and qualitatively, with less public funds. Both will be required to be more explicitly accountable than in the past for the output achieved from the use of public funds. However, there are also clearly distinguishable differences in the instructions given to the UFC and the PCFC. The distinct role of the universities and the PCFC institutions in research is made more explicit than in any previous official pronouncement. The task of the public sector in increasing access, and its greater vulnerability to fluctuations in student numbers, is made quite explicit. Universities are clearly seen to have responsibility for monitoring their own standards while the polytechnics and colleges will continue to be, at least to some extent, under the tutelage of the CNAA and Her Majesty's Inspectorate.

In many ways the 1988 Education Act and the Letters of Guidance to the Funding Councils are the clearest expression of a binary policy. Until 1988 it was always possible to see the policy as an attempt at tidying up what the government saw as the running financial sore of local authority higher education, which was spending public funds out of the control of central government. It is plausible to see the guidance given to the two Funding Councils as a recipe for two sectors growing apart, performing essentially different functions in rather different ways rather than as two sectors whose activities need to be planned and coordinated in detail and which will gradually come together.

Financial support for students

The other main factor influencing the development of higher education during the 1990s will be student finance. The policy debate on this topic is complicated by the confusion of three different propositions. The first is that the maintenance grant currently received by students should be replaced in whole or in part by repayable loans. This was the subject of a White Paper in November 1988 (HMSO, 1988). The second proposition is that students should pay a larger part of the costs of their higher education themselves. This, it is claimed, would make them think more carefully of the value of higher education to them and be more careful in their choice of courses. This is the proposition that was made by the chairman of the Universities Funding Council in an interview with *The Times Higher Education Supplement* in June 1988 and which was favourably discussed at a Cabinet seminar in July 1988. It is alluded to in the Secretary of State's letter to the Funding Councils in one of the passages quoted above. Finally there is the belief that higher education institutions would be more responsive to the needs and wishes of their students if they received a greater part of their income in the form of student fees, but the need for increased participation and equity requires that the greater part of these fee payments should be subsidized out of public funds. This is the intention of the government policy statement announced in April 1989 (DES, 1989).

On the issue of loans and grants the position of the present government is also now clear. The White Paper in November 1988 indicated that, with effect from 1990, there will be no further increase in the maximum level of full-time grants paid to undergraduate students. Instead, any increase in student maintenance costs resulting from inflation will be able to be met out of a government guaranteed and subsidized loan arranged through the banking system. Using government predictions of inflation this would result in 15 per cent of students' financial support being in the form of a loan in 1990/91 and almost 50 per cent by the year 2007–8.

There are some unknowns in these predictions. Students have not accepted the proposals and their full political impact remains to be seen. There are also persistent press reports that banks are unhappy with the requirement that they administer a scheme over which they have little control. Third, it is beginning to be realized in other countries that an interest rate subsidy is in effect a grant, and a relatively inefficient one (Johnstone, 1987). From an economic point of view it is more efficient to increase the grant component and to remove any interest rate subsidy other than the guarantee against unavoidable default. Fourth, the White Paper has been heavily criticized for making no provision for part-time students and not taking into account the effect of loans on post-graduate study.

For all these reasons it is likely that the details of the White Paper proposals will be changed considerably before the scheme is implemented in practice. However, it is a fairly confident prediction that by the early 1990s there will be in place a loan scheme for undergraduate students in higher education. It is widely agreed across the political spectrum that there is an anomaly in the state contributing so substantially to what is for most students a profitable private investment and there is growing realization of the fact that Britain remains the only country in the western world without a substantial loan component in its package of financial support for students. Finally, in an age in which 18-year-olds have been legally recognized as adults for a generation, the anomaly of the parental means test has to be recognized. While few would deny that family circumstances should play some part in determining the size of a grant received by undergraduate students, there is widespread concern that students should be dependent upon parents for a legally unenforceable contribution to cover the rest of their living expenses.

Suggestions that students themselves should pay a substantial part of the tuition costs of their education are likely to come about, if at all, incrementally as a result of competition amongst institutions rather than as a result of positive government action. The case against a general increase in the proportion of tuition costs which students will have to pay is threefold. First, it will arouse even more political opposition than the replacement of maintenance grants by loans and no political party is likely to want to have this on the political agenda, certainly not before the 1991/92 election. Second, amongst the EEC countries only Spain requires any significant fee payment by students. While there is no requirement for EEC countries to have similar arrangements for higher education funding, political pressures and the increasing mobility across national frontiers seem likely to reduce rather than increase disparities between member countries. Third, and most important, the 1990s are likely to be a period of extreme shortage of graduates in a wide variety of occupations. It is unlikely to prove politically acceptable for a government to impose financial costs that reduce the output of graduates below what it would otherwise be.

However, some incremental moves towards students, or their sponsors, making a greater contribution towards their higher education are likely. In the first place the increasing market orientation of higher education will encourage some universities to charge supplementary fees for some subjects where demand is high. At the post-graduate level there are already 'premium fees' for some Master of Business Administration courses and in 1988 and 1989 there has been widespread breaking of ranks between universities with regard to the fees charged to overseas students. It is difficult to foresee the eventual outcome of such a development. 'Up market' universities which charge premium fees across a wide range of subjects will presumably be inaccessible to students who are unable to afford the fees. However, it would be rational for such universities to take steps to ensure that they are open to the most able school leavers regardless of financial circumstances by the award of bursaries and scholarships.

The third option, finance through fees that are very heavily subsidized out of public funds, is now official government policy and is gaining increasing support amongst vice chancellors. It is hard not to detect in this a streak of opportunism. If the available resources for higher education are finite, universities are likely to obtain a larger share of the total if it is channelled through student fees than if it depends upon political choice and bargaining between the UFC and the PCFC. It seems unlikely, however, that any government, even one dedicated to the use of market mechanisms as a basis for all resource allocation decisions, will be willing to abdicate to individual, and not always well informed, consumers the complete responsibility for the allocation of public funds in higher education.

British higher education in the year 2000

The most likely outcome for the 1990s is a system of higher education in which a basic unit cost per student is paid out of public funds by the UFC and the PCFC and through subsidized student fees. The government will ensure that within each broad subject area this per student allocation will be similar for the two sectors. Some universities will charge students supplementary fees for high demand subjects and will create a few scholarships and bursaries for very well qualified applicants. In addition, universities will receive additional funding, again on a subject basis, for strategic and basic research. The polytechnics and colleges meanwhile will make special efforts to attract part-time students and others for whom the largely academic, formal university courses are inappropriate. Within each sector there is likely to be considerable diversity depending upon geographic location, the institution's history, and the existing pattern of courses.

Such a system will have many of the features of United States' higher education, as foreseen by Kenneth Baker at Lancaster University in January 1989. The casualties will be quality and access although the same humbug will be written about both as is written about them in American higher education by many British observers. It is idle to pretend that access to Harvard or Stanford is the same as access to a local community college and it is perverse to pretend that there is not serious concern about the quality of much of American undergraduate education. If British higher education is going to follow the route taken by the United States, one essential feature is the development of large, well organized, well financed, high quality postgraduate schools. So far no British political party, no university and no higher pressure group has shown itself willing to grasp this particular nettle.

The great aim of higher education expansion in Britain during the 1960s and 1970s, and it was a noble aim although currently unpopular, was that in broad terms courses of post-school education should be available for 'all who are qualified by ability and attainment to pursue them and who wish to do so' (Robbins, 1963) and furthermore that this higher education should all be broadly of equal quality and equal esteem. This was a major concern, for example, for the founders of both the binary policy and the Open University. Baroness Lee was adamant that Open University degrees were not going to be seen as second class degrees (see, for example, MacArthur, 1974). Similarly much of the debate during the first decade and a half of the polytechnics was centred on the issue of parity of esteem. It was also true of conventional universities. Until the 1980s it was a cardinal principle of the UGC grant that it was a deficiency grant to enable all universities to reach a certain minimum level of resources per student. The result was a system of higher education that was almost universally agreed to be of high average quality in which nearly every student received considerable benefit. The percentage of the age group obtaining degree and degree equivalent qualifications was the highest in Europe. The proportion *entering* higher education was fairly low by international standards and this is the indicator which has been most discussed by critics of both the left and the right. However, access to higher education for its own sake is a dubious privilege for most people. The questions which the Leverhulme Report asked in 1983 have not yet been satisfactorily answered. 'Access on what criteria? Access for whom? Access to what? Paid for how?' (SRHE, 1983) Diversity and responsiveness to the needs of students is part of the answer. The other part is resources and quality. A system of higher education in which large numbers of students know they are getting a second- or third-best higher education is not really satisfactory, however high the crude participation rates are pushed. The pressure from employers for increased participation to meet their demands for graduate recruits in the 1990s will disappear as quickly as it has appeared if increased participation results merely in higher wastage rates, or vastly greater numbers of students in inappropriate subjects, or a significant diminution in the academic performance required by those obtaining degrees. Diversity must be accompanied by fitness for purpose and the resources to achieve it. Otherwise mass higher education is simply a mirage.

References

COUNCIL FOR INDUSTRY AND HIGHER EDUCATION, (1988) *Towards a Partnership: Higher Education, Government, Industry*, London, CIHE.

CROHAM (1987) *Review of the University Grants Committee*, Cm 81, London, HMSO.

DEPARTMENT OF EDUCATION AND SCIENCE (DES) (1978) *Higher Education into the 1990s*, London, DES.

DES (1987) *Higher Education: Meeting the Challenge* Cm 114, London, HMSO.

DES (1988) Letters from the Secretary of State to the Chairman of the new Funding Council, 31 October.

DES (1989) *Shifting the Balance of Public Funding of Higher Education to Fees: A Consultation Paper*, London, DES.

HER MAJESTY'S STATIONERY OFFICE (1981) *The Government's Expenditure Plans 1981–82 to 1983–84*, London, HMSO.

HER MAJESTY'S STATIONERY OFFICE (1988) *Top-Up Loans for Students*, Cm 520, London, HMSO.

JARRATT, A. (1985) *Report of the Steering Committee on Efficiency Studies in Universities*, London, Committee of Vice Chancellors and Principals.

JOHNSTON, B. (1987) *Sharing the Costs*, Washington, D.C., The College Board.

LEWIS, P. (1971) 'Finance and the fate of the polytechnics', *Higher Education Review*, Vol. 3, No. 3, pp. 23–34.

MACARTHUR, B. (1974) 'An Interim History of the Open University', in Tunstall, J. (Ed.) *The Open University Opens*, London, Routledge & Kegan Paul, pp. 3–20.

PRATT, J. and BURGESS, T. (1974) *Polytechnics: A Report*, London, Pitman.

ROBBINS (1963) *Higher Education: a report*, Cm 2154, London, HMSO.

ROTHSCHILD (1972) *A Framework for Government Research*, London, HMSO.

SCOTT, P. (1983) 'Has the binary policy failed?' in M. Shattock (Ed.), *The Structure and Governance of Higher Education*, Guildford, Society for Research into Higher Education.

SOCIETY FOR RESEARCH INTO HIGHER EDUCATION (1983) *Excellence in Diversity*, Guildford, SRHE. This final report and recommendations of the Leverhulme Programme also summarises the main findings of the ten previous studies.

WILLIAMS, G. and BLACKSTONE, T. (1983) *Response to Adversity*, Guildford, SRHE.

WILLIAMS, G. WOODHALL, M., O'BRIEN, U. (1986) *Overseas Students and their Place of Study*, London, Overseas Students Trust.

Notes on Contributors

Kevin Brehony is a Lecturer at the University of Reading. A former primary teacher who taught in several schools in the West Midlands, he has written two course units for the Open University on primary education and is currently conducting research on school-governing bodies.

Rosemary Deem is a Senior Lecturer in Education at the Open University and also a school governor. Most of her previous work has been on gender and education and the sociology of leisure (*Women & Schooling*, 1978 (Ed.); *Schooling for Women's Work*, 1980 (Ed.); *Co-education Reconsidered*, 1984; *All Work and No Play*, 1986; *Work Unemployment and Leisure*, 1988). She is currently working with Dr K. Brehony on a study of the workings of school-governing bodies in two LEAs.

Michael Flude is a Staff Tutor in the School of Education of the Open University working in the South East Region since 1987. He began teaching in secondary schools and adult education. He spent the next sixteen years at Homerton College, Cambridge, lecturing in the sociology of education and working extensively in in-service education. He previously co-edited and contributed to M. Flude and J. Ahier (Eds) (1974) *Educability, Schools and Ideology*, Croom Helm, and J. Ahier and M. Flude (Eds) (1983) *Contemporary Education Policy*.

Merril Hammer joined the Open University in 1986 as a Lecturer in the School of Education. Prior to joining the Open University she worked as an advisory teacher for special education needs (in-service education) for the Inner London Education Authority. Her school teaching experience spans some sixteen years, mainly in comprehensive schools.

Jan V. Hardy is County Adviser for Multicultural Education in Hertfordshire. He has taught extensively in Secondary and Higher Education before taking up his present post.

Mike Hickox was awarded a BA History from Cambridge in 1962 and a PhD from London in 1976. He is a Lecturer in Sociology at the South Bank Polytechnic, a post he has held from 1966. His chief interests are the sociology of education and the sociology of industrial societies.

Sheila Miles is a Senior Lecturer in Education at Homerton College, Cambridge. She was formerly Adviser for Equal Opportunities and INSET in Haringey LEA, and a Research Associate on the DES funded project 'School Based Training in the PGCE'. She also taught in primary and secondary schools.

Chris Middleton is a Lecturer in Sociological Studies at Sheffield University. He teaches courses on the political economy of class and gender, and has published in the areas of feminist theory, the history of patriarchal relations, and gender segregation in the labour market.

Rob Moore currently lectures in the sociology of education at Homerton College, Cambridge. During the 1970s he was a social education teacher in schools in London. More recently he has had experience teaching on YTS courses in FE and was a member of the Open University TVEI Project group under Roger Dale.

Roger Murphy, currently Director of the Assessment and Evaluation Unit in the School of Education at Southampton University, has been appointed a Chair of Education in the School of Education at Nottingham University from September 1989. He has had a long involvement in research and policy debates about pupil assessment methods in both Primary and Secondary schools. Along with colleagues in his Unit he has recently produced *The Changing Face of Educational Assessment*, *The Impact of Graded Tests*, and *Evaluating Education: Issues and Methods*.

Stewart Ranson is Professor of Education and Chair of the Centre for Education Management and Policy Studies at the University of Birmingham. His work at the Institute of Local Government Studies over the past decade has focused upon the changing government of education.

Philippa Russell is Principal Officer of the Voluntary Council for Handicapped Children, National Children's Bureau. She is a part-time seconded Associate Director of the National Development Team for People with a Mental Handicap, Department of Health; and Chair of the Independent Development Council for People with a Mental Handicap. She was a member of the Fish Committee which reviewed special educational provision in ILEA, and is the author of a number of books and articles on disability and special educational needs. She is the parent of a son with severe learning difficulties.

Hywel Thomas is a Senior Lecturer at the Centre for Education Management of Policy Studies (CEMPS) and School of Education, University of Birmingham. Before that he taught in schools and worked in industry. He has published several papers on economic aspects of education management and is co-editor (with Tim Simkins) of *Economics and Education Management: Emerging Themes* (Falmer, 1987). He is the principal author of *Financial Delegation and the Local Management of Schools: Preparing for Practice* (Cassell, 1989) and author of *Educational Costs and Performance: A Cost-effectiveness Analysis* (Cassell, 1990). He was an adviser to Solihull LEA on the development of their financial delegation scheme from its origin in 1981 and has been consulted by other LEAs as they develop their local management schemes.

Dr Andrew Stillman was formerly a Senior Research Officer and Project Leader at the National Foundation for Education Research. His research included investigations into the management of educational continuity between sectors, the LEAs' implementation of the 1980 Act and parental choice, and the work and management of LEA advisory services. He has written widely on all these subjects. Having entered education as a science teacher and having worked on science assessment over many years, he is now the County Adviser for Science Education in Dorset.

Lorna Unwin is a Lecturer in Post-Compulsory Education at the Open University. She has previously taught in a college of further education, for the WEA and has worked as a volunteer adult literacy tutor. Prior to joining the Open University, she spent four years as a training and education consultant designing and facilitating staff development programmes on behalf of private companies, LEAs and public sector organizations.

C. G. Vieler-Porter, is Advisory Teacher for Multicultural Education in Hertfordshire. Previously he was head of Drama in a secondary school.

Ron Wallace is Chief Adviser in Hertfordshire. He has taught in London schools and was a Hertfordshire head for twelve years. He is the author of *Introducing Technical and Vocational Education* (Macmillan Education) which reflected his role in the early years of the Technical and Vocational Education Initiative.

Geoff Whitty is the author of *Sociology and School Knowledge: Curriculum Theory, Research and Politics* (Methuen 1985) and (with Tony Edwards and John Fitz) *The State and Private Education: An Evaluation of the Assisted Places Scheme* (Falmer Press 1989). He is currently Professor and Dean of Education at Bristol Polytechnic and, in January 1990, will become Goldsmiths' Professor of Policy and Management in Education in the University of London.

Gareth Williams is Professor of Educational Administration and Head of the Centre for Higher Education Studies at the Institute of Education London University. Previously he has worked at the University of Lancaster, at the London School of Economics and OECD. In the early 1980s he directed the SHRE-Leverhulme Study on the Future of Higher Education.

The views expressed in this collection by the authors are their own and are not necessarily shared by their employers.

Index